Ignoble

Ed Adams

a firstelement production

Ed Adams

Contains both

Corrupt and Sleaze

in one volume

First published in Great Britain in 2021 by firstelement
Copyright © 2021 Ed Adams
Directed by thesixtwenty

10 9 8 7 6 5 4 3 2 1

A CIP catalogue record for this book is available from the British Library.

ISBN 13: 978-1-913818-24-1

eBook ISBN: 978-1-913818-25-8

Printed and bound in Great Britain by Ingram Spark

rashbre
an imprint of firstelement.co.uk
rashbre@mac.com

ed-adams.net

Wise
Monkeys

The three wise monkeys "see no evil, hear no evil, speak no evil". They are:

- **Mizaru,** who sees no evil, covering his eyes
- **Kikazaru,** who hears no evil, covering his ears and
- **Iwazaru,** who speaks no evil, covering his mouth.

The phrase is often used to refer to those who deal with impropriety by turning a blind eye.

Thanks

A big thank you for the tolerance and bemused support from all of those around me. To those who know when it is time to say, " step away from the keyboard!" and to those who don't.

To Julie for that kind of understanding that only comes with really knowing me.

To thesixtwenty.co.uk for direction.

To the NaNoWriMo gang for the continued inspiration and encouragement.

To Topsham, for being lovely.

To John, for his uncompromising readthroughs.

To Elizabeth, Georgina, Roger, John, Caroline, Richard and other cover reviewers.

To the edge-walkers. They know who they are.

And, of course, thanks to the extensive support via the random scribbles of rashbre via
http://rashbre2.blogspot.com
and its cast of amazing and varied readers whether human, twittery, smoky, cool kats, photographic, dramatic, musical, anagrammed, globalized or simply maxed-out.

Not forgetting the cast of characters involved in producing this; they all have virtual lives of their own.

And of course, to you, dear reader, for at least 'giving it a go'.

Corrupt

Ed Adams

a firstelement production

Books by Ed Adams include:

Triangle Trilogy		About
1	The Triangle	Dirty money? Here's how to clean it
2	The Square	Weapons of Mass Destruction – don't let them get on your nerves
3	The Circle	The desert is no place to get lost
4	The Ox Stunner	The Triangle Trilogy – thick enough to stun an ox
		(all feature Jake, Bigsy, Clare, Chuck Manners)
Archangel Collection		
1	Archangel	Sometimes I am necessary
2	Raven	An eye that sees all between darkness and light
3	Card Game	Throwing oil on a troubled market
4	Magazine Clip	the above three in one heavy book.
5	Play On, Christina Nott	Christina Nott, on Tour for the FSB
6	Corrupt	
		(all feature Jake, Bigsy, Clare, Chuck Manners)
Stand-Alone Novels		
1	Coin	Get rich quick with Cybercash – just don't tell GCHQ
2	Pulse	Want more? Just stay away from the edge
3	Edge	Power can't be left to trust
4	Now the Science	the above three in one heavy book.
Blade's Edge Trilogy		
1	Edge	World end climate collapse and sham discovered during magnetite mining from Jupiter's moon Ganymede.
2	Edge Blue	A human outcome, after a doomsday reckoning, unless…
3	Edge Red	An artificially intelligent outcome, unless…
4	Edge of Forever	Edge Trilogy

About Ed Adams Novels:

Triangle Trilogy		About
1	Triangle	Money laundering within an international setting.
2	Square	A viral nerve agent being shipped by terrorists and WMDs
3	Circle	In the Arizona deserts, with the Navajo; about missiles stolen from storage.
4	Ox Stunner	the above three in one heavy book.
		(all feature Jake, Bigsy, Clare, Chuck Manners)
Archangel Collection		
1	Archangel	Biographical adventures of Russian trained Archangel, who, as Christina Nott, threads her way through other Triangle novels.
2	Raven	Big business gone bad and being a freemason won't absolve you
3	Card Game	Raven Pt 2 – Russian oligarchs attempt to take control
4	Magazine Clip	the above three in one heavy book.
5	Play On, Christina Nott	Christina Nott, on Tour for the FSB
6	Corrupt	
		(all feature Jake, Bigsy, Clare, Chuck Manners)
Now the Science Collection		
1	Coin	cyber cash manipulation by the Russian state.
2	Pulse	Sci-Fi dystopian blood management with nano-bots
3	Edge	World end climate collapse and sham discovered during magnetite mining from Jupiter's moon Ganymede
4	Now the Science	the above three in one heavy book.
Blade's Edge Trilogy		
1	Edge	World end climate collapse and sham discovered during magnetite mining from Jupiter's moon Ganymede.
2	Edge Blue	Endgame, for Earth – unless?
3	Edge Red	Museum Earth – unless?
4	Edge of Forever	Edge Trilogy

Ed Adams Novels: Links

Triangle Trilogy		Link:	Read?
1	Triangle	https://amzn.to/3c6zRMu	
2	Square	https://amzn.to/3sEiKYx	
3	Circle	https://amzn.to/3qLavYZ	
4	Ox Stunner	https://amzn.to/3sHxlgh	
		(all feature Jake, Bigsy, Clare, Chuck Manners)	
Archangel Collection			
1	Archangel	https://amzn.to/2Y9nB5K	
2	Raven	https://amzn.to/2MiGVe6	
3	Raven's Card	https://amzn.to/2Y8HLgs	
4	Magazine Clip	https://amzn.to/3pbBJYn	
5	Play On, Christina Nott	https://amzn.to/2MbkuHl	
6	Corrupt	https://amzn.to/2M0HnOw	
		(all feature Jake, Bigsy, Clare, Chuck Manners)	
Now the Science Collection			
1	Coin	https://amzn.to/3o82wmS	
2	Pulse	https://amzn.to/3qQlBvL	
3	Edge	https://amzn.to/2KDmYOW	
4	Now the Science	https://amzn.to/3iG5Nc2	
Edge of forever Trilogy			
1	Edge	https://amzn.to/2KDmYOW	
2	Edge Blue	https://amzn.to/2Kyq9au	
3	Edge Red	https://amzn.to/2KzJwjz	
4	Edge of Forever	https://amzn.to/3c57Ghj	

TABLE OF CONTENTS

CORRUPT

SLEAƵE

PART ONE

Beauty and Terror

"Let everything happen to you
Beauty and terror
Just keep going
No feeling is final."

Rainer Maria Rilke

Setup

Clare sensed that her iPhone would ring. She was looking out across River Thames from the Triangle's office in Hays Galleria. It still startled Clare when she saw Amanda's name come up on the screen.

"Clare Crafts," she said, "Hello Amanda! It's been a while."

Clare knew that if Amanda Miller was calling from SI6, the UK's Secret Intelligence Service, then it must be something significant. Amanda wasn't one to waste words.

"Hello, Clare, yes, it has been a while. I've another interesting situation developing here!"

"Okay Amanda, can you explain by phone, or do we need to meet?"

"I can give you the outline by phone, but yes, we should also meet," answered Amanda, "And this time it's you I need help from!"

Clare was puzzled; usually Amanda contacted Jake if it was a general request. After all, she had known Jake the longest, from that time when he'd been incarcerated by the security services, while she, Bigsy and Chuck Manners had been chasing around the deserts of Arizona. Such a long time ago...

"Ok, tell all," asked Clare.

"Well, it's once again the nature of you being 'off the radar' that could prove so useful. Clare, I'd like you to spend a little time working alone the river at the Houses of Parliament."

"Really? You know my sister Sam is there?" asked Clare.

"We do, and as a matter of fact that is one of the reasons that this is such a good fit," answered Amanda, "Samantha Crafts, Research Assistant to Mary Crestwell, Conservative MP for Darland Totteridge, in Surrey."

"She calls her Mary," answered Clare, "And seems to think she's all right, if somewhat tough."

"Yes, she has a sterling reputation. No expense wheezes, no house flips, no dirty laundry in the cupboard – Samantha struck luck with Mary!" answered Amanda.

"We are hoping you'll be able to take on a similar role, also for a Conservative MP. After all there's more of them to choose between."

"And why would I do that?" asked Clare, intrigued.

"The situation you discovered based upon that listening station out at Greenwich Peninsula hasn't gone away. There are more MPs being caught out now and it's by a mix of corruption, both sleazy and slushy."

"What? They are still trying to use the system to corrupt MPs, as a cheap way to bypass lobbying procedures?"

"Yes, although we got that Minerva listening station place by the Dome shut down just after our actions the last time."

"They must have been on to a good thing, if they have started it up again," said Clare.

"That's what we want you to find out, and who you think is involved. We've kept this from the nosey parkers in the press and overtly from the loose jawed MPs. We think there is still someone - we think it is probably the Russians - trying to exert moral suasion over some of our MPs."

"Moral suasion? You mean blackmail?" asked Clare, "Like the last time with Bernard Driscoll? I seem to remember it ended catastrophically for him. Killed in a car crash on the way to Norwich."

"Yes, and it is because you have the knowledge of this and access to your very talented friends, that I am asking you to help us. I could offer some remuneration too, but I somehow sense that your organisation has sufficient funds already."

Clare thought carefully; Amanda was referring to the substantial funds that had come to the Triangle team from past endeavours, and Clare knew that Amanda had turned a blind eye to the source of the funds. Not that Amanda was trying to exert any direct pressure on Clare.

"Of course we'll help," said Clare, "There is never a dull moment around you, Amanda. You must tell me what I need to do!"

"It'll be working for an MP called Andrew Brading; Secretary of State for Internal Affairs; you might not know so much about him at the moment, but they tip him for the top in a few years. You must read up on him before you go to their offices. Get someone to test you too.

"The next thing will be to talk to your younger sister about working in Parliament - it'll be a much better briefing than anything that I can provide! I'll take it that this is settled then? I'll make sure the path is cleared to get you inserted into an appropriate role in Parliament. One thing, I suggest you'll need to move from your apartment for this. It will be better if you are with some other researchers - that way you'll pick up the news and gossip more readily."

"Great," said Clare, "And do I get paid for this work - like as a civil servant?"

"Not enough to live on," answered Amanda, "Barely enough to buy your food every day. Most of these posts go to people with connections, usually heavily supported by Trust Funds or The Bank of Mum and Dad."

"Okay - no need to sell it," smiled Clare into the phone, "I'll get on to Sam to find out what's what."

"Excellent," said Amanda, "We'll talk again in a few days when I've set this up."

Clare heard the phone click.

Bigsy looked over, "What breaks you from staring out of the window?" he asked.

"You'll never guess what! That was Amanda - she wants me to work at the Houses of Parliament - some kind of surveillance gig!"

"What about the rest of us?" asked Bigsy.

"Oh, I'm sure we'll all be involved!" answered Clare., "If not, I'll request it from my Member of Parliament."

Cellarium

Clare had arranged a lunchtime meeting with Samantha at the Cellarium by Westminster Abbey.

"Hi Clare, we can't get much closer than this!" said Samantha, referring to them being opposite the Palace of Westminster.

Samantha had breezed in, wearing business attire. A dark trouser suit with a white blouse buttoned to the top.

"Very business-like!" smiled Clare.

"You soon get used to it, but you'll need several of this type of outfit to fit in! Dress for success but don't upstage the politicians!"

Two gin and tonics later, Clare had ordered the pumpkin gnocchi and Sam had caramelised onions and quiche. The Abbey continued the ancient benedictine tradition of providing hospitality to visitors and presented its food with panache. The Cellarium was part of the 14th century fabric of Westminster Abbey, where in olden times the monks kept their stores of food & drink. Now the

Cellarium café kept the tradition of hospitality alive, albeit at London prices.

Clare looked at Samantha, "Are you still with that Stewie Fosdick?" she asked.

Samantha looked startled, "It was Stuart Fosdyke and no, I'm not - he was a dweeb. All watermelon sweet but then I heard he was making out with some other girl. It hurt me for a while but I've moved on, I am so over it - over him."

Clare looked at her sister. She seemed clear-eyed and not in the least put out by the recent turn of fortunes.

"I hope she doesn't need to fake it like I did."

"But that took you two years?"

"Yes, it took two long years to call it quits. But forget that boy, I'm over it. Babe - Clare - I'm cool by the way."

"From what I remember you seemed fond of him...I always wondered if he was right for you - and he always scowled at me."

"I noticed - both his scowls and your looks of displeasure. And I didn't I love him, anyway. So, I decided I'd live my life... It's my life...Not following around a two-timer."

"Better without him, right on sister!"

Sam continued, "He thought he was quite the man, and he tells his friends he made my heart break. It shows he knew nothing."

"Urgh. He sound like a right head case. The big 'I Am.'"

"Yes, I did the right thing - breaking from him. Deleted all his pictures from my phone. And the sexts. Blocked him dead. He won't ever bring me down again. He is gone."

"Whoa." Said Clare, "But you still need a hug then?"

"Hugs are still good," said Samantha.

"And what about you? Any boys, or girls in your life? Who was that last one? Olivia? "

"Aurora actually. No, it didn't last. But we were both in it for the spree!"

"And you are still hanging around with that Triangle gang? I think Jake and Bigsy must be your secret boyfriends? I can see that Jake is kinda hot."

"Strictly professional. Maybe I'll meet someone in Parliament - If I was looking, that is."

Clare asked, "Tell me about working in Parliament. What will the first week be like, Ms. PPE from Oxford?"

"Are you sure you'll get the role? I mean, it is difficult to get into a Parliamentary Researcher role and quite competitive. Not to mention the awful pay. Oh, and thank you very much for helping to keep me afloat. It seems strange getting subsidies from my older sister!"

"I guess I've been lucky with 'That Triangle gang' as you put it, and we've been able to charge some impressive fees along the way. And, of course, you are tax deductible!" Clare grinned at her sister.

Samantha began, "When I sent my CV to an MP's office after graduation, I never dreamt that a few months later I would work at the heart of British politics in one of the most beautiful buildings in the world.

"Nor did I imagine that I would pound the streets during a general election campaign, sneaking into media soirees at party conference or sweating in the gym next to politicians but I have, thanks to this role, which has given me the chance to get my foot firmly in the door - and thank you, Clare - I really mean it- when I say thank you for your moral and financial help to get me started."

"Well, it's family - isn't it - not quite Bank of Mum and Dad, but along those lines!"

Samantha continued, "In Westminster, internships are common and most MP's offices will take on interns to help ease the workload. It's why I'm worried whether you'll get the job - and it's a direct jump to Researcher too. Normally it is a rite of passage to be an intern first, as MPs are wary of taking on staff without knowledge of how Parliament works.

"For some, this extra hoop to jump through is seen as a selection process, but Clare, as you know, it prices out those who can't afford to live unpaid in London.

I remember when I was going for an interview. It was with the MP's office manager and a researcher. They were both testing me, but not too formal.

They asked me about my experience and how much I knew about the MP and why I wanted the role. Of course, I had my Philosophy, Politics, and Economics degree from Oxford to wave around, plus I had done my research. So I got this six-month internship which although unpaid, includes expenses to cover my travel and food every day.

"It's really like slavery then?" confided Clare, "They all grab enormous expenses budgets and then pay you in potato crisps?"

"Don't say that during the interview," said Samantha, looking serious, "You pretend that you like the working conditions,"

"To be honest, I'll still be getting paid by Triangle, so the food money really is for food -er - or drinks."

"That's the spirit. I remember my first day clearly, trying hard not to stare as MPs I had spent three years studying stood next to me in the queue for lunch.

"I also remember how hard it was to adapt to the demands of an MP's office and the realisation that in Westminster the working day never ends at 6pm as business in the House can go on late into the night. Be prepared for that.

"As a result, my first week was one of the most exciting yet draining of my life, and I remember leaving work on Friday and wondering how I was going to make it through the next six months.

"Being an intern in such a busy office meant that for the first few weeks I was bottom of the heap and they gave me tasks such as opening the post, filing letters and emails and answering the phone. Later, they gave me more responsibility as I proved myself to the team and they trusted me.

"Sam, it always looks like you've got a glamorous job and

you never give away that there are some drudgey parts!"

"I know, and I thank you for saying that. Case in point: I remember meeting my MP for the first time and her turning to me as she strode down a corridor, me running along behind. Then she looked me dead in the eyes and asked why I wasn't a member of the party."

"What did you say?"

"A bit wishy-washy - I offered that I didn't feel able to become a member of any party as I agreed and disagreed with elements of them all. Then I watched nervously, wondering if I had just blown my chances as she studied me closely, smiled, and carried on walking."

"I'd better get some stock responses ready!"

"Yes, I learnt very quickly that you have to have an answer for every question asked, even if it's not the right one, as it might be your only opportunity to offer an opinion and people make their minds up quickly."

"So, they can make decisions then?"

"Stoppit. I know you are only doing it to worry me. The same day I went into the House of Commons for the first time (it's much smaller than you think)."

"I remember visiting it on a school trip once."

"Yes, I forgot that. But as well as the exciting things, being an intern means I also had the more mundane office responsibilities too, such as making tea, doing the washing up and stuffing envelopes. You are somehow hoping to bypass all the mundane stuff? It might be more difficult than you think."

"I'm hoping for some sponsorship from a friend."

"It'd have to be a friend in a very high place. Do you know someone in the Cabinet or Secret Service or something?"

"I couldn't possibly comment," answered Clare, smiling.

"Oh, I see you are doing Civil Servant speak now. There's more to you than meets the eye, sister dear. One of the best things about being a researcher, is the varied nature of the job.

"That first week, as I was walking to the kitchen to make a cup of tea, I met the Prime Minister, standing alone pouring out a cup of tea. He poured a second one and handed it to me. I was slightly star-struck and somehow managed to garble a thank you.

Clare smiled at the thought of her kid sister meeting the Prime Minister without a word to say.

Samantha continued, "Perhaps not the best first impression, but the opportunity to make it at all means that hundreds of cups of tea later, it's still worth it!"

"I'm sold," said Clare, "And I'm determined to get the role."

"Who is it with?" asked Samantha, " I promise I'll keep schtumm!"

"Andrew Brading," answered Clare, studying Samantha's face for a reaction. She didn't need to study it.

"Unbelievable!" said Samantha, "You've hit the jackpot there. He's tipped for the top. He's also, how shall I say 'photogenic', regardless of whether he's wearing a shirt."

"I thought he looked quite smart in the photos"

"Yes, and everyone that is around him always says he has a wonderful personality too. I can't believe it. You get one of the hotties in Parly and I get a female dragon. And I'm the one with the PPE(Oxon)"

"I'm quietly philosophical," answered Clare.

"And I'm quietly late!" answered Samantha looking at her watch. She stands. They hug.

"Does this mean I'm picking up the bill?" asks Clare.

"Ooh, would you, thank you! It means I can just be back in time!" smiles Samantha. She skips to the outside of the Cellarium. Then across the road to enter Parliament via the Old Palace Yard.

Clare paid and was walking back to Westminster tube when her phone rang.

"Hi, It's Bigsy. What you said got me thinking. Remember that Pete Burr? He was observing us at the Triangle. I remembered that I sent him some minor viruses so that we could keep tabs on him. I've just called him for a meeting!"

The Rose

Bigsy had been busy. He had tracked down Pete Burr, who had worked at the old listening station called Minerva, along the Thames at Canada Water. It had been run by dubious sorts before it was closed down. Pete had become tangled up in something involving The Triangle and seen the business end of several weapons. He'd have been traumatised except, Bigsy remembered, he was wearing a ludicrous sailor costume at the time. Bigsy wasn't sure if he'd been the one who was more traumatised by that incident.

They met upstairs at The Rose, a pub on Albert Embankment, which also has a good view across to the Houses of Parliament. Bigsy had also invited Christina Nott along, because he felt sure Pete would remember Christina from their last encounter.

Clare, Bigsy and Christina arrived together. They could sense that Pete was nervous. They worked out that he sensed that the three of them together spelled trouble.

Christina smiled, "How's business Pete? Are you still working for the Americans?"

"Hello Christina, sorry if I seem jumpy, but well - you

know. The last time I saw you there was a lot of guns involved and then we got stormed by the police. Nothing like that planned for today, I hope?"

"Everything is cool. Nothing to worry about. We were simply wondering if you still had contact with any of your old buddies from that place by The Dome?"

"What the US-operated listening station called Minerva?" he replied, knowing that they both knew all of this, but he wanted to frame it accurately.

"That's right, I guess some of the folk there would like to see their jobs continue even after Minerva got shut down."

Pete nodded, "Very astute. Actually, several of the old team moved to a new job when it was set up. As a matter of fact, I'm also still in contact with two of the Americans - you might remember them - Emily Karankawa and Anne-Marie Bristow, who were also at that traumatising event at the Lanchester."

"Did they also move with the job - I don't mean with that dubious agency- I mean with the other dubious Agency?" asked Clare.

"Ah yes, I even got paid by the Miel Doux Agency after all of that. I assume Jennifer Sussex wanted us to keep silent about everything. And, if you remember, Emily and Anne-Marie were quite junior agents, trusted for overseas work, from the CIA. Neither of them wanted to rock the boat and - remarkably - they were both awarded medals for their part in the capture of Turgenev and Yegorin - even if it didn't go quite as planned after their capture.

"Are they secret medals?" asked Bigsy, remembering something he'd seen in a spy movie on television.

"No, they were regular medals and presented in a ceremony. I can tell you that their boss Olivia was spitting nails though. She'd ignored what we'd told her, and wasn't even along for the operation."

"Operation?" asked Bigsy

"Oh yes, we had to repackage the whole event as if it had been a perfectly planned CIA operation, after the fact," said Pete, "Of course, we here all know what really happened."

Pete continued, "I decided I was well out of it after that little session. I applied for another helpdesk role. Well, I'm a small fish for some sharks at a Chinese Bank. I'm not allowed to call myself a Financial Advisor, so I'm a financial services executive. I phone people, get them interested in investments and then pass them on to someone genuinely qualified to sell them financial instruments."

"Hmm," said Bigsy, "This sounds quite on the edge?"

"Yes, it is really. It's not chop stock, microcap or pump and dump, though. The Chinese want people with good British accents to sell their financial services, We are the front line. The financial people behind us have all been poached from other British banks but then the real machinery of their banking system is run by Chinese."

"Anyway, my ex-colleagues are based in a new place, not far from here, as I explained to Bigsy when we spoke by phone. The new centre is a block of apartments opposite the Nine Elms Market at New Covent Garden. It's called

Riverside Quay."

"In other words, it is but a stone's throw from the American Embassy?" asked Clare.

"Yep, and it has line of sight to the Houses of Parliament," added Pete, "And a view along the Thames - especially from the higher floors."

"Almost a clone of the setup you had in East London, then? Asked Clare.

"It even has a similar name to Minerva - Medusa," added Pete.

"Medusa and Minerva?" weren't they sisters?" asked Clare.

"It didn't end well for Medusa," said Bigsy, "She was the one who could turn people to stone with a single glance, but then Perseus came along and chopped off her head."

"I wonder if they knew that when they were thinking up names?" mused Clare.

"Well, and according to my contacts, it is the same scam. They are once again targeting Members of the Cabinet - to short circuit the normal lobbying processes. Catch people with their trousers down or their fingers in the till and then ask them to assist passage of some highly profitable legislation."

"I think there will be more to it than that," observed Clare, "After all they are so close to the American Embassy, I'm amazed no-one has worked it out."

"That is the brilliance of staffing it with the CIA, hiding

in plain sight," said Christina.

"Okay, well, it has been great to meet you all," said Pete, arranging his backpack and looking ready to leave. He gulped the last quarter of his pint of beer.

"So soon?" asked Clare.

"No disrespect, but I don't want to get roped into another dressing-up show with firearms," said Pete.

"Okay, but thanks for coming here and being so open with us," said Bigsy. Clare and Christina smiled.

Pete stood and walked towards the door.

Christina looked at Bigsy, "He knows more than he was telling," she observed.

Minerva and Medusa

Medusa was once a beautiful woman, her beauty rivalling that of her Gorgon sisters Sthenno and Euryale.

Minerva found the god Neptune and Medusa were kissing in Minerva's own temple. In a rage, Minerva turned Medusa into a monster, replacing her ringlets of hair with hissing. From then, Medusa turned any living creature she looked upon into stone.

When the hero Perseus is sent to destroy Medusa, he used her reflection in his shield to avoid contact with her eyes, and then beheaded her. He delivered the severed head to Minerva, who placed Medusa's image on the centre of her own shield to thwart enemies in battle.

Zoom call to Amanda

This time Clare was seated in the Triangle Offices, waiting for a Zoom videocall from Amanda.

"Hello Amanda," smiled Clare, "How are things progressing?" She could see Amanda against a neutral background. It looked more like a hotel room than Amanda's office.

"Hi Clare, I'm in Paris today. But let's talk about you. You must attend an interview, just like any other Researcher. Check your inbox - I've just sent you an email. We've created your CV. It is an adjustment of your actual one but should see you through without any trouble. It still focuses on your media and graphics background, but then we have been somewhat creative with your subsequent period at the Triangle. We've said you were a lifestyle influencer, working for several high-profile companies. They will interpret that as lobbying skills."

Clare was looking through the email that Amanda had just sent her.

"No. This makes me look like a bubblehead. I'm not sure that this will do at all. She read some of it out loud.

"Listen to this...

'Having studied professional arts and music theatre in college, Clare Crafts has taken her love of being in front of a camera to becoming an online vlogger. To date, she has accumulated thousands of followers across her social media platforms, where she updates fans on her varied projects, as well as giving them sneak peaks of her day-to-day life.

'Her YouTube videos consist of fashion and clothing hauls, makeup hauls and tutorials, storytimes, relationship talks and more. She keeps her relationship with her fans as authentic as possible, as she often opens up about her personal experiences regarding her health and her opinions on various social concerns.

'Clare's empowering attitude towards female identity has become her watchword and she often takes to Instagram to exhort her values.

'Her influence throughout the online world has prompted various brands and businesses to collaborate.

'More recently, Clare has shown an interest in ethical politics and has successfully taken this to her many followers.'"

Amanda replied, "That sounds perfect. Just what they will be looking for. Someone to advise on appealing to the metropolitan female market. And we'll have put in a few good words about you too. As long as you don't say anything too upsetting during the interview, then they should snap you up!"

"Oh yes, one other thing. You'll need to find somewhere

to live. Ideally with other interns or researchers. It wouldn't look right with you living in your apartment and if you can get in with some other like-minded spirits then it should help us short circuit some of the investigation."

"Okay, I'll ask my sister where I should start looking, she seems to know her way around. When is the interview?"

"I guess you'll have Andrew Brading's office call you about that. Oh, and good luck!"

There was a gentle click as Clare realised Amanda's Zoom session had been terminated. It looked as if it was really happening- she was going to Parliament.

"Bigsy! Jake!" - She called, "I'm going to need some help!"

Clare needs digs

Clare called Samantha again, this time about accommodation.

"I'll get on to it. We have a system here that tells us about flat shares. It's on the Parliamentary intranet. I'll send you some over when I've had a look."

Soon enough a message pinged onto Clare's phone. It was a WhatsApp group Clare shared with Samantha.

"You could be very lucky...My friend Tessa is looking for someone to move into their flat. She shares with a couple of other girls, but one is moving out. This is so hot that it smokes! - See the attachment. I can put in a word if you like. S. x x x"

Intrigued, Clare clicked on the attachment link provided.

It opened.

AVAILABLE: DOUBLE ROOM TO RENT IN FLAT W/GARDEN, LIVING ROOM

Enquire here:
https://www.sparespace.co.uk/flatshare/london/bermondsey/1 667081321

Hey everyone – We're in an amazing house in Bermondsey and need a new third person to take the last room.

Price: £630, bills probably around £70, deposit is one month's rent (housing benefit should be fine, references not needed etc)

About us: 2 women in our mid-twenties, both working in politics. We're both sociable and enjoy going to the pub, watching trash tv, sitting around reading and getting out and about.

We'll both be working from home for a while and will be using the living room as a work from home space. We're generally tidy people and hope everyone will pitch in but won't expect everything to be perfect all the time, as we all have busy lives and more interesting things to do at times. Generally easy-going and love a good political discussion from time to time.

About you: we're looking for a friendly person who is up for socialising (but obviously we'll all be doing our own thing at times as well). If everything above sounds good to you then I'm sure we'll get on fine.

About the room: A small double. The smallest of 3 rooms which is reflected in the price. It has a built-in wardrobe and storage with a raised bed and storage underneath.

The house: the house is honestly amazing with a beautiful open plan kitchen living room. There's lots of hidden storage including under the window seat, cupboards in the hallways etc. There's also a sofa bed in the living room for people to stay over. There's a small garden with loads of plants, a table and seating area. It is south facing so would be amazing in the summer. There's 2 bathrooms, 1 ensuite, so you'd only be sharing with 1 other person.

Accessibility: flat is on the first floor with a small staircase up and then another down to the garden area (about 10 steps). The room also has a raised bed.

There's no lift in the building, unfortunately. There is an intercom.

Send us a message and we'll arrange a chat to get to know each other/ answer your questions about the house.

Clare forwarded the email to Jake, Bigsy and Christina.

"What do you think?" she asked.

Bigsy came back first, "It looks ideal for what you will be doing. Two women who work in Westminster, political connections, and it's so cheap for London. £700 pcm all in. Say Yes."

Then Jake, "No brainer - say yes."

Christina's reply was more circumspect, "Three single females living in a flat share in central London - what could possibly go wrong?"

Clare buzzed her WhatsApp back to Samantha - "Yes - It'd be great! I'm in if they'll accept me!"

A few seconds later Samantha replied, "This has got to be the fastest ever room grab! They will want to meet you before they agree, though. I'm with Tess at the moment."

"Okay - How about tonight? Topolski's 18:30?"

"Tess is nodding. Do you mind if I come along as well?"

"Excellent see you all at 18:30!"

Topolski's to meet the Flatmates

Clare decided it would be simplest to take a cab to Topolski's, but to stop it around the corner from the venue. She didn't want to let on that she could afford random cabs until she had met her potential flatmates.

For Clare, this was going backwards a step or two. Ever since she had made the initial money from the Triangle, she had been living in her own small but fairly luxurious apartment. No sharing, except for when she had guests and a kind of freedom which fitted very well with her lifestyle.

She was seated in the bar, looking at the drinks menu, when her new flatmates arrived. Samantha guided them over and winked. Clare knew that Sam would have 'bigged her up' for the occasion, but she had no idea what stories Sam would have told.

"Hi, I'm Tessa," smiled the short-haired one, "I work for Anne Reeves, Labour MP for West Shields"

"She's the shadow minister for something, isn't she?" asked Clare.

"Environment," answered Tessa, "I hear you are more of a Conservative?"

"Well - it looks as if that's who I'll be working for," answered Clare, "Andrew Brading, MP for Ranmore Grenville."

"Is that even a place?" asked Tessa.

"You lucky lady," said the other one, "My name's Lottie and my MP is the rather wandery-handed Duncan Melship, MP for Knutsford North."

Lottie continued, "Compared with Duncan, your MP Andrew is an absolute angel. I know I shouldn't say this of the Tories, but he's a dream come true. You watch as he rises from the pack."

"Have you been accepted yet?" asked Tessa, "Sam said you still needed to go for the interview."

"That's right," explained Clare, "This has all happened in something of a rush - but they know I've been waiting for an opening."

"Well - you sounded convinced about our flat share," said Lottie, "At least according to your sister. I'm not sure about this...sibling influences in Parliament." She smiled and Clare could see she was teasing.

"How did you know about this bar?" asked Tessa - "I mean, we live in Bermondsey - Only a short walk away - yet neither of us knew about here."

"You have to know some of the wrong people!" joked Clare.

Tessa started, "Well let's talk first about the flat. Our friend has moved out. She wants to go live with her boyfriend. It is all very torrid. That has opened up her double room, which could therefore be yours. There's a double bed, storage, a desk, a decent window with street view and access to the other rooms like the shared kitchen/diner and a lounge with the communal telly. We've decent high-speed Wi-Fi and it has been given a certificate by the House of Commons security people."

Lottie added, "It's actually only 4 stops from Westminster to Bermondsey on the Jubilee line. They are about every three minutes. TfL keeps the line open during disputes and outages, because of its strategic significance."

Clare nodded, she didn't want to say that she was a regular user of the line to get to London Bridge, and then onward to the Triangle offices in Hays Galleria. Her subterfuge was proving increasingly difficult.

"I know this area of London pretty well," she ventured, "I've worked around here too."

"Ah, that would explain your choice of here for cocktails!" said Tessa.

Clare noticed a slight accent when Tessa talked. It was well-honed London but had a slight hint of somewhere European - maybe Germany.

Lottie's accent was It-girl London. Close to Samantha's chosen voice.

"So - how did you get the flat - and the jobs?" asked Clare, " I know about my sister, but surely everyone can't be like that?"

Samantha had been able to get her appointment via a friend of the family, plus her First-Class degree, plus the funding of somewhere to live which Clare was supporting.

"Daddy knows Sir Hugo Petheridge, and they came up with a placement for me," answered Lottie.

"I was recruited to help with the positioning of DNS Industrie into the opposition Agenda," said Tessa, "My father is a President of the company in Hannover and was able to get me this sponsorship. Technically, I'm supposed to look out for sales opportunities. Land and Expand."

Clare could see that Lottie and Tessa were too highly attractive female assistants, operating in what was still seen by many as a boorish men's club even despite the increase in female MPs to around 220, or around one third of the House.

"So, tell me what it is like to be an intern or Research Assistant?" asked Clare.

"It's all about the poodles," said Lottie.

"And the labradoodles," continued Tessa.

"But never the dachshunds," added Samantha - looking towards Tessa.

"Nein, niemals der Dackel," said Tessa.

Lottie continued gesturing as if answering a phone, "OK, so you've got a problem with your neighbour. Sorry yes, with your neighbour's dog. Your neighbour's dog is jumping up at your fence and damaging your roses? Yes I do understand, it's just I'm actually in Westminster and we're quite busy at the minute so it might be difficult to come and have a look. Yes, of course we have time for you, I'll call you back."

The other two nodded. "This is top-flight research," added Samantha, "Knowing which dogs can to the most damage."

"To sanity," added Lottie.

"That's a typical constituent call, could be by phone. Now they all want to use Skype or Zoom or even Teams - but Teams buggers up everything on the intranet, so we'd rather not."

"...and Skype sounds like its underwater half the time," added Samantha.

Lottie continued, "There's a set of constituents - they are like regulars and we think they phone us more to chat than anything else. After a few calls it becomes a case of laughter as the best way to stay sane as we deal with so many similar calls, sometimes 20 a day, and hundreds of letters and emails.

"So where's the Research part of this?" asked Clare, intrigued.

Lottie answered, "Well, it sounds as if you are skipping the intern part of the process and being bumped straight up to researcher. That goes beyond casework and leads to other things. We'll all be there too someday, and the reason we get given support - like Tessa has - from DNS Industrie is because they all know how influential a trusted Researcher can be."

Tessa nodded, "We all start by making the tea and dealing with constituents, but in the course of it we meet so many other people and build amazing networks. Plus, our quiet backroom networks of intern-to-intern and among the researchers.

Samantha said, "It's like I told you, Clare - There are various aspects to casework; from answering the phone, writing letters and emails on behalf of constituents and attending advice surgeries with the MP to meet local people."

Lottie added, "It's hard to keep emotions in check as problems range from the serious or sad to ridiculous. Dealing with the correspondence is the best and worst part of an intern's job. All constituents believe their problem is important and we should drop everything else to solve it."

Samantha continued, "In some cases, we stop everything else. They often call us upon to help constituents with immigration issues, domestic violence, addiction and depression."

Tessa spoke, "Yes, what many people don't realise is that most times an MP's office is a last port of call for those who have fallen through the cracks of civil society. Often constituents start a phone call with: 'I'm sorry to call you but there's no-one else left'."

Samantha added, "Remember Clare, to help, you need patience, good people skills, the ability to stay calm and think logically. Hmm. Maybe as your sister I know too much about your skills in those departments."

The other laughed, and Clare joined in, "Ouch," she said.

Lottie added, "And remember that working for an MP gives you an insight into just how powerful a name can be; I remember my first 'don't you know who I am' moment when I used my MP's name to get through to the top immigration official at a national airport after being passed from pillar to post for an hour. I felt a mixture of pride and achievement as I got through to the right person and helped our constituent get where he needed to be."

"Okay, I'm getting the lay of the land now," said Clare, "But there's still one thing you haven't told me about..."

"What's that?" asked Tessa.

"The Boys," answered Clare, to raucous laughter.

"We'd better get some more cocktails," said Lottie.

Portcullis House Interview

Clare had another session booked in the House of Parliament. She arrived at the visitors' gate but was directed across the road to Portcullis House. There, after the formalities of being photographed, badged, and processed, they then took her to a small side area where she met two other people.

"Hello, my name is Serena McMillan, I'm the office manager for Andrew Brading, and this, here, is Maggie Shannon; she is one of the other researchers for Andrew."

Clare shook both their hands, resisted the overwhelming temptation to curtsey and said, "Hello, yes I'm Clare Crafts and I'm hoping for the Researcher Post here working for Andrew."

They had some general questions, said that her CV looked very strong, and that she appeared to have some great references including from a James Cavendish, who worked for the security services. Clare realised what Amanda had done - she'd substituted James as a referee, instead of herself. It provided some distance but meant that Clare had to think on her feet.

"Yes, James (or Jim) is a friend of my father, I suspect he may have had a hand in my sister's hiring as well."

"It is always wheels within wheels," observed Serena, "Do you also know Sir Stafford Peters, by any chance?"

Clare remembered that Sir Stafford Peters had been involved in the incident with Maximovich, Yegorin and Turgenev - but she wasn't sure how much to admit. She knew that Sir Stafford would remember her, though.

"I did briefly meet Sir Stafford Peters once," replied Clare, "We were along at the same event. I can't say I really know him though,"

This answer seemed to satisfy Serena, who scribbled something onto a corner of Clare's CV. Then it was Maggie's turn to ask a few questions. The combination of Samantha's briefing and then the questions that Bigsy and Jake had invented meant that Clare was able to answer just about everything. She was even asked if she was a member of the Party. Clare remembered Samantha's reply.

"I didn't feel able to become a member of any party because I agree and disagree with elements of them all - I hope that my time as a Researcher with Andrew Brading will help me decide."

Clare realised she had said 'with' instead of 'for' and watched nervously in case it would get picked up.

Serena smiled, " I notice you said 'with' rather than 'for' Andrew Brading. A good sign of an intelligent and free-spirited candidate. Andrew is most insistent that the surrounding people will think for themselves and bring him fresh ideas."

Clare smiled, "I think I should ask you a few things as well?" She hoped that by doing this she would push the interview beyond the tipping point. She could also see how they responded to questions.

The most obvious one is what will I be expected to do in my first few weeks as a Researcher?"

Serena answered, "Political issues are often at the front and centre of news bulletins, and the unpredictability of the field means every day will bring new challenges and obstacles to overcome.

"You'll be making and implementing change that will have an actual effect on the lives of those on a national scale. If you feel passionately about the issues, you'll experience a great deal of job satisfaction seeing plans and policies put into action that you've helped to bring together."

Maggie added, "Working as an MP's assistant is often the first step in a political career. Moving to parliament may be your next career move. The skills and experience you'll gain could see you working for high-profile politicians, working internationally, or embarking on your own political career."

"Is that what is driving you, Maggie?" asked Clare.

Maggie smiled, "For political jobs, MPs typically hire a team of people, rather than a single assistant. They usually split the team between the MP's constituency office and the national political offices in Westminster. We are all parts of a team together. However, as MPs hire their staff directly, the structure of their teams, whether they hire full or part-time staff and where their team is based, can vary.

"I started as a caseworker in the constituency office, where I provided advice and support on issues in the local community such as immigration, housing and benefits, and liaising with government agencies and local media outlets. I had to attend local and national events and help to solve problems in our local constituency community."

"Then, when I moved to Westminster, I found the jobs were more directly related to assisting MPs with their workload.

"My responsibilities (and I assume yours too) may include:

- keeping your MP up to date on key issues and policy developments
- drafting and writing speeches, articles, and correspondence
- overseeing media coverage of your MP
- liaising with the constituency office team on local and national issues
- general diary management."

Clare said, "Well, I've done similar things in the Private Sector, particularly with media coverage as a facet. My skill with graphics and social media mean that I've a head start over some more inky types."

Clare decided she wanted to push it a little to see whether the people she was to work with could be flexible.

Serena cut in, "The role of a politician's assistant can be demanding. Because of this, you'll need a well-developed skill set, including (she looked down at a sheet of paper)

- the ability to cope in high-pressure situations
- adaptability at short notice
- excellent written and verbal communication
- high levels of organisation, including the ability to multitask
- firm but fair debating skills.

And you are right to surmise that it's your work experience and enthusiasm that will make you stand out."

"This is where I give my tears in rain speech?" joked Clare, testing their reaction. She could see that Maggie understood it immediately, but Serena looked more lost.

Maggie rescued her, "C-beams glittering in the dark near the Tannhäuser Gate. Did you know it was one of Andrew's favourite quotations?"

"I had no idea," answered Clare, imagining her clenched fist and a yelp of 'Yes!'"

"Okay, " said Serena, "I'll need to talk this over with Maggie in a moment and then we will be able to let you know the outcome. We should be able to advise you this afternoon, maybe by 18:00. Do you have other questions?"

Clare said she didn't, and Serena asked Maggie to show Clare how to get out of Portcullis House. They walked along side-by-side.

"I have to show you out, it's to discourage loiterers and nosey parkers," she said, "You did fine by the way, I should think you'll get the role, especially with that CV and those references."

They reached the exit. Clare shook Maggie's hand again and then departed. A little burst of joy rippled through her body.

Stepping Out

I'm stepping out

Don't you talk to me of no responsibility
Don't you go and pull that little pout
It ain't no use giving me your abuse
Because tonight I'm stepping out

I'm stepping east
I'm stepping west
I'm gonna put my
Toot-toot-tootsies
To the test
I'm gonna do what
I do best
I'm stepping out

Michelle Shocked

Day One at the House

Day One in Parliament for Clare. She'd been through the rigmarole of getting badged and given an email account. She now felt like she was a proper Researcher sitting with Maggie in the cramped office.

Then it happened.

A commotion in the corridor. Serena first into the office.

"Oh, hello - new girl - Welcome to the team. I must do the proper walk-around and introductions tomorrow. We've a minor crisis on our hands today."

Serena walked out of the office again, and Maggie walked across from her desk crammed in the corner.

"It can be like this sometimes," she said, "Andrew made a speech in the House today. He accidentally said something that has been picked up by the media."

"Was that the thing he said about 'I don't want to single out the BAME workers in this discussion?' " asked Clare. She had listened to the Today Programme on her way into the office.

"Yes, that's right; now the Media are twisting it to imply that Andrew doesn't care about BAME workers at all, they are sending in the Pomps to cover it."

"The Pomps?" asked Clare.

"Yes, the pompous Cabinet ministers, who will run defence for the story. Defend Andrew."

"But isn't it a storm in a teacup? And won't the so-called Pomps make it worse?" asked Clare.

"Yes, but it is running interference across the really big story about the Identity Bill First Reading," explained Maggie, "Andrew has become the unwitting sacrificial goat to distract attention from the main news agenda. You remember when we were negotiating Brexit? We kept bringing the fishing rights to the fore."

"Yes - a red herring," said Clare.

"Precisely, but it was something that everyone could get behind. And we could wave a Union Flag over the fishing waters too. Remember Rees-Mogg speaking to the empty House about 'British Fish and happier for it'? - honestly!" continued Maggie, "Look, it will get lively around here for the next couple of hours. Why don't you find some pro-BAME speeches by our MP? - That'll be like a simple test for you as a researcher."

Clare tapped into her keyboard:

"Something like this?" she asked almost immediately.

"Andrew Brading, (Cons) Member for Ranmore Grenville, speaking at the Westminster Business Development Circle,

said, *'There is a perception that certain ethnic groups are not interested in politics which I disagree with. Just because I am white, middle income and come from a certain perceived class, does not mean I am not sympathetic. BAME Politicians - that's Black, Asian and Minority Ethnic - are starting to overcome the barriers to getting to those places that are really difficult, although they have to be extremely resilient.*

'I will always acknowledge the trailblazers. Bernie Grant, Diane Abbott and Paul Boateng. They were the first black MPs, all elected in 1987. These were household names growing up. They spoke up on issues I guess many people wouldn't normally talk about, like stop and search. Then we saw James Cleverly appointed as Co-chairperson of the Conservative Party, something that was inconceivable when I started taking an interest in politics. Now we need to tackle the need to get BAME representation into FTSE100 Companies, along the lines supported by the CBI.'"

"Wow, that was fast," said Maggie, "But can you tell me what's wrong with it?"

"No soundbites," answered Clare, "But give me a minute and there will be one."

Clare clicked on the text, deleting most of it.

Conservative MP Brading speaks out for Black Lives at Westminster: White conservative MP Andrew Brading notes that, "It's time to get BAME representation into the top of the biggest companies in Britain. Black Lives Matter."

Maggie said, "That's not bad at all, and it hasn't even been through the Press Office yet."

"I know - *'Brading backs blacks for big business'* is more their kind of thing," answered Clare, "Now we need to get a couple of externals to endorse the quote and there's the story. I suggest Microsoft, Linklaters and hell, the CBI itself. There's your boxout-ready copy."

"Wow," said Maggie, "Put that into an email, send it to me and copy it to Serena. You'll get a gold star on the first day!"

Clear smiled, she was earning her keep, but it somehow all seemed simple compared with things she had to handle at The Triangle.

Maggie added, "I don't want to burst your bubble, but this latest scuffle is just that. It is a dawn patrol - looking for lighted cigarettes over the trenches. A warning exchange of fire, which the generals are pleased to see happen so the two sides remind each other they are still there."

"Two sides?" asked Clare, "I see it as five: the clergy, nobility, commoners, media and fifth estate,"

"Oh - philosophical too?" asked Maggie, amused.

"Well, the fifth estate won Trumpi his victory," added Clare, "and the fourth estate was mighty peeved."

"It's great to have you here, but you'll soon find out that with this lot we are more into reactive tactics rather than strategic offensives. Deception over Depth," added Maggie.

Serena came back into the room speaking on her phone, "Yes - it was the Westminster Business Development Circle," she hung up, "Clare, thank you for that counter-offensive to support Andrew. The news cycle has shifted now, and we are talking about that Labour MP who ordered a pizza and chips as a substantial meal. Andrew will be in the clear."

Clare smiled, "But isn't this all reactive? And diversionary? What about the big stories?"

"It's our job to bury them, or to obfuscate them," explained Serena, "To be honest Andrew doesn't like this fuzziness, but for The Party, it works well and is a way to keep Power. Give the flag-wavers something they can get their heads around. Scotch eggs, caravan parks, level playing fields. All the fancy statistics are wasted on most people. The average person in the street has lower-high-school math skills. They don't want bases, decimals beyond percentages, let alone stacked graphs. Listen to the X-Factor, it's 1000 percent true!"

Clare laughed at Serena's cynicism.

"Honestly," `Serena said, "You really have to break it down for the toddlers. The Daily Mail has it on point - its why I liked your alliterative headline. The Sun or Mail could run it right down the page."

Serena grabbed a handset and flipped on a television in the room's corner. It was tuned to BBC News. An Outside Broadcast showed a pizza and chips with 2269+996= 3265 calories written across it.

"See how fickle the news can be - the story about the pizza is more of a runner than Andrew's stumble over words. And they are gunning for that Labour MP in any case- ever since he slagged off the Daily Mail in a speech."

Another person enters the room.

"This is Douglas, he's the 'MP next door' and a friend of

Andrew. Duggie, this is our new researcher - Clare Crafts - who has just been saving Andrew's reputation on live television."

Douglas smiles towards Clare; she thinks she recognises him, but then realises it is from television, rather than real life. She needs to break the reflex to want to curtsey to everyone.

"Yes, whoever came up with that soundbite needs an instant promotion! And Andrew made a mistake! One mistake! After years of dutiful shit-eating during Brexit and then twenty-hour days and sleeping in his office for half a year to get a question slot! This can be a rough house. Delighted to meet you, Clare!"

Douglas turned around, grinned wolfishly, then pulled forward a woman in a flatteringly feminine salmon-coloured suit who looked like a young Nicole Kidman.

"This is my researcher, Hannah- I'm sure you, Clare, and Hannah will get to know one another, and Maggie and Hannah can surely show you the ropes."

Hannah beamed across to Clare, "Yes, and we can tell you of some hazardous areas too, maybe over a glass of wine?"

Clare grinned, "Or a bottle?" she replied, and Hannah and Maggie both nodded.

"We must go," said Douglas, "And yes, you can call me Duggie!"

They left and Clare looked back towards Maggie and Serena. Maggie commented, "Yes he's a good one - although he nearly always has the hottest researchers.

I'm not sure how he selects them."

Serena suggested to Maggie, "Why don't you take Clare to the lobby? Show her the aftermath and make sure she gets seen a bit?"

"Good idea, I can point out a few people too,"

They walked down the shallow stone steps to the landing overlooking Westminster Hall. Clare sensed a change of mood. The Victorian gothic fantasy was replaced with the austere grandeur of the oldest part of the parliamentary estate. A vast space the length of a football field, its hammerbeam roof a masterpiece of fourteenth-century engineering. Clare remembers it now. A school trip to see Parliament. A rainy day so they could eat their picnic lunches inside this very hall.

Maggie says, "Guy Fawkes and Nicholas the First were both sentenced to death here. It's been a shopping arcade, a courtroom, a church, a concert hall, a feasting chamber. It is full of ghosts."

'Even one of mine,' thought Clare.

A sudden burst of activity.

"Maggie! How are you?"

"Rachel, and how are you?"

Rachel Crosby. A lobby journalist for The Post - one of the many papers who have just been attacking Andrew Brading, his party and his leader. Maggie suspects that Rachel is not as loyal to the party in power as her bosses believe. Rachel keeps her reports factual, and even calls for comment before she runs something. She is also a very careful gossip. Clare spots that Rachel is wearing TV make-up, which makes her look ten years younger under TV lights.

Rachel replies, "Yeah, like you care. And try no more of those print ready soundbites. You are so goddam lucky that the rags wanted to get at Philip Clarke-Smythe as our pizza-eating knight in pound-shop armour today."

"So, Maggie, are you off for one of your walks? And aren't you going to introduce me to the new girl? I'll keep you company to the edge of the estate."

"Fine. This is Clare, a new researcher for Andrew Brading. She might have been the source of that soundbite too!"

They walk down the steps together and the ceiling rises above them. Clare notices Rachel is wearing trainers. A lot of women in parliament switch into heels for any time the cameras are nearby, with trainers handy for the rest of the time when they are wandering the endless corridors, chasing division bells, bills, stories.

"So when did you join the gang?"

"Today, actually!"

"Okay, I'll go easy - Kudos though; you produced a good line to bail out Brading. You are probably wondering why I'm chatting to you too?"

"It crossed my mind, but I assume that's how you get a lot of the informal stuff? From the back-room people? It was the same for me when I was in the Private Sector."

Clare had thrown a mild swipe with her own sword. Not

the cutting edge, but the side. Enough to alert Rachel that she might think she was the cat playing with the mice, but that at least some of them could roar.

Rachel looked at them both, "I'm giving you a heads-up. And you'll owe me one. The Labour Party leadership is launching an anti-BAME investigation."

Rachel looks at them both as if she is giving away a big secret.

"A slightly tawdry freelancer called Roger Slater has whipped the editors of the Chronicle into a frenzy with the prospect of a damning expose. Your leadership might want to get out in front of the story. That piece about Brading could make for a great attack."

Clare looks at Maggie, "Here we go again," she thinks, "More noise to clog up the arterial messages. Nothing like a spat to sell Mainstream Media."

They go out through the doors and into the diesel-fumed rainy air. Three steps out onto the tarmac, Rachel puts a hand on Maggie's arm.

Maggie watches Rachel for her next move, "There - but remember me first when Brading wants to run his story. I know there is more to it."

Now they are on the tarmac forecourt, the echoing space of the ancient hall is replaced by traffic noise, the smell of the roast chestnut vendors, the chants of a small cluster of protestors with the view obscured by a line of red buses.

Day One at the flat

It was still raining when Clare left the office at around 7pm. She felt as if she'd had more than a day's worth of experiences in her first working day inside Parliament. Now she would hit the tube and get back to her new flat share in Bermondsey.

She arrived at the flat before 7:30pm and climbed the stairs. She opened the door and there was a whooping sound and party poppers exploded, covering her with thin paper streamers.

Tessa and Lottie had arranged an impromptu celebration. Three glasses of Bollinger Special Cuvée Brut were speedily poured and then Lottie proposed a toast.

"To Clare, fragrant but unbeaten on Day One!"

Clare laughed, and Lottie and Tessa cheered.

"Group Hug," said Clare, and they all wrapped arms around one another.

"We heard about your news report too. A classy piece of action to get something out on Day One and also able to defend your MP like that! - Incredible!"

Clare signed, "But you know what. I'm pooped. The day veered from adrenaline to ennui in a few minutes."

"Who did you meet?" asked Tessa.

"Oh, I still haven't actually met my MP yet - Andrew Brading, but I met Serena and Maggie, who work in the same office as me - and the office - it's tiny!"

"We all know Maggie Shannon. Serena McMillan has a bit of a reputation as a hard case though. Be glad she is on your team. Don't be surprised if it's more than a week before you meet your MP. They move around in wildly unpredictable ways.

"I met a lobbyist too," said Clare, "Rachel something - Ah yes Rachel Crosby - she seemed to know something about what was going on around the place too."

"Oh yes, we know Rachel, but it is amazing that you met her so soon. She usually loiters around the lobby and then targets people with an eye for a good story," said Tessa.

Lottie nodded and continued, "Her paper, The Post, is a bit of a muck-raker, so you need to have your wits about you when you talk to her. She can come across all friendly, but she is looking for the angle or the lead. I guess today it was because you had put that one-liner into circulation, and she wanted to know its actual source."

"Ah yes, I met another M.P. Douglas Lessiter, and his assistant Hannah. They literally just stuck their heads around the door."

"Duggy is a charmer, but Safe in Taxis. He always picks amazing women assistants - did you think that Hannah looked like a film star? She is smart too. We'll have to give you some of their phone numbers. We think that Douglas is gay, by the way, although he's not 'out' and no-one seems to be that interested in following the story."

"I learned something in the private sector about having a stash of stories which could be ready to be used, rather than already out there," answered Clare, "Usually mild indiscretions, but if played at the right time the could be hurtful. It was all in the interests of business."

"We've heard that there could be something like that operating around Parly too," said Lottie, "Although the stories are mainly innuendo and they are very difficult to pin down."

Tessa nodded, "Except when those MPs were caught at that club - for - you remember - a Gentleman's Evening or something,"

Clare realised that Tessa was talking about the very event that she had been directly involved in, with Jake, Bigsy, Christina Nott and Chuck Manners. She wouldn't be owning up to it and thought it best to let it slide.

"But what about you two? Have you ever been approached by anyone shady?" asked Clare.

"Shady? That's about half of them!" joked Lottie, "No, I'm kidding, but there are sometimes things that make you question how the system works."

"That's right,"" said Tessa, "For example, in the Register of Interests most of the Researchers show up as having

54

'Interests: None'. I did disclose my link to DAS Industrie, so I show up as a 'Consultant, digital communications' on the Register. The reality is that Researchers or others close to them may well be paid through a lobbying group."

"It will take you a few days to realise, but the lobbying system is rife around the Halls of Westminster.

Clare made a mental note to get Bigsy to chase down and provide a briefing for her on lobbying. But now she was employed, she would need to think how and when she could get to the Triangle Offices. The question from Tessa arrived next and was ideally suited to Clare's situation.

"What about you, Clare, are you seeing anyone?"

Clare suddenly realised that this was the answer - an imaginary boyfriend.

She found it coming out of her mouth before she'd really had a chance to think, "Yes, his name is Jake and he's a journalist."

Lottie said, "Alarm bells. Some of what we deal with is Secret or Top Secret. You'll have to be careful what you talk about."

Clare was thinking, 'Perfect - an excuse to visit the Triangle offices and even to go back to my Apartment - I can say I'm visiting Jake's.'

"No Jake isn't interested in politics and he writes for a lifestyle magazine. They write about billionaires, fast cars and fancy places to eat."

"Well, if you need someone to test somewhere, then I'll

be up for it," said Tessa.

"I don't mind testing any of those categories: billionaires, fast cars or nice places to eat," added Lottie.

"As a matter of fact, I'll be with him tomorrow evening," Clare lied. She thought that she could visit The Triangle and get Bigsy digging in to help her research.

Bigsy describes the Lobby

"It's lucky we start late," joked Jake as Clare arrived at just after seven in the evening. She had been working in Parliament for a week now and had started to get a routine.

"Bigsy tells me you've asked him to pull some info about the lobbying system. We decided - including Christina - that we'd all like to hear about it and about your first days in Parliament"

Christina walked over; she was carrying a bottle.

"I thought we should make this a more relaxed session," she said, as she unscrewed the metal top from a bottle of Burgundy. Then Bigsy arrived with four wine glasses and a bottle of Vouvrey.

"We kept it in the fridge. I can get some nibbles too, if anyone is hungry."

Clare started her explanation of the last couple of days. She included her impressions of the people she met, but also noted that they had all seemed to be friendly and quite open with her. She told them about her flatmates and then got to the part about her deception.

"I've had to invent an imaginary boyfriend to get away to here - and for that matter, to go back to my apartment. I told Lottie and Tessa that my boyfriend's name was - er - Jake.

Jake guffawed. The others smiled.

"It's the most logical," said Bigsy, "They saw me when I helped you move in and I introduced myself as a 'helpful friend'; luckily we didn't talk about Jake at all. You are also unlikely to get caught out if you must describe Jake or anything. And we can call you as long as we say it is Jake."

Clare looked to Jake, "Are you okay with this?" she asked.

"Clare - after the craziness we've been through, this is just the next stage of our grand adventure," answered Jake, "and I guess it is simpler than having Aurora as your current fling!"

Clare smiled, stood, walked around the table and hugged Jake.

"Thank you," she smiled and then Christina poured everyone a glass of the chilled white wine.

"We'll let the red breathe for a moment," she said, "Now we've heard all about Clare - even her love life - we need to hear what Bigsy has found out about lobbying."

On cue, Bigsy switched on a TV flat screen to present a few slides.

He began: "Lobbying in the United Kingdom plays a significant role in the formation of legislation and is used by a wide variety of commercial organisations. There are lobby groups for particular policies and decisions by Parliament and other political organs at national, regional and local levels"

"I could see, even in my quick walk through Westminster Hall, that there were many people hanging around. And they looked like they were dressed for Westminster rather than casual tourists," added Clare.

Bigsy continued, "Yes, Lobbying is a massive industry now and the professional lobbying industry has been rapidly growing since as long ago as the mid-1990s. The last in-depth report estimated it to be worth £1.9 billion, employing 14,000 people. The report also suggested that some MPs are approached over 100 times a week by lobbyists."

"We were approached in the lobby, but it was by a journalist, rather than a lobbyist," said Clare.

Jake spoke, "At least, they said they were a journalist, could you be sure?"

"Oh yes, I was with another researcher and she already knew the other person, a Rachel Crosby."

"Journo," said Jake, "I've run into her before, she writes 'colourful' pieces for the red tops."

"She seemed to know things too. Stuff that wasn't out in

the open," added Clare.

"She is very good at her job," said Jake, tapping into his laptop. Here we are - her CV -

Rachel Crosby is a British journalist and writer. A few years ago, she was an editor on ITV News. Earlier, she worked for four years as a political editor on BBC Two's Newsnight. She has co-presented a Sunday news programme for a couple of years. State school in west London and then onto Emmanuel College, Cambridge.

"She's also been a producer for the BBC, on the foreign desk at The Times and wrote for The Independent and the New Statesman.

A significant player to meet on Day One, Clare. But Bigsy, back to your story..."

Bigsy was waiting patiently, the next slide already projected onto the screen, "The original phrase "lobbying" comes from the gathering of Members of Parliament and peers in the hallways and lobbies of the Houses of Parliament before and after parliamentary debates. Nowadays - mainly because of the old free-for-all system there are also formal procedures to enable individual members of the public to lobby their Member of Parliament.

"It means most lobbying activity centres have become subtle. Nowadays there are each of corporate, charity and trade associations lobbying, where organisations seek to amend government policy through advocacy."

"I'll need to be careful then, it sounds as if they are everywhere," said Clare.

"Companies and individuals who operate in this sector commonly use the terms 'public relations', 'public affairs', 'political consultancy' or 'corporate affairs' to describe their activities. I'd say that their methods are often suspect and the new terms to describe them are partially a reaction to the negative publicity surrounding the word 'lobbyists' after the old 1994 cash-for-questions affair."

Jake added, "Yes, I remember in my journalism work. I'd run into professional public affairs agencies, representing multiple clients. They would undertake significant lobbying activity beside individual organisations conducting lobbying on an in-house basis."

Jake screwed up his face "It was all a bit shonky actually, and the companies were often taking their clients for a ride too. A case in point: The tobacco lobby - which would try to stop restrictions on ciggy advertising - they'd talk about 'sticks' - meaning cigarettes - and were quite used to being advocates for several firms at once. I interviewed a 'fast boy' who had made money from this and he said, quite seriously, that they kept a lobby presence in the UK, but that most of the action had moved out of Europe. He was part Chinese, and said China was one of the biggest growth markets and he was running his efforts there now, 'Follow the money,' I think he said it had risen from $160 billion in 2012 to around $225 billion now. I remember him saying it was around ten times the size of the biggest European market - The Germans."

Christina nodded, "It's the same with Russia - over half the men still smoke. Lung cancer is a national problem. Women less so, although it isn't fashionable compared some countries. Of course, the cigarettes are still cheap too," added Christina.

Bigsy looked back at the projection, "Since 1994 there have been various complaints by MPs about unacceptable lobbying and several police investigations. It's a corrupt picture overall. I'd characterise it as hired guns with expensable inducements."

"And quite amoral, judging by the cigarette scenario described by Jake," added Clare.

"And what about the police investigations? Was anything done about it?" asked Jake.

Bigsy replied, "You'll see in a minute; very little, just a few people caught with their hands in the till."

"What a few being made examples of?" asked Christina, "That's how the Russians do it - well maybe their methods are a little more strong-armed."

Bigsy nodded, "Yes in the UK it is very understated. Current levels of lobbying are 'causing concern' as is the so-called 'revolving door' by which industry professionals move rapidly between legislative and commercial roles in the same sectors, creating potential conflict of interests.

"Tired of being an MP? Been voted out? Thrown out even? Become a lobbyist, or even a broker for lobbyists. We all know of politicians who have jumped ship to a lucrative role in the private sector."

"I can remember we had some 'hired-gun' approach us when I worked at the media company," said Clare, "He was a suited old duffer who had 'revolved out' of Parliament and was offering to get us introductions at the upcoming party conferences season - Cash for introductions - totally legal, especially because he was now a officially a parliamentary outsider. My boss agreed to pay him a finder's fee, but then he booked himself and his female helper into a swish hotel at the Birmingham conference but none of the rest of us were allowed into any of the sessions. It was truly shocking and a total rip-off."

"What happened to the 'clear blue water clause?" asked Jake, "You know when someone couldn't work for a conflict of interest for six months or a year?"

"It was unenforceable in most cases. The argument was that it was preventing people from taking further legal employment," answered Bigsy.

He continued, "That brings us up to the current period when ministers appoint Special Advisors (SpAds) who are staff members employed by the minister personally but paid for from the public purse - like Dominic Cummings was. They are often selected from related private sector industries and have sometimes criticised for engaging in campaigning while still on the government payroll or for moving directly between lobbying roles and the advisor role."

"Like those firms that employ someone who then becomes a civil servant who can then hire their old firm to help out?" asked Jake, "Jobs for the boys? I can think of a few examples of that."

Bigsy continued, "Curiously enough, the House of Commons Public Administration Select Committee recommended creation of a statutory register of lobbying companies and activities similar to the one required in the United States, but the government rejected that recommendation."

"I guess they could see which side their bread was buttered?" asked Jake.

Bigsy continued, "Then, in 2014, Parliament passed the Transparency of Lobbying, Non-Party Campaigning and Trade Union Administration Act, requiring statutory registration of professional lobbyists. The Office of the Registrar of Consultant Lobbyists (ORCL) maintains the register as an independent statutory office.

Bigsy flipped another PowerPoint slide and added, "In June 2015 the Chartered Institute of Public Relations launched the UK Lobbying Register to replace a joint voluntary register previously run in conjunction with The Public Relations Consultants Association and the Association of Professional Political Consultants."

"We are, by now, drowning in the alphabet soup," said Jake.

"I agree, all the various regulatory bodies - yet run by the people they are trying to regulate. Like 'It's my football, so my game and my rules.'"

"None of this is new, though," said Bigsy, "For example, in 1923, Winston Churchill acted as a highly paid lobbyist for Burmah Oil (now BP plc) to persuade the British government to allow Burmah to have exclusive rights to Persian (Iraqi) oil resources, which were successfully granted. No heads turned over that little arrangement."

Bigsy flipped another slide, "Or in 1994, The Cash-for-Questions Affair reported by the Guardian when parliamentary lobbyist Ian Greer of Ian Greer Associates bribed two Conservative Members of Parliament in exchange for their asking parliamentary questions on behalf of Mohamed Al-Fayed. Various people were criticised for these deeds."

Bigsy added, "Then, shortly before the 1997 general election Bernie Ecclestone as head of Formula One donated £1 million to the Labour party; after Labour's victory and after a meeting between Tony Blair and Mr Ecclestone, the Department of Health sought exemption for Formula One from the United Kingdom's proposed ban on tobacco advertising."

Clare said, "Wow, Bigsy"

Another slide and Bigsy continued, "Save your wows, Clare. Next, we have Jonathan Aitken, previously Minister of State for Defence Procurement under John Major in 1992. He was jailed in 1999 in relation to the Arms-to-Iraq scandal. Prior to becoming minister, he had been a director of an arms company BMARC, and after losing his seat at the 1997 election he was appointed as a representative for the arms company GEC-Marconi."

"That's a whole other thing, when the politicians can have a finger in the pie," said Jake.

"You should hear about Russia," said Christina, "The politicians sold off the state in a fire sale and conveniently bought up everything themselves with money that they loaned to one another from their newly acquired ex-state banks. The rise of the oligarchs. Thank you, Vladimir."

"That explains the rich oligarchs with so much cash," said Clare.

Bigsy projected a cover picture of a book, showing a USAF helicopter on the cover,

"And I had a look at an interesting little reference work called 'Fuel on the Fire' by Greg Muttitt.

"Muttitt argues that disclosed minutes from 2002–2003 (leading up to the war in Iraq) showed that many oil companies lobbied towards a war in Iraq to seize Iraqi oil reserves.

"For example, BP plc allegedly said in their minutes that they 'are desperate to get in', describing Iraq as 'the big oil prospect'.

"'This won't be the last resource war,' says Muttitt, 'The legacy of Iraq and the many blunders of the US and UK hangs over NATO's conflict in North Africa, and the way the Western nations are pursuing their agenda in another oil-rich state.' Muttitt's book should trouble even the most ardent liberal interventionist."

Bigsy flipped another slide, "Or, more mundanely, we could also mention the fundraisers for the parties, including the Cameron 'Leaders Group'. In March 2007 the Select Committee on Standards and Privileges published a report investigating a series of fundraising events which allowed donors to meet Cameron."

Jake added, "Nowadays, of course, it is all about games of tennis with the Prime Minister."

Bigsy picked up, "The investigation concluded that it was improper to employ parliamentary staff for fund-raising purposes and that it was 'ill-advised to link directly, in promoting the Leader's Group, the issues of access to his office and party fund-raising.'

Clare nodded, "Whiffle-waffle," she said, "Weasel words

that let everyone off the hook with a gentle tap on the knuckles for a minor indiscretion."

Bigsy continued, "Lord McNally, a member of the Lords Committee, said that this was 'yet another example of how pressure on political parties to raise ever larger sums from private sources pollutes our politics'."

"So, the river is polluted - no mention of fixing it then?" asked Jake.

Bigsy grimaced, "No - everything is quite slippery around this point and there's so many vested interests. Like the London runway for Heathrow. I can't pin anything specific on the Freedom of Information request showing that Heathrow Airport Holdings (BAA) executives met the Department for Transport 117 times between 2002 and 2007, including 24 meetings with the Secretary of State. Maybe that one still needs time to mature?"

Bigsy continued and flipped another slide, "But also in October 2007 Lord Hoyle, a member of the House of Lords, was paid an undisclosed sum to introduce an arms lobbyist, a former RAF officer who worked for BAE Systems, to the Defence Minister, Lord Drayson. The lobbyist had also a security pass as a "research assistant" from another MP. Accepting money for introductions is 'frowned on', but not illegal."

Bigsy flipped a further slide, "Then, in January 2009, The Sunday Times claimed that when a reporter had posed as a lobbyist that Lord Snape, Lord Moonie, Lord Taylor of Blackburn and Lord Truscott had offered to influence legislation in return for payment. The Metropolitan Police said that no action would be taken, noting that 'The application of the criminal law to members of the

House of Lords in the circumstances that have arisen here is far from clear,' and 'there are very clear difficulties in gathering and adducing evidence in these circumstances in the context of parliamentary privilege.'"

"Ha - 'Adducing,' lawyer-speak and then a word in someone's ear maybe?" said Jake.

Bigsy nodded, "A deal more like. The House of Lords voted to suspend Lord Taylor and Lord Truscott for all of six months in the first such action since the 17th century."

"Wow," said Clare, again, "Bigsy - you have been busy and several of these are pretty major events. A war, funding an election campaign, cash for introductions, cash for legislation, using civil servants to promote a specific party."

"Oh, I haven't finished yet," said Bigsy.

"You'd better send me that PowerPoint deck," asked Clare.

"My pleasure," said Bigsy, "Let's continue, from 2010, there were several, separate developments:

"The Department for Transport were being investigated by the Information Commissioner's Office and could face a criminal investigation over allegations it had deleted, or concealed records related to Heathrow to prevent them from being disclosed under the Freedom of Information Act. The investigation followed a complaint by Justine Greening MP."

"But does it end up in the long grass?" asked Jake.

Bigsy nodded and continued, "Andrew MacKay, a conservative MP and previously a senior advisor to Cameron's team was reported to be joining the lobbying firm Burson-Marsteller after quitting parliament at the next election with a salary of more than £100,000; His wife, Julie Kirkbride, also an MP, was reported to be looking for a lobbying job as well at a similar salary. The couple were both stepping down at the next general election following their part in the MP's expenses scandal during which they had claimed second-home allowances on separate houses. They had been ordered to repay £60,000."

"A fall from grace and a grab at the scraps?" suggested Jake.

Bigsy added another slide, "Labour MP Tom Watson complained of 'unprecedented and relentless lobbying' around the Digital Economy Bill sponsored by Lord Mandelson. He suggested that over 100 people were probably working full-time to bounce it through parliament and possibly only two people representing the interests of the nation's youth. He observed that it was difficult when being lobbied by people you respect and admire. Lord Puttnam accused the government of attempting to push through the legislation without allowing for proper discussion, and that the bill as it stands was not fit for purpose."

Jake grimaced, "The aftermath from that was exposed three years later during the pandemic which showed parts of the country and population still didn't have fast access and that the reach of digital education to school kids was highly inefficient."

"Yes - and that was after the Bill became an Act," added Bigsy

Bigsy pressed the slide advance again, "David Cameron, the conservative leader, predicted that this lobbying corruption was 'the next big scandal waiting to happen. It's an issue that crosses party lines and has tainted our politics for too long, an issue that exposes the far-too-cosy relationship between politics, government, business and money'."

"What happened to that golden sound bite?" asked Clare.

Bigsy added, "Cameron suggested he would shine 'the light of transparency' on lobbying so that politics comes clean about who is buying power and influence. Ironically, Cameron himself had moved from the role of ministerial special adviser to become Director of Corporate Affairs at Carlton Communications when the company bid successfully with Granada television for license to launch the world's first Digital terrestrial television service (ONdigital - later branded ITV digital)."

Jake laughed, "So Cameron was trying to outlaw something he had been directly involved with?"

Bigsy continued, "It's murky. Cameron resigned as a director of Carlton to run for parliament, but he remained on as a consultant to the company. During a roundtable discussion on the future of broadcasting, he criticised the effect of overlapping regulators on the industry."

"It could be construed that he still had an interest in the outcome?" asked Jake.

"It's really difficult to figure that one out," answered Bigsy, "Just like that Jeremy Hunt situation with BskyB."

Bigsy reminded them all, "The then Labour leader, Ed Miliband, called for the resignation of the culture secretary, Jeremy Hunt, over allegations he set up a private back channel to Rupert Murdoch's News Corporation when he was charged with making a quasi-judicial decision on whether to allow its takeover of BSkyB."

"I remember that, accusations of fingers in the pie?" said Jake.

"Hmm, not so much in the pie as hands around it," said Bigsy, "Miliband said the Conservative MP Hunt was 'standing up for the interests of the Murdoch's rather than those of the British people, after it was alleged in evidence to the Leveson inquiry that he had provided detailed information to James Murdoch on the state of the bid, and the thinking of the media regulator Ofcom."

"Sounds like a spy in the camp?" stated Jake, "It was incredibly untidy behaviour for a Minister. I won't be surprised if it gets selected in Uni classes as a case study."

"Strangely enough, that's where I found some of the information - In the London School of Economics Media Policy Planner website!" Bigsy snickered, "Hunt said that he had asked Lord Justice Leveson to bring forward his appearance before the inquiry and was 'confident that when I present my evidence the public will see that I conducted this process with scrupulous fairness'.

"He said: 'We've heard one side of the story today, but some evidence reported meetings and conversations that simply didn't happen.'"

"Hunt implied someone was lying?" asked Clare.

"Yes, or that he was being set up." answered Bigsy, "During the appearance by James Murdoch, News Corp's deputy chief operating officer, before Lord Justice Leveson the inquiry was shown extracts from 163 pages of email correspondence from Fréd Michel, News Corp's director of public affairs for Europe during the Sky takeover bid, to Murdoch marked "Confidential", detailing communications with Hunt, often via Hunt's special adviser, Adam Smith."

"This was a master class in obfuscation, " said Bigsy, " Use of 'I don't recollect', missing pages, you name it ..."

Bigsy continued, "Cleverly, Hunt's aides suggested Michel had wildly exaggerated the level of his knowledge and contacts with Hunt's Department for Culture, Media and Sport (DCMS) during the decision-making process between June 2010 and July 2011. However, the Michel emails published by the Leveson inquiry revealed that sometimes half a dozen confidential texts and emails a day would fly back and forth between the culture secretary's Cockspur Street office just off Trafalgar Square in central London and the News Corp team promoting the Sky takeover bid."

"That's not easily forgotten or denied," said Clare.

"Murdoch, in his evidence to the inquiry, steadfastly defended Michel's relationship with Hunt's office, saying it was 'active public affairs engagement' and 'legitimate advocacy'."

"Does the gun smoke?" asked Jake, "...But wasn't that bid ultimately scuppered?"

"Yes, but because of another reason - phone hacking -

another Leveson enquiry. It finally saw the Murdoch empire off the table," answered Bigsy,

"And there's still more, and by the way, I didn't have to dig too deep for this stuff. In March 2010 Dispatches and The Sunday Times recorded four Members of Parliament offering lobbying in return for influence with the Cabinet. Stephen Byers, a former member of the cabinet was recorded as saying he would work for up to £5,000 a day and was like a "cab for hire".

"And a real fun one," said Bigsy clicking another slide on the PowerPoint, "Also in March 2010 the Advisory Committee on Business Appointments revealed that Tony Blair, who had resigned as prime minister and MP had acted as a paid business consultant to an oil firm with interests in Iraq just 14 months after leaving office. He had requested to the committee that his relationship with UI Energy Corporation should be kept secret for reasons of 'market sensitivity' and the committee agreed to postpone publication for three months against normal procedures.

"The committee then had to then 'chase' Blair and send a formal letter to his office, which he responded requesting continued secrecy. "

"I see, extending it until the public are no longer interested? - Long grass tactics again?" said Jake.

Bigsy said, "Yes, but this time the committee chairman Lord Lang disagreed, and the information was published on their website with the note 'Publication delayed due to market sensitivities'. The news raised concerns that Blair had profited financially from contacts he made during the Iraq war. Blair also earned money from the ruling family in Kuwait for whom he produced a report on the oil state's future over the next 30 years for a reported £1,000,000 fee. "

"I see, puff pieces for royalty - good fees though," said Jake.

Bigsy nodded, "A 2009 investigation by The Guardian found that Blair had put his multimillion-pound income through 'an obscure partnership structure called Windrush Ventures, which enabled him to avoid publishing normal company accounts'. Blair later went on to close down his empire established after he stepped down as Prime Minister in 2007. He used £9 million of funds from his companies to create a new non-profit called the Tony Blair Institute, aimed at making globalisation work for everyone by combating poverty."

Bigsy added, "Blair's business empire proved highly controversial in the approximately ten years he ran it. His companies provided strategic advice on economics and politics but often worked with controversial clients such as the authoritarian government of Kazakhstan and oil companies. The Sunday Times claimed Blair was involved in a secret 'cash for contacts' deal with PetroSaudi to help broker oil deals and advised the Kazakh leader on how to present the deaths of workers in the country."

Clare, "This sounds a bit off to me. I'm sure there's another side to this?"

Bigsy said, "Yes. The former Prime Minister declared he would 'retain a small number of personal consultancies for my income' which included investment bank JPMorgan and a number of private individual clients according to the Financial Times. Blair's business empire is thought to have made him millions, although the structure makes it hard to tell the exact amount."

Jake, "It certainly implies that there is money to be made as an ex-Prime Minister. All the contacts and a slightly hidden soft power."

Bigsy flipped another slide, "And another one. In December 2011, The Independent newspaper reported that lobbying agency Bell Pottinger claimed to have been responsible for a variety of activities on behalf of clients considered not in the public interest including the manipulation of Google searches and Wikipedia pages. One allegation was that Bell Pottinger, acting on behalf of Dyson, used its influence with the Prime Minister and the Foreign Office to get the Prime Minister to raise concerns about counterfeit goods with the Chinese Prime Minister."

"Are we nearly there, yet?" asked Clare, "We're already on to the second bottle."

"I made it with no headers and footers, so that it doesn't show 'The Triangle' anywhere on the slides," commented Bigsy. He flipped another slide.

"That's all, folks" it said.

"Do you mind if I do some digging, too?" asked Christina, looking at Clare, "I could ask - you know - my contacts - see if they know anything?"

"Please, answered Clare, "But be aware that I am - we are all - effectively working for Amanda Miller at SI6."

"Share a cab later?" asked Christina, "Back home?"

"No, I'm going to Bermondsey, not Caroline Terrace,"

said Clare.

"But that could be a perfect alibi," said Christina, "You are out with your imaginary boyfriend and stayed over at his!"

Bigsy and Jake laughed, "Good plan! - But you'd better text the others to let them know you'll be away!"

Clare smiled, "This could work out very nicely, but I'm going to need another toothbrush!"

Christina unearths something

Christina's FSB Handler contact was codenamed Blackbird. His real name was Fyodor Kuznetsov.

Christina knew, once again, it would restart her direct dialogue with the FSB, which was something she always tried not to instigate. Still, Kuznetsov had left her alone and not cared when she had made money from a recent series of incidents.

She rang the number for Kuznetsov. A London-based car dealership answered. "I'm interested in taking one of your vehicles for a test-drive, " she continued, " A hatch back."

There was a pause on the line and then a recorded voice asked for her reference code and the nature of her enquiry.

She gave a number, and after a moment was put through to a voice.

"And how may I help you today?'

"I'm seeking a colleague, " she began.

There followed a protocol to verify security, and then Christina waited.

"Eventually a voice said, " Hello, Christina? - Or should I call you Archangel?"

"Blackbird, " she replied, " It's been a while."

"Is everything okay?" he asked, " It is so unusual for you to make the initial contact."

"Can I ask you a question?"

"Who is asking? Is it you or are you asking for someone else?"

"No, it's just me, " lied Christina, "I thought I heard someone mention something about a Medusa project and I wondered - you know - if it was linked to the old Minerva?"

"Yes I know this one. It's a precautionary tactic," said Blackbird, "Similar to how the Kremlin operates. You know how they like to monitor everyone - it's the same idea, except instead of the Kremlin running it all from around Mokhovaya Street, they can go out into the Oblast now, past the МКАД - *Moskovskaya Koltsevaya Avtomobilnaya Doroga* ring road.

"Frankly, the FSB is more cyber-aware nowadays. There's a major phishing operation using a group of hackers called CyberBerkut, targeting over 200 subjects from around 40 countries, including members of governments from Europe and Eurasia, ambassadors, high-ranking military officers, CEOs of energy companies and members of civil society. Things have move on from the days of Minerva."

"So why does the Kremlin still run Medusa?" asked Christina.

"*Дезинформация - dezinformatsiya* - Disinformation; we run it as a kind of placement. It is a reliable way to convince the Americans and Europeans about how much and how little we know. To be frank, I think we are even too good at it. The British don't seem to even know that Minerva was replaced, and the Americans seem to think they are running Medusa. It's incredible really, and even if it gets discovered it will only set a very out-of-date place marker on our activities. They will think we are far more primitive than we actually are. Pure disinformation. When I say 'we' run it, actually I think it has been outsourced to one of the *krysha*."

"Outsourced? To a Russian gang? What? A Bratva is operating Medusa?"

"Yes, remember *sistema*? systemic corruption? Well, the size of *blat* going to and from the Kremlin has increased. Blat are no longer just small favours; they have grown through container ports and economic sectors to now being targeted toward foreign governments. One could say it is a success of modern Russia."

Blackbird continued, "Look - I need to say something *Arkhangelsk* - You must be careful you don't wake a sleeping dragon looking at this. If the GRU get a hint, then you could have much trouble coming your way. I know you are capable operative, but they won't play nice with you."

Christina realised Blackbird's warning was friendly, but also that Medusa must be the tip of an iceberg. By creating something considered outdated, the Russians could convince the west of the Kremlin's lack of sophistication while they built new cyberoffensives. It truly was the new cold war.

The dragon from the mountains

Christina, smiling, told the others the story of the dragon from the mountains.

"Once upon a time, a famous Russian Bogatyr (Knight) Ilya Murometz was, as usually, at home. A group of old men from the village came to see him and said: 'Ilya, help us, Zmey Gorynych (the dragon) is so angry, he burnt 3 villages, he ate all the hens, we are in trouble!'

No answer from the Ilya.

Some days after they came again: 'Ilya, helps us, please, Zmey destroyed 10 villages, ate all the cows, kidnapped our wives!'

No answer.

Some days after men came again: 'Ilya, it's a nightmare. He destroyed 20 villages, he ate all the domestic animals, he kidnapped all the princesses, and he is very close to us now!'

Ilya started to get up and to take his dress. The old men were so glad!

'Ilya, you are going to help us at last!!!'

'Oh, fellows,' said Ilya, 'it's time to escape now!' "

Clare goes home

Clare was back at her flat as the sense of relief flooded over her. She sprawled across her bed and made snow angel exercises with her arms and legs. She realised that she was past flat shares and thought how, in just a few days, things had jammered in her mind.

First, the new roster had come out and Clare had been reminded of dish politics, and of night-time smoked salmon food theft. She should have realised that both Lottie and Tessa had boyfriends. The evenings were like mini parties, with the two boyfriends coming around and sometimes one of them would bring a curry-carrying friend too.

They had told Clare the tale of the competitive mess-maker - Janice - who had occupied Clare's room before Clare. If Janice put something down somewhere it would stay there until she needed it again. At first the others started putting things just outside her room, but it made no difference, so they stopped. She used to take her socks off on the sofa every night and just leave them there, she would genuinely leave them until she did laundry (which was rare).

Janice never cleaned anything, so she would cook in the kitchen and wash any item that belonged to her, but anything else would be left dirty. She would wash her plate, knife, fork etc, but if she had used someone else's saucepan she would just leave it, she also never cleaned the work surfaces or hob.

Then - for everyone's benefit - there was the 'scrunchie on the door handle' warning system - a kind of 'no entry' sign.

Or the endless trash television. Made in Chelsea, Made in Essex, Made in Gateshead, The XYZ Factor. It wasn't all as Herbal Essences as they'd made out in the advert.

And then there was that evening when someone unknown was crashing around in the kitchen at 2am drunkenly cooking 'pasta surprise' for three other visitors.

Or when Lottie's drunken boyfriend Matt turned the house into a honeymoon suite with loads of flowers and expensive boxes of chocolates. But, thought Clare, you kind of must let it happen, because this is nice, and Lottie says she has been single forever, so let her have her fun, don't be jerks. Then - as night follows day - there's the reverse: Tessa breaks up with Rick and everyone has to tiptoe around, or Tess's feelings will be hurt. Oh, she'd never say so, but you can tell from the look in her eyes. You just can.

And that was just the first week. Clare would have several more, at least. She decided that she would be seeing her imaginary boyfriend quite often.

Clare's phone rang. It was Christina.

"Glad you are back at home?" she asked.

"Christina - you can't imagine how good this feels! Thank you for persuading me!"

"You looked kind of jaded when we saw you. We all figured you needed some peace and quiet."

"Yes - it is full-on at the House, then full on at the other house!"

"Well - I bring news. A little bird has told me some things."

Christina relayed the information from Blackbird to Clare.

"There's a new project in this for Bigsy, then? To find out about the Kremlin end of things?"

"Yes - but Blackbird warned me to be very careful. Not to wake the sleeping Dragon."

"Dragon? I thought that was Chinese or Japanese?"

"No - we have many tales of Zmey Gorynych - The dragon from the mountain is in our country too!"

Another day in the House

Clare had finally got to meet Andrew Brading. It had taken nearly a week, but he seemed like a lovely person. He'd been through the mill though, because of his unguarded BAME comment. A couple of the red tops were clearly gunning for him and now that the Identity Bill Second Reading had slithered though the Commons, the news cycle were looking for something else to poke and prod.

Andrew was very aware of the 'one-liner' that Clare had provided and had shaken her by the hand by way of saying thanks.

The already crowded office was now host to another visitor, the Special Advisor named Ian Harrison.

Clare noticed that Harrison was playing his role like he was on the TV show West Wing. He kept saying things like, "Walk with me," and "Talk to me," like he was too busy to stop and think.

Clare nicknamed him M.T. - Moving Target, which was also a delightful pun on 'Empty'. She also worked out he was what she called a 'rear view mirror watcher.'

Harrison could pontificate about anything after the fact but seldom had anything new to add to the direction.

Ian has been elated, deflated, proud, over-eager and depressed in half-hour bursts since Andrew's BAME clip had been uploaded. He has also taken to stumbling into the office whenever his mood shifted to share his latest thought with his boss.

Clare could see that Andrew Brading was tolerating Ian, rather than embracing him. She wondered what Harrison's daily rate was - certainly more than a couple of grand for doing almost nothing useful. By comparison, Andrew Brading showed a no-nonsense style and independence of spirit (the libertarian), and then could flip to a common-sense embrace of difficult negotiations (the patrician).

Andrew looked up from his reading as Ian entered the room for the third time today. Clare could see that Andrew was peeved but that Harrison had missed it.

"Andrew, I've just had Wilbur Griffiths on the phone!" One of the Secretary of State for Health's special advisors. A champion of health care privatisation, free market absolutist. Not a natural ally of Andrew's. Not a pragmatic market reformer, Oh no. Off the other bloody side of the dart board, really.

'Reactive,' thought Clare.

"What did he want?'
    "He'd love to have a sit-down with you to talk through some of the provisions for shifts of the trusts to profit-creating centres.'

"That's dynamite, " thought Clare.

Andrew initials the document he is reading. Picks up the next.

"But what do you think, Ian?"

Ian sits on one of the wobbly office chairs, pulls out his phone and scans it while he speaks. "He wants to establish a relationship in case the Secretary of State gets the boot and you get his job, of course."

"Not my question. I asked what you think about the situation?"

Harrison squeezes Andrew's shoulder and lumbers off without replying.

"Idiots," mutters Brading.

Brading recollects that Harrison knows about wine, and Harrison's boss at Hayter Consulting, Jason Turner, is legendary for knowing his way around a wine list.

"They all get paid too much and take us for granted," says Brading, "Clare - don't let it happen to you."

Clare smiles across to Andrew, "I find it so hollow," she says.

"Leaning together, headpiece filled with straw," answers Brading.

"Yes, the hope only of empty men," replied Clare - also quoting from Eliot.

"Come," he says, "we should get some sandwiches, and you can tell me some more about 'The New Girl.'

"Sure," answered Clare, "But less of the girl, please."

"Oh, I am so sorry," she sees a slight blush run across his face.

"That's okay, but I don't want the name to stick," she replies.

They leave the office together.

"Look, I'm sorry about that 'girl' thing," says Brading, "This place is so damned misogynistic. What do you think of what you are seeing so far?"

"It's complicated, fragmented, interrupt driven, policy led. A few people 'in government' seem to make all the decisions. Some of it is two-faced. Some of the spokespersons are plain embarrassing. I'm amazed that anything gets done."

"That's a good and a plain-talking assessment. They told me you spoke your mind - Please continue to do so. I only ask that you don't embarrass me or the office and that I'm not asked to bail you out because of something, Otherwise, please feel free to act on any matters. Oh, and I plead to your loyalty, or that you tell me when you disagree with something I've said or done."

"That seems very fair," answered Clare, "And - in my humble opinion - you seem to do a good job!"

Brading stopped and looked at Clare.

"Now, you looked as if you meant it, unlike some!" he said.

Clare was pleased; she thought she could read Brading.

"Andrew!" called a woman's voice, "Over here!" They both looked towards Parliament Square, close to the Statue of Benjamin Disraeli.

An attractive woman was standing, waving. "It's Katherine, my wife. She is in London today for some kind of event."

They crossed the massive roundabout and greeted Katherine. Clare noticed Andrew give her the mildest of kisses to the cheek and then stepped forward.

"Katherine, this is my new researcher, Clare Crafts. She joined us just over a week ago. She was out shopping for sandwiches - but so far hasn't found any."

Katherine smiled, "Well, I think she is in luck. She could join us for lunch. I've a table around the corner at the Supreme Court."

"Great idea," said Andrew, " Let's go and be Conservatives."

They walked the few steps to the cafe at the Supreme Court.

"It's with some sadness that we walk past Roux," said Katherine. "It used to be a wonderful place, just like someone's living room and serving the best food."

"Did it go under?" asked Clare, thinking back to the virus and its consequences.

"Yes, I'm afraid so," answered Katherine.

They were soon seated at a large round table.

"When did you join?" asked Katherine, Clare thought of her interview and wondered whether she was about to have it all over again. She decided to turn the questioning around.

"Oh, just over a week ago - but tell me, what event are you attending" asked Clare.

"Oh, it's a talk about mediocrity," said Katherine, "About white men in positions of power - don't worry darling, I'll wear my dark glasses!"

"You are something of an activist too?" asked Clare.

"Yes, you could say that; I work for The Tribune, as a journalist."

"Doesn't that put you into conflict with Andrew sometimes?"

"We've worked it all out nowadays - Years of marriage, two kids and I think we've devised a system."

"Do you live in London, then?" asked Clare, "I assume you have somewhere in your constituency too?"

"We are among the MPs who haven't been on the take, over housing," answered Katherine.

Clare nodded, "Yes I heard about all the profiting from second homes and MPs staying in hotels. It was quite a feeding frenzy when one of the tabloids discovered it."

Andrew interrupted, "It is what gives we politicians a bad name, all of the ones who are on the take."

"I remember, I think it was around 160 MPs accused, including, if I remember correctly, Michael Gove. I think he was reckoned to have made £870,000 on two homes originally paid for from taxpayer sources. And didn't Maria Miller, pull in more that £1.3 million? And the respectable-looking Tory chairman Graham Brady was also implicated. Parliamentary rules meant they were entitled to keep the money.

"Entitled, says it all," muttered Andrew, "You are right Clare, the Daily Mirror investigated and found out that MPs made an average profit of £255,000 on selling their homes.

"Of the 20 who made more than £500,000 in gross profit, 14 are Tories and six are from Labour. Labour MPs made an average of £193,000 profit on sales, while Tories averaged double at around £417,000. And the politicians could reclaim thousands of pounds in mortgage interest payments under the discredited old expenses system."

"What will I be reading in your column?' Clare asked Katherine, intrigued.

"Nothing as exciting as the stuff we are discussing here," said Katherine, "I mainly deal with culture and arts - that new show at the R.A. is a case in point. And the trees wrapped in polka dots along by the river."

"Yayoi Kusama! I love her work, " said Clare, "The polka dots - the infinity rooms - her agenda - feminism, minimalism, surrealism - stylish Art Brut, pop art, and abstract expressionism. She has been said to be one of the most important artists to come out of Japan."

"I think you should write this piece for me!" smiled

Katherine, "I shall certainly keep your comments in mind when I take a look."

"I knew we'd hired a good one," said Andrew.

Calling Amanda

Another week had passed. Clare was back at her own home, expecting her weekly call from Amanda.

There was a bleep and Zoom opened.

"Hi," said Amanda, "How are you and how's things going?"

"Well, I seem to be in with everyone now, including lunch with Andrew Brading and his wife Katherine. They both seem to like me. I've also met a shifty Special Advisor named Ian Harrison, who seems to specialise it borrowing watches to tell everyone the time. And I seem to be well in with my lively flatmates, although I'm going away for a couple for days each week to spend some quiet time back at my own apartment."

"Any sign of anything unusual?" asked Amanda.

Clare relayed the information she had got via Christina.

"The Medusa Listening Station must be fairly new, " observed Amanda, "And I'm genuinely surprised that they would try an identical operation twice."

"I suppose you don't expect it the second time - but also beware that they are not just using it as a distraction. If I were you, I'd get Grace Fielding or someone at GCHQ to take a look at Cyber-attacks being mounted by the Kremlin."

"Thanks for the steer on that. I won't ask where you got it from," said Amanda.

"You might want to look out for CyberBerkut too," added Christina.

Special Advisor

Ian Harrison was pleased they had recruited him as a SpAd. A Special Advisor. He would not take the risks that Dominic Cummings had taken. He was too canny to become the story. The early history was already written of Dominic Cummings. He broke the first rule. By defending himself in the Rose Garden at No 10, Boris Johnson's chief of staff entered uncharted territory. And as senior Government figures fought his corner, the rulebook was torn up entirely.

A government aide quoted: "It is a completely bizarre situation where we've got ministers, Cabinet ministers – the Prime Minister – going out and defending one adviser. It is the complete opposite to what should be the case."

Cummings was no ordinary member of staff. Few advisers were so integral to a prime minister that they would stake as much political capital as Johnson did in order to keep them in place.

But the secret of the Tories was always about Power. How to get it and how to keep it. A few reality distortions never did any harm if it allowed one to mainline on

Power.

The charge against Cummings was that he breached lockdown rules by travelling to Durham to be near his family in case he and his wife, both with suspected coronavirus, could not take care of their young child.

Then he fanned the flames by misjudging his initial response to the joint investigation by The Mirror and The Guardian. The subsequent coverage led many to conclude he should have fallen on his sword. "That really should have been the outcome," said a former aide to another Cabinet minister.

Another ex-SpAd argued: "Your job is to help the reputation of the minister and the government of the day. Rightly or wrongly, if your coverage is damaging that, then you're not doing your job. I think most special advisors would step aside."

History showed that Cummings days were numbered. It needed an excuse, but something that would make the PM look like he was in control.

Harrison realised the Cummings saga reinvigorated the public's awareness of the cult of the SpAd. Aspersions were cast about the influence this unelected cabal have and the motivations they hold. "It's as if there are all these devious special advisers who have got this grand plan to mess things up," says one. "It often feels there's not enough appreciation that it's a load of people trying to do their very best and make what's already a difficult situation better."

Harrison knew how to keep his head down. Take the money and lie low. Or was it take the money and lie?

"I sometimes call them the people who live in the dark," Clare Short, the former Labour cabinet minister, told the New Statesman way back. "Everything they do is in hiding."

Ian Harrison was enjoying being a temporary civil servant who could now walk through the walls of Parliament. They had given him a code of conduct, which set out the roles he could carry out. This included speech writing, advising, policy development and representing the views of their minister to the media where allowed. Cummings had enjoyed power without responsibility. Harrison would accept money without responsibility.

The code also stated: "Special advisers must not take public part in political controversy, through any form of statement whether in speeches or letters to the press, or in books, social media, articles or leaflets. They must observe discretion... and would not normally speak in public for their minister or the Department."

Cummings had driven a coach and horses through that one.

Harrison was in it for the hourly rate. He could rack up a decent amount and would usually have vague responsibilities and not get involved in anything too controversial. He knew how to avoid accountability and considered himself coin operated. It annoyed him that Brading had made a comment about BAME which had swung the searchlight his way.

A rule of survival for Harrison was to always know whether the bright light was a spotlight (good thing) or a searchlight (bad thing). Harrison also knew that as a SpAd, it was most important to be liked and respected by journalists, while being trusted that you're a reliable source. Another source of income.

But right now, Ian Harrison's phone had just rung. He could see it was his boss from Hayter Consulting, Jason Turner.

"Hey Ian, How's things? I bring you news. Can we meet?"

Jason Turner continued, "Look Ian, I need to speak to you in private about some things, can we meet together soon? Tomorrow maybe? Don't panic, it's not an H.R. thing."

Ian sighed almost imperceptibly. If Turner was calling him to speak direct, then it would most likely have been a Human Resources moment. He didn't want that, not now he was well and truly comfortable in his lucrative role in Parliament.

"Sure thing, where would you like to meet?" he asked.

"How about Langan's," suggested Jason, at, say, one o'clock?"

'Hmm,' thought Harrison, Langan's Brasserie, it could only be good news if Jason was inviting him there.

"Absolutely, I'll see you there tomorrow at one!"

Langan's Brasserie

Harrison arrived at Langan's. It was one of London's traditional relaxed meeting places. Smart tablecloths and sharply dressed waiters. Parisienne cafe society brought to London by Peter Langan. He had chosen Stratton Street, Mayfair, as its location. Then Michael Caine - the actor and friend of Peter Langan, became his business partner, and the pair transformed the site with original artwork, brighter lighting with mis-matched lamps and relaxed the atmosphere of the restaurant. Everyone had visited - Patricia Taylor, Marlon Brando, Mick Jagger, Francis Bacon, Muhammad Ali, Jack Nicholson, and David Hockney, to name several, and there were discreet pictures sprinkled around of the great and the good. Not to mention the artwork, which included pieces by David Hockney, Lucian Freud and Francis Bacon,

Harrison was meeting Turner upstairs, in 'The Venetian Room' which featured murals by Patrick Procktor specially commissioned by Peter Langan.

Harrison also knew that this was the site of many a boozy evening, both back in Langan's day but also much more recently courtesy of Jason Turner.

"Hello Ian," greeted Jason. He was seated at a round table with another guest. She looked stunning as if she had just walked from the set of a fashion shoot. Claret coloured dress, blonde hair and tanned skin. Ian assumed St Tropez was her natural habitat.

"Let me introduce you to Tasha, a modelling friend of mine," said Jason. Tasha moved gracefully to extend her toned arm, and Ian wasn't sure whether to shake her hand and or to kiss it. He selected the former but thought about the latter.

"Hello," said Tasha, "Tasha is short for Natasha - Natasha Makarovna - actually, Tasha seems to go well here with the informality of London."

"So where are you from?" asked Ian, aware he was drifting into areas of questioning that could be construed as non-PC.

"I'm from Moscow originally; do you know it?" asked Tasha.

Ian shook his head, "No - I've never been there. I hope to one day." He thought his answer sounded lame.

"Yes, it is a raging city. There is always something happening. The night life can be extreme. Just don't follow the tourists around and you'll have a great time."

Jason started, "Ian, I want to bring you up to date on something. It is a delicate subject, which is why I wanted to meet you somewhere private to discuss it."

Ian leaned forward, "Is it about me?' he asked, "Only I'm getting on really well in Parliament at the moment."

A server arrived with three cocktails.

"Peter Langan's Fizz, we need to have at least one in his honour," said Jason, " I think it's vodka and Champagne, with a touch of elderflower and lime."

They clinked glasses, Ian met Tasha's eyes and was instantly befuddled.

"No, it's only indirectly about you - more what you need to do than anything."

Jason paused as if to collect his thoughts.

"We've an interesting situation that has developed with your MP, Ian - with Andrew Brading."

"He's been - how shall we say - romantically involved with Tasha here. There's a terrifically detailed audit trail of his dalliances, with hotel room receipts and a few photographs of them together,"

The server returned; they each ordered some food. Jason asked for something off-menu which sounded so good that Ian decided to have to as well. Tasha had the lemon sole.

Now Jason foraged into his small case and pulled out a some 10x7 glossy photographs.

"Here, see, a handful of the photographs."

Ian could see they were slightly blurred but there was the unmistakable profile of a beaming Natasha holding hands with Andrew Brading. In the second one, they appeared to be checking in to a hotel, which looked quite like the Dorchester. A third picture showed the two of them at a table in China Tang's. The photographer had kindly placed a menu in the foreground and the distinctive chair backs of Chinese silk were quite visible.

"Em, isn't this somewhat irregular?" Asked Ian, looking towards Tasha, "I mean - we normally see the mistress (excuse me, Natasha), but seldom get to talk to her!"

"It would be if this was an ordinary situation," answered Jason, "But for this the stakes are sky high."

"What is your angle Jason? I'd have thought Andrew was as straight as a die, and faithful to his wife Katherine and his two young children?"

Natasha spoke, "Sometimes things are not quite what they seem. You will learn this over the next few weeks. The pictures don't lie and it puts Andrew Brading into a tough position."

Jason added, "But not as difficult as the other photos. They show Brading with Shanell Kinkead from Jamaica. Here, take a look,"- Jason showed Ian a similar set of photographs, this time of Brading with Ms Kinkead.

"Kinkead by name, Kinkead by nature," said Jason rather crudely. Then he looked directly at Ian.

"That's where you come in. Ian, we want you to tell Brading that you have found this out today. Tell him privately. Tell him you were shown the photographs. Tell him that this is on the edge of circulating to the press. That you have been offered a deal to broker with him."

"He'll see it as blackmail. Pure and simple. And then he'll get the police involved."

"Ask him about his dog called Barney. He'll know what you mean."

"Barney? I didn't even know he had a dog."

" A treasured family red setter - sadly, it went missing about a week ago. One minute it was in their house and the next minute it had gone. Suffice to say it was a simple demonstration of agencies unknown and their ability to access his home."

By now they were eating. Some delicious red wine had arrived. Ian felt that his head was clouding. The alcohol. He wasn't used to what was a heady mix of cocktails plus Natasha, news about Shanell and his boss.

He finished his lunch. Natasha looked over. She placed her hand on top of his.

"You'll know what to do?" she asked, "You'll be resolute about this and report back to Jason in a couple of days when you've told Andrew?"

He felt her slightly squeeze his hand. He knew that the squeeze would be much greater if he didn't obey.

Video Conference

It was a video conference call to the Triangle office.

Grace began, "Hello everyone - Grace Fielding here: it has been a long time! Thanks, Clare for remembering me when you talked about this with Amanda Miller. It's good that we can trust one another."

Everyone said 'Hello' to Grace, who smiled back at them. Amanda was on a separate session and they assumed she was patched in from SI6.

Grace continued, "Here's what I've found out,"

"The Kremlin have been increasing their cyberattacks against military and civilian infrastructure in the West. We mark them as a persistent challenge nowadays."

"We thought you'd know about all of this, from Brexit and the various elections," said Bigsy.

Grace continued, "Yes, but we are still struggling to get a better understanding of Russia's strategy and cyber actors, particularly the growing role of the military in these issues. If we can achieve that, then it can facilitate an improvement in ours and Western governments' policies to defend against future Russian activity."

"It seems the Russians leverage western systems to help themselves?" asked Amanda.

"That's right," said Grace, "Systems like Facebook, Instagram, Parley and simple social engineering have all been used with recent significant effect. Cybersecurity is perceived as a Western notion in Russian debates, while the semantic Russian equivalent is information security *(informatsionnaya bezopastnost).*

"The Russian military scholars and official documents present varying definitions of information warfare and information security, but it is well-established that information security is a component of information warfare, which is a term that has a technical and a psychological or cognitive component."

"It goes well beyond propaganda, then?" asked Christina, remembering her time at the Akademy.

Grace continued, "We can assert that although Russia's doctrine suggests a defensive and cooperative posture in response to threats in the information space, there is a preference stirred by Putin for offensive cyber capabilities and operations, shaped by Russia's threat perceptions and doctrine, and the institutional cultures of the departments within the military conducting them."

Grace added, "The chief of Russia's Armed Forces, Valery Gerasimov, wrote that the rules of warfare were changing, and revolts modelled on the Arab Spring presaged future wars where the protest potential of the non-military actors and the use of political, economic, and other non-military measures would be widely employed."

"Cheaper too," said Bigsy, "Than using military might"

"Gerasimov was a key driver for us, back at the Akademy, " said Christina, "He showed that warfare could be asymmetric and that - agreeing with Bigsy's point - use of cyber made it much cheaper than with conventional weapons - and potentially more far-reaching."

Grace nodded, "That's right, General Gerasimov re-emphasised the employment of mixed tactics and the maintenance of asymmetrical and classic potential at the 2019 conference of the Russian Academy of Military Sciences. He noted the changing character of war and the developing 'coordinated use of military and non-military measures' and even suggested the primacy of non-military measures over military power."

Grace continued, "Yes, so over the past two decades, Russia's military and political leadership has undergone a fundamental modification of its conception of warfare and the role of cyber operations in this developing view.
    "Some terms that Western and Russian scholars have used to describe Moscow's shifting character of warfare include 'hybrid warfare', 'new generation warfare', 'the Gerasimov Doctrine', 'political warfare', 'hostile measures', 'cross-domain coercion', and 'grey zone tactics.'"

"We were told it was 'The Information Sphere'," said Christina.

Grace node, "Yes, the so-called 'information sphere' and the concept of information warfare fits well within Russia's understanding of the changing character of war because, as General Gerasimov asserted, 'without having clearly defined national borders, the information sphere provides the possibility of remote, covert influence not only on critical information infrastructures but also on the country's population, directly affecting the state's national security.'"

Amanda said, "And the cyber influence will be wherever it can destabilise the state. They are just as likely to use Alt-Right doctrine as anything from the Communist manifesto. Their aim is to destabilise at a low cost. Get the people with easy access to guns running around shouting slogans. QAnon and Deep State theories are just as just as useful to create some chaos."

"We've seen examples of all of this," said Jake, "It is well past Crop Circles, Bigfoot and Loch Ness conspiracies - which are 'mostly harmless,' as Douglas Adams might say, and straight into 'Get Help' territory."

Amanda added, "We know that the cyber operations attributed to Moscow are not conducted in a strategic vacuum. They are enabled and shaped by broader geopolitical considerations and the institutional culture of Russia's military, intelligence, and political leadership, as well as by Moscow's evolving approach to asymmetric interstate competition that falls short of all-out conflict."

"In other words, Moscow - The Kremlin - is calculated about using cyberwarfare to support its aims," said Jake.

Grace continued, "To understand the motivations behind, and the constraints of, Russia's use of cyber and information operations against perceived adversaries, decision-makers must thoroughly study existing policy and doctrine, particularly its evolution from the immediate post-Soviet period until now, while striving to attain a more sophisticated comprehension of the actors responsible for executing cyberattacks and digital influence campaigns."

"Yes, and they have been doing it for quite some time," added Amanda, "We think there is more continuity than contrast between Russian cyber perspectives and practice. Russia's cyber posture, nested in Russia's concept of information warfare, is reflected in the offensive cyber operations launched by Russian government departments, whose institutional culture, expertise, and modus operandi have affected and will continue to affect Russia's cyber signature."

"So I'd better get rid of all of those Russian sounding anti-virus packages, then?" asked Bigsy.

Grace continued, "Such differences may have wide-ranging consequences for deterring Russia and understanding Russia's red lines, and for facilitating the creation of a long-term strategy that addresses the causes of Russia's behaviour."

Then she added, "Yes, and Russia's MoD 2011 'Concept on the Activities of the Armed Forces of the Russian Federation in the Information Space' provided a clear definition of information warfare:

"'...the confrontation between two or more states in the information space with the purpose of inflicting damage to information systems, processes and resources, critical and other structures, undermining the political, economic and social systems, a massive psychological manipulation of the population to destabilize the state and society, as well as coercing the state to take decisions for the benefit of the opposing force.'

"We get the various terms too:

- *informatsionnoe protivoborstvo* (information struggle)
- *informatsionnaya voina* (information war) and
- *informatsionnaya borba* (information fight).

"These characteristics render studying issues of preparation and conduct of informational activities 'the most important task of military science'. Considering its multi-faceted and unconventional nature, information warfare, and by extension cyber operations, may begin deploy prior to the official announcement of war and to achieve political objectives without resorting to the use of military force."

Grace added, "In line with the Soviet tradition of portraying Russia as a besieged fortress defending itself against constant internal and external threats, Moscow also views the struggle in the information sphere as unending."

Confusion will be my epitaph

The wall on which the prophets wrote
    Is cracking at the seams.
    Upon the instruments of death
    The sunlight brightly gleams.

When every man is torn apart
    With nightmares and with dreams,
    Will no one lay the laurel wreath
    As silence drowns the screams.

Between the iron gates of fate,
    The seeds of time were sown,
    And watered by the deeds of those
    Who know and who are known.

Knowledge is a deadly friend
    When no one sets the rules.
    The fate of all mankind I see
    Is in the hands of fools.

Confusion will be my epitaph.
    As I crawl a cracked and broken path
    If we make it we can all sit back
    And laugh.

But I fear tomorrow I'll be crying,
    Yes, I fear tomorrow I'll be crying.

Epitaph: Robert Fripp / Peter John Sinfield / Ian Mcdonald / Michael Rex Giles / Greg Lake (King Crimson)

Clare gets the bug

Clare had borrowed a couple of Bigsy's little gadgets. The little Tammano gadget plugged into a USB port and was like a miniature voice recorder. All it needed was power and a sound and it would switch itself on and record everything. Even if the USB socket has been disabled, it would still work.

"It lasts around 17 hours," explained Bigsy, "Consider it around a day. Here, take two - then you can swap one for another and cycle them."

Now she was in Andrew Brading's office and had plugged the unit into a spare USB socket. She would have a recording of the whole day's events.

It was another busy day. There was further news about a big Bill sponsored by Brading and the Opposition were kicking up a storm. There would be questions asked in the House.

Clare noticed that Ian Harrison had visited their office several times. He always asked for Andrew but didn't seem to contribute anything to the Bill debate that was raging. Serena and Maggie had gone across to another building and now Clare was alone.

In walked Andrew, "Oh hello, Clare, it's a madhouse everywhere today. They don't like my Bill about Fundamental Rights.

"It is ridiculous really, because all I am doing is re-enshrining in law something that was in place anyway when we were in the EU. The tabloids have got hung up on the word 'fundamental' - as if I'm supporting a 'Fundamentalist doctrine', which is ridiculous. I'm having to fight tooth and nail to keep the Bill moving forward."

Clare scanned through the Bill's contents pages. There were around 50 separate headings. She read a few of them and they all seemed eminently sensible and protective of the populous. Some football shirt wearing twitter lobby was kicking up a fuss, and it was being magnified through some vociferous chancers on the Left.

Clare was about to reply when there was a clatter at the door. It was a sweaty-looking Ian Harrison again - maybe on his fifth or sixth sortie to their office.

"Ah Andrew, I'm so glad I've finally caught up with you. I have something very important that we need to discuss."

"Is it about the Bill? Asked Andrew.

"Bill? What Bill?"

"The one that is pushing us into overdrive this morning."

"Oh, no, it's not about that, but it is still something very important. Can we talk here? Sorry, new girl, I can't remember your name, please can we have the room?"

Clare looked across to Andrew.

"Sorry," he mouthed and used his head to gesture that she had better go.

Clare stood and walked to the door. Ian's bulk didn't move to give her an easier path.

Clare marked him down as a bad-mannered slob and a slacker.

"Good, Andrew. Look, I have something delicate to discuss..."

That was all Clare heard as the door closed on the conversation. She walked back towards the Jubilee Cafe inside Parliament. There she spotted Serena and Maggie drinking coffee with someone else. They both looked frazzled sitting next to an calm-looking black woman with dark finger coiled hair.

Clare walked over.

"Fifty headings!!" said Maggie to Clare, "That's fifty pot shots from the Opposition; they seem to think that Andrew's Bill is incredibly toxic."

"Is it because it was ex-EU or because of the word 'Fundamental' in the title?" asked Clare, "Could we change it to 'Basic Rights' or something similar? They would have a harder time attacking that and it would make it different from the EU Legislation too."

She smiled across towards the third member of the table.

"Have you met Flore Chéron, QC?" introduced Serena, "We were going to ask her about changes to the core legislation - things like the Bill's legislative titles can be difficult to get amended."

Flore Chéron smiled across the table, "Hello Clare - they have been telling me about you! Let me introduce myself, she began, I'm Flore Chéron and I work for Lion & Freshwater LLP."

"You're a silk?" asked Clare, "My uncle was a QC for a company called Deringer, I always thought it sounded a bit like cowboys!"

"Ah yes, they are not called that nowadays, they have gone triple-barrelled like many of the other firms!"

"A triple barrelled Deringer! I suppose you want that on your side in a fight!" chuckled Clare.

"You looked surprised when Serena first mentioned it. Are you surprised that I'm Queen's Counsel, or that Andrew Brading's office is concerned enough to appoint a Queen's Counsel?"

"Bit of both. You look young to be a QC and I imagined Secretary of State for Internal Affairs would have asked one of their own many lawyers to get anything fixed."

"Well thank you, but I've been doing this for many years!" Flore scribbled something into a small Moleskine notebook. She wrote it with a fine liner instead of a fancy fountain pen. Next thing she'll be typing into an iPhone. A thoroughly modern lawyer.

"What are you doing over here?" asked Serena, "I thought Andrew was in the office?"

"He is. That Ian Harrison appeared and wanted to talk to Andrew all secret squirrel. Speaking frankly, I don't trust that Harrison. He seems to be paid a lot of money to skulk around dispensing wisdom after the fact. A rear-view-mirror jock, if you ask me."

Clare thought it was better to speak frankly and create a little damage in the process.

Maggie giggled, "You should have been here half-an-hour ago. His last invoice has just arrived, and we were talking about his value to the Department."

"Who does he work for," asked Clare, "Have they got any real credentials in Government?"

Serena answered, "It's the partner system. A partner for a big, approved firm gets some work. Then they find what they call a 'floor-filler' project and backfill it with a bunch of stringers. Stringers means that the so-called employees of the partner's firm are really all freelancers. Some of them are good, but others, like Ian, have, shall we say, 'room for improvement'."

"I must go," said Flore; "It's refreshing to meet someone so forthright. It's terrific to have you working in the office of my next Department, Clare. Goodbye, all!"

"See you in the corridors," said Maggie.

There was a pause as they each collected their thoughts. Then Serena asked, " Ian Harrison - you don't know what he wanted, then?"

Clare shook her head, "He almost barged me out of the office - he wanted it to be private, just between him and

Andrew. Who does he work for then?"

"Hayter Consultants - We make a joke about them. They are a subsidiary of ISMC which stands for International Strategic Management Consultants."

"ISMC, they were connected with Brant," observed Clare, "I had something of a run-in with Brant last year."

"Intriguing," said Serena, "You do run in some interesting circles, Clare, your uncle a QC, sister in Parly and run-ins with Brant!"

"They are all very long stories, "said Clare, and then changing the subject, "So, what's the joke about Hayter?"

Maggie replied, "Hayter Consultants - slogan: 'We don't let the grass grow under our feet.'"

Clare looked blank.

Maggie explained, " Oh dear - I'm explaining jokes now - Hayter is a well-known make of lawnmower..."

The recording

Clare had listened to Harrison's discussion with Andrew Brading. Bigsy's gadget had worked perfectly and now she was about to play it to everyone, on one of her dates with her imaginary boyfriend.

She was also going to need to ask Jake to become the boyfriend because her flatmates had invited her out with their boyfriends, to a bar called Opium in Chinatown.

"I just ran out of excuses; they were most insistent that they meet you, particularly as I'd stayed away from the flat so often. But I think I will - that is we will - be able to get more information from everyone in the social setting. Both are dating other people from the Parliamentary Estate. Lottie's is another Research Assistant - Matt Stevens - and Tessa's is a Special Advisor - Robin Hunter - although he is only a PB1"

"PB1?" asked Jake.

"Oh, sorry Pay Band 1, the lowest £40k+ to £60k+. It goes up to PB4, which tops out at £145k. See, I'm learning all kinds of things!" smiled Clare.

At Clare's request, Amanda was on the call and Grace had dialled in from GCHQ.

"I think we can see something of history repeating itself," suggested Clare, "Listen to this."

She started the playback and Bigsy adjusted the volume setting so that those remote could hear it clearly.

They could hear Ian Harrison explaining about some photographs to Andrew Brading. He talked about Natasha Makarova and Shanell Kinkead.

Andrew Brading started off sounding irritated; "was this some kind of joke? Who put Harrison up to this?" He didn't really have time for the fun and games when he was so busy with the Bill."

Harrison persisted, and Brading realised that it wasn't a practical joke. His tone changed to one of annoyance. Annoyance and denial. He didn't know these women. He had never heard of them before today. He had nothing to hide. He was fully faithful to his wife and family.

Harrison explained that he had seen photographs. That on a couple Brading was holding hands with the women. Harrison had even briefly met one of the women.

"Where?" asked Brading, now angry with Harrison, "And what is it you expect to get from this - my trust and loyalty to you. Forget it. You have just crossed the line which means today will be your last day on Crown Estate soil.

Harrison played the 'Barney' card.

"Have you recently lost your dog?" he asked, "Barney,"

Brading paused, "We have actually, from inside of our home."

"Well, it was a demonstration. Of the power that certain people wield. That they can come and go to your house."

There was the sound of Brading picking up is phone, "Security, please could you come to my office to help escort Ian Harrison off-site."

Barely five seconds later, there was a knock on the office door. A brief hubbub as two new men entered, approached Harrison and offered politely but firmly to walk him from the Estate.

They heard Brading buzzing someone and a few seconds later heard Serena enter the room.

"Serena," he said, "There is something not right. That little shit Harrison has just threatened me. He says they have got something on me. Something to do with two women. Natasha Makarova and Shanell Kinkead. He implied that I was seeing these women, being unfaithful to Katherine. It's simply not true."

There was a pause on the recording. It was difficult to tell how long because of the auto-stop start when things went quiet.

"It's okay, I believe you, Andrew, of course; we've worked together too long for me to think you'd have something running on the side. And I'm sure it is the same with Katherine."

"Thank you," said Andrew, "But frankly it's the fourth and fifth estate that I'm worried about. They can make trouble out of a minor mis-speak - imagine what they can do with this!"

"Look, I've just been speaking to a new QC, Flore Chéron from Lion & Freshwater. She's not one of our usual suspects, and I brought her in to take a fresh look at your Bill. I hate to say it, but our expensive normal advisors have tackled your Fundamental Rights Bill with such little imagination. I suggest we ask her for her advice in this matter?"

Another pause, "Do you think she can be relied upon for discretion?"

"Absolutely, and, by the way, all the women in your office seem to trust her already!"

"Okay - I'd better meet her then, could you set it up without saying too much about the subject?"

"I'll try to arrange something for tomorrow."

Clear spoke up now, "The recording continues, but there's nothing of real interest; I think what you have heard sets the scene in a manner similar to the late Bernard Driscoll."

"That could be our lucky break," said Christina, "I mean if they have used some of the old moves, then I suppose they might have used some of the old players as well?"

"Good point," said Jake, "Who were those women we met before? Marion Charlotte and her friends - they all worked for the same agency too, I seem to remember - it even hired Pete Burr for that big event in London."

"We'll have to make some enquiries," said Christina, "But what is bothering me is we don't know what they are trying to influence now. It surely can't be that Rights Bill?"

Clare nodded, "I agree, we will need to see whether Andrew handles any other big Bills."

Amanda spoke, "Clare, you have exceeded expectation in the first couple of weeks. I just need to remind you to be careful. If the people involved are as strong minded as they appear to be, then the last thing we want is for them to find out about you."

Opium Chinatown

Clare and Jake arrived at Opium. They had to locate it first.

Clare said to Jake, "Well this is a secret bar if ever there was one; My instructions are to find the jade green door and head up the long dark stairway.

They emerged into a chic, hidden venue in the heart of Chinatown. Orientally themed but an element of freshness with a twist making it modern and current. Metal finishes on mis-matched Chinese furniture produced a London feel.

"Three bars - it could take us a while to find the others," said Clare, but then noticed Lottie and her extra needy boyfriend. They waved to her and Clare led Jake across to the table.

"Hooray! You must be Clare's imaginary boyfriend then?" asked Tessa.

"Oh no, I'm very real," said Jake, "My name's Jake Lambers - please to meet you all. They went around the table doing introductions. Clare finally learned Lottie's boyfriend's name - it was Matt Stevens.

"What are you drinking?" Matt asked, and signalled to a waiter.

"A Hemingway Daiquiri," said Jake, "And a Clarified Negroni, for me," said Clare.

"We are going down in flames tonight," said Matt, "Can we have six Yam Sings too,"

"Yam Sings?" asked Clare.

"Shots!" replied Matt.

"Easy, Tiger," whispered Lottie. Clare noticed Tessa was with a First Date Situation. At least Clare assumed it was because she didn't recognise him and he seemed a little swamped in the conversations.

"Hi, I don't think we've met?" asked Clare.

"Hi - yes - I've seen you around the Estate. You work for Andrew Brading, don't you? I know Maggie quite well. I'm Robin Hunter."

"It's a small world," said Clare, "I'm Clare Crafts and this is Jake Lambers,"

Matt piped up, "Well, expect 3 bars of amaaaaazing Asian cocktails and a shelection of dim sum to get your appetite going."

Clare noticed that Matt's voice was a little slurred. He had ordered another round of slammers too. Jake looked at Clare signifying that he had also noticed. Clare knew Jake had the constitution of a seasoned journalist and a couple of shots on top of a cocktail wouldn't even dent him. Clare was slightly cannier and poured her second shot into the thriving tableside foliage when no one was looking.

Matt started, "So didn't you save Brading's bacon the other day? That's what I'd heard. A new girl wrote a five word sound bite, and it saved Andrew."

"Easy on the 'new girl', Matt," said Lottie. "We've all been called it, but none of us like it."

"Slorry," said Matt, slurring his words, "I meant nothing by it."

"I think we need another drink," said Jake, piling on the pressure. Clare realised what he was doing but let him, anyway.

"My shout for this round of cocktails." - Jake gestured to a server who wrote an order. "Oh, you'd better bring a half dozen of those nice shots as well and can you put this round on this card, please."

Clare could see that this would get out of control after the next round. She asked the server to bring some tap water as well.

"What are your first impressions then, Clare?" Asked Robin.

"Nothing like I could have predicted, totally frantic and interrupt-driven," answered Clare, "Or is that just because I am new?"

"Well - some things you should know, " said Lottie. Take my MP. Not Safe in Taxis. He's the slippery and wandering handed Duncan Melship, MP for Knutsford North."

"Yes," said Tessa, "We call him the Befummeler - fumbler. My cabinet minister has a different habit. It sometimes leaves white powder around his nose. The Blasenator. But he is also incredibly wealthy and has offshored most of it to the Caymans and Ireland. The public know about the Irish piece, but not the Caymans. And then there's that tittle-tattle about him and the porn-star. What did she say? She was 'happy to have helped the government through some unprecedented times'."

"And what about Andrew? Anything there for me to watch out for?" asked Clare.

A moment's silence.

Lottie spoke, "No - I think you landed on your feet. He seems to be the guiding light - all good."

"I heard something," said Robin, "It was only a passing remark. Apparently the very same porn-star is also a friend of Clive Haven."

There were groans from around the table.

"Brrr, he is a slimy toad," said Tessa. Lottie nodded.

"Well, he believes what he says, even if no-one else does, " answered Robin, "But this time he was talking about some new reform, which he wants Andrew to sponsor through the House. It is some kind of Health Passport, but Andrew seems to be refusing. It could cost him his next leg-up."

"I can't help thinking that if Haven is involved, then there must be something not quite right about the Heath Passport, said Lottie's.

"Surely that's like National Identity?" Asked Jake, puzzled.

Robin continued, "Not how you hear Clive Haven describe it. He says that the passport is for health identification only, There's Four levels - Tiers in the modern parlance - Tier 0 and 1, then 2 and then 3. They have linked it to the danger threats of the Tiered pathogens. But Andrew is dead against it. Some of you know that I shared an Oxford flat with Andrew when he was at Uni. He could be quite determined, even back then."

Robin added, "And the same flat also contained Maggie Shannon - who, Clare, you now work with. Andrew found the house through friends of his mum and dad. The owners were creative academics who had gone to teach at Carnegie Mellon for a year. Maggie already knew Andrew Brading from Oxford - I think he was already studying for his Masters when Maggie showed up - I think he was doing her parents a favour to let her in. I knew Andrew from when we were both doing a gap year in Thailand."

"You weren't at Oxford?" asked Clare

Robin feels himself bristle. "I was at Manchester. You?'

Now she looks up at him and flashes a quick smile, "Brighton - I studied Media. Communication and Cultural Politics, that sort of thing."

Robin relaxes a little, "No I was in Oxford already volunteering for the Party. We were hacking through analytics and could get undergrads to help us crunch the numbers. They could use their work for us also in their written work."

"And your job at this point, Robin? When you were sharing the house?'

"I was Head of Analytics for the local Conservative Party group.'

"And Andrew Brading?'

"As I said, he was studying for his Masters - although he was a local Officer in the Tory Party, even then whilst he worked for his PPE. And Maggie, she was just around - like as a Tory advisor. I'm amazed she went back to being an intern, but I think it was so she could work for Andrew. Although I don't think they were ever - entwined - but she has remained loyal to him, and him to her, ever since those days.

Matt interrupted, loudly. "If you spin a Chinese man around would he become disoriented?"

Lottie nudges him, "Matt. Stop. Inappropriate."

Matt says, Inn-a-prooop-priii-ate, In-app-rom-iate. Naughty. Wrong. Okay. I get the message."

Lottie smiles, "I think the cocktails must be quite strong," she looks over at Matt, who is staring at one of the waitresses.

"Hello," Matt says, "you have lovely eyes. Can you bring me and my friends here another round of cocktails?" He gestures around the table.

The server looks around the table for someone more approachable. Her eyes alight upon Jake.

"Shame again everyone?" asks Matt.

Jake looks at Lottie, who nods, "He'll be okay - he sometimes gets like this, but he'll pull through and become quite docile."

"Okay - these are on me," says Jake, offering his card to the server.

Jake has got their measure now. Well-connected highflyers, Head of this, Officer of that, Advisor. But still a bunch of twenty something political junkies, experimenting with job titles.

"Robin, you seem to know Andrew pretty well. Can you give any advice to Clare here?" asked Jake.

"I can tell you about when we backpacked around Thailand," answered Robin, "Any of the rest of you heard this before?" Everyone shook their heads.

Matt added, "Go on, tell us, dear chap,"

Robin smiled, "Good - it means I can make up more of it! - But hey Jake, if you are a journo, this will have to stay off the record. There's a muck-raking hack named Roger Slater who is digging around for dirt on Andrew. It's supposedly something to do with Brading's anti-BAME statement the other day but looks like a well-positioned hatchet job to me."

Jake said it was cool, and Clare said she would vouch for Jake's discretion.

Robin began, "Andrew and I arrived at Khao San together. It's best described as a decompression chamber between east and west. But when we arrive, it soon becomes clear that even this is a generous description; the Khao San Road actually doesn't feel like it's in Thailand at all."

"I was there once, actually" said Jake, "Gaining some life-skills! It was rammed with bars showing premiership football; Britney Spears and Coldplay blaring out; hustlers selling European T-shirts and fake British ID cards."

Robin continued, "Good description, Jake. Andrew observed straight away that this was a goldrush town. Designed to fleece the prospectors who were looking for nuggets of enlightenment."

Jake added, "And there was danger there too. We knew that a short time before we arrived 20 Thais were massacred in clashes between soldiers and anti-government redshirt protesters barely 100 metres from the Khao San Road. But it might as well have been 100 miles away: the Khao San's tourist festivities were barely disrupted."

Robin continued, "Then we met up with Jamie, a graphic designer from west London who 'took several gap years' and said that 'the Khao San just feels like home'.

"Andrew was immediately aware of the dichotomy of the well-heeled experience-dipper looking at another culture. We talked about it when we sat waiting by the roadside for a bus.

"I can see that too," said Jake, "That street was like Camden on steroids,"

"Yes, apart from the fat, bald westerners parading their suspiciously beautiful Thai girlfriends."

"Andrew and I were travelling onwards to the so-called Full Moon Party. We could have taken the overnight train or bus down the coast to the ferry terminal of Surat Thani. But we worked out it was almost as cheap to take the plane. After a couple of cramped journeys, we got to Koh Phangan, and it isn't long before we're talking to the cream of British gappers - paid for through Bank of Mum and Dad."

"At least I used my own money," said Jake sheepishly, "I travelled out with my then girlfriend and we shared our limited resources."

Robin continued, " We were sitting on the side of a dirt track near the centre of Haad Rin, the main tourist town on Koh Phangan, and venue for the next day's Full Moon Party. Tourists were whizzing past every 30 seconds on mopeds belching out acrid fumes."

"Every second shop is an internet cafe packed with tourists checking Facebook. Every third shop is a travel agent's filled with tourists plotting their next move. It's an odd place to visit if you don't like tourists. And particularly if you yourself are one."

"But Jamie- who we'd only just met - didn't think of himself as a tourist: he said he was a backpacker. 'Most of the people here are backpackers,' he insisted.

Robin continued, "Jamie explained, 'Backpackers are infinitely different to tourists. Backpackers will accept anyone. Whereas tourists are the people who back home would end up in fights. But backpackers have no interest in fighting anyone, do they?'

"Jamie directs this question at Pete, an even friendlier backpacker whom he met a few months ago in Vietnam. Pete, ear-ringed and wearing a vest, is 23, British and on a different kind of gap year; he' says he's been given a year's leave of absence from the army.

"For most the time, he has been working as a promoter for a bar in Vang Vieng, Laos, but he's back in past-its-sell-by-date Had Rin for one last Full Moon Party.

"Pete couldn't agree more with Jamie. 'Yup,' he says. 'Tourists are the people who spend their time fighting here. Tourists are people who go on holiday for two weeks. This is not a place where you can go for two weeks. This is a place for backpackers. Tourists may pay more money, but they're idiots.'

Jake interrupted Robin, "Do you know something, I wanted to get out- We - wanted to get out - Jan and I decided it wasn't a place for us at all. We'd travelled all the way there, but Jan and I only stayed overnight and then moved on."

"Maybe you were you too old when you went there?" asked Robin, "They say it is all about youth. Ten thousand people condensed into one area where they can do everything they want to, with no regrets. Back home, you get mortal and there are repercussions. Out there, you can do what you want. It's like Ibiza before it turned. It's way cheaper, too."

Matt chimed in, "Mortal? Getting mortal? Have you suddenly gone all Geordie on us, man? Way-eye-man!"

Lottie gently tapped Matt, "We're trying to listen to the

story. Shhhh."

Robin continued, "We could see that the drugs were another big draw. These guys knew exactly which pharmacies sell speed – and what to ask for when they're at the counter. They know where to go to buy weed and can name the three bars in town that list magic mushroom milkshakes on the menu.

Matt cut in again loudly, "Can't you just have Doctor Robert on speed dial? Add it into your address book?"

Lottie kicked Matt, "Shhhh - you'll get us thrown out."

Robin continued, "Andrew asked Pete, 'if everything here is all so western and familiar – and if they're spending most of the week off their heads – are they really experiencing Thailand?' - see the pattern emerging - Andrew questioning and with a moral compass?"

Robin continued, "But Pete was brutally frank. 'This isn't a Thai experience,' he admits, instantly, 'This is a party experience. Chiang Mai and Bangkok, you get a Thai experience. Koh Phangan is a party place.'

"'We've gone through the Thai experience,' Jamie clarifies. 'We've seen it, we've done it. For us this is just a nice way to cap it off and celebrate what we've achieved, all that we've been through. A lot of people just visit the Khao San Road and the Walking Street – and they're tourists. They're not travellers.'

Jake interrupted, "I don't know, I don't think Jan and I were either tourists or - in Jamie's words - backpackers?"

Robin answered, "That's interesting. It is what Andrew said, I think you reached a similar conclusion. He worked out that people passing through were not going to learn anything in Koh Phangan about Thai culture. But he thought that places like Chiang Mai- they were where you could learn so much about the Thai culture of respect"

Robin continued, "So Jamie and Pete invited us to a "shroom" session with some of their many backpacker friends that evening. A few hours later, Andrew and I rendezvous in a bar built high above Sunrise Beach (where, in 24 hours, the Full Moon Party will take place) – a bar nicknamed, for reasons which soon become apparent, Mushroom Mountain.

Jake nodded, "I remember there was an entire culture around the magic mushrooms. I think they contained psilocybin, which is a bit like mescaline and has psychedelic properties. But I also saw someone tipping some liquid into the mushrooms. I assumed it was a psychoactive drug."

Robin resumed, "So we are there, but turnout is lower than expected; Jamie and Pete are joined only by two second-year medical students from Nottingham – Hailey, who took a previous gap year, and Laura, who didn't. Laura had studied pharmacology and was worried by the mushrooms. She would not try any because she reckoned the dose was so variable. Jamie and Pete were both ready to partake and Pete went into a mad trancey kind of state. Jamie said he'd stay with him and Andrew and I decided we'd better heed the advice from Laura and chickened out; we walked down to the beach with the two med students."

"We both thought it. Andrew and me. Koh Phangan isn't really the real world, but it's still an experience. Andrew was astute even back then, he asked what the locals thought about being invaded monthly by rowdy westerners.

Jake, "Did they tell you about the other party? Jan and I found out about that too."

Robin continued, "Yes, we soon found out that the locals don't actually go to the Full Moon Party. They go to an after-party up the hill the following morning. The Full Moon's just for the young westerners."

Then, with Laura and Hailey, at four in the morning, we visited The Rock, a bar perched high above the sand at the opposite end of the beach to Mushroom Mountain. We can see a DJ booth at Paradise Bungalows, where there sits a Burmese immigrant DJ.

He'd lived in Haad Rin since he was 16 and this party is roughly his 100th. He's bored with playing the same electro-house on the same broken system to the same crowds. He stares at the thousands of Europeans who will soon be flying home and wishes he could one day go with them. But he could not afford the flight.

"Up and down the beach, young western men are peeing into the Gulf of Thailand. It was supposed to be an amazing experience, but neither Andrew nor I could tune in and drop out to it.

"That is so like my experience with Jan," said Jake.

"I thought you said your girlfriend's name was Clare?" asked Matt, looking more dissembled than ever.

"It is, this is Clare, she's my girlfriend now."

"We thought you were made-up," said Tessa, "To begin

with Clare wouldn't say your name, nor describe you. That's why we decided you were her imaginary boyfriend."

"Oh no, well, as you can see, I'm very real!" answered Jake, "So you think there really is some truth about someone gunning for Andrew Brading?"

"We had also heard about it from the lobby actually," said Lottie," I think the word got to us via Rachel Crosby - you know, the journalist. I told Maggie what I'd heard, but Crosby is either spreading a false rumour or very well-informed."

Clare decided she would keep quiet that she had also heard about it from Rachel. Otherwise, she wasn't sure where that particular winding corridor might lead.

"You all seem to know one another," observed Jake. "Yes, I even know Clare's sister Sam," said Lottie, "To be truthful, she probably contributed to the imaginary boyfriend rumour - I asked her who Clare's boyfriend was, but she said she wasn't aware that Clare was with anyone now. I guess she was being discreet."

"Here's to the sisterhood," said Clare, and everyone raised their glasses.

"We need another round," said Matt, "Hey miss waitress!"

Jake and Clare looked at one another. They sensed it was time to leave. "Early start tomorrow," said Jake.

"Brilliant to have met you all!" said Jake.

"Zàijiàn" said Robin, as they made their way to find a

black cab.

Onward to Clare's, where they had let the taxi go, because Clare's road led onto a busy thoroughfare served well with late night taxis - and there was always Uber.

"Jake, thanks," said Clare, "You made an excellent boyfriend, I'm sure they will talk about you back at the flat."

"My pleasure, as always," answered Jake, "And I think we gathered some new intel tonight. Quite a lot about Andrew Brading and about some scuzzy reporter named Roger Slater."

"Yes, I didn't say anything, but I'd heard about Slater as well. From the same source though, Rachel Crosby."

Clare leaned forward and kissed Jake gently on the cheek. He briefly hugged her.

"Hey - you can stay over if you like?" said Clare,

"Sure," said Jake, "Just like a real boyfriend!"

Politician bashing

They were both in the Jubilee Cafe, the Houses of Parliament's private cafe. Clare was sitting alone with Serena.

"There seems to be more gossip about Andrew floating around," ventured Clare, " I was out with some of the ladies yesterday evening and they were talking about what Rachel Crosby told us. Don't worry, I didn't say anything, but I thought you should know. They are talking about a hatchet job on Andrew."

"Yes, I'd also heard, although I've not done any digging on the reporter. I don't have a name yet."

"Roger Slater, that's who the rumour seems to be about. And it is linked to that fabricated story about BAME workers."

"Machiavelli at work, as usual," answered Serena, "Half virtu and half fortuna,"

"Ah yes," said Clare, "Political leadership - you touch on my friend Jake's high-horse: He sometimes quotes that Machiavelli line: when it comes to political leadership half was virtu -action oriented towards power and glory, and half was fortuna - or luck, or even 'a blind bitch goddess'."

"Or what Harold MacMillan called 'events dear boy, events'," added Serena, "Now we will need the political skill to turn circumstances we did not choose and events we could not predict to our advantage. Look - I've got a call - see you back at the office!" Serena left the cafe.

"Hey Clare!" It was Samantha.

"Hey Sam, Wow - you were right about this place. It is suitably manic. Hardly a dull moment since I've been here."

"Yes, sorry that your MP/Secretary of State seems to have a cloud over his head!"

"Fabricated. He's a lovely person," said Clare, looking into her sister's eyes.

"Oh - and if anyone asked you about me and Jake, say it's all true - although it isn't of course. He's my imaginary boyfriend so that I can escape back to mine away from the flat sometimes."

"Gottit, I wish I had one of those," said Samantha, "Only when I need them, of course."

They both laughed.

"Tell me then, what's happening?" asked Samantha. She had selected a prawn wrap and an exotic juice.

"There's talk of a hatchet job," said Clare, "But I can't understand why?"

"I expect he is being threatened by some lobbyist or another. It is fairly standard for the rags to build up a stockpile of bad news about everyone. They can then choose when to deploy it. It's interesting that there seems to be a rush to get something against Brading though. Maybe he is lily-white like they say?"

"My impression. He is."

"Well, it could be to do with that Fundamental Rights Bill he was pushing, but I reckon it is something else. Something where the Deep Tories are involved, pitting themselves against the UK heartland."

"Yes, the more I think about it, the more I think there is something we don't know about in play. Some kind of influence politics."

"Clare, I wouldn't have thought you believed in conspiracy theory?"

"I don't. But Tories who exploited the long-term disaffection of Labour's heartland voters and turned the red wall blue will need to be held to account. Globalisation and abandonment combined with the incoherence of Jeremy Corbyn offered a moment to transform the class basis of English politics, with Brexit as a flawed proxy."

"Yes, Clare, with Brexit supported by populists, the Labour covenant that endured through generations, was broken when the red wall went blue. Now, Andrew as Secretary of State for Internal Affairs finds that a lot of this lands with him. He needs a way to patch things up. But the predictable Tories will be worrying about their potential loss of power."

"Not helped when the worst of the COVID Tiers also tracked the old Red voters? Not exactly levelling up?"

Samantha added, "Those tiers didn't just track the red wall. Did you notice how they tracked the coalfields as well? Think of it. Elderly miners with breathing difficulties in most of the Tier 3 zones outside of the major conurbations. Privileged Londoners were allowed to drink expensive cocktails outside whilst Liverpool and Manchester remained in lock-down."

Clare smiled, "Yes, usually things spread outwards from London. This time it was the reverse, even as some London boroughs maxed out higher than anywhere else in the country."

Samantha spoke, "Well, they got London under lockdown in the end, making it Tier 4 before anywhere else, although the London Lockdown soon spread in a traditional way around much of the rest of the country."

She continued, "It revealed the lack of strategic clarity. Cummings was a bullying show-off, using academic sounding doublethink to befuddle the regular politicians. Most of them wouldn't know a pivot table or whether the origin on a graph had been manipulated. A full-on case of 'baffle them with bullshit'."

Clare laughed, "I would laugh about this if it wasn't so serious,"

They sat at a small table, facing one another, with their plates of wraps and fruit juices.

Samantha continued, lowering her voice, "Excuse my PPE lecture, Clare, but to unpack some of this: The inability to react strategically to events means that you become their prey, and the removal of Dominic Cummings only intensified the strategic void.

"Cummings mocked the government, yet he understood that the Government's programme could only be delivered outside of regulatory convergence and an active role for the state was required. There seems to be little understanding of any of this remaining within the Government."

Samantha took a bite of her wrap, "It is not fishing and transport but state aid that really matters; if they fold on that, then there will be no possibility of achieving their political goals. Yet the inability of Labour to renew itself as an object of affection for the working class or articulate a plausible economic plan for national renewal is allowing the Government to limp along."

Clare interrupted - "This wrap reminds me of one of those old-fashioned sandwiches, with curried chicken and fruit - what were they called? Oh, yes, Coronation Chicken."

Samantha continued, "You'll discover the Tesco Metro next to Westminster Tube soon enough."

Then she picked up her explanation to Clare, "Pretending things didn't happen are all very well, and it is obvious that some 'straight to camera' speeches have been made with an eye on historical reworking of events. Imagine the documentaries in twenty-year's time with Boris waving his arms about and pretending to be a statesman."

Samantha sipped her fruit juice, "Aside from a handful of politicians, there is no strategy, no narrative and very little energy. And they know that the next year could be worse. Instead of fixing any of those things, they are doing what Trump used to do, diverting attention with 24-hour news cycle gimmicks."

"We are all doomed!" stated Clare, smiling at her sister.

"Yes, but it does keep us all busy," said Samantha, "So what's this about Jake then - was I right the last time we met? He is very pleasant eye candy."

Bermondsey compression

Evening and back at the Bermondsey flat, Clare was in her room. A double bed with cupboards underneath, a full wardrobe and a small space where she could rest her laptop. She needed to appraise Amanda of the latest situation but wasn't sure whether she could be overheard in the flat.

Lottie was playing Taylor Swift's 'Shake it Off' loudly in the main room, so Clare decided that it would create sufficient noise cover.

She dialled Amanda on a voice line.

"Hi Clare, how has your week been?"

"A few new discoveries, but still nothing conclusive. I think that there must be someone out to get Andrew, but I don't know the reason. There's a journalist named Roger Slater who is digging around."

Amanda replied, "Yes, we know about Slater. He has run a couple of other smears on well-known people. It is the first time he's been involved with politicians though; the others were in business. He specialises in a kind of sleaze/smear of his target and gets paid well by the tabloids. I guess you'd call him a 'hack for hire'."

PART TWO

The Hollow Men

We are the hollow men
We are the stuffed men
Leaning together
Headpiece filled with straw.
Alas! Our dried voices, when
We whisper together
Are quiet and meaningless
As wind in dry grass
or rats' feet over broken glass
in our dry cellar

Shape without form, shade without colour,
Paralysed force, gesture without motion.

Those who have crossed
With direct eyes, to death's other kingdom
Remember us - if at all - not as lost
Violent souls, but only
As the hollow men
The stuffed men.

TS Eliot

Roger Slater

Roger Slater was in his home office. He lived in an apartment in the well-heeled Batchelor Street, in Camden. It was a row of almost identical terraced houses, each with a black front door and a window either side of it - like something a child would draw. He had bought it several years earlier before the extreme price hikes in London and he was certain he couldn't afford it nowadays. It was mainly luck that he'd bought a place in the area. He had wanted to be close to the Guardian's offices and had found that the area was well served with tube lines, buses and even the main line Kings Cross railway, which he could see from the end of his road.

Now he was working in Westminster, he could hop onto the Northern line and make one change at Embankment to get to Westminster or hop the Piccadilly to Green Park and work his way one stop back on the Jubilee. Either route took him around 20 minutes, door-to-door. And, of course, the rest of London was spread out before him. He didn't need a car and hired one if he needed to go further afield.

Like many journalists he knew, he was still single and had occasional dalliances with the opposite sex. More likely he would pitch up in a well-used journo-compatible watering hole like The Westminster Arms, St. Steven's Tavern or even a one-time legend like Ye Olde Cheshire Cheese - still on Fleet Street, although all the papers had moved out years ago. He knew his way around Greek Street and Soho too, and would sometimes stop at The Coach and Horses, where Hislop's Private Eye gang would convene every fortnight.

Slater believed that journalism was a drinker's game. He'd been left as something of a dinosaur since the current climate of multi-platform internet journalism (not to mention a more enlightened modern work ethic) had killed the functioning-alcoholic status of the lowly hack.

But he knew how to play the game, how to target someone and to gather information via the grape and the grain even if it meant, increasingly, using gastro-pubs and hipster dives to stalk his soon-to-be half-cut prey.

But right now he was worried. He'd been given an ultimatum by someone he'd fried in the press. A well-known and benighted businessman who seemed to have too many of the right connections. He'd been presented with a costly writ and an invitation to a meeting. He had been told that the writ would disappear if he could assist them in some small way. He still remembered the meeting inside a Chambers at the Law Courts. He wouldn't have believed the story if someone else had told it to him.

Law Courts

Roger Slater had made his way to the Royal Courts of Justice, the large, national courtroom building on the Strand. The building was acknowledged as one of the foremost examples of High Victorian Gothic Revival design. It was the 19th Century that saw the rise of Britain as an industrial and trading nation creating more litigation and forcing the construction of the new building.

Replacing Lincoln's Inn Fields, a green space which was regarded as one of the 'lungs of London', the present site was chosen; an area of seven acres to the north of the Strand of ancient and poor-quality housing. This slum property could be acquired relatively cheaply, and it was conveniently positioned close to the Temple and Lincoln's Inn.

These were the area to the north of the Courts and comprised many small offices - the Chambers of legal firms who had both the Royal Courts and the Old Bailey close at hand.

He was on his way to the chambers of a triple barrelled

firm, to try to understand how he could shake off the expensive writ.

He walked into the building, up stone steps and across panelled hallways. A smart woman asked for his name and then asked a male usher to conduct him to a large meeting room which resembled a panelled board room. There was water, coffee and tea available, so he poured himself a black coffee.

A door opened and in walked three men and a woman.

"Mr. Slater, thank you for coming, my name is Hugo Lawson-Parry QC and this is Sir Edgar Holland."

They each shook hands, and Hugo handed Slater an opulent business card and then continued, "My other two colleagues are from my practice: Emily and David. They are here to take notes of our discussion."

Roger Slater realised that Sir Edgar Holland was one of his recent hatchet jobs. And that Hugo had served the writ upon him. He was cornered.

"Now we all know how expensive these kinds of cases can become, when there is often a much simpler out-of-court settlement available," began Hugo.

"We know of your special skill and thought that simply hiring you to do something that we request might be a way to wipe clean any hint of a writ against you. So far, the only people who know of the writ are the people in this room."

Roger had been a journalist long enough to know that this smelled somewhat iffy. Was he being asked to do something illegal? Surely not from inside a QC's

Chamber.

"It is very simple; we just need you to find a few facts about a certain Secretary of State. Andrew Brading, the Secretary of State for Internal Affairs."

"But you don't know how this works," explained Roger, "I follow the smoke to find the fire. Andrew Brading appears to be squeaky clean."

"Perfect," said Hugo, " So he is more likely to go down in flames after you have discovered a couple of things about him."

He pushed an envelope across the table to Slater. Roger looked inside; it contained photographs. They were of Andrew Brading holding the hands of two women. On the back of the photo, in pencil, were written the names of the women. It presented a prima-face case of Brading seeing these two women illicitly. One of the women was black. That could also stoke Brading's recent outspoken comments about Blacks, Asians and Minority Ethnics.

"What do you need me to do?" asked Slater.

"Put the pieces together, " said Hugo, but use this information to gather other information about Brading. We would prefer to see his reputation unsalvageable."

"But why?" asked Roger, "Let's just say he is inconvenient," answered Sir Edgar Holland, "As Mr Slater, are you, unless we can resolve all of this."

How long?" asked Roger, aware that it would take time to build a case.

"You have until the end of the month, or things will

become difficult for you," answered Hugo.

"Is that everything? If I do this, will you destroy the writ?"

"You have my word," said Sir Edgar Holland.

Builder's lorry

Clare was at the office early the next morning. The short journey from the flat still took her by surprise. She had a quiet first hour before everything kicked off.

Maggie burst into the room, sobbing.

Clare leapt to her feet, put her arm around Maggie.

"Maggie, what is it? Are you all right?"

"It was terrible, and I saw it. You won't have heard yet, but Ian Harrison has been killed. It was a road accident. Terrible. Just outside of Parliament. He was on the pavement, ahead of me. I saw a bicycle swerve and hit him. Pushed him into the road and he was hit by a truck. The cyclist (all in black) was able to leg it out of the way. In fact, he crossed the junction at Parliament Square against all the traffic and shot up Parliament Street towards Whitehall. I'd say it was deliberate, but I don't think anyone would believe me."

"That's terrible. He was only in the office yesterday, talking to Andrew about something." At that moment Andrew appeared with Serena. They could immediately see that Maggie was upset.

"You've heard"" said Andrew, "about Ian?"

They both nodded. "I saw it," said Maggie, "He was about three metres ahead of me. It looked like something deliberate."

"Ian brought me some news yesterday. It suggests he was tangling with some difficult people," said Andrew.

"What news?" asked Clare.

"A smear campaign about me," said Andrew, "The details are not so important, but it looks as if there are people out to get me."

"Maggie, you'd better take today off," said Serena, "Clare, can you please go with Maggie and make sure she is alright. Don't worry about anything here. Use taxis. Go, please go, the both of you," said Serena decisively.

Clare looked at Maggie, "I think Serena's right; that's been a big shock. We don't want random people coming up to you today. It would be unbearable."

Maggie pulled herself together, "Thank you everyone, I didn't want to make a fuss, but it is so awful!"

Maggie Shannon

Clare and Maggie walked outside, and Clare hailed a black cab.

"Where to, Luv?" Asked the taxi driver.

Maggie gave an address in Agar Grove.

"I know, it," said the cabbie," the road further up past the gas towers?"

Maggie nodded, "Near to the Newmarket Ale House," she replied.

"Yes love, I've got it."

Clare and Maggie sat in the back of the taxi; Clare could see that Maggie was still upset.

"I was with him yesterday. I was only a few steps behind him today. It seems so callous. Shoving him under a builder's truck filled with bricks or something. He didn't have a chance."

"You talking about the RTA at Parliament this morning?"

155

asked the cabbie, "It's been all over the news. I usually drive around Parliament Square, but until I picked you two up it had been blocked off by the police. I reckon they had just re-opened it."

The cabbie went back to busily zigzagging across London. Clare and Maggie looked at London passing by. In a few minutes they were by Euston, where the cabbie said, "I'm bypassing Granary Square, we'd only get held up around there any case."

Soon, they're at Maggie's. Clare judged that it would be easy to grab another cab from that busy area, so she paid the taxi driver and then climbed the steps into Maggie's flat.

"It is so kind of you to come back with me," said Maggie, "Let me fix us some tea."

Clare decided that Maggie had settled down now. She thought she would talk about something else.

"So how did you get to know Andrew then?"

Maggie smiled, "Our families knew one another, Andrew was like a big brother to me. You can see I'm still loyal."

"Yes, I gather from some of the ladies that you'd flat shared with him when you were all at Oxford?"

"That's right. Most people think Andrew studied for a PPE Masters at Oxford, but it was actually a 2-year course to get a 2nd BA. He studied for a regular BA first, also at Oxford. But with PPE, there's a wrinkle that means if you wait five years after you get it, then it can be upgraded to an M.A.(Oxon)."

"I was studying there too, but I took the three-year PPE to get a regular BA. You can probably do the math to work out that Andrew helped me get into the house - er - flat in Oxford, mainly because our parents knew one another. I guess you'd say that 'I know where the bodies are buried' with Andrew, but - you know something - there really aren't any. Katherine and he both went to Harvard and by the time I'd finished Oxford he was married, in Parliament, and looking for an assistant. I jumped at the chance!"

"What is this strange campaign against him about?" asked Clare, "You must know about it?"

"Yes, he told me and Serena that there is someone trying to discredit him. He didn't think it was anything to do with the Right Bill, nor the BAME statement. He thinks that the BAME disruption has just become a convenient stick with which to flog him."

"I don't think he has told Serena, but Andrew thinks that the situation that someone wants to stop him on is the passing of the Vaccines Bill."

"Vaccines Bill?" asked Clare, "I'm not familiar with it."

"No, it has been kept quiet and has another title in the House, something about 'Protection of Healthcare Rights' or something similar.

Maggie brought the two teas across.

"Milk, no sugar?" she asked, and Clare nodded.

"It's builder's tea, I hope that is okay?"

"Perfect," answered Clare.

"Remember the Tiers that were used when the pandemic virus was at its worst? Tier 1, 2, 3 and 4 where 4 described the worst restrictions and 1 was originally for places like Cornwall which had very little early deaths?"

"I remember all too clearly," said Clare.

"Well, there' a consortium who are trying to use the Tiering as a blueprint for medical reform. They want different levels of vaccination and healthcare applied to Tier 3 and 4 people, compared with, say, Tier 1 and even a Tier 0."

"That sound bit like something out of Philip K. Dick!" Said Clare.

"Understand now why Andrew's favourite quote is from Bladerunner. You know - that piece where Rutger Hauer is on the roof in the torrents of rain.

"Yes - 'Attack ships on fire off the shoulder of Orion. I watched C-beams glitter in the dark near the Tannhäuser Gate'..."

"Well, imagine if they get your Protection of Healthcare Rights Bill passed. It becomes a licence to manage humanity. Decide who gets the good stuff - Tier Zero and who gets the life-shortening Tier Three or Tier Four protection." Forget about killing replicants - this is management of the human livestock.

"It always worried me when the politicians started talking about herd immunity, like the population were some form of cattle."

"Andrew told me he was concerned about this around

three weeks ago - just about when you arrived, Clare."

"He also reminded me of another scheme the had happened previously. It showed that Big Pharma or Big Chem could generate money-making schemes."

Transgenic

"You must have heard of the Monsanto cases?" asked Maggie, "Transgenic wheat?"

"I'm a little hazy on it, I remember it was something to do with Genetic Modification?" asked Clare.

"Oh, there was more to it than that. It opened an entire line of ethics questioning. Along the lines that the wheat crop was licensable - just like having to rent your Microsoft Office licenses every year, they invented something capable of forcing farmers to renew their license to grow their crops every year."

Clare asked, "So what did they do?"

Maggie answered, "It is something of a high horse of mine. In March 2015, the EU Patent Board granted patents for two plants which had been bred conventionally, not genetically engineered. These were a tomato (which had low water content) and a broccoli (which had enhanced glucosinolates). This set a precedent for patents to be granted on conventionally produced plants, and their seeds.

Clare asked, "Why is this a problem?"

Maggie continued, "If a patent is granted on a plant, the breeder not only 'owns' the plant, but gets subsequent rights on all its genetic traits. This is logical if applied to genetically engineered plants, as those plants are defined by the specific trait present only in that species."

Clare asked, "So they could then grab the rights to all apparent derivatives?"

Maggie nodded, "Yes, if patents are granted on the results of an open cross-breeding process, there will be many traits within the new plant which exist in other plants of the same species."

Maggie added, "So you are right, Clare; a single patent, say on a simple cross-bred tomato plant, can de facto cover hundreds of tomato varieties. The patent could also cover its seeds, and potentially the seeds of other varieties. This could ultimately lead to one patent owner having legal rights to all tomato plants and seeds, for instance."

"For the organic grower this raises the risk of a legal challenge when saving and swapping seeds. In effect the seed could come with a User Agreement, similar to one on a piece of software. "

"It means that plants and seeds can be patented if they are defined by a single DNA sequence that has been individually created. For example, a genetically engineered plant which has a gene inserted to make it herbicide resistant."

"This is like trying to patent all of nature?" asked Clare.

Maggie nodded, "Yes, then we get to patented seeds and plants. They can be considered the property of the patent owner – who can restrict their use and distribution. This puts our food supply in the hands of breeders, such as large agribusinesses, rather than the growers."

"All of this is happening while European patent laws are changing. It used to be that the results of conventional breeding processes were not patentable, but as of that ruling in 2015, they now are. This negates the whole intention behind the patenting process (known as Article 53b) and opens a wider pathway for patent granting.

Clare asked, "But who grants the plant patents?"

Maggie answered, "It is another comfortable little club: The European Patent Office (EPO). It is funded by the fees from patent applicants... wait for it... such as Syngenta and Monsanto and it is not answerable to the EU justice system.

"Instead, we have a closed shop system, where the EPO benefits from applications. Indeed, it is in its own vested interest to invite and grant patents."

"We can foresee a time when not just plants, but the very DNA of a seed could be patented – leading to control of our heritage seeds by the large agribusinesses.

Clare queried, " But that would affect farmers, small plant breeders, and ultimately the food supply chain."

Maggie nodded, "Yes. So that is precisely how biodiversity gets licensed. If the EPO continue to grant patents on seeds and plants bred by conventional processes, there are four important consequences:"

"Firstly, increased prices for farmers and consumers through the monopolisation of the seed market. That way small breeders will be edged out and the large agribusinesses will be free to determine the prices for their seeds, at the costs for farmers, and ultimately consumers. The three biggest companies Monsanto, Dupont and Syngenta already control around 50 percent of the global proprietary seed market. They are the ones who will decide which plants will be bred, grown and harvested - and how much they will cost."

"Is this a copycat strategy?" asked Clare.

"Not at all - each of the seed manufacturers jealously guard the way the create their proprietary seeds," replied Maggie, "And Secondly, contrary to the intended purpose, patents on seeds substantially hinder innovation. These patents can be used to block access to the biological diversity needed by other breeders and farmers to breed and grow. If permission is granted, a licence fee must be paid to the patent holder. And no further breeding can take place without permission of the patent holder. It would be like building an Office software product extension. You'd still have to pay Microsoft for the licensing rights."

"Wow! licenses to plant crops and vegetables!" said Clare

Maggie continued, "Third, As the patent owners spread their control, there will be less access to diverse agricultural varieties for breeders and farmers. Growers will have restricted choices and gradually the diversity of species and genome types will decrease.

"I can see that," said Clare, "Like stopping natural selection."

Maggie added, "Exactly, we can predict endangered food security. Given reduced diversity, crops are less capable of adapting to diseases or changing environmental conditions (such as climate change). High agricultural biodiversity is essential for our food security.

Maggie paused, then added, "That's not all though. There is the matter of the transgenic wheat monopoly that you referred to, Clare. Monsanto's MON 71800, which was made glyphosate-resistant via a CP4/maize EPSPS gene was the furthest developed. Monsanto received approval from the FDA for its use in food, but withdrew its EPA application in 2004, so the product was never marketed.

"But then Monsanto faced class action lawsuits after its genetically modified wheat was found in areas it was never approved to be in. Monsanto still claims it is mystified and that all its experimental GMO wheat was destroyed.

"The search for the rogue wheat is still ongoing. The GMO wheat, labeled MON 71800, was field tested by Monsanto in 16 US-states from 1998 to 2005.

"Monsanto had engineered 71800 to be resistant to glyphosate, the active ingredient in its herbicide Roundup, which it also manufactures. It had conceived the seed as a companion product to the herbicide. But it discontinued 71800, the company says, to focus on corn, cotton, and oilseeds.

"But now 71800 appears to have migrated from one of Monsanto's test plots. But how? And were there other farm fields pocked by GMO wheat? Had seeds of 71800 taken a ride on a container ship across the Pacific?

"Not exactly comforting to American wheat consumers

or producers. The American wheat export business is worth $8 billion and neither Europe nor Asia is interested in accepting GMO crops grown outside controls. This, along with Monsanto's political power, perhaps explains the secrecy around the story.

"So we still don't know where the abandoned mutant genetically adjusted wheat came from and Monsanto isn't talking. If MON 71800 escaped the lab then what other abandoned experiments could? If the planting was deliberate, who did it and why? Is it safe to eat the wheat?"

Maggie paused.

"So can you see how this could be applied to the Tiered vaccinations? A matter of 'Rights'."

Clare nodded, "Yes, similarly a few global conglomerates grab the 'Rights' to production and then build out a Tiered licensing vaccine model.

"But who are the people that want to support this, then?" asked Clare.

"It's a spinoff company, we think that are a subsidiary of Brant Industry. They are called the ever-so-friendly-sounding Elixanor."

Clare asked Maggie, "So what are we saying, then? That Andrew is fronting a Bill to push through the Vaccine licensing? That the UK Government can see it as a way to subtly manage the population? That somehow, some vested interests are trying to manipulate this?"

"No, to the contrary," said Maggie, "Andrew would not do such a thing. He would stand against it. Of that I am certain. That's what this Protection of Healthcare Rights Bill is supposed to be about.

"It is why they are trying to remove him, to put in place someone who will support their cause. That's why the allegations of mistresses and of inappropriate choices of words have surfaced. And back to Ian Harrison, he was the one sent to warn Andrew about all of this. My guess is that Harrison knew some of the upstream players and was considered too dangerous."

"It looks as if they could get away with this!" said Clare.

"We will need some pretty powerful players to stop them," said Maggie.

"Look," said Clare, "Both our cups! The tea leaves have formed the shape of a Triangle! You know something, I might be able to help you some more!"

Red Light District

I've seen all your qualifications
You got from the Sorbonne
And the painting you stole from Picasso
Your loveliness goes on and on, yes, it does

When you go on your summer vacation
You go to Juan-les-Pins
With your carefully designed topless swimsuit
You get an even suntan on your back, and on your legs
And when the snow falls, you're found in St. Moritz
With the others of the jet set
And you sip your Napoleon brandy
But you never get your lips wet, no, you don't

But where do you go to, my lovely
When you're alone in your bed?
Won't you tell me the thoughts that surround you?
I want to look inside your head, yes, I do

Your name it is heard in high places
You know the Aga Khan
He sent you a racehorse for Christmas
And you keep it just for fun, for a laugh, ha-ha-ha
They say that when you get married
It'll be to a millionaire

But they don't realize where you came from
And I wonder if they really care, or give a damn

Peter Sarstedt

Marion Charlotte gets minted

It was mid-evening by the time Clare got back to her own home in Caroline Terrace. She phoned Amanda to tell her about what Maggie had said.

"Hi Amanda, Clare here...A few more pieces of the jigsaw."

"Oh Hi, Clare, I'm in a hotel now, in Milan, actually. I'm with some people. Can I call you back in a while? Say around 10 o' clock Milan time?"

"That's fine," said Clare, "It'll be 9pm here. Ciao"

"Ciao Ciao," replied Amanda.

Clare decided to call Christina, to get some ideas.

"Hi Christina, I think I've found out some more."

Clare told Christina about Andrew Brading and the Protection of Healthcare Rights Bill and explained that she had found out that Maggie Shannon had known Andrew Brading from a flat share in Oxford, long before he became an MP, and even before he married Charlotte.

Katherine commented, "There's nothing particularly suspicious there, although the Protection of Healthcare Rights Bill is probably a camouflage for something else."

Clare went on to describe the two women now interlinked with Andrew Brading. Shanell Kinkead and Natasha Makarovna.

"Tasha?" said Christina, "I think I know her - from my time in Bulgaria. She was another one of the Russians sent there to play with NATO equipment. They had a nickname for us - *Kifla* - which means 'loaves' but was their slang for selfie models. It implied that we were there to get selfies of ourselves standing by Bulgarian scenes. Tasha was one hot loaf! This changes the game though. It tells me that there are Russians involved.

"What about Shanell Kinkaid- I think she is Jamaican?"

"No idea, but I know someone who might have an idea...Marion Charlotte. Why don't I call her?"

"That would be great; and I think you know Marion better than I do from that Raven business."

"Okay - let's talk again later," said Christina, "Maybe about 9 pm?"

"I can't then, I'll be talking to Amanda, but I could call you back when we are done?"

"That works for me...Speak later!" said Christina.

Christina looked through her phone to find Marion Charlotte's number, and called.

"My god," says Marion, "I was only thinking about you the other day. How are you? I can guess what this is about. It's all started up again. Minerva the listening station. They have moved it and given it a different name. I'm quite worried actually, in case they want to call me up."

Christina spoke softly, "You don't need to worry from us, but we noticed that the listening station was running again. You know it is in a different location?"

"Yes, it is near to the American Embassy now, in one of those blocks of apartments. London is crazy. You can buy a whole floor of an apartment block and no-one bats an eye-lid."

"Yes, we thought that is what they have done. Lessons from the money launderers, I suggest."

"That's right, the oligarchs have bought so much of London that a mere splash on a luxury block goes almost unnoticed."

"I'm interested in couple of people. Shanell Kinkead and Natasha Makarovna?"

"I know them both. I think you've met one of them too, Christina - Don't you already know Natasha?"

"That's right, we go back a long way."

"Well, the other one, Shanell, is Jamaican and described as an actress. Her main specialty is honey trap, though, and she has caught a few men in her time. She works through the Jennifer Sussex agency - Miel Doux Artists, just like I did."

"Did?" asked Christina, "You've stopped?"

"Yes," said Marion, "After that scrape at the Lanchester, with the guns and all, I decided I'd better find another pursuit. I'm married now, to Lord Edgar Hinton of Gloucestershire."

"Wow, that sounds impressive! So are you a Lady?"

"I am! Lady Hinton of Gloucestershire. I know what you probably think, and I'm sure most of it is true. But Edgar is both dashing and kind and seems to have a very good supply of money from his hardware manufacturing business. I am settled now, and thankful for it."

"Congratulations!" said Christina.

"Thank you," answered Marion, "Now how else can I help you today before we part company again for a long time!"

Christina smiled; she knew that her call had brought back bad memories for Marion.

"Do you know whether the two ladies have ever been around an Andrew Brading?"

"I doubt it, " said Marion, "Brading is well known as totally loyal to his wife Katherine. Anything I've attended in the past when Brading showed up, he was always alone or with his wife. I place him as steadfast and not easily swayed."

"So why would there be photos of him with other women?" asked Christina.

"I expect they have been manipulated; see if you can get

the original digital copies; I'm sure your friends Bigsy and Clare will be able to spot any irregularities. Trust me, there will be some!"

"That's brilliant, so you are telling me that the compromising photographs are probably fakes. That's very useful to know."

"Sad to say, deepfakes were becoming increasingly a way that the old Minerva operated, when it was trying to compromise MPs in the past. Some things don't change."

"Okay and who was running the old Minerva?"

"It was set up to look like the Americans, with all those Junior CIA agents, but it was really the Kremlin looking for ways to grab power. But I thought you realised that when we last met?"

"You know it is called Medusa now?" asked Christina.

"No, I didn't actually. I haven't kept up with all of that business!"

"Marion, Thank You. Er - I should say Lady Hinton, Thank You; I hope I won't need to bother you about this anymore!"

Marion said, "Thank you, Christina and *Paka-Paka*."

Christina laughed; Marion had just said 'bye-bye' in perfect colloquial Russian.

Amanda is not shopping

It was 9pm and Clare reached for the phone call from Amanda.

"Hey, so why are you in Milan?"

"I had to meet someone. They were a little bit shy about giving out information. Don't worry - it's nothing to do with your case, though."

"London, Paris, Milan... Are you sure you're not just on a giant shopping expedition?"

"Well, it is Fashion Week here now. It's amazing how Milan goes over entirely to fashion, whilst in London the whole event can be swallowed up in a couple of major venues!"

Clare replied, "Okay, well I found out a few things. Let me summarise."

Clare flipped open a small black notepad.

- Brading is under pressure
- They are trying to discredit him over his misinterpreted Black Asian Minority Ethnics statement two weeks ago in the House.
- As Secretary of State for Internal Affairs, Brading is trying to pass a Fundamental Rights Bill that is at least as good as the one passed by the United Kingdom.
- Someone has sent in an investigative reporter to trip him up
- Someone from an aggressive lobby has also sent him threats via the now deceased Ian Harrison, a Special Advisor who was deliberately killed by a cyclist outside Parliament.
- Someone is starting rumours that Brading has been seen cheating on his wife.
- There are photographs, but Marion Charlotte suggests they may be manipulated.
- One of the women implicated has links back to the FSB.
- Minerva is active again as Medusa, to corrupt and then blackmail MPs and other key figures
- The next Secretary of State for Internal Affairs Bill is for the Protection of Healthcare Rights but Brading is against it
- The Protection of Healthcare Rights Bill introduces the so-called Vaccine Law and Healthcare Passporting - Brading considers both to be immoral and unethical.
- The Vaccine Law can become a huge money spinner for a ruthless corporation.
- There are rumours that Brant and Elixanor are lobbying to pass the Protection of Healthcare Rights Bill.
- Brading's co-workers, Maggie Shannon and Serena McMillan are extremely loyal. Everyone else (such as Lottie and Tessa) only have good words for Andrew Brading.
- His wife, Katherine, is lovely and does not suspect anything amiss.

Amanda smiles, "Wow - that is comprehensive, Clare, you and the folk from the Triangle have been busy. Now, do we know more about the leverage over Brading?"

Clare answered, "No, but I assume it links to the two women and becomes a simple blackmail. Getting the Bill passed with its innocuous title then gives an unscrupulous Corporation a carte-blanche to manufacture and ship the vaccine. From a politician's point of view, it can also bring about tiered response to vaccines. It could make huge sums of money."

Amanda answered, "Yes, but think about a Russian angle on this too. I suspect they will be up to their usual tricks of money laundering. Think about it. Fast Moving Consumer Goods can be a mechanism for operating money laundering. Remember when car washes and then, later, apartments were used to launder? Now it is FMCG that provides the opportunity.

"Waste goods was so 1980s as exemplified with The Sopranos and then Breaking Bad with the car washes in the early 21st Century. Later a few property developers in Miami, London and West Coast America became stained by one man's laundering reputation. We all know who I am talking about.

"There still has to be ways to move the big money around and to clean it in the process. Hooking into the supply chain of FMCG related to vaccines makes an easy option, especially because it is being handled in such large quantities. I guess you'll tell the others about this?"

"Tomorrow night, answered Clare, I'll be visiting the Triangle offices again."

Balls Brothers, Bishopsgate

Roger Slater had arranged to meet Matt Stevens at Balls Brothers, in Bishopsgate. There were several Balls Brothers to choose from, but he wanted it to be one away from the usual hubbub of Parliament. This was more an Institute of Directors alternative hangout and Slater felt at home here.

He knew that Stevens was fond of his drink but needed to be somewhere he could keep up without it looking too obvious. The wines topped out at around £50 per bottle and he could probably pick a nice mid-range red - something like a La Galiniere Merlot, du Donjon, Languedoc, which would do nicely and could be replenished at will.

Going to a cocktail bar ran the risk of alcohol overshoot, with Matt whizzing his way through a row of slammers. This could look respectable, but Matt could also get gently pickled and thus better able to answer Roger's questions.

A few minutes after the appointed time, Matt breezed into the bar. Roger had already ordered and was sitting with the first bottle of red wine. He poured Matt a hefty glass.

"Hey, Cheers, Roger! How are you anyway? I had a bit of a binge yesterday with a few of the lads; we finished in Parly late and then headed over to Soho. Things got a tiny bit out of control and I ended up sleeping it off on my friend's sofa. He'd a supply of fresh brand-new shirts so I showered and put one on. Look carefully; it's still got the 'you pulled' lines on the front." He pointed to the remains of some sharp creases where the shirt had been folded into a packet.

Roger smiled and thought of the story he would need to tell Matt to get him to open up. He decided to talk about tax havens.

"Your MP has been busy recently with a few foreign flights? I noticed he'd been to The Caymans and then to Luxembourg. I'm not telling you anything that isn't already out there, but there's those who do and those who don't. I sometimes get a queasy feeling that something has gone badly wrong with the world economy and that's why these moves are necessary, but I'm never sure."

"Don't let it slip through your fingers, is what I say, " replied Matt, "I mean I've seen it all since I've been in Parly. I studied tax and tax havens before I came here. But if I once thought some of it was dubious, I can understand now why powerful governments don't just close them down. Apart from anything else there's the whole eco-system to consider,"

Roger poured another glass of wine, "Yes the byzantine world hosted – only on paper, you understand – by the Grand Duchy of Luxembourg, where Amazon has located its European headquarters, slashing its tax bills around the world. Remember how in 2011, Amazon revealed that the US Internal Revenue Service was chasing it for $1.5bn in back taxes."

Matt nodded, he gestured with his wine glass and Roger

noticed the red wine slide nearly over the edge of the glass, "I know, it's amazing how these stories flicker in and out of the press, but little gets done. There must be too many people dependent upon it now for the threats to have any real impact. It's similar with Google - The most famous phrase in Google's corporate philosophy, 'Don't be evil,' was been almost entirely removed from the technology giant's code of conduct."

Roger agreed, "Yes, when Google restructured into Alphabet in 2015, it replaced its simple language with vague and less specific wording such as "ethical business conduct". "The Google Code of Conduct is one of the ways we put Google's values into practice," the updated guidelines begins.

"Snore," said Matt, "It's been deliberately made to sound bland."

Roger added, "And then there was Apple - achieving in 2013 what Senator Carl Levin called, the 'holy grail' of tax avoidance, setting up offshore corporations legally incorporated in Ireland and the US – but for tax purposes, not resident anywhere. Apple shifted $74bn into one of these subsidiaries between 2009 and 2012, paying just 2% in tax on it."

"A bit more wine?" asked Roger and signalled to the nearby barman, who walked another bottle of the La Galiniere over to their table. He quickly uncorked it and poured two even handed glasses.

"Thank you," said Roger, grateful that he had Muesli for breakfast that morning.

Matt continued, "Tax havens' defenders say they smooth the flow of capital around the world, removing roadblocks and red tape. But what are those roadblocks? Taxes, regulation and democratic laws. Havens are places where you can put your wealth in order to escape the rules at home. Those rules might be around tax, or criminal laws, or rules about transparency and disclosure, or financial regulations. You don't have to put your wealth itself in the tax haven. It is the legal structure that owns the wealth – the shell company, the trust, or whatever – that usually matters."

Matt paused, took a glug of wine and then continued, "The asset itself – the thing you own – can be anything, anywhere. It could be a painting or a Learjet or a Swiss bank account, or a luxury home in Mayfair that the owner – let's say a Ukrainian oligarch – is currently using for the benefit of his daughter. Instead of owning the house directly, the oligarch owns the house via an intermediate structure in a tax haven. The land registry records won't list the oligarch's name, but the name of some anonymous offshore shell company. And when you go to find out who owns that company, you'll come up against a brick wall."

Roger noticed that Matt had now acquired red lips from the wine, "Yes, This can all take a bit of getting used to, even for people with wealth."

Matt added, "A few years ago, when Hurricane Ivan headed towards the Cayman Islands it sent a stream of light aircraft racing to Miami. They contained computer hard disks, relating to a large slice of the world's Cayman-held wealth. (Banking assets in Cayman account for nearly a 15th of the world's $30tn in banking assets.) When the storm passed, they flew them all back again."

Matt questioned Roger, "You know how transfer pricing

works?"

Roger wasn't sure, "Go on, explain," he said.

Matt began, "Well, there are many tricks used to shift money offshore, and a pinstriped army of accountants and lawyers to help people do it. The commonest technique is one called transfer pricing, employed by pretty much every multinational. Let's say MyCorp picks and packs a container-load of bananas in banana-capital Ecuador, and it costs the company $1,000. It sells them to a French supermarket for $3,000.

"The obvious question is: Which country gets to tax the $2,000 profit – France, Ecuador? The answer is, 'Wherever the multinational's accountants decide.'"

Matt continued, "So MyCorp sets up three companies, all of which it owns: EcuadorCo, HavenCo (in a zero-tax haven) and FranceCo. EcuadorCo sells the container to HavenCo for $1,000, and HavenCo sells it on to FranceCo for $3,000. That's basically it. (The bananas themselves don't go anywhere near the tax haven: this is all just paper shuffling in New York or London.)

Matt paused, sipped his wine and then continued, "But it's a shell game. Blink and you miss what happened. It cost EcuadorCo $1,000 to pick and pack the container, and they sold it on for $1,000. So EcuadorCo records zero profits, meaning no taxes. Likewise, FranceCo buys it for $3,000 and sells it to the supermarket for $3,000. Again, no profits, and no taxes. HavenCo is the key to the jigsaw. It bought the container for $1,000 and sold it for $3,000 – a $2,000 profit. But it is based in a haven, so it pays no tax. In short, all the profits have been stripped out of France and Ecuador and shovelled into the haven. Whoopee!

Then a decent slug of the red, "Of course, it isn't that shimple, defences have been erected against this kind of sharp practice, but the lawyers find 'legal' waysh to get around them, in a constant game of cat and mouse. This all transfers wealth away from taxpayers towards corporate shareholders. A kind of wealth extraction scheme. "

Roger noticed that Matt's speech had started to slur. He was also waving his arms more furiously.

Roger added, "But let's not forget all the criminality that tax haven secrecy facilitates. When multinationals use these platforms, they provide these places with immense political cover. If you are a tiny bit illegal you can hide inside the well-fortified shelter. A case of who gets the cream and who doesn't."

"Or who getsh the wine, here let me pour us both some more," said Matt.

"Have you heard about poor old Andrew Brading?" asked Roger.

"Oh yes, I think I know that one. As a matter of fact, we were all talking about him the other day," continued Matt, "About his time in Thailand."

"Oh, I don't think I've heard that one," said Roger.

With a slurred voice, and another glass of red wine, Matt
continued his recollection of the conversation they had
all had in the Opium bar in Chinatown a few days earlier.

Emily Karankawa

Pete Burr's phone rang.

"Jake Lambers," he read.

"Hi Jake, I thought we'd seen the last of one another?" joked Pete.

"Don't panic, I think we have," answered Jake, "But I was hoping you could make an introduction to one of your friends for one of our group."

"Go on..." Asked Pete, "But I'm not going to be surrounded by gangsters or soldiers, am I?

"No this is cool. I was hoping you could ask one of your contacts - preferable an American - to invite Bigsy to the new setup, however briefly. You could say he was an expert in surveillance or something."

"And why would I do that?" asked Pete, good-naturedly.

"We'd like to take a quick peek around inside Medusa station, and an invitation is quicker than us doing a breaking and entry kind of thing. Look - I seem to remember you telling me that you'd once dated someone there - Emily something?"

"Emily Karankawa - yes she's American but I think would like to be thought of as a native American. Her people lived in Texas for many centuries. She's the real deal."

"Pete, I detect a hint of longing there! Do you think you could run an introduction for Bigsy?"

"Phew, I'll have to walk across that burning bridge again," answered Pete, "Honestly - I've got some butterflies at the thought."

"Right then, that's settled - We'll have to put in some good words for you too, with Emily. Not too many good men get a second chance!"

Pete smiled, "Oh - I guess I can do it - and if Bigsy or you can get me another date with her, then that's a bonus," he said wistfully, "Come on; give me the details!"

"They are in a email. I'm just pressing Enter," answered Jake, "And Pete, 'Cupid' is The Triangle's other name. Although, come to think of it Bigsy would make a better tooth fairy."

eMail chain

Useful Contact: D. Barlow

Hi Emily,

Long time, eh? I hope you are well.

I thought your workplace might be interested in this guy who I met. He's a security specialist named Dave Barlow and he seems to know everything about surveillance.

I've attached his details below, but I can fix an introduction at your office if that's okay?

He's said he's prepared to travel although he lives in London in any case.

Best wishes,

Pete x

Peter Burr

<Attached Dave Barlow.Vcd>

On XX XXX XXXX, at 15:05, Emily Karankawa
<emily.karankawa@XXXXXX.com> wrote:

Re: Useful Contact: D. Barlow

Hi Pete,

I still have visions of those shorts.

Thanks for the tip off. I'd like to see him. Can you send an invitation to both him and me for a get-together, say next Tuesday at 13:00 at my offices?

You are welcome to also attend.

Best wishes,

Emily

Emily Karankawa

On XX XXX XXXX, at 16:18, Pete Burr <pete.k.burr@hot_mail.com> wrote:

Re: Re: Useful Contact: D. Barlow

Hi Emily,

Meeting arranged for Tuesday. Dave has confirmed.

See attached.

Best wishes,

Pete x

Peter Burr

<Attached Dave Barlow(Bigsy)/Emily Karankawa meeting.iCal>

Bigsy fails the interview

Tuesday at Riverside Quay. Bigsy and Pete Burr arrived and asked the concierge to buzz through for them to Emily Karankawa. The concierge looked like any other for an apartment block, and there were other bustlings of package deliveries, laundry and even car hire returns being processed.

They were both photographed, given a visitor lanyard and told to wait by the elevators.

"This isn't quite like a regular apartment block, observed Bigsy. Photographs and Lanyards?"

"I havn't ever visited before," said Pete, "I've only seen the outside."

The elevator door pinged, and Emily peered across to them both.

"Welcome to Riverside Quay," she said, gesturing for them both to get into the lift.

There was then what Bigsy judged to be an awkward moment whilst they all stood looking at the doors on the way to Emily's floor.

"It's right at the top," she said, "We can see parliament, the American Embassy and flights coming in along the Thames."

"Ideal spot for a listening station," thought Bigsy. He was working out that it looked as if Emily and Pete would like a few minutes alone to talk out some things. This could play to his advantage.

"We've got CR07 booked," said Emily, "Any coffee or water before we get started?"

They came out onto a busy floor. Bigsy was aware of the all-around windows and that the area had been partitioned into a series of pods. There was a corridor close to the main supporting wall and there, inset, were several glass fronted meeting rooms. The adjacent pods were filled with people wearing headsets and with either one or two monitor screens. Busy could see that some of them displayed text, but others showed picture in picture videos. Unlike some noisy 'help desks' that Bigsy had visited in his technical line of work, this was a fairly hushed environment, which gave Bigsy the impression of more incoming than outgoing calls.

"They were soon seated and Emily brought in one of her surveillance specialists to interview Bigsy. Bigsy knew he needed to be 'good, but not that good' in the interview. He wanted the interviewer to say that he was okay, but not exceptional. Bigsy dialled back his knowledge as he fiddled with the conference room's projector mouse.

The interview started and Gavin, the specialist asked a few framing questions to calibrate Bigsy's knowledge.

"I couldn't find much about you on the Internet - I tried the usual places; Facebook, LinkedIn and Twitter..."

"No, I prefer to go dark," answered Bigsy.

"Not too dark?" asked Gavin, referring to the Dark Web."

"No, I steer clear of anything with an x or a z in it," answered Bigsy.

They both laughed. Bigsy added, "or anything with pictures of bears, however fancy."

Gavin remained quiet at Bigsy's last remark which was an oblique reference to Russia's security initiatives codenamed Fancy Bear and Cozy Bear.

Gavin began asking Bigsy specific questions about security protocols, which Bigsy found straightforward enough to answer.

Bigsy made a quick reference to a fired director from the Cybersecurity & Infrastructure Security Agency (CISA) after the election beset with Russian hacking rumours and he could see that Gavin was somewhat deflated.

"It's all got so confusing, said Bigsy, "One simple little thing like the GRU Unit 26165 gets given so many different names. Fancy Bear, APT28, Pawn Storm, Sofacy Group, Sednit, Tsar Team (by FireEye) and STRONTIUM (by Microsoft). It's too much - but I guess everyone needs to have a proprietary name for the hackers?" Bigsy decided he would blow up the next question. He fiddled with the white Apple mouse some more, flicking it from hand to hand as if agitated. When he stopped, Pete quietly removed it from Bigsy's arm range.

"So, what do you think of Guccifer?" asked Gavin.

"Goosy Fur? how do you spell that?" asked Bigsy, knowing that Guccifer 2.0 was a well-known faux-Romanian hacker.

"No, Guccifer 2.0 That's G-U-C-C-I-F-E-R," replied Gavin, now certain that he wouldn't hire Bigsy.

"Nope, I'm drawing a blank, said Bigsy, "Unless it's a code name for Dimitri Badin, the GRU officer and suspected member of APT28. He's the main suspect for the cyber-attacks on the Bundestag?"

Gavin looks at Emily, he was wondering who was interviewing whom.

"Emily, I think we are more or less finished here. Dave Barlow shows a great deal of promise, but I think still needs some more comprehensive depth before he would be able to help us."

Bigsy decided to put up a small amount of resistance, "I hope you can see I'm keen and fairly well informed? It would be great to work for you, and I'm sure I could learn quickly."

He decided to wreck his chances, "I'm sure I could help you stand up some significant resistance to those damn Russian hackers."

Emily stood, "Dave, Pete, thank you both very much for coming in today, and at such short notice too. We can let you know soon after this meeting of our final decision."

"Er, I can take it. I don't think I've passed, have I, Gavin? Don't worry, I just really appreciated the opportunity."

Gavin could not play poker and shook his head, "Sorry, mate," he said.

Bigsy looked suitably crestfallen.

"Look - no hard feelings, if I could walk out with Gavin so I can get some feedback and maybe, Pete, you could be escorted by Emily?"

Bigsy wicked slyly at Pete and suggested that he and Gavin remain in the conference room for another five minutes. Emily and Pete walked to the door and Bigsy could see that they were pleased to have a minute alone.

"I realised I'd blown it on that Guccifer question," said Bigsy, "Were there any other things you didn't like?"

"Honestly, not really, you were almost too good to be true, like you knew what I was going to ask you," answered Gavin.

"Well, keep me in your address book, you never know when I might come in useful!" answered Bigsy, "It's been a privilege to meet you!"

Gavin smiled, "I guess the others will be downstairs by now. You can't keep your colleague Pete waiting."

They had walked back to the elevator. Bigsy had successfully swapped the Apple mouse in the conference room with the one in his pocket. That should give them some ability to hack into the system.

Street level. Gavin and Bigsy shook hands. Bigsy walked back over to Pete, eyebrows raised, "Well?"

"Yes," beamed Pete, "A date, this Friday! Thank you,"

Straight Ahead

Have you heard baby what's the wind blown round?
Have you heard baby?
A whole lot a people comin' right on down

Communication, yeah, is comin' on strong
It don't give damn baby
If your hair is short or long

Jimi Hendrix

How long will that watch battery last?

Bigsy was back at The Triangle's offices. He used a computer to call up the mouse he had left in Medusa and sure enough; it appeared on his screen. He had adapted it with a small computer placed inside. It was enough to get onto the intranet of Medusa and to send packets of data back to The Triangle.

Jake and Christina were looking over his shoulder and looked impressed.

"I used an Apple Watch to make a computer small enough to fit inside the Mouse," explained Bigsy, "That mouse can even tell the time!"

"And the weather I expect," said Jake.

"Let's see what we can find then?" said Bigsy, and he started up a primitive looking 'green on black' session on his Triangle office computer.

Within minutes, he was browsing some useful looking report abstracts. Let's see what we've got," he said.

"Ahah, here's one about Facebook: 'Following Facebook's announcement that it would give Congress the details of 3,000 advertisements bought by a Russian agency to sway the US election, Russia threatened to ban the company from the country during its upcoming election.'"

"Well, that's a turnaround if ever I saw one," said Jake.

Bigsy continued, "The special services have always played a crucial role in the Soviet Union and in modern Russia, and nowadays deploy 'active measures', from propaganda, espionage to actual violence."

"That's exactly what we were taught in Akademy," said Christina.

Bigsy looked at another one, "How about, in its new report, the Bellingcat server suggests that the Russian Federation is attempting to influence European politics by reaching out to youth organisations of European political parties?"

"Ha!" said Christina, "Some of the instruction given is so primitive. I remember from our training. They explained to us what a cocktail party was like, but it seemed to come from a 1950s textbook! I don't think the west has much to fear from that!"

Bigsy said, "Here's another one: A London-based think tank says Moscow's bid to establish a bloc of four neutral or pro-Moscow Balkan states has experienced major setbacks in Macedonia and Montenegro."

"I'm not surprised by that one," said Christina, "The old USSR was always territorial. I'd say Russian plans could be broken if they don't get this under control. Two pinch points. The Balkans and the Adriatic."

Bigsy added, "Russia could be on a mission to restore its Soviet or imperial glory and to prevent liberal democratic values from taking root in the Russian political system. Yet the tools used are precisely the ones that emerged during the liberal '90s and until recently were not subject much to government interventions: the online media and tech sectors. Nowadays, the Russian government builds up many sophisticated tools of online propaganda."

"Dreams of old men," said Christina, "The new guard took over Russia after the fall of the USSR. They took over the banks and then bought up all the state industries at knock-down prices. If powerful old-guard people were in the way, they got pushed out of windows. That's why there's so many gold-encrusted young oligarchs with model wives and a string of mistresses. Russia had to reinvent the Mafia to run everything. VV said, 'I'll give you this thing,' (like an oil refinery) 'you go figure out how to make money.' And if anyone won't play along, there're dozens of hungry young people waiting to grab everything that's on offer, backed up by the Kremlin. Do as you are told, pay your tithes and don't step out of line."

"VV?" asked Bigsy, "Vladimir Vladimirovich Putin," answered Christina, "or Vova"

"Here's one about leak spinning," said Bigsy, "The Citizen Lab group at the University of Toronto's Munk School of Public Affairs published a report describing a new case of the so-called "tainted leak;" stealing, doctoring and then publishing data presenting them as authentic."

"Yes, always make more out of a leak, use it to support your agenda, said Christina, "Akademy 101."

Bigsy said, "Here's one we already know about: 'A study reveals a major phishing operation of the group of hackers called CyberBerkut, targeting over 200 subjects from 39 countries, including members of governments from Europe and Eurasia, ambassadors, high-ranking military officers, CEOs of energy companies and members of civil society. Although the Citizen Lab group does not demonstrate a clear link to the Kremlin, it shows in the report that it has key links to Fancy Bear or APT28, previously accused of the attacks on the Democratic National Committee and the campaign of Hilary Clinton by the US intelligence agencies and cybersecurity firms.'"

"We really should go to that site and have a look around," said Jake.

Bigsy added, "It goes on, 'Russia's hybrid challenges continue to threaten security across the Euro-Atlantic community, which is why there is such a need for a comprehensive, coordinated strategy that will engage both the nations of NATO and the EU, and the institutions themselves. Four key categories of hybrid threats can be laid out together with corresponding recommendations; the categories are: low-level use of force, cyberattacks, economic and political coercion and subversion, and information warfare.'"

"A lot of this stuff is since Putin came to power. He is a great believer in asymmetric warfare and the use of lies," said Christina, "They gave us extra sessions on some of this near the end of our training. The media used to support it was in a different league from the old 1950s and 1960s textbook content of a lot of the stuff."

"This one is quite amusing, " said Bigsy, "Pot calling the kettle black: 'The United Russia party issued a report investigating whether and how the United States tried to influence the elections in Russia. Leonid Levin, the chair of the State Duma's committee on information technologies, presented the report in the Parliament. According to him, media outlets like CNN (which does not broadcast in Russia), Voice of America or RFE/RL were part of an attempt to interfere with the domestic electoral process in Russia'"

"Hilarious," said Christina, "Great use of mis-direction."

"Whoa," said Bigsy, "What about this one, then? 'In the NATO Strategic Communications Centre of Excellence official journal, James Rogers and Andriy Tyushka describe the Russian anti-hegemonic offensive seeking to desynchronise political developments in the regions close to Europe, to distort European perceptions of reality, split the Atlantic democracies from the European continent and saturate the vacuum with false and fictitious narrative. There are also chapters analysing the influence of Russian academic, political and public spheres on the politicisation of information warfare or examining the role of botnets in propaganda dissemination.'"

"And I thought it was Trump that was using reality distortion and Fake News! It looks as if everyone is at it!" said Jake.

"And one that strikes to the core regarding Medusa," said Bigsy, "Look, they say: 'Russia is the only country to date to have definitively combined cyberwarfare with conventional warfare. As far as the Kremlin thinks, geeks and hackers now rank alongside soldiers and spies as weapons of the state.'"

"I have to agree," said Christina, "The West needs to have

zero tolerance for cyberattacks. Where there is evidence that individuals or countries are behind cyberattacks, they should feel the full force of the law. That would not only send a political message, but also deliver a blow to these activities."

Bigsy added, "Her we go, 'It is necessary to adopt an integrated approach to cybersecurity. At present, the various aspects of what constitutes 'cyberwarfare' are not being addressed together, which could lead to gaps in security. Western countries should increase funding for cybersecurity education programmes, especially when we consider Russia's cyberattacks succeeded several times because individuals fell for phishing scams via e-mails.'"

"Yes, it's like socially engineered attacks, still relying on human frailties," observed Jake.

Christina nodded, "Yes, we were taught that civil and military contingency planning should include scenarios on which access to the Internet is limited and the internet infrastructure should get at least as much defence and protection as other strategic assets."

"Oh yes, and something else," said Bigsy, "I managed to intercept a couple of emails to Emily. One of them had copies of the original photographs of Andrew Brading as attachments. I'll be digging into them soon."

"How long will that watch battery last?" asked Jake.

Love nest scandal

Andrew was awake early. He'd heard the early news on the World Service, before Radio 4 had re-awoken. He seemed to be the main story of the morning. Someone had leaked a lot of information about him and then restitched it in a most unrealistic manner.

He glanced down towards his phone. There were some missed calls and a few texts from Serena and Maggie. He knew that they must have heard the story.

Now he needed to see it written before he responded.

He started his laptop and selected The Echo's home page. There was his photo, from yesterday judging by the suit and tie he was wearing. And there were a couple of old photos too. One he recognised and another he didn't.

He worked out that one of them was from someone's Instagram but the other one wasn't anything he recognised. It showed him with a slim dark-haired woman. They were crossing a street into what appeared to be a hotel. They were holding hands. Characteristically, the Echo had done two blow-up circles from the photo. One was of the hotel sign and the other of the hands linked together.

He decided he would need to read the story. The headline ran as:

Brading BAME Beauty break.

MP-shocker as BAME-critic in love-nest scandal.

He read the story. It was densely packed with lies. He had never met this woman. He had never visited the hotel described. The article further described him as a free spirit (true) who didn't mind the occasional magic mushroom (not true). The photo he recognised was of him with an old girlfriend - Jan - with whom he had backpacked to Thailand. It was unimaginable that Jan would tell tales about him, when they split, they were still fond of one another and it was mainly because Jan had been offered such a fantastic job in L.A. That caused them to part company. And anyway, Katherine knew all about Jan, so there was no angle there.

Andrew decided he'd better alert Katherine to what was happening. She was away on business, in Brussels, but he knew she would be awake and probably already at work. The hour was later in Europe in any case.

He called, "Hi Katherine,"

"I've seen it. I didn't call you because it was so early. I don't believe any of it, by the way."

"Thank you, Katherine, I was just going to reassure you of that. It's someone's idea of a vendetta. Let me tell you it won't work. There are three pictures. One of me (yesterday). One of me with Jan - many years ago and another of me holding hands with a woman I've never seen before, allegedly going into a hotel."

"Can you sue?" asked Katherine, "Defamation, Libel? I mean it must be a hatchet piece, I'm going to use my contacts to find out who wrote it."

"No need. I'm pretty certain it was a Roger Slater; that was the rumour going around here, anyway. He's a freelance hack and well-known for hatchet pieces, usually on businesspeople. He must be branching out. By the way, the woman is Jamaican, so I expect they will link this up with the BAME stories."

"Don't worry - remember I'm media trained," said Katherine, "And in the business, so to speak. You should get someone to warn that woman that she becomes an accomplice in the Libel if she says anything more, by the way. I'll only say we are in love and that I don't believe a word of the story. I'll also say that there is no other story. I suggest you get legal advice as well, so you don't accidentally ruin any case against the Echo. Love you, gotta rush, Bye."

Andrew breathed a sigh of relief that Katherine was so instantly understanding and also so practical about the situation. He had one less thing to worry about now and some useful suggestions about what to do when he got to the House.

He called Serena back.

"Hi Serena, I've seen it now. Don't believe a word of it. Katherine knows and will support me. She suggests I get a lawyer to help build a case against the Echo."

"Okay, Andrew, I'll inform the office that it's a made-up story and tell everyone to stay tight-lipped. It begs the question though, what do they want to get you for?"

"I know, I guess it's one of my current string of Bills," answered Andrew.

Deepfaked

Clare was back in Parliament. She noticed the additional reporters hanging around and the media teams setting up across on the grass across from Victoria Tower. She realised that they were all interested in following the Andrew Brading story now and she was quite pleased that they still didn't recognise her.

Then she caught Rachel Crosby from the corner of her eye.

"Hello, Clare," began Rachel, "It looks as if my prediction has come true. That Slater is ruthless. Where do you think he dug out that story from?"

Clare looked at Rachel and tried to assess if she was genuinely quizzical or just fishing for some quotes.

"Off the record," said Clare, knowing that would give her a few sentences which Rachel couldn't attribute.

"Well played," said Rachel, "I don't believe the story, so I'm interested in getting to the truth."

"None of the allegations in the story are true," answered

Clare, "I'm going to try to get to the bottom of this. How about we cut a deal?"

"Sharp for a 'new girl!' answered Rachel.

"Yes, I've played with media before. I know how it works. You stand by for an exclusive that counters the allegations against Andrew. I know the moves, but we're not there yet."

"You sound confident?" queried Rachel.

"Oh, very!" said Clare, knowing that to waver now would diminish her position.

"Okay, you've got my number. Come to me first and I'll splash it across the paper!" said Rachel. "But every day the story loses value,"

"I know," said Clare. In her bag she had a memory stick containing the photographs which Bigsy had filtered from Emily Karankawa's email. Bigsy had looked at them on his computers and shown Clare how to prove to Serena and Maggie that they were fakes.

She moved towards Andrew Brading's office, ready to reveal the photographs. She wasn't even sure whether Andrew had seen them all.

Inside, Serena was looking despondent.

"Hi Clare, we had had so much bad coverage today. The photograph clinched it. They are now saying that Andrew is hypocritical. Seeing this woman - Shanell Kinkaid a Jamaican - with Andrew and yet him allegedly saying anti BAME statements in Parliament. My head explodes.

Clare smiled, "We should look at the originals then - it is part of a set of photographs. There are plenty of things wrong."

Clare placed the memory stick into her laptop. "Don't ask me how, but I've managed to acquire the originals of the photographs. There are two of Andrew with Shanell and three others of Andrew with another woman, Natasha Makarovna,"

"Who?" asked Andrew, "I have never heard of this woman,"

"So we will soon be able to prove," said Clare, "My friend Bigsy has been busy with some analysis software. Nothing fancy, just Adobe Lightroom. He imported the pictures and then showed me how to look at the hidden information. Here we are:

Clare showed the five photographs as if they were a little film strip on her laptop. To the right was displayed a series of numbers and other information.

"This other data is called the EXIF information. It stands for Exchangeable Image File format and it is recorded by the camera taking the picture and includes the lens, the shutter speed and so on. Let's look at your photos, with the two different women."

Clare dialled up the pictures one at a time on the Lightroom display, which showed a big picture surrounded by data.

"First, there's the two of you crossing the street with hands held together. Isn't it strange that the two incidents should only be around five minutes apart? You must have been busy, Andrew. Now let's look at the two of you outside of the hotel. Here's one with Woman A, and five minutes later, here's one with woman B."

Now, the final picture of you with Natasha at China Tang's. That's along Park Lane and maybe a 20-minute cab ride from the hotel shown here. But look at the timestamp. Another 5 minutes later. You must have used a motorcycle. According to this, you used the same camera, see, the serial number!"

Serena shook her head, "This is great Clare, but it would be difficult to disprove any of this in the press with an explanation about date stamps, camera data and locations."

"I know, but my colleague Bigsy found something else. In the rest of the EXIF data is a log of any amendments made to the picture. Usually, it covers cropping the picture or, say, boosting the brightness. Well, on all of these it also shows that there have been further edits made - with Photoshop."

"That's more like it!" said Serena, "If we can prove the photos have been doctored!"

"It is what Bigsy did next," explained Clare, "He used another piece of software - ForensicPhoto, which looked at the whole image and then found areas where there had been manipulation. For example, the spacing of the pixels changed or there was a change in the blurriness of the photograph."

"What did he find? " asked Serena, looking excited.

"He showed me that the road crossing and the approach to the hotel was accurate. It's just that the person, allegedly Andrew - is someone else. The photos have been posed and then had Andrew's face blended in - like a deep fake. That covers all of the photos of Andrew crossing the street and checking in to the hotel."

Maggie chipped in, "So the pictures of Andrew have been doctored to place him with the two women!"

"Precisely," answered Clare, "And it is easy to prove!"

"That's better, " answered Serena, "And it can be captured in a single headline too! - 'No cheating here, Brading exposes fake photos!' " said Maggie.

"Brading deepfaked by enemies," said Clare, "That'll give use the high ground again."

"Yes," smiled Serena. Andrew looked relieved.

Andrew goes on the offensive

Andrew asks from his office "Okay, so do we attack?"

Clare added "Serena, I know you might think it is playing with fire, but I've made an arrangement with Rachel Crosby."

"You learn fast, " said Serena, "What did you discuss?"

"Well, I knew she didn't believe the hatchet piece, and so I agreed with her that if I could get some evidence to disprove it, then she would run it - but we must move fast before the story times out."

"Impressive, Clare," said Serena, and Maggie nodded.

"It will be so good to clear Andrew from all of this mess," she said, "But I'm wondering who leaked the stuff about Thailand?"

"I can rule the list down to six or so people," said Clare, "Including me - but it wasn't me!"

"Well, who then?" asked Maggie.

"You know we went out for that ladies' night in Chinatown?" said Clare, "It was me, my boyfriend Jake (It wouldn't be him), Lottie, Tessa (my flatmates) and their boyfriends - Robin and Matt."

Maggie said, immediately, "Not Matt Stevens!" and looked at Serena, "You see I know Robin really well, but Matt is a walking legend of indiscretion. Everyone knows that (sorry Serena) he can't hold his drink and that he blabbers every rumour he is ever passed. If you want to make sure a news story leaks, pass it to Matt. He's an idiot."

"He was rather drunk the night we met him," said Clare, "and kept ordering rounds of tequila and other shorts. To be honest, I'm amazed if he could remember any of it."

"No, Matt is a hardened drinker," said Maggie, "He has a reputation around these parts."

Clare was intrigued that Maggie had said, "Sorry Serena," and wondered why.

Serena started to speak, "Yes, it was me that originally sponsored him into a role. I was under some pressure to find him something a few years ago, but I've regretted it ever since. But Matt Stevens is a two-year man. A year to mess things up, and then a year on special disciplinary measures before he gets moved. Then it's the same thing all over again."

Clare said, "Well I think Lottie should know and perhaps we can prepare something 'special' for him!"

Andrew smiled, "Clare, thank you for being such an instant asset to our team. Now we need to think through what we are going to do about this situation."

"Okay," said Clare, "I'm going to call Rachel Crosby and also one of my friends who might help with Roger Slater. Right now."

Clare stepped outside. There was so little private space inside the main offices and outside all the corridors were busy. She decided to go outdoors and to contend with the traffic noise. Rachel picked up.

"Hi Rachel, I bring you a story!" announced Clare.

"Wow, that was quick!" said Rachel, intrigued that Clare had been so busy, "You must have already known something when I saw you this morning!"

"Let's meet!" said Clare, "Outside of Parly - somewhere quiet if they is even possible!"

"Okay," said Rachel, "Across the river? - How about the Marriott?"

Clare smiled, it was the very venue she had chosen with Bigsy and Jake when they had first met Chuck Manners.

"That's perfect," said Clare, "How about at 3pm?"

They agreed to meet, and Clare then called Christina, "Hi Christina, how do you fancy playing a strong-arm tactic towards a reporter?"

"Tell me more..." Answered Christina, "I assume this is the reporter who has tried to destroy your MP - Andrew Brading? Where are you tough? It sounds so noisy!"

"You're right about the reporter and I'm staining in one of the Parliament car parks, looking across to place barriers," Clare explained the evolved situation to Christina and gave her a free hand to 'frighten' Roger Slater without causing any actual bodily harm.

Then it was time to cross the River Thames to the Marriott's cocktail bar. A haven of tranquillity just behind one of the main tourist drags.

Brant Shareholders' Meeting

Jake, Bigsy and Christina went along to the Shareholders' Meeting of Brant. It was at the Elizabeth Hall, almost opposite Parliament.

"We'll get some refreshments at the event, they will want to ensure everyone is in a good mood," said Bigsy.

They were shepherded through industrial airport scanners and made to put their phones into little pouches.

"It stops the signal to the phone, like a Faraday Cage," explained Bigsy. They are doing it more frequently at pop concerts nowadays."

"We must bring back the Zippo lighters to make the candle effects then," said Jake, "Instead of holding up our phone torches."

Jake and Bigsy scanned down the list of presenters. Aside from a major bank, there was Miller McDonald, a Texan MVP at ISMC. He was hosting the event. Jake, Christina and Bigsy all recognised him from prior Raven events. He seemed to be a Raven Corporation fixer. It was his company that had facilitated various celebrity events, including the ill-fated one when everything kicked off at the Lanchester.

"I'm amazed he is still able to do any of this after the Lanchester," said Jake.

"He must know where an awful lot of bodies are buried," added Bigsy.

"I remember Chuck called him a tanned, drive-by handshake," said Jake.

Then there was Trudi Hartmann, Chief Executive Officer, Brant, who they remembered as a close ally of McDonald.

"She used to work for ISMC," said Christina, "That's an interesting change as she is now the CEO of Brant. I seem to remember there were rumours about Hartmann intertwined with McDonald too."

"Yes, there was quite a lot of collateral damage around them, I recall," said Christina,

"Remember Bernard Driscoll- that rude idiot of a Minister who was compromised by the efforts of ISMC, acting on behalf of Raven. We think he was killed by the Roslavl Bratva run by Tima Maximovich. If so, that would have been orchestrated by Vassily Turgenev."

Jake said, "How could we ever forget that."

Christina added, "Then Sir Charles Frobisher - also threatened by Turgenev. He disappeared after saying he was going on a helicopter flight to Nice airport from

Monaco. A likely death at sea caused by Vassily Turgenev."

"Oh yes," said Bigsy, " That was when we were investigating Brant."

Christina continued, "And Gerhard Schmidt - who I met at a Raven event - later blown up, with seven others on a yacht off Monaco. Almost certainly an American smart mine attached to the vessel. The suspect was Vassily Turgenev."

"Maximovich and Turgenev were both killed, too, in that helicopter explosion outside of London," said Christina.

Jake added, "And then, I see Michael Tovey, MP is attending this meeting. He has sailed through everything relatively unscathed. Amanda's people believed he was duped until they unearthed a significant Foundation Fund in the Caymans. Tovey had made the same stupid mistake as Driscoll and was funnelling money into it via a well-known bank. Amanda thinks Tovey is further up the decision tree than he is letting on."

Jake added, "And there's a Norwegian who we've never seen before: Arne Holstad, Ph.D., Chief Science Officer, Elixanor, who seems to be the new kid on the block. He's sitting on the intellectual property that Brant wants to acquire."

Raven Corporation was a complex company. It had spun off another company in the last two years called Brant and then through Brant it was in the process of acquiring a further pharmaceuticals research company, named Elixanor.

They were presenting a press release about their latest

strategic acquisition and it appeared to turn Brant from a sell-off afterthought company into a strategic asset of Raven.

Jake, Bigsy and Christina watched the glossy shareholder show from some seats near to the back. The presentation glittered with the best and probably the most expensive Event management.

Brant and Elixanor Pharmaceuticals, Inc. (Elixanor) have entered into a definitive agreement for Brant to acquire Elixanor.

Elixanor shareholders will receive $60 in cash and 2.1243 Brant American Depositary Shares (ADSs) (each ADS representing one-half of one (1/2) ordinary share of Brant, as evidenced by American Depositary Receipts (ADRs)) for each Elixanor share. Based on Brant's reference average ADR price of $54.14, this implies total consideration to Elixanor shareholders of $39bn or $175 per share.

The boards of directors of both companies have unanimously approved the acquisition. Subject to receipt of regulatory clearances and approval by shareholders of both companies, the acquisition is expected to close in the next three weeks, and upon completion, Elixanor shareholders will own c.15% of the combined company.

Trudi McDonald, Chief Executive Officer, Brant, said: "Elixanor has established itself as a leader in complementary biology, bringing life-changing benefits to patients with rare diseases. This acquisition allows us to enhance our presence in immunology. We look forward to welcoming our new colleagues at Elixanor so that we can together build on our combined expertise in immunology and precision medicines to drive innovation that delivers life-changing medicines for more patients."

Arne Holstad, Ph.D., Chief Executive Officer, Elixanor, said: "For nearly 30 years Elixanor has worked to develop and deliver transformative medicines to patients around the world with rare and devastating diseases. I am incredibly proud of what our organisation has accomplished and am grateful to our employees for their contributions. This transaction marks the start of an exciting new chapter for Elixanor. We bring to Brant a strong portfolio, an innovative rare disease pipeline, a talented global workforce and strong manufacturing capabilities in biologics. We remain committed to continuing to serve the patients who rely on our medicines and firmly believe the combined organisation will be well-positioned to accelerate innovation and deliver enhanced value for our shareholders, patients and the rare disease communities."

Both companies share the same dedication to science and innovation to deliver life-changing medicines. The capabilities of both organisations will create a company with great strengths across a range of technology platforms, with the ability to bring innovative medicines to millions of people worldwide. The combined company will also have an enhanced global footprint and broad coverage across primary, speciality and highly specialised care.

Brant's mixed portfolio includes a growing scientific presence in healthcare. Brant has developed a broad range of technologies, initially focused on small molecules and biologics and with a growing focus in precision medicine, genomics, oligonucleotides and epigenetics. More recently, Brant has increased its efforts in immunology research and the development of medicines for immune-mediated diseases.

Elixanor has pioneered complement inhibition for a broad spectrum of immune-mediated rare diseases caused by uncontrolled activation of the complement system, a vital part of the immune system.

Elixanor's franchise includes nano-engineering solutions as well as blood management solutions including the Tropus (a managed vaccine and healthcare delivery mechanism), additionally a first-in-class anti-complement component 5 (C5) monoclonal antibody. The medicine is approved in many countries for the treatment of patients with paroxysmal nocturnal haemoglobinuria (PNH), atypical haemolytic uremic syndrome, generalized myasthenia gravis and other related spectral disorders. More recently, Elixanor launched Tropus and TiC(Tropus-in-Cartridge), a second-generation C5 monoclonal antibody with a simple and convenient licensed monthly dosing regimen.

Elixanor's immunology expertise extends to other targets in the complement cascade beyond C5 as well as additional modalities, with its deep pipeline including Factor D small-molecule inhibitors of the alternative pathway of the complement system, an antibody blocking Fc receptor (FcRn)-mediated recycling, and a bi-specific mini-body targeting C5, among others. The FcRn extends the half-life and hence the availability of pathogenic immunoglobulin G (IgG) antibodies.

Brant, with Elixanor's R&D team, will work to build on Elixanor's pipeline of 11 nano-machine enhanced molecules across more than 20 clinical-development programmes across the spectrum of indications, including tiered-licence support for healthcare remediation.

Elixanor's leading expertise in complement biology will accelerate Brant's growing presence in immunology. The Elixanor acquisition adds a new technology platform to Brant's science and innovation-driven strategy.

The complement cascade is pivotal to the innate immune system. It plays a crucial role in many inflammatory and autoimmune diseases across multiple therapy areas, including haematology, nephrology, neurology, metabolic disorders, cardiology, ophthalmology and acute care.

By licensing the solutions on a tiered basis, the healthcare solutions become affordable to national governments and can be cost-effectively targeted across wide populations.

In contrast, Brant's capabilities in genomics, precision medicine and oligonucleotides can be leveraged to develop medicines targeting less-frequent diseases. Combining Brant's capabilities in precision medicine and Elixanor's expertise in rare-disease development and commercialisation will enable the new company to develop a portfolio of medicines addressing the large unmet needs of patients suffering from rare diseases.

The combined companies will bring together two rapidly converging, patient-centric models of care delivery with combined strengths in immunology, biologics, genomics and oligonucleotides to drive future medicine innovation. Brant has already established Bodø, Norway for its research centre for nano-engineering and is examining London for its corporate Headquarters, capitalising on talent in the London medical research arena.

Brant's acquisition of Elixanor, with its strong commercial portfolio and robust pipeline, will support its long-term ambition to develop novel medicines in areas of immunology with high unmet medical needs.

Elixanor achieved impressive revenue growth over the last few years, with revenues of $5.0bn in the last year (21% year-on-year growth). Elixanor has exhibited skilful commercial execution in building its 'blockbuster' C5 franchise. The success of the franchise is demonstrated by the effective transition of over 70% of patients from tradition medicines to Tropus-based dispensation of medicine in less than two years from launch in its key markets, including the US, Japan and Germany, as well as the strong pipeline of additional indications for Tropus and TiC.

Brant intends to build on its geographical footprint and extensive emerging markets presence to accelerate the worldwide expansion of Elixanor's portfolio.

The acquisition strengthens Brant's industry-leading growth, underpinned by its broad portfolio of medicines, which will enable the new company to bring innovative medicines to a broad range of healthcare practitioners in primary, speciality and highly specialised care. The combined company is expected to deliver double-digit average annual revenue growth across each of the next five years.

The end of the presentation arrived. There was loud music and the lights twinkled across the stage.

"That was some show, topped off with a Muse track. I'm surprised they didn't hire the band," laughed Jake, "Management and Science buzzwords supreme. I bet most journos just copy the Press Release into their articles!"

Bigsy laughed as well, "Yeah! A right portfolio of medicines convergant, patient-centric models of care delivery with combined strengths in immunology, biologics, genomics and oligonucleotides, yet wholesomely addressing the unmet needs of patients suffering from rare diseases."

Jake and Bigsy both laughed, and several people turned their heads to see who was making the noise.

"Boys! Shhh! They are playing down the other activities of Brant," said Christina, "For example, how it builds military bases and stocks them with contractors."

Jake nodded, "Well, they seem to have struck lucky with this situation, but I guess they need to get it through Parliament. That must be why they are pushing the lobby processes."

"And leaning on Andrew Brading," said Bigsy.

Chumocracy

Rachel Crosby wrote her commentary for The Post about Andrew Brading.

It blew the scandalmongering out of the water. The next day Katherine Brady did her own opinion piece about the Red Tops in The Tribune. It had enough retaliatory firepower to make the very printing presses shudder.

Andrew Brading also went on the attack about self-interests in Parliament. He knew that the lobbying against him was being done to further the creepy self-interest of a few MPs.

Brading stood in the House of Commons.

"They used to call it 'jobs for the boys'. But times have moved on. These days, well-connected insiders securing plum government contracts to resolve Government difficulties are as likely to be women as men. The Tory establishment is no longer simply an old boys' network. It's a chumocracy at the heart of government

"Barely a week goes by without another revelation: the vaccine chief who went to school with the prime minister's sister and is married to a treasury minister; the test-and-trace chief married to an MP (who happened to be the UK's official anti-corruption champion); the string of well-connected firms granted six- and seven-figure contracts to supply, consult, research, poll.

"Another scoop about a man who lived near to the health secretary and pulled him pints in the local village pub. Surprisingly, he then wins around £30m of work supplying plastic vials to go into medical test kits even despite having no prior experience of manufacturing highly regulated medical products.

"Nice work if you can get it.

"Of course, denials were issued at first, until, ridiculously, a bouncy castle manufacturer said it had been asked to make an inflatable clean room for the medical test supplies.

"I wish it would stop there. Now I see that a Founding Partner and Chief Executive of Tribalistic Capital Management, a $7bn Global Emerging markets specialist investment company has been appointed to the Department for International Trade. I note that Tribalistic moved from onshore to offshore ahead of Brexit and has made additional arrangements with the Cayman Islands to protect assets on behalf of its bond holders. I could comment further that I see a member of our very own government is involved with this company, but I realise that this will do neither me, nor the country any good.

"Instead of scurrilous hatchet jobs, the free press of this country should turn its eyes towards proper investigative journalism. Media scrutiny of the contracts I mention and the placements I describe and whether they are efficient and value for taxpayer's money?

"Such scrutiny is vital because many are awarded without the normal competitive tender.

"Proper scrutiny safeguards against cronyism and corruption."

There was silence. Several people looked towards the Prime Minister.

Then a hubbub.

Too many MPs had realised that this could turn into the early 21st Century expenses scandal all over again.

They could be caught out.

Yes, that agreeable lunch at Rules. That trip to Royal Cheltenham, escorted by those lovely ladies. The modest loan of a holiday home in Tuscany. Of course, it was lobbying. Lobbying fair and square.

"Order, Order," called The Speaker, several times whilst motion papers fluttered to the floor.

Plate glass corner office

A quiet, well carpeted corner office. A view across the entirety of London. Plate glass.

Trudi Hartmann was expecting visitors.

"Hello Michael, I expect Miller will be here in a minute. We have something to discuss."

She beckoned to her assistant, Nicole, who came into the middle of the office.

"Nicole, could you get us both coffees, please."

Michael Tovey acknowledged the courtesy, "Thank you, Nicole,"

Just at that moment Miller arrived, "I'll make that three," said Nicole, as she walked past Miller McDonald.

"You decided to stay on, then?" asked Tovey.

Miller's voice carried its distinctive Texan drawl, "As a matter of fact I live in London nowadays; at least for half of the year," He looked towards Trudi and Michael all at once remembered that Miller and Trudi were 'an item'.

Nicole reappeared with a dainty tray, with three bone china coffee cups, a milk jug and a silver pot containing more coffee. Miller gently lifted the tray from Nicole and continued with it towards the oblong coffee table at the meeting-room end of the office.

They all moved across and sat in the comfortable chairs, whilst Nicole moved to the outer annex of Trudi's office, "Call me if you need anything," she stated quietly.

Michael found himself seated between Trudi and Miller.

"Well, what are we going to do about Andrew Brading, then?" asked Miller.

Trudi and Miller both looked expectantly toward Tovey.

"Em, he seems to be making more noise of late. I think that scandal shook him up," said Tovey.

"Yes, but he is capable of stopping our plans," said Trudi, "The point of Brant taking over Elixanor was to monetise their products. To deliver tiered healthcare support to the UK population."

"It's why we put through that narrow bill about licensing of healthcare products a few months ago; we needed to position the main Bill," continued Miller.

"There's a whole group of interested parties waiting for this. Michael, you should know that after you presented at the Healthcare Research Group session a couple of months ago," Trudi looked at Michael Tovey with something that could only be regarded as an icy stare. Tovey noticed that she pronounced his name as Mik-a-el.

"We have provided you with considerable funding for your Tovey Healthcare Research Trust and the separate funding that goes directly into your Cayman Islands investment," said Miller.

"It's about time we had a little something in return," said Trudi.

"Tell me what you need," said Tovey, sipping his coffee and trying to look unruffled.

"Neutralisation," said Miller, "Neutralisation of Andrew Brading. There are various ways but if he were to lose his spot in the Cabinet, whether by scandal or by some other means, then we could move someone more - er - patriotic and sympathetic to our cause."

"Me?" asked Tovey.

Trudi spoke, "Well you are a good example, a moderniser, well liked, connected, photogenic, and as far as we know with little back-story beyond those slightly awkward funds in the Cayman Islands."

"But you will need to move swiftly," said Miller, "We want that Protection of Healthcare Rights passed, so we can capitalise on the initiative."

"You can't become a direct stakeholder this time, either;

we will have to invest on your behalf and put the funds into Tovey Healthcare Research Trust. It will be untraceable that way."

Yes, but lose the Tovey, from the name, change it to Tovarich or something," said Trudi.

Miller smiled, "That's quite an ironic name! Maybe something that sounds scientific, Psidium - maybe?" said Miller.

"But how can I 'neutralise' Brading, as you put it? They are his Bills, and I can't stand there from the same side of the House and critique them?"

"No need, we can drop more innuendo into the lobbies," said Trudi, "Brading may survive one critique, but he won't survive a second loss of trust."

"Let us introduce you to a specialised colleague of ours, Anatoly Yaroslav. He has been most helpful in other situations requiring speedy results," said Trudi, "I took the liberty to pass on your contact details but did ask him not to be in contact until after our session today."

Tovey's brow furrowed, "I assume with a name like that, he is Russian? I'm not sure that it is a good idea to be seen with Russians around the House."

Miller said, "Don't worry, Boris Johnson was doing it all the time, remember that the Russian-born billionaire newspaper proprietor Evgeny Lebedev was nominated for a peerage on Johnson's watch. Come to think of it, so was his brother Jo Johnson. The Evening Standard and Independent owner Lebedev held a party in Italy attended by Boris Johnson when he was foreign secretary, Lebedev was said by many to be a surprise name among Boris Johnson's life peerage nominations granted, which have led to accusations of "cronyism" against the prime minister.

Trudi added, "Boris Johnson showed 'fearless leadership' when giving his friends peerages, but most importantly signalled that the Tories had no wish to reduce the size of the House of Lords."

Miller added, "Yes, we couldn't get away with anything so blatant in America. That Johnson could get away with it shows what a private member's club your House is. The Lords was already the largest second chamber in the world. Now, with over 800 unelected peers, voting on our laws for life and The Lords is stuffed with party loyalists."

Tovey said, "I supposed I can see what Brading was alluding to in his 'chumocracy' speech. I can also see his speech was disloyal to the government and that his waves disrupt getting his own Department's Bills passed. Yes, I'll talk to Yaroslav."

Killer Genie

Michael Tovey decided he'd better check out Yaroslav before he met him. He was dismayed when he saw his history. It was that of a Russian Mafia thug.

When the Southern District Court of New York had attempted to prosecute Anatoly Yaroslav on charges of racketeering and conspiracy he was acquitted when the case against him fell apart.

Yaroslav, was depicted as a stocky, five-feet-four frame and wrinkled face which belied his jaunty personality. He had been in a scuffle whilst on detention. Among his fellow detainees at one point were Martin Shkreli, the snarky hedge fund manager and pharmaceutical CEO, and Vincent Asaro, the elderly Bonanno family mobster whose life served as the inspiration for the film Goodfellas.

Yaroslav had nothing to do with the initial altercation. It began as a verbal dispute between a fellow Georgian named Giga Gakharia and some Latin Americans.

Only after it escalated into a brawl did Yaroslav enter the picture, rushing into the fray to give his outnumbered compatriot a hand.

Gakharia, of course, was more than just a countryman to Yaroslav. As a *vor y zakone*, or 'thief-in-law,' a high-ranking honorific given to select members of the ex-Soviet criminal underworld and whose usage is thought to have originated in the gulags of the 1920s, Gakharia was the kingpin behind a vicious Brooklyn-based Russian mafia (or Bratva) for which Yaroslav allegedly was a key henchman.

Thus, Gakharia was effectively Yaroslav's boss. Whenever a problem emerged with the rank and file, say, with a messenger who was late on a payment or an employee who did not offer sufficient *obshchak*, or 'tribute,' Gakharia would allegedly summon Yaroslav to mete out a disciplinary solution. But there are clues that their relationship was not purely transactional.

Gakharia was star-crossed from the moment he set up his US operation. The FBI had wiretaps and informants homed in on Gakharia, recording what would amount to several years' worth of evidence. Headquartered in Brighton Beach, Brooklyn, where Gakharia ran an illegal poker house above a restaurant, the group had bases in at least six other states.

Gakharia ran his lines of business as a dizzying array of criminal schemes, in which blue-collar rackets coexisted with ostensibly white-collar ones. The scams included the sale of contraband cigarettes, the defrauding of casinos by hacking into slot machines, identity theft, credit card fraud, murder-for-hire conspiracies, and using femme-fatales to seduce well-heeled victims and later drugging them with traditionalist chloroform.

Gakharia's eclectic, high-minded ambitions for his enterprise were in line with his villainous heritage. Indeed, the *vory/vor y zakone* as a subculture had been making inroads in the US since the early 1990s, back when the FBI had not quite smartened up to their dealings. From the outset, though, the *vory* were noted for their special brand of ruthlessness. Even John Gotti is reputed to have once said of the *vory*, "We Italians will kill you. But the Russians are crazy—they'll kill your whole family."

Gakharia's fledgling criminal outfit, however, would never get a chance to flourish into the kind of interstate empire of which he dreamed. Gakharia, along with more than twenty-five of his alleged associates, was arrested in a sweeping federal roundup. That included Yaroslav, who was charged on two counts: one for participating in RICO conspiracy, the other for participating in wire fraud conspiracy.

Unlike many of his co-defendants, Yaroslav did not strike up a plea deal with the government.

If there can be said to be a crucial difference between the Italian American mob (La Cosa Nostra) and Russian organized crime, it is that the Russians have a culture of "flipping".

Clearly, Yaroslav didn't share this sentiment. Indeed, Yaroslav's refusal to cooperate was a source of frustration for one of his previous lawyers, who later resigned, citing his client's supposed stubbornness.

The government believed it had a watertight case against Yaroslav, arguing that as the "primary enforcer" for Gakharia's group, Yaroslav someone whose role was "breath-taking and extraordinary."

In other words, the prosecution contended that Yaroslav wasn't just kept in the dark and then trotted out for a routine beating; he was a valuable member of the Gakharia dynasty, privy to the larger conspiratorial designs of the group.

According to court documents, Yaroslav's defence lawyers briefed an account of at least four key errors made by the trial judge.

It explained why some of his peers received sentencing below federal guidelines but Yaroslav was the only one not issued with a sentence. By comparison, Gakharia, who was facing life, received forty-five years.

Five months later in an interview conducted and translated by his previous counsel over email, Yaroslav was asked to describe his detention surroundings. "I have never been in such a company before," he wrote. "Murderers, terrorists, fraudsters."

"The genie is out of the bottle," thought Tovey, "A killer genie."

Don't look back

he not busy being born is busy dying

Bob Dylan

blow your harmonica, son

Christina was at the Triangle offices when Clare appeared for her next debrief and update to Amanda Miller.

"You have got trouble," said Christina, "I just heard something from Blackbird. He says that the Kremlin are interested in what happens next in the UK and that Andrew Brading is at the heart of it."

They were on Clare's weekly conference call with Amanda Miller. "Yes," said Amanda, "I don't know specifically about Brading, but I have heard that Anatoly Yaroslav has come into the UK on a diplomatic passport."

"Yaroslav?" asked Christina, "He was the one who saw off Turgenev and Yegorin, when we were trying to ship them back to Russia. He used a Pechora SAM - a surface-to-air-missile - in Surrey! - and blew their helicopter out of the sky. We think he was working for Maximovich, who was working for the Kremlin.

What do we have?" asked Amanda, "It looks as if The Kremlin are trying to remove Brading. That their soft power approach with innuendo didn't work. Brading was too clean for the mud to stick. Now they want to use a Kremlin enforcer. We'd better upgrade Brading's security."

"Remember if this is some kind of Kremlin inspired threat, that they simply don't care and won't uphold any of the niceties of international law," said Christina, "Think of the Salisbury poisonings or even back to Litvinenko and the Polonium in a teapot. The Kremlin will use what it takes and simply lie about their involvement to everyone."

"What is the driving force behind this? The motive?" asked Bigsy.

"They want Andrew Brading or his replacement to support the Protection of Healthcare Rights Bill otherwise there'll be trouble coming every day" explained Amanda.

Clare nodded, "Yes, it is one of the Bills in Andrew's 'hopper'. He has to pass the Fundamental Rights Bill first. They were interfering with that one, but I think the bigger game was to tarnish his reputation in the House."

"There are too many vested interests," added Jake, "If they can lose Andrew Brading as the Secretary of State for Internal Affairs then they could put a tame puppet in place instead."

"Who are contenders?" asked Clare, "There is no-one obvious"

"We should wait to see which names start to gain currency one the next few days. I expect it will be someone new and probably a little less well-known," said Jake, "It's standard play."

"But what is their game?" asked Bigsy.

"It's what Andrew has referred to as the chumocracy at work," explained Clare, "If they can get the Protection of Healthcare Rights through, they have an open route to bring in as much 'tiered' healthcare as they like."

"I see," said Christina, "Couple that with the recent acquisition of Elixanor by Brant, and it is like a licence to print money."

"And the icing on the cake is that the vaccines they would produce can be classified as FMCG - Fast Moving Consumer Goods - That is also music to the Bratva's ear. They can mix their tainted money into the cash stream and cleanse it all together. A new source of money laundering is born."

"There are so many aspects to this," said Jake, "Is Andrew Brading aware?"

Amanda spoke, " We should brief him. I really think it should be at SI6, here at Vauxhall Cross, where we can provide the necessary 'Theatre' around it. We can also stress how much danger Brading is in, with his resistance to passing the Bill."

"But do we know who else is involved?" asked Jake, "Aside from the likelihood that Yaroslav has been activated?"

"Our best guess is that it is some of the people we saw at that recent Brant/Elixanor Shareholders' Meeting," answered Bigsy.

"And that points back to some of the same people that

were involved with Raven the last time," said Christina, "Miller McDonald, Trudi Hartmann and that MP - Michael Tovey?"

"Tovey, the backbencher?" asked Amanda.

"Sorry, we didn't mention him previously, because it didn't seem significant. It does now though," said Jake.

Christina looked pensive, "I'm worried by that. The usual move by Yaroslav is to do a substitution. The conventional Bratva tactic would be to destroy Brading and replace him with one of their own - in this case it could, perhaps, be Tovey."

Jaffacakes and regulation

Clare was seated back in Andrew's office in Parliament. The office was busy. Andrew Brading was there, as were Serena and Maggie. Maggie was opening a packet of Jaffacakes, which she had bought in the nearby Tesco Express.

"I'm going to sound callous when I say this, but I've not noticed a single difference since Ian Harrison's demise," said Andrew Brading.

"I was thinking the same," said Maggie, "You'll have to make me into your Special Advisor!" She offered the Jaffacakes around.

Maggie smiled across to Clare. They were both surprised when Serena said, "Andrew, that's not such a bad idea! You would have someone you trusted acting as your Special Advisor!"

They all looked across to Clare, "What would you think if Maggie becomes a Special Advisor?"

"I think it would be terrific!" said Clare, "I mean, if Maggie is in for the long haul then it has to be a good decision."

Serena said, "Okay - we can start the process, but we mustn't be caught out by the 'chumocracy' that Andrew spoke up against in the Commons the other day." She was delicately holding a Jaffacake and nibbled at its circumference.

Andrew smiled, "We've some other fish to fry at the moment. I need to get the Fundamental Rights Bill passed, and then we can concentrate on what we intend to change in the Protection of Healthcare Rights Bill. It is like the European Research Group - The title of the Bill has little to do with its implied objectives - remember ERG - it was totally opposed to Europe and quietly manoeuvred by Jacob Rees-Mogg."

"Yes, but I suppose the Fundamental Rights Bill is the umbrella one under which the individual Bills get proposed?" asked Clare.

"That's right, and actually it means we in the UK are more or less tracking what the EU is doing on these topics," reiterated Andrew.

Maggie spoke again, "The topics, again, are: Dignity, Freedoms, Equality, Solidarity, Citizens' Rights, Justice and General Provisions."

"But they've not been 'polarity adjusted?' " asked Clare.

"No - they are what they say they are," answered Andrew," Simple Rights, and simply expressed."

So why are the lobbyists after you, then?" asked Clare, perplexed.

Andrew began, "They don't like where it may all lead. No business organisation other than the lobbyists, has such an extensive network of contacts with government ministers, MPs, civil servants, opinion formers, and the media.

Clare said, " But surely lobbying is the means by which big businesses seek to influence politicians in order to increase their profits?"

Andrew nodded, " There is some truth in this, of course: businesses lobby politicians in order to increase their profits."

Clare nodded, "Yes, I suppose high profile business scandals like the collapse of Enron and Arthur Andersen only add fuel to the fire."

Andrew interrupted, "Precisely. However, many other groups and individuals engage in activities aimed at influencing politicians, building relationships with the media and other stakeholders, and raising political issues with policy-makers."

Serena said, "We see it all the time. The British policy-making process is dynamic, fragmented, and subject to a great many influences from a diverse range of organisations hoping to shape policy decisions by communicating with Parliament, government, and one another in the interests of promoting (or resisting) change.

Andrew again, "Yes. Direct or indirect lobbying of policymakers and other stakeholders is widespread and deeply ingrained in our democratic system. Indeed, it is symbolic of a healthy pluralist democracy."

Serena answered, "But we all know that the size and shape of the contemporary lobbying community and its techniques have been influenced by wider social and political change; changes within government and Parliament, and the growth of supranational institutions which have affected the locus of decision-making."

Andrew was looking riled," Yes, so the effective communication of political issues and agendas to policy-makers has come to involve a great many disparate and diverse activities which are not about directly approaching government or Parliament at all – activities as varied as government relations, grassroots campaigning, stakeholder management, partnership building, branding, reputation management, strategic planning, legal advice, media strategy, and corporate social responsibility initiatives."

Clare asked, "Which kinds of organisations are in the business of influencing and shaping policy in Britain?"

Serena continued, "Corporate lobbying in the UK is big business, although public affairs professionals working in the consultancy or corporate in-house sector have long worked under a shadow of mistrust and scepticism.

Maggie added, " Yes, it is very difficult to get a clear idea of the number of people involved in private sector lobbying and how big the industry is, giving the impression that it is secretive and, therefore, unsavoury.

"But isn't there a list?" asked Clare. She plucked a second Jaffacake from the packet.

"No, that's part of the problem," said Maggie, "There is no official register or list. And even if there was, the main obstacle is the fact that the precise forms of activity which constitute 'public affairs' are ambiguous and diverse, and hence, the number of people engaged in it is blurred and difficult to find out."

Clare asked, "But could there be other agencies at work? We know about the Russian click-farms. What about other more clandestine forms of influence?" She was thinking about the original Minerva station and now about the newly discovered Medusa station but didn't want to let on to the others.

"It can be an expensive business," said Maggie, "Any figures do not take into account the enormous number of other consultants, advisers, and experts in other professions and sectors who provide public affairs support in one way or another.

Serena nodded, "Yes, many PR agencies which specialise in the corporate and financial sectors offer strategic advice to companies on a range of issues such as brand reputation and crisis management, which involve many of the kinds of activities commonly associated with public affairs, but which are not always labelled as such."

Maggie added, "Then there are the management consultants who also offer advice in areas and on issues which often overlap with those dealt with by public affairs specialists. Investment banks, in offering advice to clients on mergers and acquisitions and such like, often advise on how to deal with the complex legal and political issues which surround financial markets, crisis management, perceptions management and corporate relations. All of which is entirely or peripherally covered by the term 'public affairs'. Law firms regularly provide counsel to companies and individuals on a range of issues to do with legislation and the changing nature of UK and EU regulatory frameworks, which again fit directly within the ambit of public affairs."

Andrew spoke, "Yes, there area a lot of fingers in the pie. The picture is complicated even further because on top of all these consultants there is also a huge and thriving community of in-house public affairs practitioners, legal advisers, corporate communications specialists, financial advisers, public relations experts, and strategic planners who work throughout the private sector on issues which can in be termed 'public affairs'. Finding out the number of people employed in these positions poses an even greater challenge than working out the size of the consultancy sector. "

"But it is one thing to use direct statistics and science to drive a point of view, quite another to use moral suasion against an MP or Minister," declared Clare.

Andrew nodded, "Exactly. The second reason lobbying and public affairs activity within the corporate sector remains controversial stems from a wider scepticism about the role and influence of business in public life more generally. Lobbying on behalf of big businesses who want to increase profits for their company shareholders and expand their market share seems, for many, qualitatively different from lobbying on behalf of, say, endangered animals, and feeds easily into widespread worries about the power of business to usurp government and dictate policy for its own ends."

Serena added, "The increased globalisation of international markets and the increased fragmentation of the policy-making process have led to a growing fear that it is becoming easier and easier for corporations to find their way into the policy-making and decision-making process and use their commercial might to influence global political decisions away from the public interest and toward their own interests and the interests of their shareholders."

Andrew nodded, "That's what George Monbiot called the 'corporate takeover' of Britain. He said that the growing dominance of big business on the national and supra-national stage has meant that conventional democratic institutions are being squeezed out. As he puts it '...seizing powers previously invested in government and using them to distort public life to suit their own needs. The provision of hospitals, roads, and prisons in Britain has been deliberately tailored to meet corporate demands rather than public need. Urban regeneration programmes have been subverted to serve the interests of private companies, and planning permission is offered for sale to the highest bidder.'

Clare spoke, "That's like the old song 'Selling England by the Pound'. It is also reminiscent of what happened in Russia after the collapse of the Soviet Union. A chosen few could buy up the state's assets at knock-down prices and then make huge profits from them. The natural resources were a classic example, oil, energy, refineries, mining. Systems that had long run-rates upon which to capitalise."

"And that is my worry," said Andrew, "we introduce our Fundamental Rights Bill but then see it get hijacked by a few sneaky additions, like that new Protection of Healthcare Rights. The Bill has been drafted to do the exact opposite of what it says in the title. It externalises the run-rate of medicines and vaccines, making them ripe for monetisation. There is a great pressure being brought on me to move it forward, although I am resisting."

"But how can that be?" asked Clare, looking bewildered,

"Surely you run this Department?"

"I do," said Andrew, "But it is a complex mechanism. There are permanent Ministers and many units within the Department who are under other influences. Fundamentally, I suppose we are seeing corruption because of corporate lobbying. People in the Department get lobby-sponsored trips to Wimbledon, The Races, best seats at the ballet. 'Just delete a sentence from the Bill, could you?'

"Think who owns the debentures, the corporate boxes? The reputation of the lobbying industry in Britain has been hand in glove with high-profile scandals which have led many to assume that underhand tactics and nefarious practices are endemic among lobbyists. They always seem to have 'something' on people in power or influence."

Serena said, "Yes, there are the old examples: I'm thinking of the famous 'cash for questions' scandal in which an established lobbyist (Ian Greer, of Ian Greer Associates) was accused of paying MPs to table parliamentary questions.

"Then Derek Draper's all too public claim that he was on intimate terms with the most important people in the Government and that he could, for a fee, approach them on behalf of clients. Together, the scandals that surrounded these two events brought those who worked in public affairs under the intense and hostile glare of the UK's media."

Maggie said, "Yes, and so the industry responded by setting up the Association of Professional Political Consultants. It's a self-regulatory body for public affairs professionals. It requires members of the APPC to publish the names of their clients, the names of any paid staff who are involved in the provision of public affairs services and are bound by a statutory code of conduct aimed at improving transparency. Firms are not legally required to join, and so they need only sign up if they think it will be in their commercial interest to do so.

"There is a concern that any code of conduct which seeks to restrict the activities of member firms in the interests of transparency will cause those firms opting out and pursuing their commercial interests more effectively outside the code. This is exactly what some big public affairs agencies have done."

Clare asked, "But what about state actors, for example, the Russian, Chinese or even the Americans?"

"And even the Europeans nowadays, ever since the UK left the EU," said Serena.

"It could lead to a systematic form of corruption," said Andrew, not realising how much Clare already knew, "We are defending against major and clandestine players."

Serena said, "You know what...I think I feel a speech about Regulation is required!"

The others nodded their agreement.

Old fashioned tactics

Clare was back in Bermondsey. Lottie and Tessa were both home and Tessa's boyfriend Robin Hunter was also sitting on the sofa in the lounge.

"Hi Clare," he said, "Tessa and I are going out in a while - to The George - to meet up with a couple of friends - as a matter of fact I think your sister Samantha will be along as well. You are welcome to come along if you'd like?"

"No, I'm zeroed out," answered Clare, "I've done so much today!"

"Okay - I get it - first few weeks can be tough on anyone!" answered Robin, "Er - by the way - it wasn't any of us that gave the Brading story to that journalist."

"I'm less sure," said Clare, "It has to be one of the 'Opium' group, judging by the fidelity of your story, as described in the press. I expect it was someone 'under the influence,' you know."

She could see Robin's brows furrow and then ping back as he worked out - suddenly - who had probably done it.

"Your office is remarkably unlucky, what with leaks and that SpAd killed - Ian Harrison - wasn't it? I heard he was run over by a builder's truck outside Parliament?" he added as if just remembering.

"A terrible accident," said Robin, "But he's not the first SpAd to meet his fate either," he added.

"No?" asked Clare.

"A couple of years ago, a friend of mine, Stan Daly was helping a Minister resolve sort of security situation, when he O.D'd on LSD."

"I didn't think LSD killed you?" asked Clare.

"Not directly. But he stood on a balcony ledge and then toppled off, straight onto a car roof six floors below. I knew him quite well but didn't even know he did drugs."

"Unless someone spiked him?" asked Clare.

"I know, we were all trying to work it out at the time. And the rumours were that the Minister was mixed up with the Russians."

"Who was the Minister?"

"It was a Minister called Bernard Driscoll. Come to think of it, Driscoll was killed too, in a road crash maybe a year later."

Tessa appeared in a tight-fitting dress.

"Wow! Hot!" said Robin, "Okay - shall I say Hi to your sister if I see her?"

"Yes, do, you can say that you've met Jake too, if you like!"

Imaginary Boyfriend Day

It was one of her 'imaginary boyfriend' days again, and Clare was back at the Triangle offices.

Amanda was dialled in on a video link and Bigsy, Christina and Jake sat with Clare as she described the situation.

Clare spoke, "Andrew Brading admits he is under pressure. They want him to push through the doctored Protection of Healthcare Rights Bill which will derestrict the ways that vaccines and other health care are provided. He seems to be pressurised by vested interests. He knows that the photos used to blackmail him had been faked and can prove it.

"He intends to come out all guns blazing in the next few days and to make a speech in the commons about Regulation."

"Does he know about the Listening Station and the dirty tricks being deployed?" asked Amanda.

"He's on the receiving end, but I don't think he knows just how well orchestrated it all is," answered Clare.

"Plausible deniability, that's good," said Amanda, "But I've arranged for his security status to be uprated. He gets the same treatment as the PM around Parliament now. Black support vehicle and a couple of outriders to clear the route. I want to send a signal that we are on to them."

"What? A signal to Yaroslav? I don't think he'll mess around; you know. He seems to be totally ruthless."

"I know; the one thing we can't defend against is a broad daylight attack with guns - but I'm afraid that's what he might attempt."

"Well, he used a Surface to air missile when he was in Surrey, can't we just arrest him?" asked Clare.

"Unfortunately, not. He's on a Dip. Passport and travels around on CD plates. Like a bubble of protection around him. We'll have the Embassy shouting about diplomatic rights if we try to pull him in."

Christina smiled, "Classic, textbook stuff, just like we were taught at the Akademy. But you must pay particular attention because he is likely to go dark, and that is when he will most likely strike."

"He won't break cover though, surely?" asked Amanda.

"No, you are right, he will hire a crew to do whatever he is planning. He might even use Brits or another country's nationals to throw you off the trail. And as for hardware. I can remember being in Paris when my flatmate Galina had a Swiss Arms 511 sniper rifle delivered by courier. It could fire a .50 around 3 kilometres."

"Interesting..." said Amanda, "I always wondered about that G8 working party in Paris."

"No comment," answered Christina, archly.

Clare looked at Amanda on the Screen, "Amanda, we've found out a lot for you now. We know that Andrew Brading is under a threat. We've found the Minerva replacement and potentially uncovered the Protection of Healthcare Rights Bill's commercial purpose. We even know that it could involve Raven and Brant, via the new Elixanor company. What else do you want from us?"

"Honestly. You've done great. And you are undetected in all of this. That is the beauty of the approach. If I send in regular SI6 employees, they will be identified very quickly, whereas you go completely under the radar. Having these sessions is also a clever idea, and the fact you can bring in extra people from the wider team is excellent. I really think you need to stick with this now. We could uncover the whole conspiracy."

Christina nodded, "Amanda is right - It has the hallmark of Russian involvement, with the direct links back to the old Minerva and also to Raven. I always thought that Raven Corporation was like unfinished business. This could be a way to tie it off. And Amanda's right, you are still a clean skin, so very valuable!"

"Hmm. Clean Skin... I'm not sure I like the sound of that," said Clare, with twinkle in her eye.

"How about squeaky clean?" asked Jake, laughing.

"Stop!" said Clare, "You may be my imaginary boyfriend, but that doesn't give you any special rights!"

"Ahem, no, certainly not," Jake coughed.

"Okay? We continue then?" asked Amanda.

"Okay - let's keep going, but from here on I'll reserve the right to bail!" said Clare.

Backhanders

The House of Commons chamber was packed. Andrew Brading was just standing to make a speech on the subject of Regulation. It occurred to him it could be his last. They could take away the whip if he was too disloyal. Or perhaps even worse. But he needed to send a signal that he was not being played.

He started, "Britain likes to delude itself that it is better than the rest of the world. That the 67 million citizens of this cluster of islands are somehow a little bit elevated from the billions living elsewhere on our planet."

There were mild shouts of bafflement from both sides of the House.

"Order! Order!" bellowed The Speaker.

Andrew continued, "This strain of self-defeating exceptionalism is especially noticeable when it comes to the issue of corruption."

There. He had said it. Corruption.

There were further shouts and a few coughs. The Prime

Minister shot him a glance as if to say - "Take great care"

He continued, "Our leaders preach about the sanctity of democracy, sneer at dodgy elites in developing nations, hold summits to promote transparency and pose as protectors of probity in politics. They are right to rail against the curse of corruption since it is 'one of the greatest enemies of progress,' as David Cameron once said."

Now there was a loud shout from his side of the House. This was irregular. He would expect the kerfuffle to come from the Opposition benches.

"Order! Order!"

"We are fortunate that we do not have to grease palms every time we deal with officials; in some nations, this has been shown to account for about one-third of salaries. Yet what a shame that successive prime ministers failed to practise what they preach, instead presiding over a business and political culture riddled with corruption."

"Order! Order!" Andrew could sense the walls closing in on him.

"Britain has passed tough anti-bribery legislation and measures to combat money laundering. Yet it does little to clamp down on tax havens under jurisdiction of our flag that enables wealthy people and major firms to avoid contributing to the public purse. Now that "Singapore on steroids' is being bandied about, it becomes a clear sign that Britain is to become a deregulated business playground.

Brading continued, "Governments even hand huge contracts to the shameless corporations that encourage and benefit from such disgraceful practices. Note also how often thieving autocrats and their allies stash stolen assets with the help of our accountants, bankers, estate agents and lawyers.

"Order! Order! Will the Right Honorable Gentleman please make his point?" asked The Speaker.

"At the root of this problem lies a political system that sanctions corruption. Not the overt plundering seen in some places with politicians taking vast backhanders for deals and contracts. The expenses scandal showed Westminster was engaged in lesser but similarly tawdry practices. Instead, it is the constant drip-drip of corruption."

"It is the world of private dinners, party donations, lobbyists, favours and questionable relationships."

"As we put forward our Bill of Fundamental Rights, we should clarify that these are not self-serving for our political and chattering classes. That instead, we are doing something for every citizen of this glorious land. And we should not try to dilute the Bill by substituting clauses from further Bills, which attempt to trump the statements in this Bill."

"Trump!" shouted someone.

"He'll be wearing a baseball cap next!" shouted someone else.

"Order! Order!" barked The Speaker, attempting to bring proceedings under control.

Andrew Brading continued, "Corruption, whether personal or systemic, is a cancer that eats away at the body politic. It destroys public faith. It fosters a system of patronage that benefits the elite and disempowers those lacking the right connections. It fuels state capture by powerful corporate interests while disadvantaging challengers.

"It is wrong on moral, economic, political and social grounds. When will Britain finally accept that even our nation is not immune to this disease and demand the disinfection of a tainted political system?"

The House of Commons had erupted. There was paper throwing, loud shouts and the fury of many MPs from both sides of the House. How dare this MP - admittedly a senior member of Cabinet - challenge their integrity?

"Order! Order!" once more called The Speaker, "I will close this session if we cannot behave in a more moderate and courteous manner."

Brading knew he had made his point. He also realised that it had been deflected by the huffing and puffing of other members. The playground bullies. He caught an eye from the Prime Minister. He could see the PM was not happy.

Take a ride

Outside the Chamber was chaos. There was a phalanx of MPs from both parties attempting to get to Andrew Brading. He felt someone sidle close and then a woman's voice whisper in his ear, "You want a platform? I'll give you one." It was Rachel Crosby.

Serena noticed and pulled Rachel from Brading. She turned towards Serena and spoke, "I'll help Andrew make his case through my column. It will be good counter to the obvious swipes he will get from the red tops. Let me help you."

Serena nodded, "Our office will be in touch. Right now, is too busy to handle this but we are interested."

Rachel looked Serena in the eye. "Okay - we have an agreement."

The security detail attached to Andrew Brading was now hustling him towards the Category 1 area where his car was parked. His driver was waiting, and they were soon outside the Estate, escorted by the outriders and a black Range Rover with an added security detail.

Andrew Brading was alone and could feel the adrenaline rush subsiding in his body. It was like feeling gravity suddenly pulling him back into the leather seat. A few moments of respite from everything and no-one talking to him, not even a phone call. He pulled the palm of his hand over his eyes and let it rest there for a few seconds.

So peaceful.

Suddenly he felt a bump and the car lurched to the right. He opened his eyes and looked out of the window. There, to the right, at eye height, he could see a small drone. He wondered if it was trying to take his photograph and he thought that someone was breaking the rules around the Parliamentary Estate, which had a strict no-fly zone policy toward drones.

His driver called out, "Danger, Sir, Lay down in the car,"

To begin with he felt sluggish and slightly embarrassed to do this, but then the driver called a second time "GET DOWN!"

He pulled himself flat along the seat. So much for a peaceful day. He could hear a metallic thump on the roof of the car. Surely it wasn't a bomb?

There was a loud crash and he felt himself tumbling. The roof of the Jaguar car had gone, and he could see daylight. He was aware that he was being flipped over and he gripped at the other seatbelt to steady himself. As he looked down he could see a huge amount of blood. His driver also appeared to have gone. There were a couple more thumps and he could only see grass and a kerbstone. He lay where he was, unsure if the car was about to explode, but unable to move to free himself from his own seatbelt.

He realised he was still conscious and as his hearing returned, he was aware of blue lights and shouting, "Stay Clear, Stay Away!"

Then he blacked out.

St Thomas Hospital

Brading awoke. He was in bed. He looked around the room and could see two bulkily armed policeman talking to one another. He noticed the paraphernalia of monitoring equipment.

One of the policemen noticed him awake. "Mr Brading? Mr Brading? We've just called through for a doctor. They say you are okay, Sir."

He could tell as a doctor approached the bed. "Mr Brading? You are in St Thomas Hospital. Can you hear me? The doctor was shining a light into his eyes. She looked over towards the equipment.

"Your vital signs are good. Can you tell me the month?"

He realised he was being tested for his level of recall. He tried to answer the questions but could not speak. He gestured.

"That will be because we had to intubate you when you first arrived. We had to stick some pipes into your mouth and down your throat," she explained, "We were worried about your breathing and potential loss of oxygen supply

263

to the brain."

Brading nodded again. He understood.

He could see the two policemen looking towards him. The second one looked like he was going to faint. Brading realised he might not look too pretty at present.

"The policemen are here to provide protection. You have a mild concussion from the explosion.

The doctor continued, "It will take you one to two weeks to recover. You will need to get plenty of rest and avoid stressful situations. Have someone stay with you for the first 48 hours so they can look out for problems such as changes in your behaviour or difficulty concentrating or understanding. Take the medication we provide. Increase your daily activity very slowly. Don't return to work or drive until you feel you've recovered. Avoid sport or strenuous exercise."

"I'm telling you this so that you realise that it is not as serious as it looks. These policemen are contacting your wife right now."

Brading felt the scene slipping away. He was so darn tired.

"It's okay," said the doctor, "The body is a marvellous system. Right now, it is trying to recover and is telling the patient it will be quicker if he sleeps."

Serena and Maggie were already on their way across to the hospital, but Clare had said she would stay in the office. She decided to phone Christina to get an external viewpoint.

"Yes, I saw it come up on my phone, as Breaking News" said Christina, "It looks as if a drone was used to deploy a bomb directly onto Brading's car. They could have steered it from anywhere in the vicinity. My guess is from across Parliament Square. It gives a great view and has many routes of escape. I guess the drone would only need to be in the air for less than five minutes."

"Do you think this was Yaroslav?" asked Clare.

"Almost certainly he will have arranged the hit, but would not be nearby, on purpose. He will have paid others"

Clare could see an incoming call - it was Amanda. She added Amanda to the call with Christina.

"Hi Amanda - I'm talking to Christina at the moment."

"Hi Christina, Hi Clare. We've seen the footage from Parliament Square - it was a manually operated drone. It looks as if someone in the Square was operating the drone and made their escape as soon as it exploded on the roof of the car.

"Andrew Brading survived although his poor driver was decapitated by the blast. Andrew Brading is in a secure ward at St Thomas' Hospital now. He can't speak but that is because of short-term intubation. He has concussion but they reckon he'll be functional again in a few days. His wife Katherine knows. The drone and explosive showed a middle eastern origin. We've got some footage from across the Square of a couple of Arab-clothed men hurrying away from the area."

"I'll guess this is simply laying a false trail," said Christina, "It's how we were trained in the Akademy.

Confuse your pursuers."

"Yes, that's what we thought too. They both hopped into a cab in Great George Street and headed toward Birdcage Walk."

"That's toward the Palace," said Clare.

"Yes, but it is also toward plenty of tourists," said Christina, "They are going to melt away."

"You are right, Christina," said Amanda, "That is exactly what they did. Disappeared."

Singapore

We sail tonight for Singapore,
We're all as mad as hatters here
I've fallen for a tawny moor,
Took off to the land of nod

Drank with all the Chinamen,
Walked the sewers of Paris
I danced along a colored wind,
Dangled from a rope of sand

You must say goodbye to me

Tom Waits

Ideology

Back at the Bermondsey flat, Tessa and Lottie were very interested in Clare's latest gossip.

"That's three or four headline events in your office since we've known you!" said Tessa, unscrewing a bottle of crisp, chilled Chablis.

Lottie added, "Yes Brading has been all over the papers. There was that BAME comment first, then the fake indiscretion with those two ladies - One could say the 'cheating on his wife scandal'..."

"Then, Andrew Brading's SpAd gets knocked down in the street outside Parliament and then, barely 100 metres from the site of that happening, someone tries to blow up Andrew Brading! What is going on?"

Tessa poured some generous glasses of wine, "Don't panic - there's another one in the fridge," she said.

"...Neither of the slurs about him were true," said Clare, "The BAME story was manufactured from nothing and then the photos of the two women were proved to be fakes,"

"Something you'll come to realise in this game is that it is not whether it is true, it is whether it is perceived to be true!" said Lottie, "Take the Boris Johnson as an example: With one throw of the dice, he broke the Brexit interregnum. After three years of frantic inertia, he resolved the impasse through transforming the class basis of the Conservative Party. A conjuring trick."

Tessa added, "Yes, but so effective. His sleight of hand renewed his party for a generation and ripped into the Labour heartlands by aligning Brexit with national renewal and exposing the class divisions within Labour by siding with the poor. Remember all the Red Wall narrative? As a political strategy it was brilliant - less so when the 'wall' turned blue and became kind of neglected."

Clare smiled, "Hmm - Levelling Down instead of Levelling Up!"

Lottie continued, "Although the Conservatives led across every social class, their lead in the skilled and unskilled working class was particularly emphatic. It was similar to Thatcher's 'Cortina Man' strategy. Boris had no equal in the cabinet. There was also no coherent opposition, his majority was impregnable, and all his MPs signed up to his agenda. Hail Caesar. Meet the new King of Merry England. Implausible 'Good King Boris.' "

Tessa added, "Now we in the Party are all being told that the Tory goal is to make domination hegemonic through two measures. The first is to identify the Tories with the working class and the country towns and to distance them from London and finance.

"But surely that is class polarisation against the ruling

financial and cultural elite?" asked Clare.

Lottie agreed, "Yes, it is, but it is even more subtle because of all the places you won't get blow-back. Remember the Conservative vote went down across the home counties, and especially those areas nearest London. The party concentrated entirely on the towns and villages of the North and the South, the country shires and the post-industrial working class, the basis of what was the Brexit coalition. The Conservatives positioned to be more northern and proletarian. Watch the skeezy PM drink beer with his new MPs in the many bars in Parliament.

Clare smiled, "It's a case of the Cavaliers lording it over the Puritans."

Tessa nodded, "Yes - It is a SpAd powered strategic Power Grab. Nothing to do with Party politics or conventional ideology."

Lottie sipped the wine, "The second step is a break from fiscal orthodoxy and to embrace the activist state. Expect to see cynical propaganda around the country lanes of England in partnership with local government. Expect a chummy house building boom. Expect to see the state sell-off whatever it can get away with. It's the Russian model, but with a state better equipped to manage financial matters. It's 'Liege and Lief' - from the Middle English as 'loyal and ready,' a pledge made by peasants to the lord of the manor. The peasants' fealty will be to the Cabinet. A group of nouveaux lords presiding over the riches, or spoils of state. 'I can give you the means - you must make the money,' as Putin would say.

Tessa poured into each wine glass, "And make no mistake: The government will violate EU rules on state aid and competition law with relish. 'Singapore ne plus ultra,' as it has been described."

"Out of the mouths of Etonians," said Lottie, "electi videntur ius hereditabunt terram."

Tessa laughed, "Die Elite glaubt, ein Recht zu haben, die Erde zu erben - The elite think they have a right to inherit the earth!"

Clare added, "I think there should be a phrase about show-offs too!"

Lottie sipped again, "They say it is an era of change. No. It is a change of era. Jumping the S curve. The old era and consensus were defined by four shared assumptions: that the nation state, democracy, the working class and conservatism would matter less. The dominant forces were the educated middle-class, globalisation, written constitutions and liberalism."

Clare asked, "But what about the Opposition?"

Tessa walked towards the refrigerator, "They Lost. Big Time. The family from hell. The responses of blame, avoidance, denial, anger, displacement, and depression are all both shocking and predictable. Labour is full of hate and blame and unable to understand how it got sidelined. With a few exceptions, it is no longer a tribe and has lost its homeland."

Lottie looked at her empty glass, "Now, glimpse a future where a progressive mind can only be reactionary, nostalgic and backward looking. The left can't see that the decisive role of the working class will be in ironic assertion of national sovereignty through its democratic vote. The consequence? To renew the ancient institutions of Parliament and the common law. This new era will be a foreign country for those who thought the arc of history was with them."

Clare asked, "Okay, so I see the Conservatives positioned to sell off the state. Where does Andrew Brading fit into this?"

Tessa had unscrewed the second bottle and was pouring more wine for everyone, "He doesn't. That is just it. He wants to stand up to this flagrant rip-off. That is why he is fronting the Fundamental Rights Bill. To give the populous a say in their own rights. It is also why he wants to curtail the Protection of Healthcare Rights Bill - which was cynically selling healthcare rights to the highest commercial bidder."

Clare asked, "And who is behind the Protection of Healthcare Rights Bill?"

Lottie answered, "That's just it. We don't know. But I think there will be a Big Pharma Corporation poised somewhere to make the government an offer which will put the Big Pharma onto a gravy train."

Clare decided she should keep quiet about Raven and Elixanor, although speculation was already rife.

"So, should we all invest in Big Pharma?" she asked instead.

Beauty and the Devil are the same thing

Christina was on her way to visit Roger Slater, at his home in Batchelor Street. She knew it would have more of an impact if she visited him on his own doorstep, rather than in a venue that one of them had selected.

She knew he would be in. When he was between stories, he seemed to be a creature of routine habits and would usually be back by around seven 'o clock in the evening.

She rang the bell. She'd decided to wear a leather overcoat, for maximum threat level, but had unbuttoned it so that he would see her vivid red dress when he answered the door. She carried her Mulberry bag on her shoulder.

There was a clunk as the door opened. Before her stood the noticeably quiffed Roger Slater.

"Oh," he said, "I was expecting someone else."

"Roger Slater?" asked Christina, "My name is Alya. I have some news for you. May I come in?"

Christina smiled and she could see Slater melt in much the same way he melted his targets with a concoction of alcohol and probably rohypnol to get the information he required.

She took in the room.

'Mapplethorpe/Rodin' said a large poster of a male nude next to one of Rodin's almost identical sculptures. Then the stairwell contained a cropped picture of leather trousers. And another wall contained a picture of Debbie Harry in a white vest sitting in a leather chair. Big clues about Slater's penchants everywhere.

She resumed her pace, "Yes, I have some news for you. My name is Alya Sokolova. I'm from the GRU. That's Russian intelligence. I've been asked to give you a warning. You are playing with fire, writing that hatchet piece about Andrew Brading. I don't think you know how much trouble you are in."

Slater looked amused, "Look, love," he said, "I think you'd better turn your tight little cheeks around and leave. I don't know what you are talking about."

Christina pulled something from her pocket, "Look, I don't want to be more demonstrative than I need to,"

Slater was staring at the blackened cobalt vanadium blade of a Russian Spetsnaz Predator knife, held by his unexpected visitor.

"Yes, 17 centimetres of blade, with the last four serrated, stab and rip... Love, " she explained, "Now I'm going to need a little information from you today, but my knife is very clean and I really don't want to mess it up."

She could see that Slater was entirely out of his depth.

"Okay, okay..." He said, "What do you need to know."

"Simple enough really. Who put you up to the story about Brading? I want names and the organisation."

She could see that Slater was thinking quickly about ways he could fob her off with lies. He did the obvious 'tell' of looking up and to the right to seek creative inspiration.

"No. Don't try to lie to me, or I'll have to show you what's in the Mulberry," she said.

Slater changed his mind quickly. She could see his eyes move down and to the left, he was accessing facts now.

"Okay, it was a routine assignment. They just paid me well. It was a company who asked me to do it. Something to do with lobbying. ISMC, they were called, but I think they were working for someone else. My main contact was Miller McDonald."

Christina stiffened as she heard this name. Miller McDonald had worked for ISMC supporting the incentives to tarnish MPs when she had been investigating Raven all of that time ago.

"Okay - but anyone else?" she asked.

"A woman...Trudi something or other, I seem to remember," he answered, "and an MP... Michael Tovey was his name. Oh, and someone from Elixanor - Arne Holstad."

Christina looked at Slater. He had folded quickly but he

seemed to be telling the truth. She thought about whether a grand reveal was necessary.

"Thank you, Mr Slater, you have been most helpful. Let's just think about this for a moment. If you were to mention this to your employers, or to the police, about our little meeting, there is every chance that word would get back. That means you might suffer reputational damage as a journalist who can't protect his sources. But worse than that, some of the people who have employed you would carry a grudge. Let me show you something."

She opened the Mulberry and lifted its content into view. A SIG Sauer Copperhead sub-machinegun.

"Pretty isn't it? It is surprisingly quiet with the built-in noise suppressor, more of a rattle than a bark. Now I'm not the one you should worry about. It's the men in Mapplethorpe leather jackets who come in through your doors and windows at night if you were to spill our little secret."

"I get it; I won't say anything. Will you be leaving now?" he asked, weakly.

"Yes, thank you for our little chat."

Christina walked back to the front door and let herself out. She had secured the weapon in her bag and the knife in her coat and was almost skipping along the road. Sometimes it was good to let the training kick in.

Bodø

Christina and Jake were on a plane bound for Oslo.

They had followed up on Slater's information and Jake had positioned himself as a journalist prepared to write a largely puff-piece about the technological breakthroughs occurring at Elixanor, fronted by Arne Holstad. To do this, they had to travel to Oslo and then on another plane to Bodø, which was on the west coast of the Nordland peninsula, and within the Arctic Circle.

"I suppose this feels like going home to you?" asked Jake.

"Not really, the Norwegian landscape might be like Iceland, but their language is different enough. We kept the old Norse in Iceland, but the Norwegians decided to adopt other words and phrasing from Germany. I can usually work out what they are saying, but it is much harder for a Norwegian to understand me talking in Icelandic," answered Christina.

They had both looked up the facts about Bodø, including the climate and were prepared for snow underfoot and nights to be light, but when they finally arrived it was almost as temperate as London.

"It's not like Reykjavik at all," observed Christina, "We'd have pretty consistent snow at this time of year. This seems to be quite an anomaly."

"Maybe it has something to do with global warming?" hazarded Jake as they both climbed into the back of a taxi-van and were whisked lite-night into the town centre and down to the town's harbour where their hotel was located.

"It's late," said Jake.

"Yes, see you tomorrow morning!" said Christina.

In the morning Jake and Christina met in the lobby of the hotel. Christina had ordered room service for breakfast, whilst Jake had taken a breakfast in the restaurant. Christina was carrying a canvas khaki bag with leather straps and Billingham written on the front. She looked the part, like an artsy photographer.

"You know how to use those things?" checked Jake.

"Do you know how to operate a Kalash?" she replied, "How complicated can it be?"

"Point taken, and we don't really need the pictures in any case."

"Maybe not. Although we can get some useful ones of the surroundings."

A car arrived to take them to the Elixanor facility. They had been told that it was far easier to go in a company car than to try to get into the secured facility in a taxi. They also knew about not discussing 'business' in the company car, which could well be recording them both.

They were soon in the Visitor Suite of Elixanor. Someone came to greet them.

"Hello, my name is Runar Teig, I'm here to accompany you around the building so you won't get lost," he explained, "First, we have a small annex with breakfast, just in case you haven't eaten."

He escorted them to a room with a beautiful view across the water and several hotel-style hotplates with a variety of 'help-yourself' breakfast offerings. Next to it were some altogether more Norwegian-looking items. Scrambled eggs mixed with smoked salmon served on breads and toast, a distinctive brown cheese, some dainty rolled pancakes, and a large flask containing a dark, black coffee.

Christina helped herself to the coffee and a small pancake and looked around for the butter.

"You have some cinnamon butter?" she asked.

"Ah, someone who knows how to eat a lefsa," smiled Runar, "Here - although I also like them wrapped up with Gravlax. Here- try this - it's gravlax with treacle and dill."

Christina smiled and as she bit into it felt a rush of her childhood in Iceland. They were just like her Pabbi used to serve for breakfast in the cold months.

At that moment another person arrived.

"Thank you Runar, I'll take it from here. Could you wait for our guests in the office annex?"

He strode forward and shook Jake's and Christina's hands. A handsome chiselled man, Christina decided he didn't have much body fat and looked as if he spent a lot of time in the fresh air, probably climbing mountains and running.

"Yes, I'm Arne Holstad," He continued, "I'm pleased to welcome you both to Norway and to our little facility here in Bodø. Let's go on through to the meeting area. Will you want me anywhere in particular for the photograph?"

They walked into the next room and Christina could see it was set out like an informal lounge, with an enormous plate glass window looking out toward the sea. It screamed Scandinavian design and looked effortlessly cool.

"There will be places here for us to photograph you. I'll probably take several pictures," she said, "Although it would make more sense to have a picture of you in one of the labs. You know, it will go with the cutting-edge science theme of the article."

"Ah - I hadn't allowed for that. We would need special permits to go into the laboratories. I'll ask Runar to see what he can do. I guess it doesn't matter what you have as the background science?" he smiled.

"No," said Jake, "Although something fancy with dials and screens always looks impressive. Ideally with lots of white walls."

"I think we can provide that without too much trouble," smiled Arne.

"Now, what would you like to know?"

Jake asked some questions about Arne's background and how he got into science. Arne's well-rehearsed replies could have come from a Wikipedia article. Then Jake changed tack.

"What about the recent action with Brant?" he asked, "I'm sure our readers would love to hear about life in the fast lane."

"If I speak directly to you, I will need your word that you won't attribute it back to me," Arne said.

Jake nodded, "Of course, we can show the article as coming from a number of sources. I could even stop the attribution after your background bio."

"To be honest, I think I am due to be replaced here," Arne continued, "No-one has said as much but at the last couple of strategy meetings it was abundantly clear that I was against the hasty monetisation of our recent discoveries."

"How so?" asked Jake.

"We have designed a vaccine here and a distribution mechanism which was to reduce the inconvenience of regular injections. We created a small cartridge delivery system, like the cannulas that are used in routine surgery."

"I know - those little inserts that they can plug drips into!" interrupted Christina.

"That's right, except the ones we designed were smaller and had a nano-engineered component. The nanobots could control the flow of vaccine and literally count the number of drops dispensed. It makes for a very fine and granular delivery system."

"I see, but can you control the nanobot system as well?" asked Jake.

"Yes, that was the latest addition to the system. The bots can read a tiny marking on the cartridge to know how much to dispense and over what period."

"That is an incredible breakthrough," said Jake.

"Yes, but the unintended consequence is the ruthless ways that it can be monetised," explained Arne.

"What do you mean?" asked Jake.

"Well, suppose that you identify a pure form of vaccine. The dose can then be regulated at various degrees. A higher quality dose for the rich and a lower quality for the poor. The 'bots can also turn off the dose at intervals, requiring more of the vaccine to be supplied. It is like the recipient has a short-term usage licence. It is like seed licensing all over again, but this time the crop is human life."

"But surely no-one would do this?" asked Jake, "I mean it is so immoral!"

"Quite," said Arne, "But consider the revenue flow. Millions or billions of people requiring regular top-ups of the vaccine."

"Why would you tell us this?" asked Jake, "And surely you do so at some risk to yourself and the company?"

"Yes, but I'm really worried. We have invented something so dangerous if it falls into the wrong hands. Think also of the implications of vaccine tampering. Too hideous to contemplate."

Christina took a few photographs, "You know, I think we'll need some from the lab too. And with you looking a little more upbeat."

Jakes looked across at the ashen-faced Arne, "So why are you telling us this? Do you want us to do something?"

"I really want the whole thing stopped. I have made my feelings known to the company and to Trudi Hartmann, but Miller McDonald and Ms Hartmann are more intent on replacing me now. Sometimes I fear for my life, although they keep saying they are going to pay me off."

Runar re-appeared, "Hello again," he said "I have arranged for you to visit one of our low security facilities. They are taking a couple of pieces of scientific equipment across as we speak, to make a good background for the picture of Mr Holstad. We have transportation outside."

The four of them walked down to where a Volkswagen bus was parked outside the doors of the briefing centre. They all climbed aboard and were driven to another building, which said Lab Facility 12 on the signage.

"L12 - Here we are," said the driver, punching a button for the side door of the bus to open it. They all climbed out of the VW bus. "It is usually faster to travel around the site on the buses than to call for a car, even when I'm the CSO," said Arne.

Runar handed out some new badges on lanyards. "You will need these inside or otherwise you won't be able to move around. Please don't lose the pass and give it back to me afterwards."

They walked towards the main entrance to the lab. Christina readied her camera and took a couple of exterior shots.

Then they were inside. Christina could sense the air pressure inside. The room was set to expel air, and she assumed that somewhere else there would be an air-scrubber for incoming air.

"You will soon get used to that hum," explained Arne.

"It reminds me of being on a plane," said Jake.

"Ah - it is actually considerably quieter. It runs at around 46 dB, which is just above home noise but lower than background music," explained Arne, "You are simply attuned to it when we first enter the space."

Christina could see a couple of men shifting a new piece of shiny white kit into position. She noticed they were talking in Russian.

"Just plug it in anyhow, they only want it for a photograph. Let's make a few lights come on," one was saying to the other. A third person appeared with a smaller piece of equipment, "Hey Dmitri, put it over there, but leave it so that it can be wheeled around!" called one of the Russians, still speaking Russian.

Arne spoke to the three men, in Russian, "Thank you all, we can take it from here!"

They moved away leaving the group of four visitors to be arranged by Christina.

"Mr Holstad, if you could stand so that we can see the dials on that piece of kit, please, and then Jake, if you could be talking to Mr Holstad..."

Christina took a few photographs and then said she was finished. Runar called for another security guard to escort them back outside. Christina noticed that the security guard also spoke Russian.

Code Words

By the next evening, Christina and Jake were back at the Triangle offices. They had invited Clare along and had called up Amanda for the briefing. Amanda had also called Grace Fielding from GCHQ.

"This must be serious!" joked Jake, seeing Grace appear on the Zoom call, "Now we have GCHQ as well as SI6!

"Hello Jake," smiled Grace, "it's been a while!"

"Yes, and we've just arrived back from Bodø, in Norway," said Jake, "But no snow on our boots!"

"No, it is surprisingly temperate in that part of the Northern peninsula," replied Grace, " I spent a few months further north in Svalbad - that's the separate islands off of northern Norway. We were making some adjustments to a satellite array for tracking unusual movements in the Arctic Circle. We had the snow but somehow they managed to keep the main routes cleared."

"What did you find out?" asked Amanda.

Jake and Christina explained that Arne Holstad had seemed on edge when they met. That he'd told them about the designs of the vaccine dispenser and how it could be operated by nanobots. He had expressed his misgivings about the way that Miller McDonald and Trudi Hartmann planned to monetise the patents through licensing the limited use dispensing of vaccines and other healthcare products.

"And we know that Michael Tovey, the MP is also involved," added Christina.

"And you may not know the latest news," said Grace. "In the Financial papers today, it states that Elixanor is holding an Extraordinary General Meeting."

"That is unexpected," said Jake, "I could understand if we'd published the article about Arne Holstad, but otherwise..."

"Not really unexpected," corrected Christina, "He said he was likely to be replaced and that McDonald and Hartmann were already lining things up. Do we know who his replacement will be?"

Grace shook her head, "No - there's only rumours, but nothing definitive. A couple of names in the frame are a well-qualified Russian scientist named Belochkin Mitrofan Timurovich or possibly a Norwegian scientist named Mikael Bjornstad. My money is on the Norwegian, simply because I think they would draw too much attention to themselves with a Russian fronting the scientific efforts."

"That's a good point," said Christina, "There seemed to be many Russians working there. I saw three from the science facility - all Russian-speaking and then a security guard - who was also Russian fluent. Even Arne Holstad spoke Russian to the other workers."

"We'd better check the FT tomorrow to find out what has been happening then," said Bigsy.

"There is something else," said Grace, "Someone has found a way to hack some of the information. It could be a leak, but I suspect it is someone monitoring our communications. We have traced one end of it to Medusa, but the other ends seem to terminate somewhere in Whitehall."

"What was the leak about?" asked Jake.

"It was about Yaroslav. They seemed to know that we knew he was here in London. There have only been a couple of direct references to him - he is usually a code word - Besheny."

Christina giggled.

"I see you like the irony," said Amanda, "*beshenaya sobaka* - rabid dog. It seems appropriate for Yaroslav.

"That's right, but they also referred to Q in Whitehall as their source."

Bigsy was intent, "Q? I know that code. It's an old BT code. I used to work in comms with an old fella named Albert. He retired, but before that he was fond of talking about the good old days as a British Telecomms engineer.

"He and some others wired up a series of tunnels under Whitehall with loads of comms gear. There were also situation rooms built. I guess the most famous is the Cabinet Office War Room behind Downing Street. But there's supposed to be miles of tunnels. He referred to it as 'Q.Whitehall.' I always remembered it because of the James Bond character named Q. You know - Desmond Llewelyn, then John Cleese and then Ben Wishaw."

Amanda interrupted, "That's right - Pindar was the official code name. It still is, as a matter of fact. Pindar was the house left standing after Thebes was razed in 335 BCE. The space under Whitehall is still a crisis management and communications centre, principally between the MOD headquarters and the actual centre of military operations, the Permanent Joint Headquarters in Northwood. It is connected to Downing Street and the Cabinet Office by a tunnel under Whitehall."

Bigsy said, "I can remember Albert saying that the tunnels were long, too. He used to get about in them on a bicycle. One end was at the Horseferry Road Barracks and the other end was right up by Trafalgar Square. The tunnels took in The Treasury, Downing Street, The Foreign and Commonwealth Office, Minister of Defence and went right up to the Admiralty Citadel. You can still see access points as anonymous doors on the side of a few buildings along that route, as well as rotundas and even still functional lift shafts."

Amanda nodded her agreement, "You are quite right, Bigsy, and there's even more than you describe."

"I always assumed that the big underground complex at Kingsway was tapped into the system," said Bigsy, "And there were rumours that the cable routes went all the way out to Bethnal Green."

Amanda nodded, "Correct, Bigsy, although this hasn't been a state secret for many years. It is, however, pretty galling if someone has applied an old-fashioned wire-tap to it."

"That's my guess," said Bigsy, "With so much wire to select, it wouldn't be difficult for someone disguised as a telecom engineer to get in and tap into a few of the cables - literally a wire-tap."

Jake added, "But it will be damned difficult to find now. It's around 1.5 miles of cable run and presumably a rat's nest of wires. An immense amount to trace."

"Albert knew a thing or two about tracing faults," said Bigsy. "He taught me a few golden rules. One was that 'the causes of 95% of faults were in the access boxes'. The second thing was to 'never forget the need for power' - and that's beyond the 50 volts DC carried on the phone line. Another thing I remember was to 'find the cleanest line and work down.' - For tracing a fault that is. Oh, and a last one, 'look for the handprints' - he reckoned that many faults were the consequence of human intervention."

"I reckon we could chop the problem into smaller pieces. We'd still need a bunch of technicians, but we could scan for a Wi-Fi signal to the outside, trace the lines for both faults and ultra clean lines, and inspect the access points for signs of tampering."

Jake and Christina looked at one another, "This still sounds like a lot of work! And its based on the theories of long-retired telecoms technician," said Jake.

"Get me a bicycle, and a torch," said Bigsy, "I'll start the hunt!"

"No offence, but we can do better than that," said Grace, "We can send you a team from here, GCHQ's finest, with some modern scopes too. That should speed things along. But do tell them Albert's rules!"

"We have a plan then, to find the source of the leak."

"It's not enough," said Amanda, "I want to bring this thing down. Enough is enough. We need to destroy both Medusa and Elixanor and bring whoever is running this to justice."

"Would you like me to dig into Elixanor?" asked Grace, "I'm sure we can find some dirt."

"Please go ahead," requested Amanda, "I'll clear all of this with Jim Cavendish. He'll be pleased to know that we are finally stopping all of this noise in the system."

Extraordinary General Meeting

The Elixanor EGM was scheduled for London, in a headquarters building of Brant. Arne Holstad arrived and noticed several other people waiting in a lobby area outside of the meeting room.

He entered and could see Trudi Hartmann, his CEO, as well as Miller McDonald from ITMC and Michael Tovey as well as a few people he didn't recognise.

"Let me introduce one another," began Miller McDonald and started to go around the table. Two names stuck in Arne's mind. Anatoly Yaroslav and Mikael Bjornstad.

Arne knew what was coming.

"Yes, we invited you here today as part of our restructuring plans," explained McDonald.

"We have decided that your extensive and highly credible record inside Elixanor has earned you a place as a special member of our Board. Arne Holstad, it is with our deepest thanks that we have designated you as a Special Scientific Advisor to the Board, with a one-off payment, in fully vested shares of 200,000 shares. You will also qualify for an immediate payment in money of US$1.2 million the moment you walk out of here, and an annual retainer for as long as you work as SSA of $100,000. None of this will affect your pension rights and you can consider this to be a per diem of $25,000 - in other words, four days' work per year."

Arne looked shaken by the sum. His quick calculation meant that he would never have to work again. They were buying his silence. He could also see Yaroslav in the room, smiling. He knew of Yaroslav's reputation and realised that if he was difficult about any of this, then Yaroslav would arrange something unpleasant for him. Truly carrot and stick, a large carrot, and an even larger stick.

"I assume you will want me to accept this straight away?" asked Arne. Trudi nodded, "Yes, we can vote you off of the Board, but this seems like an altogether more gracious and fitting way for you to leave. See, I have arranged for our attorneys to be present to witness the event."

Arne thought for a moment. Selective witnesses and a fait accompli.

"I accept," he said, "But you will need to give me time for my lawyers to process the paperwork."

"We took the liberty to invite them also," said Trudi, "They are waiting outside the meeting. I provided them with advanced copies of our agreement. I believe they found everything was in order."

Arne thought for a moment, 'what was the English phrase - ah yes Stitch-up' - he had been well-and-truly stitched-up on this occasion.

"Let me ask Mr Yaroslav to escort you from the room."

Yaroslav stood and Arne could immediately see the intimidatory nature of the way that he moved, like a huge, coiled spring, ready to release.

Yaroslav crossed to Arne and gently pressed his palm into Arne's back: "Here, let me show you the way. You should be pleased; you are a very lucky man, on any number of counts."

Arne was now outside of the room $1.2 million wealthier. Well-recompensed but muted under the threat of who knew what, if Yaroslav was unleashed. Yaroslav spoke softly, in Russian, to Arne, "I suggest you take the money and then we will never need to meet again." Arne recognised it as a threat.

Inside, as Yaroslav returned, there was more discussion. "Okay, so how do we move Michael Tovey into Andrew Brading's role?"

"You want me to finish it?" asked Yaroslav, "I have people in the hospital. One word and it is done."

They all looked towards Miller McDonald.

"No. We can finish him another way. Politically. Expose his Cayman Funds."

Tovey looked confused, "But Brading is squeaky clean?"

Miller McDonald replied, "Not if he has your funds. You didn't make the name change from Tovey, so I arranged for our lawyers to do it. The new name of your accounts isn't Tovarich. No. It is Andrew Brading."

Tovey looked crestfallen, "But that was my money!"

Miller continued, "No. It was money you fronted. Your payments start when we have positioned the new company and started up a few government contracts. You will be rich beyond your wildest imaginings."

Miller explained, "We have leaked the story about Brading's Cayman investments to the UK tabloids, with documentary evidence. After all of the other noise and disinformation about Brading, he is finally finished. Any denial by Brading will just dig him a deeper hole."

Trudi addressed Tovey, "And in the meantime, Mr Tovey, you can quietly assume his position in Cabinet, with responsibility for his Fundamental Rights Bill and Protection of Healthcare Rights Bill."

Trudi looked Yaroslav.

"Did Arne Holstad seem in agreement?" she asked.

"I don't think he will be making any fuss," said Yaroslav, " I think I can head back to Moscow."

"Before you go, there is one other small thing," stated Trudi.

"Oh yes? What's that?" asked Yaroslav.

"I'd like you to make a visit to Roger Slater. He is the reporter who helped us with the Andrew Brading situation. Nothing difficult, just to remind him who paid him for the work and of the need to remain silent"

"Just a friendly visit?" asked Yaroslav, "Can't you get one of your local people to do that?"

"Not really, I think you have some compelling ways with people."

"You want me to encourage his co-operation?" asked Yaroslav.

"You and maybe one other person?"

"What to hold him while I talk to him?"

"You seem to have the measure of it," answered Trudi, "Just be 'unforgettable' with him."

One-way ticket

"This isn't a ride you can take again,
but one, I'm guessing,
that is simply impossible to get off."

— *Scarlett Thomas, The End of Mr. Y*

Rachel Crosby

Clare had phoned Rachel Crosby to arrange a meeting. They sat in a small cafe across Westminster Bridge from Parliament.

"You said you'd be interested in stories about Andrew Brading?" asked Clare, sipping her coffee, "I think I've got you one."

"Hmm, Brading is becoming toxic now," observed Rachel, "You've seen the stories about his Cayman Island accounts, no doubt?"

"Seen it, but don't believe it," said Clare, "The real story is that he has been comprehensively framed."

"You'll have to give me more than that," asked Rachel, looking into her flat white coffee.

"Well let's go through the sequence of events. He gets mis-quoted on a BAME matter."

"I'll agree with that," said Rachel.

"Then he gets put into a faked photo or two with various

women."

"I'll go with that too - he has always been such a goody-two-shoes. And I assume you can prove the photos were faked?"

"Yes, naturally. Then he gets bombed. By unknown, presumed Arab parties,"

"Yes, although the Arab connection was never proven. But I agree he could have died like his driver did in that low-tech drone attack."

"But he didn't die, and then a story emerges about him having money offshore in the Cayman Islands."

"I agree it doesn't seem very likely. There are other MPs I'd place higher on the list than him."

"Quite. We did some digging. Brading's company in the Cayman's had a recent name change."

"Interesting."

"Yes, from Tovey Holdings to Brading Holdings."

"Surely no-one would be that stupid?" asked Rachel, "To put real names on the company."

"Unless the whole thing was a setup," Clare passed a paper across to Rachel, "See the name of the legal firm that facilitated the transfer? They have to be worth an investigation."

"I'm not going to print anything without more proof. I've stayed away from the original story. I'd need to come in with hard evidence to change this around. Like the organisation that the legal firm were acting for."

"Okay, but suppose they are trying to damage Brading. They have knocked him off the games board now. Who will his replacement be? Michael Tovey? Tovey who is linked with Brant?"

"Interesting. You think someone acting for Brant has tried to tarnish Brading and to conveniently substitute Tovey?"

"That's about the size of it," said Clare, "And we think that Brant's fixer firm ITMC is also involved - through a Miller McDonald, who seems to be -ahem- romantically linked with Trudi Hartmann from Brant. As a matter of fact, Trudi used to work for ITMC."

"This is getting somewhere now," said Rachel, "This has more of a Sunday papers exposé about it! Double page spread with diagrams and pictures!"

"Excellent," said Clare, "You'll have to let me know what else you need!"

"Coffees are on me," said Rachel.

Due diligence

In the Triangle offices, Bigsy smiled," Look what has just come up on the Internet!" - He routed the link to Clare, Christina, and Jake.

"Wow," replied Jake, "I think Grace has excelled with this one! Why Brant wouldn't pause when they uncovered some of this. Next we must show it to Rachel Crosby."

The Triangle office fell quiet as they each read the due diligence about Elixanor that Grace had identified.

Elixanor due diligence

Elixanor is a privately held health technology corporation. It was initially touted as a breakthrough technology company, with claims of having devised blood tests that required only very small amounts of blood and could be performed very rapidly using very small, automated devices the company had developed. The use of nanotechnology to achieve this was revolutionary and paved the way for the subsequent refinement of vaccine technology.

However, the original blood test claims later proved to be false. Founded fifteen years ago by 19-year-old Patricia Watson, Elixanor raised more than US$700 million from venture capitalists and private investors, resulting in a $10 billion valuation at its peak some six years ago.

Elixanor was hyped to its investors and in the media as a breakthrough in the blood-testing market, where the U.S. diagnostic-lab industry posts annual sales of over $70 billion. Elixanor claimed its technology was revolutionary and that its tests required only about 1/100 to 1/1,000 of the amount of blood that would ordinarily be needed, and the cost of testing was far less than existing tests.

A turning point came around five years ago, when two medical research professors and an investigative journalist questioned the validity of Elixanor's technology.

The company faced a string of legal and commercial challenges from medical authorities, investors, the U.S. Securities and Exchange Commission (SEC), Centers for Medicare and Medicaid Services (CMS), state attorneys general, former business partners, patients, and others.

Four years ago, it was estimated that Watson's personal net worth had dropped from $4.5 billion to virtually nothing. The company was near bankruptcy until it received a $100 million loan from Leningrad Associate Bank secured by its patents.

Elixanor received sanctions from the CMS, including the revocation of its CLIA certificate and prohibition of Watson and other company officials from owning or operating a laboratory for two years. A new Chief Scientist was hired: Arne Holstad. He announced Elixanor would work on research into miniature medical substance dispensing machines. Three years ago, Elixanor said it had reached a settlement agreement with CMS related to the blood testing.

Then, Elixanor, Watson, and former company president Yagovkin Lavro Kirillovich were charged with "massive fraud" by the SEC. One section of the complaint says Watson falsely claimed that the company had annual revenues of $100 million, a thousand times more than the actual figure of $100,000.

Elixanor and Watson agreed to resolve the charges against them, with Watson paying a fine of $500,000, returning the remaining 20.9 million common stock that she held, relinquishing her control of the company, and being barred from being an officer or director of any public company for ten years. It was at this time that Elixanor was taken over by Brant, itself a subdivision of Raven Industries.

According to the Brant agreement, if Elixanor were acquired or otherwise liquidated, Watson would not profit from her ownership until more than $800 million was returned to investors and other preferred shareholders. Elixanor and Watson neither admitted nor denied the allegations in the SEC's complaint. Kirillovich did not settle. Then, less than a year ago, the U.S. Attorney for the Northern District of California announced the indictment of Watson on wire fraud and conspiracy charges. Kirillovich was also indicted on the same charges.

....

"Wow, a hundredth to a thousandth the normal blood amount for testing is almost homoeopathically small quantities!" observed Clare.

"Tropospheric!" Jake added, referencing the Scarlett Thomas book - The End of Mr Y.

"It seems suspicious that Patricia Watson was so young," added Bigsy, "I know that VCs often start young, but raising $700 million at age nineteen seems way off the scale."

"She has to be a front," said Jake, "An unwitting name put forward.?"

"I think Rachel will be pleased to receive this," said Christina.

"Pleased," said Bigsy, "Ecstatic, more like."

They all paused in thought, looking out of the window at drizzly grey skies freeze-framed like TV-static hanging in the air.

weasel words from a professional

Clare and Serena were sitting in Andrew Brading's office. Serena was fuming.

"That shit of an MP Michael Tovey has moved into Brading's position. He's also done a Gove and denied stabbing Andrew in the back."

"Ah yes," said Clare, "I seem to remember Gove's doublespeak at the time. He denied betraying his former ally Boris Johnson when he stood against him for the Conservative leadership, saying his weasel words that he believed the Tories had made the right decision by making Theresa May prime minister.

Clare continued, "What a slimy line in defence too, I remember him on maybe World at One saying something along the lines: 'I wouldn't say I stabbed him in the back but I certainly came to the judgment in the immediate aftermath of the referendum campaign that, while I had originally thought he was the best person to be prime minister, for a variety of reasons that I won't go into, I didn't think he was the best person at that point.' - Nothing like convoluted doublespeak, is there?"

Serena nodded, "Then he went on to attempt to cover it up with the priciest of reasoning, 'It's not treachery. I explained my reasons at the time. The water is under the bridge.' Do you see how he did that? A forward reference to the reason and then a backward reference but with the actual reason conveniently missing!"

Serena looked more annoyed, "Well, he came out into the open later, when he ambushed Boris by bidding against him for Premiership. Do you remember when he stunned Johnson and the rest of Westminster by announcing just three hours before nominations closed for the Conservative party leadership – that he had reluctantly concluded his old chum Boris was not up to the job? Truly a twist of the knife."

Serena continued, "Well hold that thought about Gove. It's tantamount to what Tovey has just done to Andrew in this latest move."

"Look at Tovey's egotistical statement, 'Now with the benefit of hindsight and the opportunity to spend time on the backbenches reflecting on some of the mistakes Andrew Brading has made and some of the contrary judgments that I concluded, I think I am the right person at the right time,' "

Serena grimaced, "If ever there was a clumsily scripted speech then this must surely be it."

"Is there anything you can do?" asked Clare.

"I think there is. I met Flore Chéron from Lion & Freshwater a few days ago. She was introducing herself to Andrew and Katherine. She's a Queen's Council and seemed very positive toward Andrew and offered her card for services. I think she'll be interested in this situation, which is most unconstitutional lobby placement."

"I guess you'd better tell Andrew and Katherine what you are thinking," observed Clare, "I mean the whole womanising thing is mixed in with this and could get messy."

Serena smiled at Clare, "You know something, Clare? Andrew and I have worked together a long time and know how one-another tick. Trust me, he'll be pleased to know I'm working the system for him. You know what? You should come along when I get the meeting."

Fielders Court Chambers

Clare and Serena were sharing a taxi to Fielder's Court Chambers, where Lion & Freshwater were based and where Flore Chéron had an office.

"Have you ever met a silk before?" asked Serena.

Clare was bashful in her response, having known various members of the legal profession because of her father and her uncle, who was a QC himself. And then there were a couple of scrapes that The Triangle had been involved with, where legal cover had proved useful. Clare decided to answer blandly.

"I've met a couple of Legals before, but I can't remember how 'high up' the system they were. But I know that a silk is a big deal!"

"Flore's the real deal. Looks the part, and very quick witted; reminds me of you, actually!" said Serena.

In a few minutes they were in Flore's office, which looked like something one would expect to find in a Charles Dickens novel about the legal profession.

"Nice panelling!" greeted Clare they shook hands.

"Oh, I know! We have two offices actually. This is the one for private clients - they usually expect a legal office to look like this and be all quill-pens and wig powder. The other corporate office is completely different - Plate glass and steel. But I thought it would be more convenient to meet here, rather than traipse over to Canary Wharf."

Serena smiled, "Thank you for seeing us, I didn't take the decision to call you lightly. And I also admire your reputation and the standards you drive."

"Well thank you," said Flore, "Let's see if we can make some sense of this. Actually, you remember that you did set up a brief meeting for me with Andrew when he was considering what to do about his Fundamental Rights Bill?"

Serena gathered her thoughts. She tried to turn them into things which Ms Chéron's yellow pad could handle.

"Yes - I remember. It's been a whole catalogue of recent events. We suspect a covert campaign to discredit Andrew and substitute Michael Tovey. We believe it will have been lobby inspired."

Flore looked up from her pad.

"I'll need to stop you there. I'm not sure I can handle a case that might be based upon innuendo?'

Serena nodded. "Andrew is like most politicians. He humanly screws up sometimes. First, it was a mis-reported quote about him being anti-BAME. Then an accusation of womanising via a rogue reporter. Then the bomb. And to top it all, the fraudulent banking receipts apparently showing him with Cayman Island interests. I've known Andrew a long-time, and this is too much to conceive and entirely out-of-character. Someone wanted him moved out of the way and was prepared to stop at nothing to achieve it."

Flore had been taking more notes, "You present it all as a conspiracy, which might work in a John Grisham novel, but I'm afraid won't work in a regular court case. There is too much supposition involved. Let me take your story to pieces."

She walked across the wall to the panelling, pressed one of the panels, and a whiteboard appeared behind a hinged door.

"There is a secret door as well," she said, smiling.

"What about a cocktail bar?" asked Clare.

"You are looking right at it, said Flore, "But it is a bit bloke-ish, filled with men's drinks and some token wine. Come on, we'll open it."

Flore pressed a different panel and a small bar appeared, with a mirror behind it.

"Personally, I find it a bit like a James Bond set," said Flore, "But at least the wine is chilled,"

She picked up a marker and wrote down the four items.

1) Anti BAME quote
2) Womanising
3) Bomb
4) Cayman Tax retreat.

"I'm ruling out getting involved with the bomb - which should go to the anti-terrorist squad. Cayman Island - you need a forensic accountant. It leaves two and I'd say the most straightforward to pressurise is the rogue reporter attempting to implicate Andrew in womanising."

Serena and Clare stared at the whiteboard. Clare felt that this was usually her role when they were planning something at a Triangle meeting.

"With the reporter, we can get him on Libel - if you say he has manufactured the allegations and passed them on, then it would be damaging to Andrew's reputation and there is the basis for a case."

Serena said, "Frankly, it is too late to rescue the situations that Andrew finds himself in. They have done too good a job, but I'd be interested in trying to understand who has been doing this to Andrew."

"Well, there's a couple of things you could try," said Flore, "Look you don't need to hire me for this - and my Chambers would cost you a pretty penny. I can, however, give you some informal advice here and now. I like Andrew and can see that the government will need other help over the coming years. I'm more interested in getting Lion & Freshwater onto the approved list than trying to make up a case based upon what you have told me."

"That is remarkably honest and forthright of you," said Serena, "Let me thank you now, before you have even given me the advice."

"Okay - let's see. Who did you say the reporter was, and who does he work for?"

"It's Roger Slater and he is a London-based freelancer."

"Okay - we can assume he is a hired gun then. No newspaper to leverage; you will have to make this personal. You don't have good grounds for any form of police action either. Under PACE - that's the Police and Criminal Evidence Act 1984, you can't even legitimately search Slater's home or office. He can play the journalism card to prevent access to anything."

"What can we do then?"

"Legally, you could request an injunction against Slater. To stop him from hounding Andrew Brading in the future."

"That's a good idea," said Clare, "It would show Slater that we are on to him and could be reputationally damaging to him as well. People won't want to hire him for further shake-downs!"

Serena looked pleased, "Flore - I think you have cut to the quick of this. We can alert Slater and see where he runs for cover. It doesn't require the police to rattle him either. It is certainly a start."

Flore smiled, "I'm only sorry that I could not be of more service, and may I please remind you to look kindly upon Lion & Freshwater for your next public interest situation!"

Flore closed her notepad. Serena and Clare noticed how she had stayed scrupulously polite throughout their meeting, but some of her pointers made them both uneasy. If she could break it down into a few words on the whiteboard, then whoever was running the vendetta could just as easily add additional steps. It wasn't over yet. The troublemakers could be back, but the bomb the next time could have a touch more explosive. This situation would still require some significant steps to dismantle.

Ship and Shovell

Matt Stevens is rattled. There seems to be rumours going around that he was the leak who passed the information about Andrew Brading to the reporter. Even his girlfriend Lottie had told him he had been found out.

Matt was meeting meet Roger Slater again to tell him that he was not, under any circumstances, to reveal his source. It would cost him his job, and he'd only been paid in wine for what he had let slip.

They were meeting at a Victorian pub, The Ship & Shovell in an upstairs area, which was enough of a walk from Parliament to mean they could be private. The pub was also unique, being split in half by an alleyway which ran through the middle.

Matt had not dared tell Lottie that he'd spilled the beans about Andrew's background because of the trouble that Andrew Brading had been involved with. He was sitting in a corner, sipping a glass of beer when Roger Slater arrived.

"How much time have you got?' Roger says as soon as the 'hellos' are out of the way.

"I've a ton to do, but no meetings till later,' Matt replies. Slater is looking calm and carefree, as if his expenses budget could run for the entire afternoon.

"I'm in trouble," says Matt, "And I think it's because of what I told you when we last met. To be honest, I can't remember what I said - well not all of it anyway."

"You are fine," says Slater, "There's nothing you said to me that I didn't already have from another source."

"Will you protect your sources though?" asks Matt.

"Of course, even if they subpoenaed me, I'd still be able to claim a journalist's right to protect sources."

"But you are close to Parliament with this story," says Matt.

"The story is over. There is no follow up, I've been paid and will walk away."

Another man enters the upstairs bar, carefully carrying two glasses of wine on a small silver tray. Slater lowers his voice, "You have nothing to worry about,"

There is a minor crash. The new man who has entered the bar sees his wine flip around and smash onto Roger Slater.

"How clumsy," says the man, "But I'm not sure whether I'm the one who should be sorry?"

Roger Slater stands looking toward the darkly tanned man. To Matt, the man looks as if he can carry himself. You'd want him on your side in a fight, that's for sure.

The man glances across to someone else, who neither Roger nor Matt had noticed sitting in another corner of the room.

Now, Corner Man stands and walks across to the scene of the accident.

"That didn't look like an accident to me," he says, in a heavy accent,

"No," says the other man, "It wasn't - it was for Slater,"

Roger Slater looks alarmed that they have mentioned him by name. He appears confused, dripping with red wine in his ruined shirt. Matt wants to be somewhere else. He is not sure whether Slater has somehow brought this on, but it doesn't look as if it will end well.

"Here," says Corner Man, "Take my handkerchief. I don't care if it goes red."

Roger Slater takes the handkerchief and turns back to Wine Glass Man.

"I think you'll find a message on that handkerchief, " says Wine Glass Man.

Slater still hasn't said anything but now asks, "Who are you?"

"We are friends of your employer," says Corner Man, "They have asked us to remind you about confidentiality."

"Silence," says Wine Glass Man, "One way or another."

"Goodbye now," says Corner Man and the two of them

walk downstairs without looking back. The silver tray and the glasses are on the table where Slater sat talking to Matt.

"My god," says Matt, "That was intense. Were they people you knew? Or what did you do to upset them?"

Roger Slater was looking at the handkerchief, now red stained like his shirt.

On the handkerchief was written, "Spilt wine before spilt blood."

"Are we finished?" asked Roger Slater, "Only I need to go now, and don't worry, I won't be saying anything."

Matt sat surveying the damage as Roger exited towards the stairs.

Superinjunction

Slater was back at home. He was thinking about the last few days. First, a mad woman threatens him at home with a knife and then he gets a warning treatment from two men in a bar. He has so much red wine on him that the first taxi driver refused to take him as a passenger.

Now he was back at home. There is a sudden knock on the door.

"Damn," he thinks; he's still not got a security camera installed.

He puts the chain across the door, opens it a small amount and peers outside.

A slight man dressed in a suit and tie stood outside.

"Mr Slater?" he asks.

"That's me," says Roger Slater.

"Well, here is a court order, served to you in person," says the man, handing over a buff-coloured envelope. Too startled to reply, Slater took the envelope.

"You have a pleasant evening," said the thin man as he turned and was gone.

Slater looks at the envelope, then picks it open by a corner.

It was a court order. A damn injunction against him. He read it quickly. It was plainly to stop him publishing anything about Andrew Brading, yet it had been "anonymised" – using initials apparently plucked at random – so that no one could tell who was bringing the action. The claimant was listed as "KJS" rather than Brading.

No one searching any court list could ever guess that this was a well-known politician going to court. Further defendants were listed as "persons unknown" because the lawyers didn't know who leaked the information to Slater. Slater realised he was obligated to inform the paper that had published his article about this injunction. He also realised that it was reputation limiting. He would be bound up in legal red tape and unable to function as a journalist.

The order began by warning of the possible penalties for infringing the breach of a court order.

He looked through the wording for the key features:

1A: Slater agrees not to publish any further part of the KJS Report, or cause or authorise anyone else to do so.

1B: The publishing newspaper has to keep any copies of the document it may have. This can be significant if the claimants want to try to have the document returned or if, for instance, they want to see if they can identify the source who leaked it.

5a: Here the judge worries about the possibility that publicity about the injunction could "unfairly damage the interests of KJS." He therefore orders that the court hearing must remain a secret: no one is allowed to describe it, or the claim.

5b: The judge orders the "alphabet soup" approach to naming the case. No one will be able to see KJS has been to court.

5c: Just in case there's any doubt about the total secrecy of the proceedings, there can be no reference to any "persons or places" related to the case.

6: All the papers relating to the case will be sealed. That means no one (snooping journalists or MPs, for instance) can inspect any of the witness statements or any other papers to do with the case.

7: Having effectively put a wall of secrecy around the whole affair, it moves on to the injunction itself. It says that everything about the KJS article and further investigations is secret and nothing about it can be published.

10: Then more blood-curdling clauses about the secrecy of the proceedings. Neither Slater, nor newspapers, must publish any papers, documents, witness statements or letters to do with the case.

13: Costs. The order makes no specific order about costs at this stage - this is because the judge is not able at this point to decide where the overall merits of the case lie. Slater realises it was like a bottomless pit of costs.

18 The order was directed at Slater, but through him to newspapers. This clause warned that anyone who was aware of it and knowingly breached it would also be in contempt of court and could be locked up or have their assets seized.

...

Slater throws the paper onto the table. He realises it was a gagging order. More than that, it was worded like a superinjunction. And worse of all he would be obligated to tell newspapers he dealt with about being served with the injunction. But he could not tell them the basis. No-one would want to give him work after this.

Three things, the woman with the gun, the two heavies with the red wine and now a super-injunction. He couldn't even talk about his own tribulations.

Well, maybe one answer - to turn to the crown and provide evidence. Instead of water into wine, he could turn superinjunction into supergrass.

But first, a bottle of Lagavulin's finest.

Bigsy and the Tunnels

Bigsy had made it to the tunnels. He felt a mild excitement that he was now in the very area where his old work-buddy Albert had once worked. Albert had been old school, already close to retirement when Bigsy met him, but he always seemed to have practical ways to solve problems, many of which were not in the official manuals. "RTFM" was for Albert a last resort. "Read the flippin' manual" as it might politely be considered.

Now, Bigsy was with team organised by Grace from GCHQ and they were inspecting the miles of cable-run inside the tunnels of Pindar, looking for something that shouldn't be there. Bigsy remembered another one of Albert's little phrases - "New wires", which was another fast way to diagnose a problem. Albert reckoned that most of the cables which lay undisturbed would not go wrong unless a workman put a digger through them or something else, like a flood occurred.

So Bigsy was less intent on scouring every inch of the grubby tunnels to locate the wiretap which had been added. He tried to think about it logically. Where were the main switching centres in the tunnels? Where was a good supply of power and even a way to get a Wi-Fi signal to the outside world?

He decided it would be in a control centre close to a lift shaft. Maybe even one with some kind of public access. It narrowed the search somewhat. The Cabinet War Rooms were open to the public. They were also close to Downing Street. It seemed like a likely spot. Bigsy fired up 'The Lollipop' which was a small gadget that he had used for some years to detect spook signals around his offices.

It composed a bright orange dome underneath which was a slim handset with a few buttons and a LCD display. Although simple to look at, it could scan for all signals between 50MHz right the way through to 3.5GHz. It was easily enough to locate a rogue Wi-Fi or other encrypted signal and was a high-tech version of the units used by spies in James Bond movies.

To his amazement, when he switched it on in the Cabinet War Room, he was greeted with a couple of signals - one was for Wireless Internet Direct - which was the Wi-Fi which reached across much of the Parliamentary estate, the second one was for chibis, which Bigsy initially though was a fast food joint. Closer inspection revealed its signal strength to be much too high for such a purpose and he also noticed that the signal had been set as 'hidden', although his PCE-29 Electromagnetic Field Meter was picking up the signal clear as a bell.

He gestured to one of the technicians from GCHQ.

"Look, I think this is the signal. His colleague soon triangulated it and they found a small wiring closet in the main corridor. It was surrounded by a clock, fire extinguisher and even a kind of fire hose in a glass cabinet.

"Plenty to distract the eye around here," observed the GCHQ technician. They opened the wooden fronted cabinet and could see the cabinet had a distinct left side and right side.

"Oh my god," said the technician, "Rats' nest!"

Bigsy was less phased by the interior of the cabinet. He had seen early wiring closets and knew that the wires ran in on the right and were then clipped together in the left-hand side of the cabinet. Sure, enough in the middle was a kind of ruler marked from 10 to 90 repeating and with 100, 200, 300 marked at where the hundred marking would be.

"It's the individual extension markings," explained Bigsy, "See the twisted pairs of red and white wires going to each terminator point?"

The technician looked and Bigsy pointed, "Do you notice anything else? See that? A blue and white twisted pair. I wonder where they go? Let's see. The main buss of the cabinet. This is a wiretap."

The GCHQ technician looked and pointed to the base of the unit. A dusty small black plastic square was visible.

"Oh look!" said the technician, "A raspberry Pi! I wonder how that got there?"

He shone a torch on it and Bigsy could see a couple of small lights were on. The card-deck sized device was active.

The GCHQ technician made as if to unplug the unit. "No wait," said Bigsy, "We should consider this carefully before we remove it, we might want to send some new signals along it first!"

The technician smiled, "Have you worked with us before?"

Get it On

"for meanwhile, I'm still a thinkin' "

Marc Bolan

Meanwhile, back in Bermondsey

Clare was back in Bermondsey. She was listening to Lottie telling a story about her boyfriend Matt.

"He was in the bar with Slater when he was approached by a heavy thug. The thug tipped a bottle of wine over Slater. Matt says he tried to intervene but was blocked off by a second even more intimidating thug. Matt says they looked as if they had come from central casting and were dressed like a couple of Russian gang members. Matching leather jackets, shaved heads, lots of tattoos. They roughed Slater up a bit and then left. Matt isn't even sure what caused it , but he is rattled now."

"Why was Matt with Slater anyway?" asks Clare, "Wait. Was it Matt who leaked the information about Andrew?"

Clare sees Lottie is embarrassed.

"Clare - Please don't tell anyone - Matt is an idiot sometimes and does get rather drunk. I'm sure he didn't mean anything by what happened."

Lottie adds, "Funnily enough, there's no love lost between my MP Duncan, and Roger Slater. Slater exposed Duncan's wandering hands a couple of years ago in a similar hatchet piece. Duncan never forgave him."

"But was it true?" asks Clare, "About Duncan Melship?"

Lottie shrugs, "Oh yes, we all used to warn one another about him. He didn't get the nickname "Handyman" for nothing!"

Tessa added, "Nor the Befummeler!"

"Handyman! Befummeler!" Clare laughs and then shudders, "So maybe Slater had his uses?"

"He would only ever do anything for money," says Lottie, "Maybe now it has backfired upon him?"

"What does Melship think? Will he support the new man?" asks Clare.

Lottie answers, "Yes, I think so; He's under the whip and so he will do what he is told."

Tessa adds, "You have to remember my MP is Labour so we have to think differently."

"Oh yes, I was almost forgetting - The beloved two-party system!" replies Clare.

That secret entrance

Andrew Brading was making his way back to Parliament using the Tube. He decided that his first day back after the bomb would need to be cloaked in some secrecy. At the top of the deep escalators in the grey caverns of Westminster underground station, most passengers either make for the exit straight ahead on to Westminster Bridge or duck right to come out on Whitehall.

But Andrew Brading headed left before taking a sharp right along the underground walkway and disappeared through a badly lit revolving door, on the inside of which is a police guard.

He was using one of the lesser-known ways into the bubble that contains the British parliament.

Having shown his green and white striped security pass, and passed through the security gates, he avoided the hassle of bag-searches or x-ray machines that visitors have to endure at the main entrance.

Then he was on another underground walkway. Turn left and he could walk through a tiled passageway between a stone unicorn and a crowned lion, to a colonnade to take him towards the main House of Commons debating chamber.

To the right is New Palace Yard and the MPs' underground carpark or the other side is Speaker's Green and Speaker's Court.

On most days, this walkway is crammed with people walking purposefully in both directions. He could blend in here and would have avoided the theatre of a re-appearance in front of the media.

Recognisable by their security passes, if not always by their faces; some MPs seem to find coming to Westminster a bit of a drain on their time and prefer to stay away.

Other MPs still look bewildered and lost, because they are.

"It takes about a year for them to find their way round," one of the many machine-gun-carrying policemen remarked. "You can tell, because that's when you become invisible to them. At the start, they are always friendly, saying hello and holding doors open. Then it stops. I'm sure they are not bad people, but they just become part of the bubble."

The police recognise the nuances of the badges.

The peers by their red and white striped passes. The media are identifiable by their brown badges, the Palace staff by their grey ones. Lords' assistants and researchers are issued with straight reds, green and white stripes are the MPs but the most terrifying species of all are those with straight green - Commons advisors.

Now Brading needs to find out a few things - but he would do so from the covert area of his office. He turned the corner and slipped in. There was a muffled cheer. Serena ran to greet him. Maggie and Clare stood back and watched him take his seat.

"Well, they've bombed me, although I feel terrible about Derek, my poor driver- and his family. The experts said if it had been a few inches further back it would have taken off my head, instead of leaving me with terrible headache. Thank you all for the wishes and chocolates and everything. My visitors polished off most of the chocolates, although I did manage to hide the Toblerone bar."

Serena smiled, "We thought flowers would be a little bit -er - final in the circumstances."

"I understand; now we need to come up with a plan to get the bastards!"

Vauxhall Cross and the Plan

Amanda had called Jake. She had asked for a further meeting, but time it was to be at Vauxhall Cross instead of over a video link.

"I'm concerned that we don't get overheard this time," explained Amanda, and I'm bringing Grace in for the session as well.

Jake alerted Clare and all of them piled into a couple of taxis around to the dramatic-looking building housing SI6 and overlooking the Thames and Vauxhall Bridge.

"It's like Gotham City has been given a good clean," commented Jake.

As they approached the building, Jake said to Clare that it was bringing back all kinds of awkward memories. He had been locked away in an adjacent building while Bigsy, Clare and Chuck Manners had been touring Arizona on an earlier adventure.

"It reminds me somehow of a post-modernist Aztec Temple," observed Clare, looking over the structure, "And considering it is supposed to be secret, it is interesting that every taxi driver in London knows where it is."

They heard the taxi driver chuckle. He came onto the loudspeaker in the back of the cab. "Luv, I was already driving when they built this place. The one before it was at Century House, near Waterloo and was just as well-known. I dunno what we'd do if we ever really had a cold war. They put this up really quick, though when Mrs Thatcher told them to look sharpish."

"They say that there's almost as much underground as there is above ground?" said Clare.

"Yes, there's a lot below surface." answered the taxi driver, "Its somewhere to lock up all the spies. And did you know there's a tunnel under the river too? It goes all the way to Whitehall."

In the other taxi there was a similar conversation, but in this one Christina was telling how the Russians had, in 2000, supplied an RPG-22 anti-tank rocket to some local dissidents who had fired on the building from the adjacent Spring Gardens.

"All it did was help justify the cost of the triple glazing," said Bigsy, somewhat drily. "Yes, but it also showed how vulnerable most of London is to unsolicited attack," added Christina, "And I remember, we used to think of the Netta - RPG-22 - as a disposable asset. The firing tube was made of fibreglass. Truly fire and forget."

After complex security procedures, they were inside the building, albeit without their locked-away cell-phones. Amanda had appeared and was to escort them to the room.

"We are in the Dick White Room," she announced, "It's quite a big deal to be on that floor."

Christina smiled, "Dick White? Wasn't he a founder of SIS?"

"Not exactly," answered Amanda, " He helped the move of MI6 to its previous building and was also the head of both services - MI5 and MI6. The floor is the only one to have the rooms named instead of numbered - There's Mansfield Cumming - he was the founder, Paul Dukes, one of the first superspies, Hugh Sinclair - from when we were at 54 Broadway - which we outgrew. Oh and a few others too."

"But not a James Bond room?" asked Jake, "You are not the first person to ask that question," said Amanda, evasively.

They arrived at the floor. It was like an office executive suite, with its own receptionists and coffee stations. Amanda led them to the meeting room. Jake caught a glimpse of another door, "James Bond Suite," it said, printed onto official-looking signage.

Inside the room, Grace was already seated, everyone exchanged greetings and then Jake asked, "I've just got to ask, that James Bond Suite. Can I look inside later?"

Amanda and Grace both smiled, "I think you will be very disappointed; it's a storage cupboard which someone had the wit to name. Nothing to see there, except cleaning materials."

"Or is it?" said Bigsy, also smiling.

"Okay, to business," said Amanda, "I wanted this to be

face to face to avoid any unnecessary security exposures."

"First, some new developments: Roger Slater has turned himself over as State evidence. He says he has been threatened and hounded for long enough and he now wants to declare everything he knows."

"That is consistent with something I heard from one of my flatmates," said Clare, "Lottie - who is the girlfriend of Matt Stevens, said that Slater was threatened by two Russian-looking gentlemen when they were in a pub."

"And why would your flatmate's boyfriend be with the reporter?" asked Grace, confused.

Clare added "Well, it's a long story, but we flatmates all went out together with a chap called Robin Hunter, who was dating Tessa. Robin told some stories about Andrew Brading, which Matt then drunkenly passed on to Slater. To be honest, I get the impression that Matt is somewhat rattled too after the Russian encounter."

Clare looked a little guilty, 'I must come clean too about another one of the threats to Slater. Serena and I visited a well-known QC who suggested we should serve a court injunction on Slater to stop him from pestering Andrew Brading. By the time it had been written it had turned into a very heavy-duty super injunction."

"No wonder Slater wants to run for the hills!" said Amanda. Christina decided she would keep quiet about her encounter with Slater. The piece of the story about the sub machine gun might not play too well inside SI6.

"Another very interesting facet is the discovered back-channel - based upon a wire-tap inside Whitehall. We can thank Bigsy here for helping track it down and for preventing it from being decommissioned. Now it could be a useful asset for us to send false information to whoever is listening."

"We should also remember the findings from our trip to Norway," said Jake, "Arne Holstad, The Chief Science Officer of Elixanor was to be replaced. He told us that the nano-delivery of the medicines didn't work, yet we know that the system is about to be sold to several governments."

"And it isn't even the first time that Elixanor has been caught being economical with the truth," said Grace, "They lied about a blood testing system once before and were caught and fined by the U.S. Securities and Exchange Commission."

"There's something else," added Christina, "I received a phone call yesterday from Marion Charlotte - except she's Lady Hinton nowadays!"

Amanda looked interested, "Lady Hinton - married quite recently to Lord Edgar Hinton of Gloucestershire?"

"Yes, but we all knew her in a previous life when she worked for an escort agency. It turns out she knew the people that framed Andrew too, both Natasha Makarovna and Shanell Kinkaid."

Christina decided to edit around her own knowledge of these people and the agency. It could otherwise get too complicated to explain, especially to the British Security Services.

"Well, Marion called me yesterday. She said that as I'd been asking about Tasha, I might be interested in the latest gossip. That Tasha was now dating Michael Tovey."

"That's hilarious!" said Clare, "Have you seen Tasha, and then Tovey? Tasha's a model - slim, fashionable, delectable and a head turner. Tovey is - how shall I say - someone you'd cross the street to avoid."

Is it another set-up?" asked Jake, "Like the time that Raven and Brant were plying MPs with all manner of experience to get their way."

"I'm beginning to see why you have called us all here," said Clare, "and to this fancy meeting room!"

"I want this whole situation to stop, and we are the people who can do it." answered Amanda, "And with that in mind, I've asked some others to meet us here, " Amanda pressed a button, "It's okay, you can show them in."

A door opened and they could see one of Amanda's assistants, ushering someone in.

It was Andrew Brading.

"Oh, a whole roomful of people," he said startled, "Which one of you is Amanda?"

Then, Serena followed him into the room. She looked around the faces.

"Clare?" she said, looking surprised.

Andrew now looked more closely, "Clare?" he repeated.

"I have some explaining to do to you both," started

Amanda, "And I must apologise for the clandestine way we brought you here. We did not want there to be any security leaks."

Grace had turned the earlier discussion into a chart, which she now displayed on the room projector.

Andrew and Serena still looked baffled.

"Clare, I'm confused. Are you part of SI6 or something?"

"No, not at all, I happen to know Amanda and she asked me if I could assist with something,"

"It certainly accounts for your quick-wittedness," said Serena, "I knew you had an above-average IQ - just the way you fixed that first problem for Andrew..."

"Pure luck," said Clare, modestly, "Although I have been in somewhat similar situations before."

"So Samantha is really your sister?" asked Andrew.

"Oh yes, although Jake here isn't exactly my boyfriend!" smiled Clare.

"Hello, yes, I'm Jake. A co-worker of Clare's"

"And I'm Christina - another co-worker,"

"And I'm Dave Carter - call me Bigsy - we all work for a small outfit called The Triangle."

"Well, I'm pleased to meet you all, but I assume you are some sort of security consultants?" asked Andrew.

"They are a mixture of security consultants and other

capabilities," answered Amanda, "And this is Grace Fielding, from GCHQ."

Grace started to stand, sat down again and smiled.

"GCHQ, SI6, Vauxhall Cross, Security Consultants...You are pulling out all the stops," said Andrew, "I hope it is worth it!"

They all looked back toward the image that Grace had projected. Amanda explained everything for Andrew and Serena.

Brading

- Brading reputation damaged by Slater innuendo
- Brading bomb perpetrators (unknown?)
- Brading Unconstitutionally replaced by Tovey
- Slater turning State evidence

Elixanor Deal

- Elixanor a sham company with bad technology
- Arne Holstad replied by Mikael Bjornstad
- Tovey to push through the Healthcare Bill to facilitate Elixanor deal
- Tovey associates are Miller McDonald and Trudi Hartmann working for (unknown?)

Dirty Tricks

- Medusa listening station in use
- Wiretap discovered
- Yaroslav as suspected enforcer on behalf of (unknown?)

Clare looked at the list and had a secret pang of envy that Grace had summarised everything so well. No wonder Grace was an information officer at GCHQ.

"So what do you expect to do about the situation?" asked Andrew, "I'm kind of resigned to being outwitted by the scourge of the media."

"I have several plan objectives," answered Amanda, "Let's list them, Grace!"

1) Find out who is running Medusa
2) Stop the Protection of Healthcare Rights Bill in its current form
3) Discredit Elixanor
4) Capture McDonald and Hartmann and identify their bosses.
5) Curtail Yaroslav and his gang.

"I'm not sure we can guarantee to put you back in position, Andrew, but we'll give it a shot as well."

Andrew and Serena both smiled. Serena asked, "Look, can we tell Maggie about this? She would otherwise be the only one of our office out of the loop?"

Amanda considered, "She is trustworthy? The Triangle people have worked together for a long time, as have Grace and I. We also know the Triangle organisation very well. It would be important to have a similar trust in Maggie?"

Andrew spoke, "I have known Maggie since she was a teenager - let me rephrase that - since she was eighteen. She is determinedly loyal. I would have no reservations about having her included."

Serena nodded, "I have to agree. And it would be more difficult to work around her. She is very capable and would soon work out something was going on."

"Okay, then, it'll be this group, plus Maggie and my boss Jim Cavendish."

Serena looked surprised, "Jim Cavendish - wasn't he one of Clare's referees for when she got the job?"

"Oh yes, it was better to decouple Clare from me," answered Amanda.

"So now all we need is a plan," said Bigsy.

"Grace and I might just have an idea about that!" declared Amanda.

PART THREE

Politicians

*"Politicians were mostly people who'd had
too little morals and ethics to stay lawyers."*

George R.R. Martin, Ace in the Hole

Identity Bill, Second Reading

Once again, the Commons is crowded. It is to be the second reading of the Identity Bill, over which Andrew Brading has unwittingly become the headline news ever since the first reading was sneaked through the House. He hopes that Amanda's Plan will work.

Andrew Brading takes to the floor and launches the first part of the Plan:

"They have done it. The right wing of the Conservative party has won its historic victory."

"The UK has become a sovereign 'third country', with its limited trade deal with the EU. The UK, right-wingers believe, has been reconciled to its true history as a nation of offshore islanders. We have our own sandcastle upon which we can fly our own flags and create our own policy. We have taken back control, so long as it doesn't irritate anyone else, nor impinge upon the scallywag plans of the elite."

There is scuffling and rustling of papers.

A quiet "Order, Order," issues from The Speaker.

Andrew continues, "But those same right-wingers have also failed, according to their own terms. Theresa May's 'red, white and blue' nation is long dead, and a hastily-patched hustler deal turned out to be better than no deal at all."

Andrew hears muttering from behind him. His own backbenchers are getting ruffled.

"Order, Order!"

He continues, "Of course, our EU friends will not be supplanted by a great new Europe where British trade flows unimpeded; there are now frictions and barriers, not least in services. Witness our lorry queues. The strange absences of tomatoes, the difficulty of selling sausages abroad. Confused fishing legislation connected to a time-out in a few years creating landed catches which cannot be sold. But that's not all, the same confusion applies to components and to large items stored in containers. Deregulatory moves by the UK are already being met with EU retaliation."

"You say Tomato," bellows someone.

"And I say Tomayto," shouts someone else.

"Order! Order!," calls The Speaker.

Brading continues. This would get him into the papers, that was for sure, "In short, the UK has repatriated economic sovereignty and discovered that, far from allowing it to humble the EU, it has harmed itself. Our Leaders who supposedly stood up for the greatness of the renewed British nation have been revealed as 'champions of free trade' who only understand the underbelly of the modern economy and as boastful flag-waving nationalists who don't realise that great British rulers once looked down on such tinpot antics."

"Tinpot speech," shouts someone from his own party.

"Listen!" shouts a cross bencher.

"Order! Order!" beckons The Speaker, now raising his voice.

Brading resumes, "As things now stand, the UK has made its pointless gesture, a politics of headlines in which sovereignty is performed by bleating world-beating absurdities. We have a promise without a plan. We have a selection of political tinkerers, intent on adjusting the table to their personal advantage. We have broken out of one regime of international relationships into a holding pattern worse than that which came before, but with a blind hope of redemption although, more likely, stagnation or damnation."

"Order! Order!" shouts the Speaker, just to make sure that the speech could conclude,

"Will the Right Honourable Gentleman please consider reaching a conclusion,"

Brading smiles, "Yes, Mr Speaker, I will make a point and list some pertinent though vulgar considerations. We might end up with a renewed plebiscitary and parliamentary democracy in which the people take back control, but not just from Brussels."

The speaker looks intrigued at where Brading's argument may lead.

Brading continues, "Now it is cronyist faux Tories making the EU's bureaucrats look like models of honest and transparent politics; our politicians use systematic mendacity, abetted by a loyal red-top press and unconstrained by a whip-controlled parliament. The game can be revealed. The pie was in Brussels. Our politicians want it closer to get their hands into it. We've seen Russia drift from oligarchy into kleptocracy. Now our moneyed and ruling classes want the same for Britain."

"Vulgar," shouts someone.

"Sermo Vulgaris," shouts someone else.

"Give way," calls a third.

Brading continues, "No. 'Nemo mortalium omnibus horis sapit.' - Of mortal men, none is wise at all times - And so, in their failure as champions of free trade, Britain has repeated a failure of the 1950s, an attempt to create a western Europe-wide industrial free trade area that led instead to the UK seeking entry to the European Economic United Kingdom in 1961. Perhaps they might reach back even further into history, to the aspiration of an earlier generation of Tory press lords, who pushed for 'empire free trade' in the 1920s and 1930s. These people – who had 'power without responsibility', in Baldwin's famous phrase – also failed, as India and the dominions remained protectionist.

"Ironically, the imperialists and press lords of that era wanted to create a trading bloc to rival the United States; today's politicians would prefer a deal with the Americans, handing control to Washington rather than Brussels. But the US, even after scurrilous Trumpism, is still protectionist and deeply committed to exporting hormone-enriched science-project foods."

"Chickens!" someone shouts.

"Fried Chickens!" calls another.

"Order! Order! You must let the Right Honorable Gentleman continue and desist from these childish cat-calls." says The Speaker.

Brading again: "We could develop a Cayman Islands model: merging the UK with an archipelago of tax havens run from the Caribbean, to create an even bigger tax-avoidance paradise than the one we already have.

"Don't be fooled, we could give up on the rest of the world, and focus on national renewal, on so-called levelling up of beyond the red wall. But we already have some indication of how this is going."

Brading pauses and looks around the House. He could see the Prime Minister giving him the same look that he'd been given for his speech about the Fundamental Rights Bill. This time he could also see the red-faced whip standing behind the Speaker and looking about as angry as it was possible to be without hitting someone.

Brading continues, "The creation of new national

business is, in reality, contracts for cronies - even shamefully through the national emergency of a pandemic - and dodgy startups angling for subsidies, while chummy businesses actually invest overseas. We should hardly be surprised that "levelling up" turns out to be a cynically small pork-barrel fund for financing better bypasses.

"Yet this ideological maelstrom gives an opportunity to abandon old nostrums and re-energise with a new national mission.

"We should disabuse ourselves of the cosy and outdated notion that Britain's ills are caused by imperial hangovers and a consequently incompetent upper-class elite. We should wake up and offer an alternative future to contest the rich-boy narrative – one that amounts to more than just better welfare and more administrative competence.

"We need a revised agenda: of greater equality, of common purpose, of rising wages, of meaningful work. We could embrace the idea of a refreshed democracy, of really taking back control, of an anti-elite politic rather than a reheated technocracy.

"We should speak in realities, not celebratory fantasies, and seek to create a truthful democratic politics, which is essential to any real programme of progressive change. The bonfire of national illusions may have only just started, and current circumstances force an essential understanding of Britain's place in the world.

Brading gestures slowly with his hand, no fingers outstretched lest they look like daggers, "We are no longer a potentially 'top nation'. Britain will not escape the orbit of Europe; it never did, even at the height of its power. It must imitate far more than it innovates.

Inserting 'UK discovery' and 'UK first' into the illusory Premier speeches fools no-one, not even Gogglebox.

"Understanding these truths is crucial to a genuine national reconstruction, which should aim to create a real better country, not to fake being the best."

"Gogglebox!" someone shouts.

"Order!" commands The Speaker, adding "You are so predictable."

Brading continues, "And so, Mr Speaker, I conclude. A policy of national reconstruction, for the foundational economy, for the support of better everyday life, needs to be built on a double critique: of the failed policies of the past 40 years, and of the ultras seeking an even more disastrous turbo-Thatcherism. If we think about this properly, we can instead write a new history for the British nation."

He stops. Looks around. Silence. A solitary clap from the Visitors' Gallery.

Someone passes him a small piece of yellow paper. "See me in my office," it reads. Signed by one of the Whips.

Truth to Power

The next morning Andrew Brading used the same route to work via the Tube entrance to Parliament.

He slips quietly to his office, where he is greeted by Serena, Clare and Maggie. They had a bottle of Dom Perignon ready and Serena asks Andrew to open it.

"Uh, I'm a bit bleary after last night's TV circuit!" answers Andrew, "But it was amusing to see the Pomps chasing around after me."

"And the short, ultra-pompous, terminally slippery, bespectacled headmaster was on the radio this morning at around 8 o'clock trying to explain the philosophy behind your remarks. It was priceless."

"Take a look at the papers, I bought physical copies this morning, I think the assistant in WH Smith was quite bemused," says Clare, "Look!"

She spreads the headlines around the desk.

BRADING SPEAKS TRUTH TO POWER
(The Guardian)

RIGHT DEFENCE
(The Telegraph)

GOGGLEBOX MENTIONED IN BRADING
PARLIAMENT DEBATE
(The Mail)

BRADING SPEECH IN FULL
(The Times - full transcript behind paywall)

DIANA'S ORIGINAL PLEA TO END CRONYISM
SUPPORTED BY BRADING
(The Express)

MODERN LIFE IS RUBBISH - SAYS BRADING
(The Star)

BRADING BLAMES TOMATO SHORTAGES ON EU
(The Sun)

"Well, Part One of Amanda's plan seems to have worked rather well. Now we need to send that invitation to Tovey."

Fashion

Michael Tovey was having a hectic week. Now that Andrew Brading had self-destructed in Parliament, his way getting the Protection of Healthcare Rights Bill out seems assured. He had felt like celebrating and then, boom, out of nowhere he'd received an invitation from a supermodel to go to London Fashion Week.

He'd met Natasha Makarovna a couple of times with Miller McDonald, and she'd always seemed to like him, but now she'd asked him to accompany her to London Fashion Week. Well, not to the whole week, but to a couple of events on Wednesday.

"It is always good when we go with someone. Usually, I turn up with a couple of other models, but sometimes it is good to be seen with a politician or racing driver. You know the kind of thing, I'm sure."

Michael was delighted at the prospect and even asked Natasha (call me Tasha) what he should wear.

"D'you know, I don't think it will matter, but I can suggest you go classic politician. Dark suit and maybe some braces for a hint of classic. Then remember a funky

353

tie and a different nonmatching pocket square. You could bring a hat too. And dark glasses!"

Michael had written it down into a shopping list and headed over to Saville Row to get something that fitted the bill. He'd been told to go to Armani when he'd blinked at the prices and sure enough the Emporio in Knightsbridge had fitted him out with a suit, shirt and some accessories for under £3000, which was less than half what he'd have spent in Saville Row.

"And trust me," said the assistant, "The fashionistas will recognise this as Armani, and you'll be thought of as one cool politician."

Michael decided that it was probably expensable in any case as working attire.

London Fashion: Wednesday

Another day in Andrew's office. Clare was more interested in the online and social media today. She'd been looking around Facebook, Instagram and a couple of fashion magazines and found several closeups of Michael Tovey with Natasha Makarovna.

Some of these were syndicated press pictures too, so they were all properly captioned with the event and the people in the picture. Michael Tovey was well-and-truly seen with Natasha.

The Daily Herald - Jasmine Richards - Fashion Editor

FOR ALL THE DEDICATED FOLLOWERS of fashion there has been only one place to be in recent days. The annual London Fashion Week has put aside the sale signs and recession fears dominating the industry and got people talking about clothes and designs again.

WEDNESDAY MORNING: The British influence on the global stage is at an all-time high. Our home-grown designers are at the helm of some of the biggest luxury brands in the world and our designers are shaping trends and making a huge impact on the global catwalks.

I dragged my man Carlton with me. It was clearly going to be a chore for him to spend the day watching 5ft 11in models strut their stuff on the catwalks.

We stopped at the 18th Century Spencer House first, it's the historic home of Princess Diana's family and venue for a new designer Edith Sparrow showing off her personal brand. Before that, Sparrow had worked on Giorgio Armani's Black label for five years. Sparrow had launched her collection last year in Milan and it was intriguing to see the interest generated.

Fleets of people-carriers ferried VIPs to the venue. Cameramen, photographers and the all-important fashion editors were arriving. We immediately spotted so many big hitters.

Among them were editors from the main fashion press and our back-stage pass meant we caught a glimpse of Edith in action manoeuvring the models and clothes. It's where we caught the stunning supermodel Tasha dressed by Edith Sparrow. Tasha explained she was taking a rest from modelling on this occasion. Her beau for the day was political man Michael Tovey, who had got the memo and was dressed in an Edith Sparrow designed piece of Armani suit, although he claimed it was 'pure luck' that he was in the right attire.

We were ushered upstairs to three gilded rooms, with high ceilings and priceless artworks lining the walls. The regal setting was fitting for this luxurious collection and being one of my most favourite designers, Sparrow did not disappoint.

The statuesque creatures displayed flashes of feathers, fur, crystal studs and beaded linings. Hand-painted cashmere and prints onto stretch cotton and duchesse satin provided an entirely opulent collection from Sparrow.

As the audience cheered and when Edith Sparrow took the customary walk round, you could see the relief across her brow. This was a huge success, and she could tell by the audience's face that they loved it.

A select few were invited for a glass of champagne - of course. I bumped into Edith's mum, who had come down for the show. Air kisses and congratulatory words were fired across the room while cameras were trying to grab the main lady for a few words. I was accosted by a photographer. How exciting I thought, she wants to take my picture. Well almost - she was doing an accessory feature and wanted to take a picture of my shoes. Oh well. However, on our way out another photographer asked if she could take a picture of the Edith Sparrow dress that I was wearing. You see, loyalty pays.

MID MORNING: Onwards with the style pack to the British

Fashion Council tent. I had been invited to meet Charlie Dassault, fashion god.

We had been asked to join her at the Jonathan Bryht show. We stood in line to collect our passes and I couldn't help but notice this wonderful array of colour from the crowd.

There were no recession blues in sight.

There was a big Eighties revival thing going on and girls were wearing neo-orange lipstick, which incidentally I also saw on the catwalk too.

Interesting.

Before the show we bumped into Natasha Makarovna again, still with her MP in tow.

Makarovna said she was particularly interested in a smaller pre-show collection, inspired by what were referred to as ladies of the night. In fact, that was her tame reference to what were a well-cut and edgy collection from Londoner Amy Slice. There was a couture feel in the weight and structure of the garments. The highlight of this collection was the innovative rucksack dress. A little bonkers but remember where you heard about it first.

AFTERNOON: Then it was front row at the packed-out Jonathan Bryht show. Magnificent fabrics and textures with pronounced shoulders and seriously padded hips. Nude chiffon flapper dresses. Then time for a dash to Soho House where Ellie Yellow was exhibiting her new collection. Ellie is a hand embroiderer who studied at Central St Martins College in London. Known for her vibrant colours, contrast and craft, Ellie produced her most refined collection to date. A colour palette of ginger, hard pink and her signature electric blue formed the core to this season. There were biker jackets, mohair coats, sheep skin miniskirts and mirrored denim bodices.

My 6in platform shoes were beginning to irritate me, although good exercise for my calf muscles. My assistant Julie also didn't let the side down, directing and filming in her 5in red suede heels. We even got some of our tame MP closely admiring Tasha's outfit.

Upon reflection, we all agreed that the feeling here in London was uplifting. Yes, there was plenty of talk of tightening purse strings, a certain downturn in consumer spending, but most designers feel that these shows are a critical part of their marketing campaigns.

EVENING: Dom P. What else can I say?

Slater's interview

Roger Slater knew that turning State's evidence was effectively ratting. He would technically be a criminal defendant giving testimony to prosecutors about other alleged criminals.

He'd want a deal though. Immunity from prosecution.

After all, he was helping to ease the caseload, and prosecutors could get on with successfully prosecuting the most pernicious of criminals.

He called in his intentions a few days ago and been given an appointment to attend Islington Police station to make a statement. It all seemed remarkably civilised.

He'd gone by taxi. The parking restrictions around the outside of the Police station were legendary.

He'd also called up his usual solicitor and explained the score. The article, the injunction, the threats. Charles Hardy, his routine Brief, had agreed to meet him at a nearby Italian, before they go on to the cop shop.

Roger Slater walks under the sign for Chapel Market and

toward the small Italian cafe which serves a great breakfast with all the trimmings.

Charles is already there, suited and booted, "Hi Roger, This is a bit off-piste for you, isn't it? Super injunctions and so forth?"

"Yes, I'm afraid I've got myself in rather deep this time. I took some very generous fees but forgot the rule."

"What rule?"

"If it looks too good to be true, it probably is too good to be true."

Hardy adds, "There's some other news too. They have informed me that there will be a Home Office observer at the interview. You are shaking some trees, that's for sure."

"I hope the right apples fall down," answers Roger.

"We are due to be there in ten minutes, we'd better press on."

Roger pays the bill for their coffees and they leave.

Walking toward the Police Station, Slater has a sense that he was being watched from a parked car. He thinks he sees a flash of glass from a telephoto lens. They turn the corner to the right and walk along the edge of a yellowish 90's brick building without any ground floor windows. Then around the corner they see the blue light. Police Station. They walk inside for processing.

They are soon escorted to a tiny interview room. There is a glass wall - which Slater assumes contains a one-way mirror - and a panic bar around the room about a metre from the floor. A recorder is bolted to the interview desk and seems to include DVDs rather than the more conventional cassette tapes used by many police forces in TV dramas.

Slater couldn't help wondering whose bright idea it was to move from one outdated technology to another one. Still, it said 'Made in Luton' on the front of the unit.

"Good Morning, Mr Slater, I am Detective Inspector Evan Davis, and this is Constable Lillian Grant. We are being joined today by an observer from the Home Office, given the nature of your statement. This is Alex Smith."

They sit across the table from one another. Slater decides that the combined age of the three of them interviewing him would be less than 100. Alex, in particular, brought the average age right down.

Lillian starts the recorder, which consists of placing three individual DVDs into separate slots, then pressing a cassette-tape deck style record button. Slater decides that the specification for the new system must have been to make it as much like the old one as possible.

DI Davis leads the questioning. He seems to write a lot onto his notepad.

"It's for the transcript of the interview," he explains.

Slater describes the situation he'd been placed in. To be offered above average fees to get some dirt on Andrew Brading. That the people he was working for had provided him with the women, and the photographer. He'd written the piece, published it but then the trouble had started. He'd been warned first by a mad woman with a knife and gun, then by a couple of Russian gangsters and finally by the threat of a super-injunction.

"My client wishes to make it clear that he is a victim of circumstance in all of this. Had he known that the photographs had been faked, then he would not have written the piece," explains Charles Hardy.

"Yes, but now I'm concerned both for my innocence but also because the people harassing me seem to know where I live. The red wine they spilled was a warning. They left a message along the lines that next time it would be my blood. Look, I've told you the names of the people involved - Hugo Lawson-Parry QC and Sir Edgar Holland. I've still got Lawson-Parry's business card actually, I put it in my wallet."

He fumbles with his wallet, then hands DI Davis the card, as if by way of proof. Then he continues, "I admit I did an expenses scandal piece on Holland a year or so ago, and that he served me a writ. I seriously didn't expect it to escalate."

Slater notices Alex Walker writing something down.

"And I'll need protection," says Slater. "Ian Harrison was the SpAd to Andrew Brading. He was literally pushed under a truck. Brading was bombed. If I leave here without a deal to protect me, then you'll be reading about me in the papers next week. It'll be on you."

He sees DI Davis squirm in his chair. It was too rich for him. To his surprise, the Home Office 'girl' pipes up. "We can fix this. But you'll need to grow a beard. Come with me after the interview, I'll arrange something."

Slater looks at Charles.

"Too good to be true?" asks Charles.

"No, to the contrary, this is Slater's one big lucky break. It is a one-time offer. Come along or take his chances. When I am gone, I am really gone."

Charles looks at Slater, who seemed to be having a minor meltdown. "You want my advice? Go with the lady."

"You can both come along if that makes you feel any better," says Alex, "I have a car waiting outside."

The two police look at one another. This interview has gone sideways. They were uncertain of what to do.

"I have this, also," says Alex, "It's a warrant for the removal of all evidence of the interview, the DVDs, your notes, that business card."

Alex produces some paperwork.

"This is highly irregular," says DI Davis.

"Not where I come from," says Alex. She looked in her bag and produced a second identity card and a smaller card with phone number printed upon it.

DI Davis looks at the identity card: Alex Smith, Secret Intelligence Services, Police Liaison Officer.

Then he asks, "That's not even a proper phone number, beginning with 333?"

"Trust me," says Alex, "It works and will put you through to my controller. Oh, and here is my Warrant Authorisation for the Removal of Evidence."

She opened a slim envelope and flattened the paperwork onto the desk.

TOP SECRET - the paper was headed and then went on to authorise the removal of all evidence of the interview with Roger Slater.

"I'll need to check this with my superiors," says Davis.

"Check away, but please don't take too long. The car is waiting outside to transfer Mr Slater and his solicitor to somewhere safe."

Davis leaves the room, leaving Lillian seated and in charge of the interview.

"I've never had anything like this happen before. But I suppose you are going to say I can't tell anyone?"

"That's right, I'll remind you of your commitment under The Official Secrets Act (1989). And I'll even add that means you can't tell 'just one other person.' We all know where that leads. And I'm afraid the people we are dealing with don't mess around. Guns and bombs; we've already heard about it from Roger, here."

DI Davis returns, "It's pukka, Lillian. I don't know how you've managed it, but I hope you are doing something worthy to protect the country. My boss tells me I've got to sign something as well?"

"That's right, both you and Lillian need to sign this Official Secrets Act addendum. It expressly forbids you from referencing this meeting... Forever."

They both scribble signatures onto the beige-coloured

forms that Alex produces.

"Thank you," she says, "You have both been most co-operative. Now I'll leave with Mr Slater and Mr Hardy and we'll be out of your lives in a matter of moments. Put the last hour down to an extended coffee break or something."

Alex ushers the two men out of the interview room and along a corridor, which leads to a green metal side door exit from the Police Station. A black SUV is waiting. They all climb aboard.

"Let's go," says Alex.

Slater hears the driver on his radio, "Package, plus one, collected."

"I think you are my plus one," he says to Charles Hardy.

They crossed town, the driver skilfully weaving through traffic and around little-known back roads. Suddenly they were on the Embankment, heading west. Slater had, by now, assumed they would be going to the SI6 building south of Vauxhall Bridge, and he was surprised when they pulled up along Millbank by a slightly grubby looking garden railing topped with high security fencing and large overt CCTV cameras.

"Welcome to MI5," says Alex, "This is where we will process you."

"At least it's not a deserted car park with a gang of men in leather coats!" says Charles.

They all walk in through a wide entrance and to a small desk, surrounded by plate glass. The security appears to start more overtly behind them, through what looked like a kind of airlock chamber.

"You must get some temporary badges to go any further," explains Alex, "But note that they will time out in 12 hours."

They were each processed, noticing that Alex didn't receive the same treatment. They walk through the airlock system and were inside. The air seems fresher inside the system and Roger Slater realises it must be treated and cleaned.

"We are going to meet a couple of the bosses," says Alex, "Behave and look respectable if you want to get what you need."

She takes them to a meeting room on the first floor. Out of the windows they can see the River Thames. There are two people in the room.

"Hello Alex," says the woman, "Any problems?"

"No, it went like a dream, Amanda,"

The man speaks, "Let me introduce ourselves, Amanda Miller and James Cavendish. We both work for the security services. We were most interested in what Roger Slater knew from his interactions, and as importantly, who sent him to discredit Andrew Brading."

"I've told the police all that I know. Barrister Hugo Lawson-Parry and Sir Edgar Holland commissioned me to write the piece and even supplied the photos and evidence. I should have thought more carefully about diligence. Look, I asked the police about doing a deal. I think I am in danger now - I've been threatened a couple of times and am also under a super-injunction."

Amanda keeps quiet that she had brought the super injunction to flush Slater out.

"Well, in the capable hands of Alex, we can find you another identity. It will literally be today and you will have 48 hours to move your assets around. You won't be able to tell anyone where you have moved or of your new identity. As a safety feature, we will, if you wish, advise one other person - your solicitor - of your new identity. But you must be very sure that you trust Charles and his ability to keep secrets.

Roger looks at Charles, "Oh yes, I trust Charles implicitly"

Amanda states, "In which case, we will have considerable processing of you to do. We have arranged for you to be kept in a secure apartment in Dolphin Square until the end of the week. You won't be able to leave, but we have the fastest and securest internet access so that you can set your affairs in order. And you'll be moving to another part of the country. We will sell your property in London through a third party and pass the funds to you."

Amanda adds, "I wouldn't come back to London for at least three months and alter your appearance somewhat by that time. After a month we will withdraw all protection and you will be on your own. You can move around freely, but it would be plain stupid to revisit old haunts. And every person you tell of your identity change, beyond Charles here, will further increase your chances of discovery. After three other people know, those looking will certainly find you."

Charles looks at Roger, "Are you sure you want to do this, old chap?"

Roger looks back, "It's this or being blown up or gunned down."

Chocolate Paradise Peachtree

Amanda had called the meeting of the Triangle. Clare was seated with Christina, Jake, and Bigsy in the Triangle offices. Grace was on a link from GCHQ. Bigsy was staring at a big blue box of chocolate covered biscuits.

"Well, so far we are running to plan," says Amanda, "Slater folded easily enough and we are relocating him now. He gave us a couple of unfamiliar names, one of which was a Queen's Council with a tainted reputation: Hugo Lawson-Parry and Sir Edgar Holland.

Grace replies, "I looked through the usual places, but Lawson-Parry has a huge question mark by his name for helping a client who later turned up in a Serious Fraud Office report. Slater says the meeting was in the Chambers of Lawson Parry, but I've tracked it down to a rentable meeting room in Chambers."

Bigsy cracks open the box of thick chocolate-covered biscuits.

Amanda asks, "So what is the story with Lawson-Parry?"

Grace explains, "The SFO secured convictions against

three former oil executives who conspired to give corrupt payments to secure contracts in Iraq. The contracts were scripted by Lawson-Parry."

"In the years of reconstruction following the overthrow of Saddam Hussein, three men conspired with others to pay bribes to public officials at the Iraqi South Oil Company and, and to the Iraqi Ministry of Oil, to secure oil contracts for the oil company and its clients.

"Making profits from the reconstruction work. That's like what we heard Brant was doing when we looked into them?" asks Jake, finding a round biscuit covered in orange tin-foil.

Grace continues, "The post-occupation Iraqi government commissioned the oil company to run projects as part of a 'Master Plan' to rebuild Iraq's oil industry and thereby expand the country's oil export capacity. It seems that middlemen were expected and paid off, in a number of cases the transactions were certified by Hugo Lawson-Parry."

Bigsy smiles, "Lawson-Parry claims he has clean hands?" Bigsy had stacked several of the biscuits in front of him in case the box went out of range.

Grace adds, "Yes, 'a clean skin'. Lawson-Parry said his role was purely to ensure that the contracts for installation of offshore mooring buoys and new oil pipelines were drafted comprehensively. He claimed no knowledge that the oil company benefitted from these state-run projects, nor that the defendants conspired to bribe public officials at the oil company and Ministry of Oil to secure contracts with the oil company and its offshore counterpart."

Clare interrupts, "Well, he would say that, I suppose, although I'm sure it must have damaged his reputation?"

Grace replies, "Less reputational damage than you might think. Now Lawson-Parry is on the radar of crooks and money launderers, because he can possibly draft them a good deal."

Grace adds, "The SFO case became almost like free marketing for him. The bribes totalled over $6 million to secure contracts worth $800 million for the supply of oil pipelines and offshore mooring buoys. Two of the co-conspirators were found guilty of paying over $500,000 in bribes to secure the $55 million contract for the offshore mooring buoys. The curious thing is, I found Lawson-Parry, by referencing 'solicitors', but couldn't find him listed as a barrister or QC."

Amanda adds, "What despite Lawson-Parry effectively setting the peg rate for bribery?"

Grace adds, "Yes, afterwards, the SFO Director said: 'These men dishonestly and corruptly took advantage of a government reeling from dictatorship and occupation and trying to reconstruct a war-torn state. They abused the system to cut out competitors and line their own pockets. It is our mission to pursue and bring to justice those who use criminal means to weaken the integrity of business.' - Think about it. If you were like these men, wouldn't you like a lawyer like Hugo Lawson-Parry?"

Grace explains, "And Sir Edgar Holland isn't exactly untarnished either. The most interesting references were in the Paradise Papers. That's a huge set of documents that show how the world's biggest businesses, heads of state and global figures in politics, entertainment and sport have sheltered their wealth in secretive tax havens.

It's a case of Sir Edgar Holland sheltering his funds in Britain's offshore empires."

"I can remember the Paradise Papers, but not so much of the detail," says Bigsy, noticeably well through his chocolate biscuit pile.

Grace continues, "It was a leak of 13.4 million files that exposed the global environments in which tax abuses can thrive – and the complex and seemingly artificial ways the wealthiest corporations can legally protect their wealth. Nowadays, even terabytes of data can become exposed. The Paradise Papers were around 1.4 Terabytes, which is only a single hard drive."

"The material, came from two offshore service providers and the company registries of 19 tax havens, and was famously obtained by the German newspaper Süddeutsche Zeitung and shared by the International Consortium of Investigative Journalists with partners including the Guardian, the BBC and the New York Times.

Grace pauses to catch her thoughts and then continues,

"These so-called Paradise Papers revealed:

- Extensive offshore dealings by Donald Trump's cabinet members, advisers, and donors, including substantial payments from a firm co-owned by Vladimir Putin's son-in-law to the shipping group of the US commerce secretary, Wilbur Ross.

- How Twitter and Facebook received hundreds of millions of dollars in investments that can be traced back to Russian state financial institutions.

- Extensive use of Cayman Island trust funds as money protection vehicles.

- Aggressive tax avoidance by multinational corporations, including Nike and Apple.

- How some of the biggest names in the film and TV industries protect their wealth with an array of offshore schemes.

- The billions in tax refunds by the Isle of Man and Malta to the owners of private jets and luxury yachts.

- The secret loan and alliance used by the London-listed multinational Glencore in its efforts to secure lucrative mining rights in the Democratic Republic of the Congo.

- The complex offshore webs used by two billionaires to buy stakes in Arsenal and Everton football clubs.

"Well, that is pretty comprehensive stuff, but what about Sir Edgar Holland?" asks Jake.

Grace answers, "Yes, there's details of a previously unknown $450 million offshore trust that has sheltered the wealth of Sir Edgar Holland. And of course, Sir Edgar Holland has been a leading donor to the Tory Party."

Grace adds, "Here, we can see the information."

Grace shares her screen with everyone.

She reads it:

'Sir Edgar Holland, 68, one of the Conservative party's biggest donors, faces fresh questions over his offshore affairs after the Paradise Papers revealed a previously unknown trust sheltering his vast overseas wealth.

'Scores of emails and financial statements chart the inner workings of the Bermuda-based Sullivan Trust from its creation just after he became knighted.

'The documents show the offshore law firm Peachtree, acted as trustee but terminated the relationship, a decision questioned at the time by Holland's representatives.

"I remember Peachtree," says Jake, "The source of much press gossip when it was first discovered, although it seems all but buried nowadays,"

"Exactly; the power of the press to manipulate events," says Bigsy, "I guess there were too many cronies likely to become exposed?"

Grace continues reading. 'The value of the Sullivan Trust fluctuated, but a leaked financial statement recorded it as having assets of $450.4m (£341m) in 2006.

Grace adds, 'Intriguingly, several emails show concern being expressed by Peachtree about the way the Sullivan Trust was being run. The concern was that Peachtree, as trustee, was in effect being asked to rubber-stamp decisions it believed it should have been informed about in advance.

'A senior lawyer for Peachtree wrote in an email: 'There

have been very large sums of money involved and I am very concerned that there has been inadequate supervision of both transactions and distributions ... To put it bluntly, we seem to be told nothing, whereas we carry the responsibility of acting as trustee.'

Grace continues, 'Then we see that Sir Edgar Holland is a former party treasurer and deputy chairman who has given millions to the Conservatives, including £800,000 towards the party's most recent campaign. He is influential in British politics through his polling company and the website GoTory, a centre-right blog aimed at grassroots party activists.

'Holland's spokesman, Quentin du Barry, said the peer had never engaged in tax evasion, abusive tax avoidance or tax avoidance using artificial structures, and "any suggestion or implication that he has will be vigorously challenged".

Grace smiles, 'Balance that with Holland being turned down for a knighthood twice because he was a tax exile in Belize. He gained his title after saying he would take up permanent residence in the UK again.

She adds, 'Then there was a political storm when he confirmed he was still a "non-dom" and did not pay tax in the UK on his earnings abroad. Holland then promised that he would abandon his non-domiciled status to comply with a change of law.

'The Sullivan Trust was set up whilst he was a "non-dom", with his three children named as beneficiaries. Ashcroft was named as the settlor and a beneficiary, the only one entitled to income for life.

Grace continues, 'That's when the trust became the focal

point for a series of multimillion-pound capital distributions, loans and share transactions. A typical example of trust activity is a document saying the trustees agreed to forgive a loan of $29.5m to Ashcroft.

'Oh, and to cap it all, the original trustee was the Brant (Offshore) Trust Services Company, which was taken over by Peachtree Services (Bermuda) Ltd.

"Oh my god," says Bigsy, "My head will explode! Did you say Brant, Grace? There's a direct link from Peachtree to Brant?"

"Only 'kind of'," answers Grace, "This is a takeover of Brant by Peachtree, not the other way around."

"I'm not so sure," says Christina, "Ever heard of a reverse takeover? Raven are good at that. When they took over Brant, instead of calling it Raven, they kept the Brant name. I wonder if they have done something similar with Peachtree. A friendly name hiding Brant underneath, as well as a vehicle for all manner of backhanders?"

Amanda comments, "Yes, I suspect you are right, Christina. It would be useful for Raven/Brant to have something like Peachtree for quartermastering."

Christina bit her tongue to decide not to correct Amanda. In the Russian Army the quartermasters were conventionally considered to be responsible for intelligence operations.

The Burma Road

Serena was back in the Houses of Parliament. She was on a third-floor corridor, known as the Burma Road. To reach it, she had to walk up a rather bleak, stale-smelling, winding staircase. The press organisations are based along this corridor. Politicians seldom visited the Burma Road in person. But their spin doctors, policy advisers and press officers are an almost daily distraction, attempting to portray events to their leaders' advantage. Serena knew she would be in competition with others as she started to spread her news story around.

It's a dance that is generally played out with good humour and politeness; many party press officers are former hacks themselves, hired because they understand the system and know the characters involved.

Unlike outside Westminster, everyone really is in it together. There's no point falling out with people you've got to work alongside every day, unless it's really worth it. Serena was typical of Conservative spinners who were, without fail, polite; it's as if finishing school was part of their training.

If the news is not good, the spinners' task is to try to

minimise the damage by telling anyone who will listen that down is up and not everything is quite as bad as it seems. In 2001, Jo Moore, a spin doctor in the Department of Transport, was forced to resign after sending out an email on 9/11 that said: "It's now a very good day to get out anything we want to bury." Her mistake was to put it in writing.

Trying to bury bad news is still standard practice. If a government has good news, it will usually try to make sure that dominates the headlines for the day, so other good news may be held back. Having two pieces of good news on the same day is a waste of good news. Bad news, however, is best dealt with wholesale. If the government releases several reports on the same day, it is odds-on that there is something it doesn't like in at least two of them.

Serena knew she had something confusing to put out and so carried it around as printed sheets of almost copy-ready material. She also had a fall-back position. She would give a supercharged version of the story to Rachel Crosby, with enough exclusive material in it to make sure that Rachel won the battle of the headlines.

Mistaken Identity

Michael Tovey exposed as Brading imposter
By Rachel Crosby

Tovey's love tryst with supermodel Natasha Makarovna is exposed during scenes at London Fashion week. Tovey is seen all over London with model Tasha including photographs of the couple returning to their bolthole at The Dorchester. Speculation abounds that earlier photographs of Tovey were doctored to implicate Andrew Brading in Tovey's lustful grab for power.

Michael Tovey recently took over Andrew Brading's role as Secretary of State for Internal Affairs, after a silent and bloodless coup during which Brading was implicated in an almost identical love triangle.

Katherine Brading, Michael Brading's journalist wife, commented, "I have never been in any doubt as to Andrew's loyalty and fidelity."

Margaret Tovey, wife of Michael Tovey was unavailable for comment.

Critics of Brading's replacement noted that Tovey was appointed in secrecy, by the Prime Minister, without a normal Cabinet selection process.

Background sources close to the Prime Minister revealed that a significant Conservative party donor directly influenced Tovey's selection.

Further shock revelations show that Tovey had a Cayman Island fund later credited to frame Michael Brading. Named the Tovey Fund, it was renamed to the Brading Fund, via a series of meetings at Peachtree Services, George Town and represented by Hugo Lawson-Parr, QC.

When asked about this, Andrew Brading commented, "I'm very surprised if my colleague Michael Tovey would go to such lengths to take over my role. If these allegations are true, then he must be suffering from a mental illness and we should offer him our sympathies. I am only pleased that the truth has finally come out and that the situation no longer places any strain upon my marriage."

Michael Tovey has a keen interest in the promotion of the Protection of Healthcare Rights Bill, a Bill for which Brading wanted substantial reforms to before publication. Sources close to Brading indicate that there may be commercial interests associated with the Bill in its current form.

Shake it off

'Cause the players gonna play
And the haters gonna hate
Baby, I'm just gonna shake
I shake it off, I shake it off

Heartbreakers gonna break
And the fakers gonna fake
Baby, I'm just gonna shake
I shake it off, I shake it off

Shake it off, I shake it off
I, I, I shake it off, I shake it off
I, I, I shake it off, I shake it off
I, I, I shake it off, I shake it off (Whoo-hoo-hoo)

Hey, hey, hey Just think while you've been
gettin' down and out about the liars
And the dirty, dirty cheats of the world
You could've been gettin' down
To this sick beat

Taylor Swift

The Globe Tavern

Michael Tovey surveys the messy traffic-clogged street at the borders of London Bridge station and London Bridge itself. A stumble from the Barrow Boy and Banker onto the stairs down to the Borough Market. Street food and French country cheeses. Across the way he spies the pub. The Globe Tavern. Used by and lived above by Bridget Jones, at least in the movie.

He enters the surprisingly quiet pub and Tasha is waiting, hair pulled back and in a dark trench coat. She is with a man and another woman, in a leather coat with military-styled epaulettes. He senses this will be a war council.

Tovey has already spent the morning in the Westminster trenches and is ready for some hand-to-hand combat if that is what it takes. With a short smile, Natasha disarms him.

"Who has been a naughty boy, then," she says, and looks first towards him and then to her companions.

"This is Hugo Lawson-Parry QC and Shanell Kinkead,"

Tovey looks at the stunning black woman, who smiles back at him.

"Weren't you also a friend of Andrew Brading?" he asks.

"No, I've never met him," answers Shanell, "But I'm pleased to meet you."

"Look, dear chap," says Lawson-Parry, "You seem to be in a bit of a pickle now. In fact, I've been asked to give you some advice. You need to drop the current plan and even relinquish your position in the House. It's time to fall on your sword dear chap, and that way, with modern politics, you can be up and running again in - oh - I daresay two years. Tops. Probably back in Cabinet."

"But what if I'm happy to tough it out?" asks Tovey.

"I think there's another sword involved as well. A very Russian one and I think you know who carries it." Lawson-Parry was referring to Anatoly Yaroslav, and Tovey knew it.

"But it is not all bad news, the fund in the Cayman has been redesignated to you. I know it has because I personally supervised it. Call it carrot or stick. Take the money - or run. And even better, Brant has just finished its takeover of Elixanor and both shares have benefitted-You should be substantially better off. Now if you don't mind, Tasha and I will leave now, but I think Shanell has something else for you. Oh, and I nearly forgot."

He hands Tovey a small carrier bag containing a bottle. On the bag is written, 'Cayman Islands Airport Authority.' Inside is a bottle of Seven Fathoms Premium Rum from the Cayman Spirits Co. Tovey places the bag on the small round table.

Tasha and Lawson-Parry stand to leave.

Tasha whispers "Goodbye, and be careful, *Lyubimaya*!" And quietly kisses him on the right cheek. Tovey realises he will never see her again.

Then Lawson-Parry shakes his hand, "Think carefully, dear chap, it's not worth getting hurt over this."

They both leave, leaving Shanell, who then leans forward so far that he could feel her hair brushing his cheek.

She whispers, "They have all decided to go along without you. You'd best play their game." She delicately kisses him on the same cheek as Tasha, then stands and leaves the bar.

Tovey fiddles with the bag containing the liquor which he absentmindedly stands it on the bar table. He'd just received a double, or even triple warning.

"Excuse me, Sir, but you can't drink that in here," comes a strident and somewhat amused tone from the barman.

Tovey decides to leave and was soon outside in the brightness of daylight. He feels his twice caressed cheek but decides he's really had several rounds in a boxing ring.

Surprise pizza

That evening, Clare was back at the Bermondsey flat. Tessa and Lottie had been asking her for more information about Brading and Tovey.

"It's such a complicated story. Why would Tovey want to take over Brading's life - and his lovers, come to that!" says Lottie.

"It's been one intrigue after anther since you joined the flat," says Tessa, "We've never had such excitement nor mystery!"

"Pure coincidence," says Clare, "I didn't even know Andrew Brading a couple of months ago! And I've never met Michael Tovey."

There was a buzz at their front door. Lottie presses the entry phone.

"It's a pizza for you, Clare? From Domino's?"

"I didn't order one," says Clare, confused.

"More mystery?" says Lottie, "Here, I'll go get it, so long

as I can have a slice!"

Lottie disappears downstairs and comes back with the pizza.

"Mmm, it looks delish, Veggie Supreme, with slaw and wedges! Are you sure you didn't order it?"

Clare shakes her head.

"Look the guy gave me this envelope - maybe it'll show who made the order then? Could it be a strange love token from Jake?"

They open the envelope. It contains three photographs. A pub somewhere. Michael Tovey, being kissed by Tasha the model. Then one of him being kissed by a very attractive black woman. And a third one of them sitting around the table with a small carrier bag on it. The words Cayman Islands Airport were clearly visible on the carrier.

"Wow, wow, wow!" says Tessa.

"You never disappoint," adds Lottie.

Clare looked a little surprised, "Erm, I don't know where these are from, nor how they got my address."

"Do you think they have been sent anywhere else? Like to the press or anything?" asked Lottie, "I mean, these pictures are dynamite and just about corroborate that story from Rachel Crosby."

"Do you think she has got the pictures too?" asks Lottie, "I mean they could do a lot of damage."

"I need to call someone," says Clare, "This is most unexpected."

She walks across to her room and dials Jake.

"Jake, guess what I've just received? - Only a set of incriminating pictures of Michael Tovey with Tasha and another woman. Just like the Brading set-up, only I get the feeling these will be real rather than photoshopped."

Jake pauses, "We should call Amanda and let her know - My guess is that Tovey is being ditched by his previous accomplices and they want to make sure it is comprehensive. I'll call Amanda and the others and tell them of the development. Can you photograph the pictures, please, and send them to me in an email?"

Clare did as she was requested.

"Expect to hear from me later," says Jake. Clare walks back to the living room, where Tessa and Lottie were already two thirds of the way through the pizza.

"Mmm - Great pizza - Any news?" asks Tessa, "You should have more mystery callers bearing illicit photographs!"

Two separate women

Amanda answers Jake's call. She listens whilst Jake explains.

Then she says, "They are dumping Tovey. This is just to make sure. I'm guessing the pictures have gone to Tovey and a member of Brading's office - They probably picked Clare as the most lowly - even if she technically outranks Maggie, they know that Maggie and Brading are good friends.

"I imagine that if Tovey doesn't take these strong hints, then they will go after him. Another tragic road accident, probably. Other than the two women, who seem to be 'paid extras' there doesn't seem to be any trail leading back to anyone.

"But there is a man's suit on the edge of the 'carrier bag' shot," says Jake, "I think there were four people at that rendezvous, not three."

"Well spotted," says Amanda, "Shall we pull in Natasha Makarovna?" We could ask about the meeting. She can hardly deny it."

"Do you think they have sent it directly to the papers?" asks Jake.

"I doubt it. They are showing the players what they know. And they have considerable leverage over Tovey before it gets published. He's a lost man after it goes to press. They must know that."

"Very good!" says Jake, "I compliment you on your knowledge of how these things work!"

"I've been involved in enough of these situations," says Amanda, "The only unusual thing about this is that the two women appear separately most of the time. I suggest we have a video meeting tomorrow evening. We should wait to see how things play out."

Kensington Gardens

Michael Tovey was not used to being given such an extensive security detail. Now, as he walked home across the Kensington Gardens, he had two concealed armed men in front of him and a similarly armed man and a woman walking behind. He was the dot in the middle of a five on a dice.

Tovey had started to use the walking route during the pandemic. It meant he could spend less time on public transport and the route gave him space, air and exercise. He could also people watch with impunity and yet he would quickly be back in his pied-a-terre in Bayswater, all at the taxpayers' expense.

Tovey didn't expect any trouble. He'd been given a gentle warning - well three gentle warnings when he was in The Globe Tavern and had no plans to open his mouth about any of the business.

He would do what was suggested by Lawson-Parry. Fall on his sword and yield control back to Andrew Brading, who he assumed would be ready to take over again.

He paused as if to consider his route. Today, he'd go directly from West Carriage Drive in a diagonal fashion to the little gate that came out by the traffic lights on the Bayswater Road.

As this blew over, he could quietly retreat to the back benches, having also moved the small number of millions of dollars from the Cayman Islands to somewhere else secure.

He'd been reading the Offshore Financial Center report, which described jurisdictions providing corporate and financial services to non-resident companies on a scale that is incommensurate with the size of their economies.

Traditionally, OFCs were assumed to be small, low-tax jurisdictions in remote location - like The Caymans. More recently, The Netherlands and the United Kingdom were edging up the rankings. The current government was good for this financial re-engineering, even if it did only affect a small portion of the population.

He looks across the park. A red-setter is running at break-neck speed, and he assumes it was off the leash. He hears a whistle, and it turns and bounds back to its master. Then a metallic click. Behind him. He turns towards it just as a man falls from his bicycle to the ground. The four security detail are running to the man. Tovey can see a weapon laying on the ground. One of the security detail kicks it into the grass by the side of the path.

The woman speaks to him urgently, almost a shout,

"Come with me now!"

He sees a black SUV driving from the road inside the park and bumping across the grass toward him. The woman bundles him in and then climbs into the front passenger seat herself. Her colleague clambers into the other passenger door and pushes his head down.

"Let's get him away from here," she barks to the driver. Tovey suddenly realises he had taken on more aspects of Brading's life than he expected.

Not a bomb this time, but a cold-blooded shooting attempt in the middle of a public park. Heck, it was a Royal Park. The gunman was on Royal property.

The BMW SUV was revving hard. It skitters back from the grass onto the road and starts a siren. Tovey was aware that a blue light was flashing from somewhere as it picked out the cars around him. He marvelled at the ease with which the driver slid through the London traffic and how quickly he was back along the Embankment. He had a feeling that he would be going to see the security services.

The black vehicle approaches some formidable looking security gates. There are two large, yellow-and-black chevron-painted metallic barriers in the road looking like two giant bulldozers, yet the driver hardly slows as he approaches them. Sure enough, they fall away, and they enter an internal road, then turns sharply left down a ramp and into an underground car park. Only then does the vehicle slow and appear to be following a light system like planes use at Heathrow airport. He taxies to a bay and everyone gets out of the SUV.

Immediately, several soldiers surround him, and they all are escorted into an underground bunker-like structure, where it was clear they were to be processed like so many drunks on a Friday night.

The woman walks over to Tovey. "Hi, I'm Alex Smith, I'll

be your case officer while you are here. The man on the bicycle in the park was attempting a hit. Lucky for you, his gun jammed. A failure to feed. He must have been practicing the hit and not noticed when the magazine became dislodged. A rookie error actually. You were very lucky."

"I want to thank you all," says Tovey still somewhat disorientated, "And where exactly am I?"

"You are under SIS, in one of our hidden levels. Before you can go any further, we will have to process you. Then we can take you to my boss, Amanda Miller."

The meeting

Amanda had set the call for the evening. She has a lot to tell.

She notes the full turn-out from the Triangle and asked Grace to link into the session. Amanda is seated next to Alex Smith, who has been particularly busy, first with Roger Slater and then with the aftermath of the attempted hit on Michael Tovey.

"Hi everyone, we have had a busy couple of days - mainly thanks to Alex Smith here, our plan is still on track."

She looks towards Alex, who waves at the screens.

"Bigsy muttered, "Alex Smith? That's gotta be a made-up name?"

Amanda says, "Bigsy, you of all people would know how sensitive these microphones are!"

"Oops, sorry," says Bigsy, "Sorry too, Alex Smith!"

"Well, thanks to your discovery, Bigsy, we have been able

to trace the monitoring of the Whitehall communications. As we suspected, it goes right the way back to the listening station. Thanks to Grace, we've also been able to add in a little trick of our own, which means we have been able to pick up some of the chatter from Medusa."

Grace chips in, "Yes, and fascinating it has been. We suspected that Miller McDonald and Trudi Hartmann were running things, and it transpires that they have been, but also using Antanov Yaroslav as an enforcer. Yaroslav is linked to the Roslavl Bratva, which is run by Tima Maximovich.

"We brought Tovey in after the attempted hit, He folded up like a Chinese lantern. The hitman did most of our work for us. We even had to buy Tovey some new trousers. Although I expect the pair he was wearing were at the taxpayers' expense."

"What did Tovey tell you?" asks Jake.

Alex answers, "Well, he was quite shaken and emotional actually. He didn't want to die, nor for his family to be implicated. When we'd calmed him down, we asked him who he'd been with and he told us that he had been manoeuvred into the new Cabinet position by Miller McDonald and Trudi Hartmann. He said that Anatoly Yaroslav was their enforcer, and McDonald and Hartmann had used Yaroslav to encourage him to take on the new role."

"That's pretty much what we'd all suspected," says Jake, "But it's good to get it corroborated."

Alex continues, "Well, Tovey told us how he had been threatened. He'd been set up by Natasha Makarovna and been in pub with her and the other woman in the photographs - Shanell Kinkead, although he said there was also another man present - A Queens Council named Hugo Lawson-Parry."

"Ah, the suit in the photo," says James, "That makes sense!"

"Not actually," says Grace, "Lawson-Parry turned up earlier in this investigation, but when I looked for him the records, I couldn't find anyone with that name. Tovey said that Lawson-Parry was definitely a Brit, but I'm less convinced."

"Whoever he is, he mixes with some hardball company," says Jake, "I mean Yaroslav - wasn't he Maximovich's enforcer when we were investigating Raven Corp?"

Christina nods and then chips in, "Maximovich used Yaroslav to terminate Yegorin and Turgenev when they were due to fly back to Russia. But I seem to remember that you, Amanda, were trying to install Maximovich as a mole?"

Amanda nods, "The law of unintended consequences again, I'm afraid. We let him run and then, after his symbolic violence in the UK, he simply melted back in with his compatriots. But now, we need to deal with Yaroslav."

"I thought Yaroslav had already left the country?" asks Jake.

"We did too, initially, but then picked up some chatter from Minerva. Miller McDonald asked him to stay longer, as an insurance policy linked to Michael Tovey."

"Well, based upon the Medusa messages we intercepted,

it looks as if Yaroslav is finally going back to Moscow. He used a 'stunt double' to exit the country the first time, so that we would think he had already gone. This time he is using 'Terminal Six'.

"Terminal Six?" asks Jake, "That used to be a nickname for Northolt? It was where all of the well-heeled and well-connected used to fly from during the pandemic. Fewer questions asked."

"Correct," says Amanda, "It still functions as a quiet way for civilians and military and Royals to enter and exit the country from close to London."

"How the other half live!" says Bigsy.

"It got rather busy during times of lockdown," says Amanda, "although there's still a cap of 12,000 civilian flights a year on it."

"I remember, it's officially a military airport," says Jake, "Plenty of the people I interviewed for my old magazine 'Street' used it. It even had concierge parking arrangements, and who wouldn't mind having their Lamborghini guarded by military? I seem to remember the runways were resurfaced a while ago and it caused an uproar because the well-heeled couldn't use it and had to make do with Heathrow. But the new runway can take massive planes like Hercules and Dreamliners. Then to have a Bentley waiting to whisk you away. What's not to like?"

"Yes, Boris Johnson's Uxbridge constituency running an airport using the same services firm as City Airport, with maybe only a fifth of City's number of flights, but all of them VIP. It would make for some fascinating reading."

"It's been done," says Bigsy, "But if you add 50% to cover the military manoeuvres, you still only get to 18,000 - or maybe 20,000 flights per year. That's only a quarter of, say, Bristol or Newcastle."

"But highly lucrative, I daresay," says Jake, "All the politicians, posh people and oligarchs."

Amanda interrupts, to keep the meeting on track, "Well, Yaroslav is to exit there tomorrow. He's due to be on a Ukranian private jet to Moscow."

"Will you require anything special?" A new voice cuts in. Jake recognises it as Jim Cavendish, Amanda's boss at SIS.

Amanda speaks, "Hi Jim, yes, I think we should prepare a special reception for Yaroslav."

Amanda looks as if she is considering what to say next, "Yaroslav ran the hit on both the Special Advisor Ian Harrison and on Michael Tovey. Yaroslav was just lazy and used the same cyclist as a hitman twice. We pulled him after the attempt on Tovey. The hitman was wounded but we kept it secret that he had survived. His name is Stefan Kostyantynovych Tarasenko, a Ukranian in London on a Canadian passport. He speaks with a very passable Canadian accent and claimed to be Steve Wheeler, which proved to be about as convincing an alias as that of those two Salisbury Cathedral enthusiasts."

"What, the two who went after Skripal?" asks Bigsy, "Hilarious when they started reciting Wikipedia."

"Not so hilarious for the brutal poison they spread around Salisbury," says Grace.

"No; point taken," says Bigsy, "but 'Wheeler,' a cyclist assassin?"

"That's where we had to get a little more creative with the interview technique," says Alex, "They patched up Steve Wheeler aka Stefan Tarasenko and we did a little digging. It turns out he was, despite his bungling, something of a big deal. He was what's known as *novyy afganskiy*, brutalised by the aftermath of the original Russian/Afghan war.

Alex continues, "He wasn't even involved in the original conflict, but only in the last few years, when Russia has been running strategies to recover its position."

She adds "Tarasenko was one of the coverts sent in by Russia which was betting that the situation in Afghanistan would be stabilised leading both to the withdrawal of Western forces from Afghanistan, and more importantly, from Central Asia.

"This would have opened up the possibility of Russia's economic expansion and the overall growth of its influence in Afghanistan. At that time Tarasenko was a serious player."

Christina chips in, "I knew a couple of people - *afgantsy* - both edgy and they both died young in normal jobs in Russia."

Alex continues, "With the deteriorating security situation and the expansion of the Western presence in Afghanistan and Central Asia, Russia became more interested in maintaining the Western presence inside Afghanistan itself.

Alex continues, "They still needed a pot-stirrer. That's where Tarasenko came in. He was sent into increasingly wild and dangerous situations to engage the US and NATO's forces, resources, and political attention in that country, thus weakening them by default.

"Asymmetric," says Christina, "Use a few to distract many."

Alex adds, "It gave Russia an additional tool, by means of transit services and transportation, to obtain political and economic benefits from them. Tarasenko was like a match being used for his bright flame, but also cynically being burnt down."

"It reminds me of the ten classifications for FSB agents; he'd be near to the bottom, " says Christina, "Always expendable, if only he knew it - How the mighty fall."

Alex nods, "Correct. Russia increasingly sought to exploit the problem of Afghanistan, in order to increase its presence in Central Asia and strengthen its cooperation with the countries in the region. Tarasenko was still a player in that increasingly concealed conflict, but he'd have been living on the edge of his nerves. It probably gave him the PTSD we can see in him since he has been captured by us.

Alex continued, "Tarasenko came back raw, shocked and angry, either bursting with tales of horror and blunder, or spikily or numbly withdrawn. He did what people usually do in such circumstances: Adapted, coped. His nightmares were less frequent, the memories less vivid.

"I see," says Jake, "Then Yaroslav meets him. Wiry, intense and morose, Tarasenko has that brittle and dangerous quality that Yaroslav needs. Give him money, at a time when most were eking out the most marginal of lives, even living with parents and juggling multiple jobs.

"Yes, make him a torpedo!" says Christina, "'torpedo' – a hitman," she explains, "Excuse my Moscow slang."

Amanda nods, "Yes, we see a once mighty player reduced to a war victim and then falling into the pay of the mobsters. Not even as a bodyguard, but as a straightforward killer. Car bombs, drive-by shooting and knives in the night."

Alex adds, Yes, but with the rise of the kleptocracy, even the gangsterism had reached its end. No wonder a somewhat sketchy hitman arrives in London on an e-Bike."

Clare speaks, "He was still lethal though. Have you matched him to the traffic cam footage from outside Parliament yet? To see what happened to Harrison?"

Amanda speaks, "We have. It positively identifies Tarasenko. Too arrogant to even wear a face mask and sloppily using the same e-bike and bike helmet for both hits."

Jim speaks again, "It is instructive to think of the Russians when we see what is happening in London now. Commentators have dubbed Russia a "mafia state". It is certainly a catchy epithet, but what does it actually mean? "

Jim continues, "It means, I think, that the Kremlin rather than being under the control of the criminals, is a shadowy puppeteer making the gangs dance on its strings. But the truth is more complex."

Jim adds, "The Kremlin does not control organised crime in Russia, nor is it controlled by it. Rather, organised crime prospers under Putin, marching in time with his drum. Putin has publicly acknowledged, time and time again, that corruption is widespread. However, after many years of his rule, we have seen little evidence that he has ever intended more than a public show of resolve and a periodic purge of officials fallen from favour who serve as disposable scapegoats."

Amanda speaks, "So we can see the early signs of this behaviour now in the UK?"

Jim again, "We can, but it is uncertain from where it originates. It could be simply the well-heeled elite of Britain, out for quick money, or it could be a leveraged attempt from, say, Russia or China, to infiltrate and divert Big Business."

"Now let's think how we can stop all of this," says Amanda, "We need to stop Raven and its chain of subsidiaries for once and for all."

"Okay," says Clare, "We can ask Andrew to help, Andrew Brading. He's made himself unpopular in Parliament but is probably about to be re-awarded with the post of Secretary of State for Internal Affairs. After all, he was cheated out of it by Tovey and now there is proof."

"Yes," said Jake, "And we know their plan was to introduce a Bill which would open the way towards tiered medical support. The richer you are, the better medicine you receive. Tier 0 for the politicians, Tier 1 and 2 for the well-heeled and elite. Tier 3 and 4 for the rest of us."

"Andrew can simply expose that, in another one of his

inflammatory speeches. We can have Rachel Crosby pre-briefed too!"

"But what about the actual company - Elixanor?" asks Amanda.

"We can use Arne Holstad to help with that. He can speak against them."

"And the capture of McDonald and Hartmann?"

"I've a feeling that when this plan unravels, someone else like Yaroslav will be sent to tidy things up. We should simply be there first and get McDonald and Hartmann to tell us what they know."

Jim's voice cut in, "It sounds, Amanda, as if you have the start of a plan. Call me if you need anything, but otherwise I'll assume Amanda is running things, goodbye, all."

There was a click on the broadcast and he was gone.

PART FOUR

How to execute a plan

A goal
without a plan
is just
a wish

The Little Prince - Antoine de Saint-Exupéry, 1943

PLAN 01 – Remove obstacles

Dusted

Yaroslav was dusted. He'd taken some of that Guyanian cocaine from a meeting in Docklands yesterday. Dealing with the Cali cartel was just about at the edge of his comfort zone. The Cali were highly leveraged through their calculated attempts to legitimise their business. It meant if he was dealing with them, they could look all friendly and business-like, with respectable people in business attire, yet have rented the whole floor of the conference suite and have other men with guns sitting ready to deploy.

He'd been supporting the negotiation of a new route using the "gancho ciego," or "rip-on rip-off," method in which full-size containers are tampered with at sea or as they await export. The route was from Guyana to Rotterdam, but the cargo was supposed to be coconut oil. The people he was supporting were keen to see it extended to Guyanese timber export or something bulkier to increase the size of the shipments.

So now he'd lost his mind on some of that white powder. He was on his way to the airport and knew he could sleep it off on the flight back to Russia.

They enter the gates of the airport, which looks like a

military compound. Northolt, it says on the sign. He's not been here before although he has heard that Maximovich and several others from the top had all been through the so-called Terminal Six. The car stops and the driver speaks with a smiling woman in the control booth.

"Yes, you can drive the car up to the doors of the plane, but you know we have to put our own driver in? Airport safety protocol. Or you can transfer to one of our cars, or simply wait in the VIP lounge? - It's your choice?" she smiles at the driver.

The driver turns and in Russian asks Yaroslav which he would prefer.

"Let them drive us in the Bentley, " Yaroslav answers. It means they don't need to transfer the luggage and he could soon be asleep in the comfort of the executive jet.

Another liveried man jumps into the driver seat of their Bentley. "Hmm," he says, "Mulsanne extended wheelbase. Very nice. I had a go in a Flying Spur the other day, but this is much nicer. I've to watch out for all the plane lights as well as the normal traffic signals. See that amber light? it means that the AN-32 wants to taxi. We have to wait on this line so that it doesn't hit us with its wings."

Yaroslav looks over. He notices the plane's registration is EW, which he recalls was the old Soviet Union.

"Belarus plane in today, they come from all over, " said the driver, "I've got to look out for a Lunajet Challenger 350 - They don't usually fly from here - they are usually from Farnborough."

He pauses at another white line with traffic lights. A

military jeep pulls up alongside and then an untidy looking green Volvo saloon behind.

"These aren't like normal lights," explains the driver, "Sometimes an aircraft manoeuvre takes much longer than you expect. It's one of the reasons we have to drive you around the airport. Also it'll stop you from taking a wrong turning at the runway."

By now there was a short queue of traffic, including an airport bus, which looks as it if was ferrying a few soldiers to a military plane.

Then a gentle tap on the side glass of the Bentley, almost unheard inside through the double glazing. Yaroslav and the driver both look around. It is an SA80 combat weapon. The driver slides the window down.

"Freeze," says the soldier holding the gun, in a very polite tone.

"Now will the driver and front seat passenger please leave the vehicle."

"Nice to meet you gents, and this is a first, too," says the exiting driver, as he is escorted away. Jaroslav's driver reaches behind his back for a pistol but gets clubbed to the ground by another soldier.

A bulky, camouflage-dressed soldier takes the driver's seat. He is wearing a green beret.

"Welcome to my world," he says, and slams the car into drive, accelerating rapidly across the airport to where the shape of a military Hercules could be made out. He races up the back ramp and into the plane, where he gracefully stops the vehicle.

"Now for a ride, but only after we've disabled the Bentley's tracker and your cell phone."

Another green-bereted man steps forward with something resembling a metal detector.

"The tracker is behind the heater ducts. Yaroslav has two cellphones and there's another one in the glovebox. The car also has a built-in SIMM."

A woman in camo-gear gestures for Yaroslav to hand over his cellphones, finds the one in the glovebox and the slot for the SIMM in the inside of the Bentley. The soldier with the metal detector prises off some trim and reveals a large grey battery and a small device.

"It's the tracker - It was the tracker," he says, clipping off the battery's wires. Then he re-tests everything with his scanner.

"Clear now, no signals," he declares.

"Such a waste to make it fish food," one soldier remarks as he looked at the Bentley.

They manoeuvre Yaroslav forward in the plane and take him to a row of uncomfortable -looking red webbed seats. This was not what Yaroslav had planned.

"Bumpy ride ahead," says one of the soldiers.

Yaroslav notices that they all have tags over their names. He makes out the red dagger patches on their battledress. Royal Marine Commandos. He sees that the grubby Volvo saloon has boarded the plane and is secured behind the Bentley, away from the rear hatch.

The commandos take a row of red-webbed seats and strap themselves in. Yaroslav is being accompanied by a whole squad of marines. He does not think they are taking him to Moscow.

The rear hatch raises and the judder of four turboprops signals the start of a flight.

He felt the queso blanco drifting around his brain.

Disappearing

Yaroslav's plane's engines change tone. He senses they are low, but he has an intense pressure in his ear. He's not sure whether it is from the descent, or from the white powder. By the angle of the plane, they have been flying in a circle. He wonders if they are due to land. Then a bang. The rear hold door is opening. After his eyes adjust, he can just make out the sea. They are flying low. Over the noise of rushing air, he hears another sound. It is a winch. He sees the Bentley moving towards the open hold.

Then, a bang and the car lurches forward, over the end of the plane, into the sea.

Yaroslav realises he is being 'disappeared'. He has done this to enough other people to know the moves. Disappeared without trace. The rear door of the plane is closing again. The marines had cheered when the Bentley rolled into the sea. The plane had skipped up in the air, but he reckoned it must have been the release of a couple of tonnes of metal, so no wonder.

Then a second reduction in the plane's engine sound. He heard another clunk sound from underneath. Wheels down. They were going to land. It had been around a ninety-minute flight. Paris? Too close. Amsterdam or Brussels, also too close. Frankfurt, maybe? But they were near to water. Hamburg then, or Bremen.

The plane does a navy landing, all wheels down onto the tarmac at once. Like a carrier landing would be. So different from an air force landing which rotates the nose down after the back wheels are all on the ground

He looks out of the plane's hold. His eyes fix upon the vehicles. They still have UK number plates. He has not even left the U.K. Unless this is a very elaborate set-up.

The woman marine walks up to him.

"You are in Prestwick, Scotland. We have a few questions for you here. Answer them and we'll keep hold of you. Fail to comply and you'll be transferred to the plane over there."

Yaroslav sees the white plane. It looks like a Boeing 737, but he recognises it as a C-40 Clipper. Along the side of it is written 'United States Navy'. Yaroslav realises he could be transferred from the UK government to the US. Extraditioned through Prestwick.

The woman adds, "Oh, and don't mistake the outside of that other plane for anything familiar. The Americans strip out the seats and install cargo webbing. Our Hercules is far more comfortable. You can come with me now."

She guides him toward the green Volvo car and into a back seat. A camouflaged driver takes the driver's seat, and she sits in the front passenger seat.

The driver reverses the car at high speed, off the plane and onto the tarmac. Then he selects forward, and they race off towards a hangar along the perimeter of the airport.

They drive inside and Yaroslav can see a single small plane and the rest of the hangar is taken up by a large concrete structure.

"This will be your home for a while. I recommend you talk. It will make things so much more pleasant for you."

Yaroslav weighs his options. They are between this woman Devil and the deep blue sea where his Bentley is already residing. He looks at his watch. He'd been on the road into Uxbridge 3 hours ago.

Red line around

Yaroslav is in what he considers to be an interrogation suite.

"What do you want from me?" asks Yaroslav, displaying a certain arrogance.

You were brazen in arranging those attacks," answers the first interrogator - a tanned well-set man with long dark hair - he could advertise tobacco on television if it was still allowed - "First, Ian Harrison and then attempts on Michael Tovey,"

"But I thought another man was responsible for both of those situations?" asks Yaroslav, "If he blames me, he is simply trying to save his own skin."

The second interrogator is an athletic blonde-haired woman - power dressed in a dark trouser suit, "He does blame you, and furthermore he showed us pictures of you with him and even of you passing him money - twice actually. Once £10,000 for Harrison and then £20,000 for Tovey."

"I see, a Special Advisor is worth less than a Member of Parliament?" says Yaroslav.

"The bicycle technique is hardly original either," says the male interrogator, "Just like Zelimkhan Khangoshvili in a Berlin park on his way home from midday prayers at a local mosque.

The woman adds, "Someone on an electric bicycle shot Khangoshvili twice in the head and once in the shoulder. The assassin was arrested by German authorities within a few hours of the murder, ridiculously having been spotted throwing his gun and wig into a nearby river."

"Neither that, nor the Harrison and Tovey events have anything to do with me," says Yaroslav.

The man continues, "On the contrary, it fits neatly into a broader pattern of international attacks perpetrated by Kremlin agents in recent years. Targeted assassinations are nothing new in the intelligence world, but the air of plausible deniability exhibited in the past seems to have disappeared today."

The male interrogator adds, "What's more, killings like the Berlin attack or the bike rider in London fly in the face of Russia's international commitments and cause significant damage to the Russian government's credibility. Despite that, the death toll continues to mount."

The woman adds, "These murders show the Kremlin's readiness to hunt down foes across the globe with little regard for the laws of host countries."

"I have told you. None of this has anything to do with me," answers Yaroslav.

The man continues, "These attacks allow Russia to intimidate perceived traitors while sending a chilling message of defiance to the country's international adversaries and reflect the increasingly hostile dynamic between Russia and the West since the 2014 invasion of Ukraine.

Yaroslav adds, "Victims of Putin's assassins serve as symbols of what happens to anyone accused of betraying the Kremlin. I don't want to be on that list."

The woman begins, "Sergei Skripal, who survived being poisoned by two Kremlin agents during an operation in Salisbury, England, had earlier been imprisoned by the Russian government for slipping state secrets to the West. I think you are finding yourself in a similar situation now."

Yaroslav is determined to stay calm, "I am no spy, certainly not working for the Russian government."

The woman continues, "Maybe not, but your employers have direct links with the Russian State - they employ you, so you are consequently an agent of Russia - and blundering around, typical of the kind of errors that they make."

She adds, "For example, the poisoning of Bulgarian Emilian Gebrev was linked to his role in the arms trade, where he frequently foiled Russian attempts to make deals in Africa and Asia."

The man grins and says, "Both Skripal and Gebrev survived, as have numerous other targets, suggesting a decline in professionalism as Russia seeks to deploy greater numbers of assassins abroad. We think, Mr

Yaroslav, that you are one of them."

Yaroslav replies. "Maybe there's an element of sticking two fingers up at Western countries here, as if Russia is saying 'we don't even really care if this works or not,' - but remember, I'm not involved."

Yaroslav was having difficulty working out who was the tough one between the two interrogators. That Columbian cocaine was still strong.

The woman continues, "Soviet hit squads were a routine feature of the first Cold War. Following a brief lull during the 1990s, President Putin reopened the door to Kremlin assassinations on foreign soil when he backed a new Russian law allowing extrajudicial killings abroad under the guise of "combating extremism and terrorism."

The man adds, "Then we saw the troubling nature of this Putin law raised early on by London-based Russian defector Alexander Litvinenko, who warned that it could target Putin's personal enemies."

The woman again, "Within months, Litvinenko was dead. Using rare radioactive polonium to poison Litvinenko turned his death into a protracted public execution that served the Kremlin's purposes admirably. It left exiled opponents of the Putin regime in no doubt of the fate that might await them, while allowing Moscow to protest its innocence."

The man speaks again, Yaroslav thought that the two of them made a strong tag-team, "I guess he is probably preparing something for you now, Putin... His use of international assassinations has escalated significantly. The Russian seizure of Crimea and subsequent military intervention in eastern Ukraine are watershed moments in the history of Moscow's post-Soviet relations with the Western world."

Yaroslav replies, "You are clutching at straws. Putin isn't interested in me. There are huge traitors to pursue; just pick up a copy of Pravda and you'll see."

The woman answers, "You are right, of course, it is not what Putin thinks that counts here. It is what those who commissioned you think. If they are trying to develop new business, which links back to Russia, or to develop new secret service tactics to corrupt our political structure, then they will be most upset if you tip up their apple-cart."

Then the man, "The Kremlin engages in an escalating campaign of hybrid hostilities against the West. Targeted assassinations are only part of this global confrontation, which also includes everything from cyber-attacks and disinformation campaigns to election meddling. You know it is being unpicked slowly, but Putin is pleased because for the Kremlin it is a cheap way to conduct warfare."

The woman again, "Russia has already paid a price for its increasingly aggressive actions, with its spree of Kremlin-linked killings proving particularly damaging to the country's international standing. The US government expelled 60 Russian diplomats and closed a Seattle consulate in 2018 in response to the Skripal poisoning. That had a serious effect on the capabilities of Russian services to operate abroad. When your name is properly linked with British diplomatic actions against Russia then I suggest your card will be well-and-truly marked."

"No-one in Russia will believe it," says Yaroslav, "Least

of all Putin. He won't even have heard of me."

The man smiles, "It's irrelevant. You've done this at exactly the time when the US and its partners need to increase the pressure on the Kremlin. What does that mean? We can simply hand you over to the Americans. Hop on their nice white plane for an extraordinary journey and give thanks to Barack Obama for his law ceasing rendition torture. Then pray that you don't end up in Egypt or earmarked as a terrorist."

Yaroslav smirks, "You don't have the power to hand me to the Americans, anyway. And it would create a huge diplomatic incident back in Moscow."

The woman speaks again, "That's your opinion. Now that the Kremlin's use of assassins throughout the Western world is in danger of becoming the new normal, fresh options should be explored that will introduce escalating costs on Putin's regime while also galvanizing public opinion.

"You could, Mr Yaroslav, become very famous. With the Russians as a botched hitman and a killjoy for their business development. Or with the Americans as a ruthless enactor of the Kremlin's asymmetric threats."

The man adds, "You could wind up as famous as the Russian opposition's man Navalny. Poisoned, taken to a Berlin hospital where he was in a coma. Then, recovered, he went back to Moscow. "

"Yes, to serve time in Matrosskava-Tishina prison."

The woman says, "You are well informed about the political opponent who exposed Putin's Winter Palace in Gelendzhik. Was that poisoning another one of your commissions? This time, Mr Yaroslav, it is different. You are not a provincial insurgent but a connected member of the Roslavl Bratva. Try as you might to decouple these London incidents from the Kremlin in policy terms and in the public imagination. But given the futility of sanctions or expelling diplomats as means of punishment towards Moscow, the only face-saving alternative seems to be your disappearance.

"Heck, you might get the powers-that-be drawing their own red line around you."

Yaroslav goes quiet. He wishes he could clear his mind. The residual cocaine magnifies the threats against him and gives him jitters.

PLAN 02 – Enrolment

Garrick

The business card Lawson-Parry had handed to Tovey had made him easy enough to contact. Alex had taken the card and then called him directly.

"Mr Lawson-Parry? Hello this is Alex, the Personal Assistant of Sir Stafford Peters. He has recently been passed your name related to membership of the Garrick Club. Apparently, you have been on the waiting list for some time?"

"Er, Gosh, I can't say that I even remember, although I am certainly interested in joining. I know that many of the legal profession are members and that it can provide a helpful way to liaise with one another."

"That's just what Sir Stafford Peters said. Apparently, over 100 QCs are members of what must be one of London's last remaining gentlemen's clubs."

Alex continued, rather sternly, "Speaking as a female, I'm not so certain that I agree with the Garrick's men only attitude, but I do understand it is a forum where senior members of the legal profession socialise with each other.

Sir Stafford Peters says that men get a unique opportunity to form connections with senior legal practitioners to support their professional aspirations."

"Well, Alex, thank you for contacting me, I would certainly like to follow up on this most courteous invitation. Where would Sir Stafford Peters like to meet me?"

"Why, at the Garrick, with you there as his guest!" says Alex, "I'll send you an invitation. I believe I have your correct email address on this business card?"

They continue for a few minutes to arrange the meeting.

Alex smiles as another part of Amanda's plan has now been set.

Lawson-Parry now relishes a comfortable leather chair inside the Garrick waiting for Sir Stafford Peters. Instead, Michael Tovey and James Cavendish approach him. Tovey identifies Lawson-Parry and now the two of them sit down beside him.

"Oh, Michael, I hadn't expected to see you here," said Lawson-Parry, taken aback.

"We're here to see Sir Stafford Peters," said James Cavendish, "My name is Jim Cavendish, I've some things in common with a few friends of yours."

James gestured to a steward, who appeared and looked quizzically toward Lawson-Parry.

"Single malt, dear chap? The Garrick's Club Single Malt is pretty good stuff and you can't really get it anywhere else. Smokey and peaty. It must come from Islay and it reminds me of an Ardbeg or a Lagavulin."

"Yes, please, I'll have one then, thank you."

"A gentleman's full measure?" asks the steward.

"What, oh, yes please," stutters Lawson-Parry, trying to regain his composure.

"You'll probably need the drink, when we've finished this little conversation," says James Cavendish.

"You see, we had a delve into your records. We found you listed as a solicitor, but there didn't seem to be anything about barrister, nor, for that matter, Queen's Council."

Lawson-Parry looks flustered, "I can explain. My original barrister listing was in the Register, but under the name William Clark. I changed my name, but the Bar has had difficulty keeping up. Look in the records for William Hugo Clark and you'll find me." He takes a gulp of the whisky.

"But why would you want to practice under another name?" asks James Cavendish. He notices Michael Tovey looking similarly intrigued.

"It was those damned Panama Papers. I'd help draft a few of them, and it was only a matter of time before the system would catch up with me. It was altogether easier to adopt another name, which worked out well for me as it happens." Lawson-Parry took another slug of the whisky.

"Another name where you also promoted yourself to Queen's Council?" asked James Cavendish.

"It seemed so easy at the time. I had to fill in some forms and tick some boxes, I didn't intend to practice as a QC, but I thought it would give me some additional gravitas when dealing with certain clients."

"Until you were discovered, anyway," says Cavendish. He notices that Lawson-Parry has downed the whisky.

"Another?" asks Cavendish gesturing toward the empty tumbler.

"Oh, yes please, you are right, it does seem to be having the required numbing effect."

"Okay, well I haven't fully introduced myself," says Cavendish.

"You're from the Service?" guesses Lawson-Parry, "There was a word that you were getting close, I've been waiting for something like this to happen."

"Correct," says Cavendish, "SI6. And we take a dim view of a gunman in the Royal Parks shooting at a Member of Parliament."

"I wasn't involved in any of that, nor on the hit against Harrison," says Lawson-Parry.

"But you know the people that were?" asks Cavendish.

"It depends...I'd need protection to give away any information. You can see they don't mess around."

"Well, that's what we have in mind. For you to assist us but for your colleagues-in-arms to be unaware that you've done anything."

"What - a double agent?"

"In a manner of speaking. Frankly, it's your best chance now. Think about it.

A. You are exposed as a fraudulent barrister and dozens of contracts come crashing down, creating many angry enemies.

B. Your colleagues get wind that you've been talking to SI6 and seek their own punishment for you - perhaps invoking Anatoly Yaroslav.

C. You help us; we get what we want (which isn't you, by the way). It keeps you clear of any wrongdoing and then you go back to your current life.

Tovey chipped in, "I'd say it was an easy decision really, wouldn't you Hugo?"

Hugo pauses, twisting the second, now half full glass of whisky in his hand.

"You know, half full is better than half empty. What will you want me to do?"

"You'll have to come with me, to join a few others and be briefed," answers Cavendish.

Rolling

Amanda's briefing room is almost full. They have Grace, Alex, Lawson-Parry, James Cavendish and the people from The Triangle present.

"I want to thank you all for coming along," says Amanda, "The first part of our plan is working well. We have Yaroslav captured and now Mr Lawson-Parry has agreed to assist. Next Andrew Brading must expose the Protection of Healthcare Rights Bill for what it is and implicate Elixanor and Brant Holdings. After that, we can let nature run its course. A television interview with Arne Holstad and then we can let the stock market decide the fate of Brant and Elixanor."

"We'll need Andrew to make another one of his inflammatory speeches?" asks Clare.

"Correct," answers Amanda, "and with Rachel Crosby well-briefed, we should be able to get Arne Holstad and also you, Mr Lawson-Parry onto the evening's 'News in Focus,' TV show."

Amanda adds, "A few well-placed questions and I'd expect Brant Holdings to want to call an emergency

Summit with Elixanor, in London."

Lawson-Parry interrupts, "You realise this could finish Elixanor. They have only just completed their takeover by Brant. Their stock is worth more now because of the Brant investment, and Brant's stock is now more dependent than ever on the fortunes of Elixanor. A double whammy of a broken product and a refusal by the UK Government to pass the Protection of Healthcare Rights Bill would ruin many months of plans and many millions of dollars of investments."

Amanda smiles, "Exactly."

PLAN 03 – Light the Touchpaper

Brading on Corruption

House of Commons. The Chamber was packed. Andrew Brading was to give another speech about his Fundamental Rights Bill, which would pave the way for the Protection of Healthcare Rights Bill. Several pundits were expecting fireworks when Brading stood up.

Madam Deputy Speaker:

"We now come to the Fundamental Rights Bill Committee statement. Andrew Brading will speak for up to 10 minutes, during which no interventions may be taken. At the conclusion of his statement, I will call Members to put questions on the subject of the statement, and I will call Andrew Brading to respond to those in turn. I call the Chair of the Fundamental Rights Bill Committee, Andrew Brading."

Brading speaks:

"We set up the Fundamental Rights to protect the citizens of this country. We may have based it upon the work of the United Kingdom, but that is no bad thing. It is paving the way for universal and Fundamental Rights for everyone and to prevent some of the scurrilous behaviour we see today."

"A Remainer's speech!" someone call from the Opposition.

"Order! Order!"

Brading continues, "A recent case springs to mind, related to housing and a planning deal. It is the stuff of television drama and yet it is still rife in our economy. Our housing minister is typical of the current crop of Cabinet ministers, an insipid character rising without trace and doing what he was told by that unelected and bullying Special Advisor to whom the Prime Minister reported."

A rustling of papers.

"This hapless Minister was most notably headlined for breaching the demand for people to 'stay at home whenever possible' during pandemic lockdown. He sat gloriously at a Tory fundraising dinner next to the former owner of a national newspaper who was being challenged by a London council over a £1bn housing redevelopment at an old newspaper print works in London. The Minister had been called to approve the scheme."

"Hear, hear!" called from the Opposition benches.

"That Tory donor texted to say: 'We don't want to give Marxists loads of dough for nothing!' Oh, no, he wanted to avoid paying any citizen related levy for the redevelopment. A case of 'don't let them eat cake'. Not even bread.

"This isn't Bake-Off," yelled someone from his own party.
   "Order! Order!"

Brading continued, unabashed, "Then, the following month, the donor sent another text urging hurried consent to avoid paying £45m in a new community-benefit levy. The Minister caved in, gave permission, even overruling officials in his own department and councillors hoping to spend their windfall on education and health in one of the country's poorest boroughs."

"Disgraceful," comes a shout from the Opposition.

"Order, Order," calls Madam Deputy Speaker.

Brading continued; he was used to this type of treatment when he made speeches, "Two weeks later the ex-newspaper owner handed £12,000 to the Conservative Party, small change compared with the huge sum he had sidestepped paying. The decision was challenged by the London borough, then the minister agreed to a court quashing his move after admitting it looked "unlawful by reason of apparent bias".

An unexpected silence from the Chamber.

"There. That's an example of the bypass of Fundamental Rights. Go to the right dinner parties. Lobby the right people and suppress any levelling-up payments. A small 'bung' at the end should round things off nicely."

Huffing and puffing from both sides of the House.

"Order, Order!"

"Meanwhile, pictures have emerged of the Prime Minister with his arm around his grinning donor. The saga stinks from start to finish. It reveals the hypocrisy of a government that claims to be on the side of ordinary people while doing the bidding of billionaires."

Brading notices, once again, the steely glare he is receiving from both the PM and one of the whips.

"There is nothing surprising about this scandal (except perhaps the rather small size of the magnate's donation-more like a tip than a fee).

"It shows again the sleazy nexus of money and power that lurks behind the doors of Westminster and Whitehall, one in which rich people can buy access, favours, knighthoods and even seats in the upper house of our parliament, plus a planning system that is woefully open to abuse. Every party knows the problem and has been stained by similar scandals. They are happening all of the time."

Cries from the Opposition benches, "Get your own people in order!"

"Order, Order!"

Brading continues, "Let's wind back. Think of Tony Blair and the Bernie Ecclestone affair, when the motor racing tycoon switched support from the Tories, bunged Labour £1m and lobbied successfully for his sport to be exempted from a tobacco advertising ban. Or Cameron's party treasurer Peter Cruddas resigning after being embroiled in a cash-for-access row.

"Blair even admitted in his biography that party donations were 'prima facie buying influence', adding that 'once in government no one believed a big donation could be made from the goodness of heart'."

Brading paused and looked around the Chamber.

"Many politicians loathe the need to suck up to rich hustlers. But it a cost of staying in power. And yet nothing gets done, even as Britain slides in the global ranking for transparency.

"The disagreeable whiff is not helped by a prime minister failing to release a report about Moscow's penetration of our political system.

"Disagreeable whiff - hot air more like," shouts someone.

"It highlights once more how the corruption bedevilling Britain is not just about money. It is about access, accountability and influence in the shadows of Westminster. These scandals flare up repeatedly. Sometimes they lead to resignation, but never to real reform. Any actions are tokenism."

Brading looks around again, "Yet corruption, whether personal or systemic, is a rot that erodes away at the body politic. It destroys public faith. It fosters a system of patronage that benefits the elite and disempowers those lacking cash or the right connections. It levels down, fuelling state capture and rent seeking by powerful corporate interests while disadvantaging challengers. We are building a kleptocracy."

"This is wrong on moral, economic, political and social grounds. That is why I launch and promote the Fundamental Rights Bill. But I resist the attempts of saboteurs to derail it in its later stages."

"There have been overt attempts to interfere with and influence the Protection of Healthcare Rights Bill. To subvert its purpose and to nullify its effectiveness. A powerful lobby exists to attempt to couple it together with the Identity Bill and then to tier citizens into strata according to heaven knows what 'science and fact-based criteria'."

"The real purpose? To monetise healthcare, and to place it in the hands of the elite. To structure healthcare so that those deemed Tier 0 and Tier 1 (Politicians and Elite) get the best products and this further down the tiers the Tier 2 - professional and middle classes and Tier 3 and 4 - everyone else, gets delivered with an economised and less effective form of treatment. It is the danger of building the castes of Brave New World, the Alphas to the Epsilons. The population has already been indoctrinated with ideas of Tiers from the times of the global pandemic. Now they can be levelled down - not up - by the disgraceful reforms being smuggled through by lobbyists in this new set of Bills."

Silence.

Brading continues, "I may preside in some futility over the Bills and the process by which they are created. I cannot control the ways that the individuals are influenced to adjust and tarnish the intention of the original offering. When I have intervened, I have been attacked, not with words, but with bombs. Someone has uttered something facile about taking back control. Well, 'they' have. They - the elite and power hungry - They - the fat cats - now have more access through closeness to the pie and the trough. We are being levelled down and it is by our own government."

Now, the Chamber erupts, with cries of "seize control!" and "Order, Order!"

Serena, Clare and Rachel Crosby are watching from the Visitor's Gallery.

"That should get the headlines tomorrow!" says Serena.

News in Focus TV show

With Rachel's assistance, Serena had managed to get a slot on the evening news programme, "News in Focus," for both Andrew Brading and Arne Holstad. John Morden from the Labour Party Cabinet is also present. Now that Andrew Brading is hot news again for his third inflammatory speech in Parliament, there was even talk of him creating his own new party.

They were all seated in the studio with Victoria Ford. They had been introduced and now a TV package of Brading speeches was playing, with a voiceover.

"Ahead of Tuesday's votes on the Fundamental Rights Bill, attention has focused on the rights and wrongs of the House of Commons seeking to 'seize control'."

The voiceover ran along the lines that there was nothing unusual about a democratic parliament controlling its own procedure and business. Indeed, the core principle of parliamentary sovereignty already gives the Commons control by default.

Victoria starts: "Well Andrew Brading, you stirred a hornet nest with your remarks about Parliament and corruption earlier today."

"Yes, Victoria, I did, but now I'm concerned that even this usually balanced programme is being influenced by an external agenda. This is NOT - I emphasise - NOT about anything to do with seizing control or creating a new party. I see those lines of questioning as deflections, something this government is very good at."

Brading continued, "No, I want to return to the principle of Fundamental Rights. That a Newcastle shop-assistant should have the same basic rights as someone in Uxbridge who happened to go to Eton or Oxford."

"And furthermore, that the follow-up Protection of Healthcare Rights Bill should not use the Identity Bill to classify strata of the population and determine different heath regimes according to which stratum a citizen is deemed to belong in."

Victoria cut in, "But your accusations in Parliament were quite cutting. You implied that there is a level of corruption running through the place, influenced by the lobbying activities of big business."

Brading smiled, " Yes, that's exactly what I implied, and – let's be straightforward here - all of those examples I cited have been well-exercised in the media. It is just that nothing gets done. An occasional paper tiger is stood up, but then, like the Russian interference paper, it gets kicked into the long grass."

"John Morden, what do you have to say about this?"

Morden, middle-aged, dark-suited, edged forward in his chair,

"That hidden report refers to Britain 'welcoming oligarchs with open arms'. However, it says the UK government's building of links with major Russian companies has been counter-productive."

Brading interrupts, "Yes, in that it offered ideal mechanisms by which illicit finance could be recycled through what has become known as the London 'laundromat'. Their money was also invested in extending patronage and building influence across a wide sphere of the British establishment. PR firms, charities, political interests, academia and cultural institutions were all willing beneficiaries of Russian money, contributing to a 'reputation laundering' process."

John Morden tried again, "But Andrew, won't this make you a laughingstock? A major conspiracy theory, and the threat of toppling your own party?"

Brading replies, "The media are already calling London 'Londongrad' implying that Russian influence in the UK is 'the new normal', and there are a lot of Russians with very close links to Putin who are well-integrated into the UK business and social scene and accepted because of their wealth.

"This level of integration, in 'Londongrad' in particular, means that any measures now being taken by the government are not preventive but make up damage limitation."

Victoria interrupts again, "Mr Holstad, welcome to the debate. You were the Chief Science Officer for Elixanor, a company implicated in the Protection of Healthcare Rights Bill. What do you have to say about Mr Brading's allegations?"

Arne Holstad begins, "Well, I know less of your British Parliamentary system, being from Norway, but I do understand how the suggestion for tiered healthcare, as suggested by Mr Brading, might work. We attempted to build exactly such a drug dispensing system in Elixanor. It was for the graduated care of existing patients, rather than to create a tiered healthcare structure. It just wouldn't be the Norwegian way. Unfortunately, the law of unintended consequences came along when some foreign investors monetised the invention."

Victoria asks, " So who were these people? Was it, as Mr Brading implies, lobbyists trying to affect a political outcome?"

Arne replied, "Well, as a matter of fact, it is an academic question, because the truth is, we could never get the invention to work properly. Inside the drug dispensing used nano-machines but they were inherently unstable. It means we had a good idea, but no product."

Serena and Rachel were watching from the control box in the studio, "This is great," whispered Rachel, "He's just blown the lid off the whole proposition - and it is the second time that Elixanor have been caught misrepresenting a product."

Rachel wrote something on a piece of paper and handed it to the show's producer.

"Ask about Patricia Wilson..."

The producer looked at Rachel, then whispered something to someone miked into Victoria's headset.

"Ask about Patricia Wilson."

"...Thank you, Mr Holstad, you seem to be suggesting that Elixanor may have exaggerated their claims? It's not the first time is it? Can you remind us about Patricia Wilson?"

Arne Holstad paused and looked back at Victoria.

"It's probably a long story, I'm not sure I can tell it here."

"That's perfectly fine, Mr Holstad, you can go ahead."

Holstad begins, "Well the original founder of Elixanor was Patricia Wilson, who raised US$700 million to start the company. Unfortunately, in its enthusiasm, Elixanor faced a string of legal and commercial challenges from medical authorities, investors, state attorneys, former business partners, patients, and others. It looked as if powerful interests were stacked up to acquire the company after devaluing its stock."

"Elixanor received sanctions from the regulatory authorities, including the revocation of its Clinical Laboratory Improvement Amendments certificate and the prohibition of Pat Watson and other company officials from owning or operating a laboratory for two years. That's when I was hired to run things and I announced a new direction for Elixanor working on research into miniature medical substance dispensing machines. It was the start of the new nano-engineering direction for the company. But Elixanor had to pay off some serious lawsuits and fines to recover its position."

"Thank you, that was a great summary for us all," said Victoria, now being fed information about Elixanor into her earpiece.

"And I believe Patricia Wilson was only 19-years-old when she started the company?"

"That's correct, although she did have seasoned backers for the original company formation."

Brading cuts in, "It illustrates my point though. Here's a company which has already misrepresented its offering once now attempting to link with a government Bill on Healthcare. In effect to monetise its product."

Victoria nods, "And Mr Morden, any concluding thoughts?"

"Yes, with a Labour Party in power instead of the current government, there would be stringent Party rules to prevent such abuses of power."

"Well, thank you all for joining this debate; now we must move on to another topic. Britain's roads have long been pothole-ridden and now a scheme to keep the potholes as a means of speed management has been proposed. More on this after the break!"

Rachel looked towards Serena, "I think that will have clinched things. We should call Amanda and tell her what just happened. And it is, of course, on the back of Brant's recent acquisition of Elixanor. I suspect the market will open lower for both companies tomorrow."

PLAN 04 – Reaction

Stock Market

Clare was back at the Bermondsey flat.

"You've done it again!" says Tessa, "Another day of headline grabbing for Brading!"

"I've just come from that very TV studio," replies Clare.

"What - were you there when Brading and that scientist were talking? - on 'News in Focus?' - it was great telly!" says Lottie.

"I reckon it will crush the share price though, of - what were they called? - Oh yes - Elixanor!"

Robin appeared from the direction of Tessa's bedroom.

"I overheard you talking! - Hey Clare - good to see you - I've just taken a look at the price of Elixanor. It's tanking, down more than 30% and still heading south. And the financial papers are saying it will pull down Brant too; quite a disaster!"

Clare smiled, "Andrew is quite principled. He could tell that something was amiss and I think his speech this afternoon in the Commons has flushed it out. The thing is, we still don't know who is pulling the strings."

Robin looks thoughtful, "Well I guess you could follow the trail back into Elixanor. See if there are any other interesting people loitering on the edges? They are bound to have a pow-wow after that lot has gone down."

Clare's phone rings, Amanda speaks: "Tovey has been invited to a meeting tomorrow. It's at the London boardroom of Elixanor. He's asked for some backup. We are sending Lawson-Parry and as his assistants Alex Smith and Christina."

"I can understand Alex, she's one of yours, but why send Christina?"

"She asked to be included. She'll also be able to keep track if there are any Russians involved. If there's any trouble, she'll also be quite useful and perfectly deniable!"

Clare smiled; she would want to check with Christina for herself.

Dubious funders

Clare was in the Triangle offices. She walked over to Christina.

"Hej,"

"Hey, so what's the I heard about you supporting the Elixanor meeting?"

Christina answers, "Yes. Have you seen their share price today! It has crashed and taken Brant with it!"

Bigsy looked up.

"Yes, it's true, Amanda asked me to go along."

Clare asks, "She said you volunteered?"

"In a manner of speaking. I'm working off a couple of situations with British Intelligence. It's all good humoured, but I do really still owe Amanda until after this."

"You sure you'll be alright?"

"Yes, and I think I can provide good back-up for Alex and even for Tovey, you know something? I think that Russia could be behind this. When I heard that Yagovkin Lavro Kirillovich was involved in the funding of Elixanor, it started to make sense. Lavro Kirillovich is a well-known Bratva member, quite close to Prigozhin, actually."

Bigsy speaks, "Is that Prigozhin, the same one that set up the "troll factory" which used fake internet accounts and fake news to influence US voters in the 2016 presidential election?"

"According to the US intelligence services, yes, from St Petersburg," answers Christina, "He was indicted by a US Grand Jury over that election interference. Prigozhin famously shrugged off the indictment, saying: 'Americans are very impressionable people; they see what they want to see. I'm not at all upset that I'm on this list. If they want to see the devil, let them see him.'

Bigsy reads something from his screen, "It says here that Prigozhin, his family and associates keep their luxuries, like yachts registered in the Seychelles and Cayman Islands offshore tax havens.

"US individuals and firms are now prohibited from doing business with him or providing services for his jets. Although his jets have flown many times to destinations in Africa, the Middle East and Europe in recent years, the US statement says."

"It sounds as Prigozhin is above the law," said Clare, "or at least laughing at it."

"So, what is the Kirillovich link with Prigozhin?" asks Bigsy.

"Good question!" says Christina, "but still a mystery!"

PLAN 05 – Execution

Elixanor Business Strategy Meeting

It was the time of the Elixanor Business Strategy Meeting.

Michael Tovey, Hugo Lawson-Parry, Alex Smith and Christina Nott arrive in an SUV driven by MI6, and a further group of five SI6 people wait outside at ground level.

"Remember," says Alex, "If both my hands go up in the air, hit the floor," she looks around at each of them as if to check they have understood. She demonstrates - with a small gesture more like a surrender rather than a goal has been scored at Wembley. Alex is in a black business dress, looking for all the world like she is about to give a PowerPoint presentation.

They all look towards a glass windowed tower block in London. It has a prestigious city address, but nowhere on the building does it mention any of the names Elixanor, Brant or Raven.

"Nothing so tame for the people from Elixanor," says Christina looking towards the sky. A red and blue civilian helicopter is landing on the roof of the building.

"H-130," says Alex, "Pretty helicopter,"

Christina is impressed that Alex seems to know so much about hardware, "I used to ride around in H-145s," she said, showing she was also knowledgeable.

"That's serious kit, military, twin engined; suitable for light attack. What were you, some sort of black-ops commando?" asks Alex.

"This and that," smiles Christina.

They pass through security, which was reassuringly lightweight after some of the situations they had all been in. 'Bags and beeps' said Christina quietly and Alex smiled.

Then they are escorted to an express elevator and onwards to the top floor.

There's an outer lobby and a group of men sitting around.

"Security," hisses Alex.

They walk through one set of double doors to the meeting room. It breathtakingly shows off its full-length plate glass windows looking out across the City of London and toward the river and Tower Bridge.

Already seated inside were Miller McDonald, Trudi Hartmann, Sir Edgar Holland, Mikael Bjornstad as well as a six other thick-set tattooed but suited individuals.

"They must be the bankers!" jokes Christina to Alex.

Christina and Alex scope the room on entry. Two exits and the tats were marking them. Altogether six security people in the room. Odds were against if it turned difficult.

Alex put two fingers on her face and ran them up and down. She was signalling that the security was armed. Christina quietly nodded.

Then the doors at one end open and in march another two strangers. Christina recognises one as Lavro Kirillovich and whispers it to Alex. Kirillovich looks tanned and at ease in the situation, more like someone that has just spent a week vacationing on a yacht than about to enter a hard-ball meeting. The other guy looks like a flustered bagman - probably the accountant, and they are surrounded by another six-security people, this time four men and two very attractive women.

Alex says to Christina, "Odds are stacked, we'll need to use my tag. Wait for my signal."

Alex fingers her security lanyard. Attached was a attached slim ATEX - which was a military version of a lone-worker alarm. A sophisticated device, it provided a high-performance GPS tracker and Active Response Center pings in case of emergency. It also contained amber alert mechanisms which would detect sudden increases in activity, like running or diving for cover.

Alex was trained to use the device such that she would not create false alarms and its slim format meant it looked like just another security card on her lanyard.

Christina and Alex could see what they assumed to be Kirillovich's dark blue-black helicopter clearing the building and flying away towards docklands.

Christina recognises it as a Kazan Mil Mi-38. Unmistakably Russian, but one of their less clumsy looking designs. Most Russian helicopters looked as if they had been designed by a child with some tin plate toys and a few crayons.

Kirillovich moves to sit at the head of the table, offset from Miller McDonald who looked as if he was to chair proceedings.

Miller starts to speak, "I want to thank everyone for coming. This is one of the gravest situations we have faced in a long time, and I want to ensure that we give it our fullest attention. The main board is unaware of this meeting. But right now, it is better to light a candle than to curse the darkness."

"Stop," says Kirillovich, quietly, "Brant is down 35% and Elixanor nearly half its previous valuation. This has all happened in a day. Where I come from the candles would be used for other purposes than to shine a light. My *derzhatel obshchaka* - bookkeeper - says we have an unrecoverable position. The Tambovskay Bratva have run out of patience. Someone in this room is accountable and must pay the consequences."

Kirillovich stands. "You allowed rings to be run around yourselves. First, the Member of Parliament makes damaging speeches. Then you substitute him for the man seated over there. He points to Michael Tovey. You can't warn him off nor get the Bill positioned in Parliament. You bodge the bomb attempt."

456

Kirillovich grimaces and his gaze moves from Tovey back to McDonald.

"Then, to finish it all off, you provide a broadcast on live television which destroys the credibility of the new company. We created this to operate as a new money-making machine, supplying legitimised drugs to the health service. It didn't matter whether they worked, as long as people believed in them."

He looks now at Trudi Hartmann, "And you, Trudi understood the nature of them as Fast-Moving Consumer Goods. We could mix other Bratva money streams with them and cleanse most of our money. Was it too much to ask? That you'd follow the plan?"

"I've lost one of my main operatives during all of this too. Anatoly Yaroslav has disappeared. He'd approve of our current plan; of that I am sure. I've decided that you are all to pay for this. It is the only way that I can recover the situation with the Tambov clan. Putin will pay a particular interest and I don't want him thinking that I don't rebalance after a failure."

Christina could hear another helicopter outside the building.

Kirillovich smiles, "Yes, I've got another transport for you all. You'll be out for a replanning session that I've booked for us all in Rotterdam. You'll go there by Mil-26. It's one of the strongest helicopters around. It has even rescued Chinooks from Afghanistan.

"Only, this time, it won't be able to cope with all of you. I've arranged for a short one-way flight for you all. To somewhere in the North Sea.

"Sadly, there will be a rotor failure and the copter will crash into the sea. It will be tragic. My security detail here is from the 16th Special Purpose Brigade, its a Spetsnaz Brigade, based in Tambov. They are perfectly used to jumping out of planes into the sea and for this assignment are getting very well rewarded. Four years' salary for this single mission for every man. He spoke some Russian which Christina understood.

"Round them up, I can hear the helicopter approaching."

Alex raised her hands in the air. Christina pushed Andrew Tovey to the floor and saw as Alex did the same with Hugo Lawson-Parry. There was a huge explosion as the plate glass windows crashed into the room. The Spetsnaz pulled out firearms, but Christina kicked one of them and his submachine gun slid across the floor towards Alex. She racked it back, but at that exact moment there was a further crack as two smoke grenades ignited. The meeting room was filled with dense purple and green smoke.

"Stay down," shouts Alex, as she slithers on her elbows though the smoke.

Christina realises the grenades were civilian rather than military and the smoke was less choking than she was used to. It was the type of effect used in a film rather than in a conflict situation.

She hears loud voices and a short rattle of suppressed sub-machine gun fire. It could have only taken five seconds for the new troops to gain control of the room.

The gunfire sounds like warning rounds rather than a firefight.

Christina hears the Spetsnaz commander stand down his men, barking instructions in Russian upon seeing they were massively outnumbered by people in full combat gear.

Military under Alex's command have reached the building and rounded up the meeting occupants. The dozen Spetsnaz surrender, having brought small arms to a full-fledged war zone. Christina looked at them, idly wondering if there was anyone she would recognise.

Christina is impressed at the way Alex carries herself, emotions ran ice cold in Alex. She's also instructed that Christina, Hugo and Michael were moved to another part of the room.

Then a bulky, dark-combat dressed man hands a gas mask to Christina. "Here, it's got comms and IR too," he said as she donned the Mira CM-7M mask. Suddenly she could breathe better, as well as hear commentary on what was happening.

The Spetsnaz had been rounded up and she could see that there were additionally around 20 commandos in the room. They had blown the glass with Brisant - a form of high explosive with a good shatter profile. Then they had swung into the room just like in the movies, throwing a few colourful smoke grenades around.

The Section Commander from the commandos spoke to Christina, "I expect you could hear our chopper outside. We had drop 20 men on the roof, without landing. We intercepted their Mil-26 with a couple of Typhoons from Lincolnshire. I think some residents will have heard the sonic boom over Cambridge. The Mil pilot surrendered immediately he saw the two combat planes."

The smoke was clearing quickly, aided by the new open-plan look of the floor, with its missing windows and a very long drop to the ground. Noisy fire alarms ring out and Christina wondered what the story would be about this building's sudden damage. Instinctively everyone was standing on the other side of the room from the open air.

Christina sees Tovey and Lawson-Parry. She'd heard about Tovey's change of trousers after the assassin incident and thinks he'll need a whole suit this time. It looks Armani, as well.

Lawson-Parry is pale but lightly covered in tomato and chilli dips from the refreshment table. She assumes that it had tipped over on to him. Alex is standing with another of the commandos, quietly chatting. Christina notices she is carrying an SA-80 rifle. Christina realises that a commando must have passed it to her.

Alex borrows this commando's radio and is clearly talking to the operations Commander. Then she flips out her iPhone and calmly calls Amanda.

"We're all safe and everyone has been rounded up. They were going to put us on a helicopter and drop us into the North Sea," she quietly explains, "It's more like something out of a James Bond Playbook." Christina realises Alex must now appear how she herself once did when she was just starting out. Young, unruffled, and as tough as nails, yet with command over a conflicted situation.

"Nicely done," says Christina, to Alex.

"Yes, thank you. I wasn't sure whether the troops were already in place when I pressed the button, but I realised it was just about the last moment that we could contain everything inside the building. A roof-top firefight would have been more difficult - probably we'd have had some casualties too, especially if we'd had an HC-4 chopper up there." She presses her business dress back into shape as she adjusts the weight of the gun's shoulder strap on her shoulder.

Christina admired Alex's logic. Alex Smith was one cool customer.

"I was just speaking to Amanda," says Alex, "It seems the other half of the plan has worked as well!"

"And what might that be?" asks Christina.

"Let's save it for the debrief," suggests Alex, "We can update Clare and the others too!"

VIP check-in

It was time to visit Amanda's office once again. Clare, Bigsy, Jake and Christina made their way by taxi and expected the long security clearance procedure.

This time Alex greeted them and whisked them into a separate VIP check-in where they were sent through security clearance swiftly, and the Alex showed them to a meeting room, less impressive than the last one, but still a decent size and kitted out with modern projectors and other office trappings.

"Hello," says Amanda, "I think all of our plans turned out rather well!"

"What was the other mission that you were doing while some of us were at Elixanor's meeting?" asks Clare.

"Well, we though that the Minerva and Medusa operations had gone on long enough, so we had a go at shutting them down. It was indirect, however."

Jake looks as if he had worked it out, "You used the Americans, didn't you?" he asks, "They were running it and could put a stop to it!"

"That's right," says Amanda, "We told the Americans that we'd discovered that Medusa had been bugging Whitehall and they folded almost immediately. It could cause a diplomatic incident if they were seen to be spying on their allies. Five Eyes and all that."

Amanda referred to The Five Eyes intelligence alliance comprising Australia, Canada, New Zealand, the United Kingdom and the United States. These countries are party to the multilateral UKUSA Agreement, a treaty for joint cooperation in signals intelligence.

"Did you give them any form of proof?" asks Bigsy, "I mean the hack to the wiring closet was pretty plain to see."

"Yes, actually, I escorted one of the American chiefs to the same spot in the Cabinet War Rooms and showed him what we had discovered. He knew about the tunnels, obviously, but had no idea that the cables were being used for spying."

"The whole Medusa operation has been closed down," says Grace, "They simply left and then a couple of days later some removals vans pulled up and took most of the kit away.

"It was a massive embarrassment being almost outside of the American Embassy.

"They have left behind a perfectly usable telephone call centre. I'm wondering if we can use if for GCHQ, actually."

"And what happened to the staff?" asks Clare, "How was that handled?"

Grace answers, "Well, most of the staff were Londoners, with a few American controllers in place. The Americans have returned to Washington and New York and the Brits have generally been relocated to other forms of call-centre.

"A few people left the organisation, and we think they may have been the plants arranged by Moscow. Altogether it has been a productive few days."

"So, what have we achieved?" asks Clare.

"I'm glad you asked," answers Grace, firing up a wall projector.

1) Andrew Brading reinstated as Secretary of State for Internal Affairs
2) The Fundamental Rights Bill prepared as legislation
3) The Protection of Healthcare Rights Bill stopped in its current form
4) Elixanor products exposed as sham
5) Brant and Elixanor diminished in the marketplace
6) Key lobby blackmailers captured including Miller McDonald and Trudi Hartmann
7) Enforcers Anatoly Yaroslav and Lavro Kirillovich captured. Both with strong cases against them.
8) Medusa spy listening station closed down.
9) An entire Spetsnaz section captured and to be used in diplomatic trade.

"That's a pretty good set of outcomes," said Bigsy, "However you look at it."

Amanda adds, "Yes, although I see that Raven is launching another Bio-engineering company now called Biotree. I guess it has at least put their plans back some years."

Grace added, "Not to mention the minor players like Roger Slater the tilted reporter, that fake barrister Hugo Lawson-Parry and the medium-sized corrupt politicians like Sir Edgar Holland and Michael Tovey.

"When the debrief gets written the Serious Fraud Office will have a field day!"

Amanda looks towards Clare, "I guess you'll be out of this now?"

"Yes, I've been thinking about that. Mainly what I'll tell my sister Sam; she'll think I've wimped out of the life, yet it is a life that she enjoys. And I have to decide what I'll tell my flat mates. They already think I have a raucous lifestyle."

"You should invite Samantha to meet you with your flatmates. Tell everyone together, then get out a 'Men In Black' gadget and wipe their minds!" says Bigsy.

"Not such a bad idea, actually; have one story for everyone and tell it once," says Alex.

"Yes," says Clare, "The trick will be to somehow make it believable!"

"I've an idea!" says Jake.

Sleaze

Ed Adams

a firstelement production

Ed Adams

First published in Great Britain in 2022 by firstelement
Copyright © 2022 Ed Adams
Directed by thesixtwenty

10 9 8 7 6 5 4 3 2 1

ISBN is for 'Ignoble' , the combined Corrupt and Sleaze

Printed and bound in Great Britain by Ingram Spark

rashbre
an imprint of firstelement.co.uk
rashbre@mac.com

ed-adams.net

Live the questions now.

<u>*Rainer Maria Rilke*</u>

PART ONE

Singapore

We sail tonight for Singapore
We're all as mad as hatters here
I've fallen for a tawny moor
Took off to the land of nod

Drank with all the china men
Walked the sewers of Paris
I danced along a coloured wind
Dangled from a rope of sand
You must say goodbye to me

We sail tonight for Singapore
Take your blankets from the floor
Wash your mouth out by the door
The whole town's made of iron ore
Every witness turns to steam
They all become Italian dreams

Fill your pockets up with earth
Get yourself a dollar's worth
Away boys, away boys, heave away
The captain is a one-armed dwarf
He's throwing dice along the wharf
In the land of the blind
The one-eyed man is king, so take this ring

Tom Waits

Fringe benefits

"Clare, we'll miss you and your fringe benefits!" said Tessa. She looked dreamily at the first remover and he winked, "Any chance of a cup of tea?"

Two lads with a white van were assisting Clare Crafts leave Bermondsey and her researcher life in Parliament. Lottie Trevethick and Tessa Maier, her two flat-shares, were sad to see Clare go, but perked up as soon as they saw the two fit-looking young men emerge from the van.

The first remover sounded well-spoken and Lottie asked him, "So, is this your main job?"

"No, Hugo over there runs a hot air ballooning business and I'm an actor. My name is Bjorn, and so you can probably guess that my mother is Swedish." He didn't have a trace of accent and sounded as if he was from west London.

"Have I seen you in anything?" asked Lottie, and Bjorn answered, "Only 'Prime Suspect', but it didn't end well for me. Apart from that, I do some stage acting to keep the wolf from the door. Oh, and this man-in-a-van stuff, too. And some contract gardening."

Clare smiled. It was turning into another typical day in the life of the flat and she wondered if she would miss it. Then her phone rang. 'Rachel Crosby' it said on the screen. Rachel was a lobby journalist for The Post - someone whom Clare had met on her very first day as a Researcher in Parliament, and even been warned not to trust. But since those early days, Clare and Rachel had worked out that they worked better together than in opposition.

"Rachel! An unexpected surprise!"

"Hello Clare. A little birdy told me that you were moving on now the business with the manipulated politicians has passed?"

"They are literally moving my stuff out of Bermondsey as we speak!"

"Well, I think I may have something for you. Assuming you are still interested in cases of extreme corruption?"

"It can't be on such an industrial scale as the last situation," answered Clare.

"No, agreed, but this one has a way to make vast amounts of cash through the chumocracy," answered Rachel, "I've received some tipoffs. It'd mean more work inside Parliament."

Clare had originally been asked to work in Parliament clandestinely, to support Amanda Miller, who was a special services long-term acquaintance of Clare and the others who made up an informal working arrangement known as The Triangle.

Working with Rachel was an altogether different thing. Clare was aware that Rachel was an investigative journalist and that this could go in any number of directions.

Previously, Clare with Jake, Bigsy and Christina had uncovered systemic corruption of the lobby system in Parliament through what would best be described as moral suasion (also known as blackmail). It had proved to be a very cost-effective way to get lobbyists into position and to influence the direction of government.

Once the whole situation had been closed with the involvement of SI6 and other agencies, Clare had agonised over whether to move away from Parliament, or whether to continue providing support to her MP Andrew Brading. Brading was now the Secretary of State for Internal Affairs, a senior governmental position.

Clare paused for a moment, then replied, "Well I guess we'd better meet!"

"How about Caffè Concerto, in Whitehall?" asked

Rachel.

Clare knew it as an informal Italian cafe and, whilst on Whitehall, it was also somewhere to escape from the usual Parliament set.

"Great!" answered Clare and arranged a time for their meeting. She would bring someone else along. Someone from the Triangle.

"Always in demand!" said Lottie, noting that Clare had finished the call.

"They may want me to do something else," answered Clare, "Still with Parliament!"

"Oh. Do stay on!" exhorted Lottie, "Even if you want to live in your fancy west-London apartment!"

Caffè Concerto

Clare knew the Caffè Concerto well. It was the one a short distance from Trafalgar Square and nestled between a small library-style pub and a MacDonald's.

Inside the Caffè was mirrored glitter and sparkling chandeliers. The friendly waiter approached and showed Clare and her accomplice Jake to a table. One side was a long banquette seat, so it would be possible to squish many people in when the need arose. At this quiet time, the venue was almost deserted. Rachel arrived within a minute and they all sat around a small table for four.

"Hello Rachel, you already know Jake, don't you?"

They all stood and greeted one another with hugs.

"Yes, when that business with the Medusa Station was unfolding,"

Jake spoke, "Hi Rachel, this sounds intriguing, but

I'm wondering whether you are going to need some further support, based upon what happened in that other incident."

"You know, I was hoping you would say that. I'll tell you what I know, but I am concerned that I've got in somewhat deep."

Jake and Clare looked at Rachel. She was normally calm and collected, but this time looked a little unsettled.

Jake spoke again, "Ground rules first, no hidden recording devices, please."

"You have my word, " answered Rachel, "And you also?"

They all laughed.

A waited came across and took an order. They skirted around the Luxury Afternoon Tea and settled for a coffee and a cake each.

"Prosecco as well?" asked the waiter hopefully, but they all shook their heads.

Rachel began, "You'll have seen some articles in the news about Pay to Play lobbying and Cash for Questions. It's even more convoluted than the press has so far discovered. And your old friends Brant are involved."

"I don't think we'll ever get away from them," said

Clare.

Jake nodded, "Brant and Raven Holdings and I think they have set up another subsidiary called Biotree now, as well."

Fleet's In

Rachel explains

"It stated when I visited Douglas Lessiter, MP at his home. Remember he is also a slightly improbable Minister of State for Infrastructure. It was his idea actually and I met him with his researcher Hannah. You must know Hannah - she looks like Nicole Kidman?"

"Yes, I met her during my first day, and we've become friends over my time in Parliament. She has helped me navigate some of the tricksier situations. Oh, as well as Lottie and Tessa, of course. And if Lessiter is a Minister of State, he's a level below Andrew Brading?"

"Yes, that is correct - although he can still attend Cabinet Meetings and his single function title is somehow more powerful than the top jobs with titles like: Secretary of State for Levelling Up, Housing and Communities; Minister for Intergovernmental Relations. If you know what I mean."

Rachel pauses and then says, "Well, I'll come clean. I was looking around for any sort of story from after that Andrew Brading faux-pas when he got caught in that mis-quote about Black Lives Matter. I seem to remember that you, Clare, fixed it with a couple of sound bites. Nicely done, and it diverted attention away so quickly. Then that pizza story broke and everyone was on to the next thing."

"Oh yes the 24-hour news cycle," mutters Jake.

"Well, I was interested to know if Andrew Brading and Clare were working in tandem and that it was some kind of stunt pulled by Serena McMillan - Andrew's office manager and that other researcher Maggie Shannon. I wondered if the whole thing was somehow staged to take attention from another story."

"I see," says Clare, "That's why you went to Duggie? Because he's the MP next door in Westminster. You wanted to find out whether Duggie or even Hannah knew anything?"

"I always knew you were cute," says Rachel, "You are exactly right."

Clare notices Jake nodding at Rachel's admission.

He says, "You remind me of my time working for the ladmag 'Street', which was always looking for after-dirt on any celeb stories. I guess you are doing the same thing for politicos."

Rachel smiles, "I didn't know you'd worked for Street! I had an ex who worked for them - Rafe Chesterton? Maybe you knew him?"

"Oh yes, we all knew Rafe - he was one of the founders of the magazine - We used to laugh about the way he pretended to be a gangster, until we realised, he really was one.

Rachel smirks, "Yes and Street was only one of his publications, all of which were very close to the gutter. Oh, sorry, no offence meant. I first met this apparently lavish and chivalrous man, but soon realised he was a two-timing liar frequently operating on the wrong side of the law. It didn't stop him from amassing money though. Now he's got a property investment company which leases High Street stores and I think he's got something to do with a Premier League team."

"Maybe it's a handy laundromat for him?" snickers Jake.

Rachel continues, "Yes, well back to Douglas Lessiter. He poured out the wine and attempted to answer my questions. I think I learned more about him than I did about anything to do with Brading during that session. Hannah was dutifully supporting him, but I could see that she'd been made to come along. I think Lessiter was aiming for an impression of some sort of frisson between them, but I could see it was all a sham. I mean, he had a Paul Cadmus on the wall - 'Fleets In', with the

French bread-sticks and men on bicycles."

Jake shakes his head, "No I don't know that piece,"

"It's a piece of iconic symbolism of a particular kind," explains Rachel, through raised eyebrows.

"Oh - I see! Likes men! The penny has dropped," splutters Jake through his pastry.

Rachel and Clare both laugh.

"Well in addition to his self-image polishing, Lessiter also mentioned something else. That there was still a type of politician who could get very rich by adjusting the terms of their service. Not only that, but there were also several support structures to help them conceal what they were doing."

"But does this have anything to do with the old situation that we uncovered?" asks Clare.

"No, Lessiter was very clear that this seemed to originate from within Westminster and was mainly of interest to those in higher positions. He said it seemed to be we'll-funded and could be ruthless with people who stood in its path. I watched Hannah's reaction to the story, and I had the distinct impression that she was hearing it for the very first time. Lessiter didn't think Brading was involved or even aware of it. And both held the opinion that Brading was as straight as a die."

Rachel continues, "I just have a chance to look

around the room when Hannah says they are pushed for time. She's rumbled that I was looking for something about Brading, not Lessiter. I get the impression that she thinks Lessiter said too much about the illicit operation in Westminster. I notice that there's an obvious workstation at one side of the living area with two huge computer screens. I realise it must be Hannah's and then I realise that she must be a live-in assistant."

Rachel continues, "The living space is divided from the kitchen by a dining table. There's another computer, a laptop this time, and a stack of cardboard folders, several of which were opened as if research was in progress. I noticed that the word 'Silverstone' seemed prominent, like it was the name of the file collection."

"Silverstone - car racing," says Jake," and traffic jams."

"I did the 'glance at watch' thing, 'I guess that's our time over, thank you for the hospitality.' Lessiter stands up, smoothes his tie. He looks as if he's sorry to see me go."

"Then he said it: 'Have you heard the latest stupid rumour about me?' Hannah caught my eye over Lessiter's shoulder. A sympathetic if slightly pained twitch of her mouth. I watched as she tucks her blonde hair behind her ear with a free hand, then reaches for a fresh glass of wine like a woman who really needs a drink. Lessiter continues, 'One of the red tops, is gunning for me now. Innuendo, but the third day of it. I was hoping...' Then his voice trailed off. I thought he should change his decor at least and maybe get a photoshoot to promote his all-new alpha image."

Rachel continues, " 'Look, I'm not sure how I can help you,' I said, all the time thinking that he had given me some potentially big news, not about Brading, but about a whole system of sleaze operating within the corridors of power."

"So that's when you left?" asks Jake, "I'd call it a result. You got a whole new story, plus hints of the Lessiter situation."

"Yes, but I'd need a photographer along for the Lessiter segment. 'Hottie dates MP' etc. That'd do it."

Jake laughs, and Clare notices several people in the Caffè look toward him.

"We're creating a small scene in here," Clare hisses, and looks carefully around to ensure there were no faces from Parliament around.

"Okay, well, I thought you'd like to know that the situation you ended is still dead, but a replacement scam has been initiated by some of Parliament's actual participants. We could work together on this?"

Then, from Rachel, a short nod. She looks away, starts to wrap her hair around her fingers, twisting and unravelling it as she talks. "This isn't just about me. It's about my brother. David. Dr David Crosby. He was a computer scientist who founded and ran a UK/Israeli data security start-up in Liverpool. They had a big contract with the UK Government. Something to do with message filtering." Clare notices Rachel's use of past tense.

"He killed himself just over a year ago."

"Oh, I'm so sorry," says Jake, "Can you talk about it?" He looks concerned and Clare realises she was watching two professional news gatherers both on their best game.

Rachel replies, "I don't, actually. You are now part of a handful of people who I've told - outside family, of course."

"So, what happened?" asks Clare, gently.

"No-one really knows. He drove to the coast and drowned himself. Wallasey. His body wasn't even in the sea. He was in a Marine Pool at Wallasey. His car was neatly parked but there wasn't even CCTV coverage of him arriving in the area.

"Wallasey? That's near Birkenhead?" asks Jake.

"Yes, in the Wirral, right where the Mersey turns into open sea."

"They wanted his body to be found, then?" says Jake.

"They?" queries Rachel.

"We'll, I'm guessing an open verdict," says Jake.

Clare notices water in Rachel's eyes.

"Jake, stop," she says.

Rachel turns to them both. She gently wipes away tears, "We journalists are a suspicious lot. I couldn't believe David would have just fallen into the water, which is what the coroner said."

She continues, "I received an email from him before I even knew he'd died. It said his security system had noticed some unusual messaging traffic from around Parliament. He suspected there was something untoward happening. He even attached a file, which was a log - all in computer-speak."

"Did you look into it?" asks Jake.

"I did at the time. No-one could work it out and I didn't want it to become a big thing, where I started to become the story. You, Jake, know how it is. My experts told me that the log seemed to imply that someone was setting up a new kind of lobbying operation,"

"Medusa mark III?" asks Jake, "Not again!"

"Well - At the time I linked the two events together. David's computer discovery and Lessiter's implication that there was well-funded clandestine lobbying operation at Westminster."

"Or is it just what you want to believe?" asks Jake.

"I wondered that too, but I didn't tell the experts looking at the computer logs anything about what Lessiter had told me."

Clare grimaces, "Hmm, but let's face it, Lessiter is not the most discreet of individuals."

"Agreed, but Lessiter seemed to be telling this story for the first time. I could tell that Hannah had not heard it before."

Rachel pauses, then continues. "The thing is it is very similar to what my brother had discovered. It makes me think that cutting one head from the serpent only reveals another one hiding behind."

"Rachel, can we think about this, please? I'll be able to give you an answer but it could take me a couple of days."

"Sure, that's fine. I've sat on this for a long time already. Knowing you were about to leave Parliament gave me a catalyst to act."

Clare smiles back at Rachel.

"I just wish we'd been able to be this frank sooner."

"I know, it's amazing the difference when someone isn't directly connected with the Westminster Bubble."

Clare looks at Jake, as if to say, 'time's up.' Jake gets the message and stands.

"Look, Rachel, it has been very pleasant to meet you today and I think you've put some interesting ideas in front of us both. I'm certain we'd have ways we could help, but you can understand that Clare needs time. After all, she was planning to leave Parliamentary duties today."

Rachel also stands. Clare and Jake can see her look of pleading for help, although she is too professional to ask for help directly.

"Okay, we'll see how this works out over the next few days. May I call you, in say three days?" she asks Clare.

"That's fine Rachel, I'll look forward to our conversation. Jake settles the bill and the three of them leave the Caffè, Rachel almost immediately hiring a cab for a fast get-away.

"You' coming around, and I'll call Bigsy so that we can talk?" suggests Jake.

Clare nods, "Good plan."

Cold beer and delivery pizza

By the time they reach Jake's, Bigsy is already there. He is sitting on the doorstep and stands as they approach.

"I thought you had a key?" asks Jake.

"I do, but I wasn't sure you'd remember," replies Bigsy, "Anyhow, I've only been here for a few minutes."

Jake opens the door and the three of them step into Jake's flat. Ground floor, with a large living room at the front, and a smaller kitchen and dining room at the back. Wooden table, metal fittings, industrial chic. A big industrial clock on the wall behind their heads

Without ceremony, they seat themselves around the dining table. Jake pulls three cold beers from the fridge.

"Okay, so what have you two been up to?" asks

Bigsy.

"We met with Rachel Crosby today. It was Clare's last day in the apartment."

"Oh, yes, I'd semi-forgotten. How did it go?" asked Bigsy.

"Fine, in terms of the move, less so in terms of the overall outcome," answered Clare.

"There's good reason for Clare to stay on longer," explains Jake.

They recount their meeting with Rachel to Bigsy.

Then, as they finish, there is a pause.

Bigsy breaks the silence, "It looks like you'll be staying on in Westminster for a while, Clare."

Jake nods and Clare gives a palpable sigh of relief. "Oh, that's great - I wondered if you thought I was mad to do this?"

"No, I guess we owe Rachel one for her help with the Medusa thing, and it also sounds as if she has some unresolved issues of her own linked with all of this," answered Bigsy.

"We'd better inform Christina too," says Jake, "She'll be back from Amsterdam tomorrow afternoon."

Clare looks at both Jake and Bigsy.

"We're forgetting one fundamental thing. I no longer have access to Parliament. My green badge and contracts all finished today."

"But has Andrew Brading already hired your replacement?" asks Bigsy, "Couldn't you say you'd prefer to stay on?"

"I guess that would be Serena's decision - she's the office manager, " answers Clare.

"Right - you must have her mobile number?" asks Jake, "Call her now, before events overtake us."

Clare stands, "I'm going into your living room. I hope that's okay?" she looks at Jake.

Jake nods, "What will you say?"

"I'll simply ask for my old job back!"

Clare walks out of the kitchen, along a short hallway and into the living room.

Bigsy looks at Jake.

"She's so well thought of, they'll be delighted," says Jake.

Ten minutes later, Jake had found three more bottles of beer, and Bigsy had ordered delivery pizza.

Clare reappears. She is smiling. "Job done! I'm back

in business. Serena was quite excited. She was going to tell Andrew Brading and Maggie Shannon tonight. I'd better check my phone is charged!"

"Best to call Rachel next," says Jake.

"What about your flatmates?" asks Bigsy, "Won't Lottie and Tessa think it a little strange when they see you in Parliament again?"

"They were next on my list. At least I've been able to tell them about my Apartment in Chelsea and they won't be at all surprised at my sudden change of direction!"

Jake walks back to the fridge. This time he returns with a bottle of Bollinger Brut and some pre-chilled champagne flutes.

"Ahah!" says Bigsy, "Good enough for Double-0-Seven, good enough for our clandestine operator!"

"Cheers, everyone," says Jake, "And congratulations to Clare on the start of another adventure!"

They clink glasses.

"Okay if I use your living room for a while to make some more phone calls?" asks Clare.

Back, once again

The next day, Clare had some of the feelings that she'd had on her very first day in Parliament. She'd called up Samantha, her sister, and explained about leaving and then not.

"Why am I not surprised," came Samantha's reply, "I guess you've some undercover reason for returning, too?"

Clare gave a light explanation that she might be helping someone but steered clear of any detail. She was aware of how leaky the whole network around Westminster was.

She arrived early, but and was surprised to see both Serena and Maggie already in the office. They looked pleased to see Clare, but almost immediately Maggie asks, "So what's the angle this time? – So that we can help you, of course!"

Clare answers, "There seems to be more clandestine lobbying. This time it is away from Andrew -- Thank

God - and apparently it is quite targeted."

"Well, I had a phone call from one of your supporters early this morning," says Serena, "From Amanda Miller. She said you didn't' know she was calling ahead, but that she wanted to underwrite that you'd have similar support to the last time."

Clare looks startled. Amanda Miller ran a department in SI6 - the security services - and they had worked together on a couple of assignments, with her associates from The Triangle. Amanda liked the ability to use reliable 'off books' people to assist with her investigations.

"No, you are right, I didn't have any knowledge of this, and I can't work out how Amanda would even know that I was coming back here!"

She thought back over her outgoing calls from Jake's. One must have been picked up. Jake, Lottie and Tessa, or Rachel. It had to be Rachel's phone that had been intercepted. A well-known investigative journalist with good access to Parliament. It had to be - but it was stranger that Rachel didn't realise.

She decides to meet Rachel in Parliament's cafe to warn her of a possible phone hack and texts Rachel to set it up.

Clare hurries through the underground tunnel to the Jubilee Café and to her surprise Rachel is already there, sitting at a corner table, which Clare reckons would have a good view of most of the room.

"Old habits?" she says as they meet, waving her arm around the room.

"Oh, I see what you mean. Just sometimes it is useful to see who is talking to whom. Case in point, that's the Energy secretary talking to his opposition number. There is probably some kind of a deal going down - one they want people to know about."

"I see, otherwise it would be somewhere far more discreet?" asks Clare.

"Yes, you have learned his place fast, Ms Crafts!" smiles Rachel.

"I wanted to warn you about something," says Clare, "I think you have been hacked."

Rachel looked interested, "How so?" she asks.

"I only told a handful of people about my staying on, yet by today everyone seems to know about it. I worked out that there can only be a few people who could be the source, however unwittingly, of the leak."

Rachel smiles, "Yes, that'd be my leaky phone," She delves into her voluminous Mulberry and plucks out a handset. "This one - my iPhone. Did I ever tell you I have an iPhone and a MyPhone? They can be very useful in situations like this."

Rachel rummages further into her bag and produced a second iPhone. This one was red.

"See, I have two phones. Only very few people ever make it to the red one."

"So, you knew we'd be overheard?" asks Clare.

"Intercepted, more like. This is how it stacks up. I'm an investigative reporter who stumbles across secrets. Who wants to know? Amanda Miller and her friends along at Vauxhall Cross. It's so much better when they discover a new tidbit. It keeps them comfortable thinking that they are monitoring me."

"But why now?"

"Despite the demise of Medusa, it is still a boom time for lobbyists. Although the Prime Minister pretends to squash lobbying, especially by Ministers and Members, he still knows what he is doing. Rush a Bill through and leave the edges ripe for a thousand unintended consequences. You only have to blend in the normal warp and weft of parliamentary business and then the actions of any specific MP disappear into a void of diary and note management: 'I can't remember. I don't recollect.' They are useful statements if ever anything approaches a Hearing."

Clare notices that Rachel looks tired.

"Let's just say that Duncan Melship gets that new

Ministerial post. Department for Transport Efficiency- DfTE. No one will have time to check his background credentials nor have much of a mind to do so. And anyway, they can soon float that DfTE is quite like DAFT, so here will be any number of puns and silly pictures flying around."

"I see, the usual thing where distraction is used as a cover-up," agrees Clare.

"Are you sure you haven't done this role before?" asks Rachel, "I mean before you turned up at Andrew's doorstep?"

"Well, it's handy because I know Duncan Melship quite well. My ex-flatmate Lottie is his Assistant and she invited me along to a few of his bashes," answers Clare.

"Hmm, you know about his - er - wandery hands?" asks Rachel, looking slightly surprised.

"Yes, and so does everyone else on the inside of Parliament," answers Clare, "But he does throw a good and rather lavish celebrity bash, and I can normally tell quite quickly whether it is worth staying."

Rachel points to her lanyard, "See the brown badge. That's what stops me from getting to most of those events. Your green one tells a whole different story."

"Yes, but you are savvy and know how to tap information, " said Clare, smiling, "And I'm sure you can expense the odd lunch or two? I guess some of those middle-aged men will be forming a line to get away from school dinners to have lavish lunch with a glamorous member of the fifth estate?"

Rachel laughs, "Yes, however harrowing the experience might be!" Then she gathers her Mulberry and the two phones. "Right, I'm moving now, but it is good to know that SI6 considered me worthy of intercepts. You'd better not tell Amanda about my second phone though."

Clare made like she was zipping her mouth.

"Always a pleasure," she says, "Although I guess we'd better not be seen together too much or someone will infer something."

"See, I knew you were good!" smiles Rachel as they hug and then Rachel leaves the Caffè.

Before Clare has a chance to move, there is a loud noise behind her, and she turns to see Lottie and Tessa giggling towards her.

"What are you hiding, Clare? You leave one day, return the next - typical Clare I might add," says Lottie.

"Then the very next day we see you with super-journalist/investigator Rachel Crosby. There has to be something going on?" adds Tessa.

"No, we were just catching up on the outcome from

that Medusa thing. All those MP's being persuaded to lobby because of their little indiscretions."

"It sounds like the whip system to me," says Lottie, "Men behind the men who vote, telling them how to think."

"Not always men," says Clare.

"No but mostly men as whips," says Lottie, "Except for Ann, Jacquie and Hilary over the years, maybe - but you get the picture."

"But have you heard the latest?" asks Lottie, "My MP Duncan Melship is to be the Secretary of State in the new Department for Transport Efficiency- DfTE. It's such a shame that the newspapers are already using headlines like 'DAFT Appointment of Melship to new role' and they are already calling him Daft Duncan. It is so unfair."

Clare senses the irony in Lottie's tone as she relays this information.

Tessa speaks, "But think of all the new parties! and with automobiles come even bigger celebrity personal appearances!"

"We are going to need a crash course in cars!" says Clare.

They all laugh and Tessa continues, "Everyone knows about Duncan Melship's parties and no-one wonders where he finds the money to throw them.

Now he has a whole new source."

Lottie says, "I'll wait for all of the new invitations for Duncan to speak and attend various functions. He will be sure to choose wisely."

"But back to the central question," says Tessa, "Clare, you are still working for Andrew Brading, but must have something else going on in parallel? What is it - you know we want to help."?

"All in good time," says Clare, "For now I want to ensure that Andrew Brading's next Bills get through the Commons in an unadapted form!"

Clare realises that she would need a cover story to tell Tessa and Lottie. She knows from experience they could be very persistent.

I'm in love with my car

The machine of a dream
Such a clean machine
With the pistons a pumpin'
And the hubcaps all gleam
When I'm holding your wheel
All I hear is your gear
With my hand on your grease gun
Oooh, it's like a disease, son

I'm in love with my car
Got a feel for my automobile
Get a grip on my boy-racer rollbar
Such a thrill when your radials squeal
Told my girl I'd have to forget her
Rather buy me a new carburettor
So, she made tracks, saying
"This is the end now"
"Cars don't talk back"
"They're just four-wheeled friends, now"

When I'm holding your wheel
All I hear is your gear
When I'm cruisin' in overdrive
Don't have to listen
To no run-of-the-mill talk jive

Roger Meddows Taylor

Triangle office

The next morning Clare made her way on the Jubilee Line around to the offices of The Triangle. These were situated along the South Bank in an area known as Hay's Galleria.

They had acquired a small space in the property after the destruction of their prior offices in Hoxton. The new building was well-equipped and conveniently situated for their trips around London and was not too far from any of their apartments.

'Hiya," said Bigsy as Clare walked in, "The gang's all here!"

She looked over and saw Jake talking to Christina, who had been a late addition to the original trio of Jake, Clare and Bigsy. Christina was a star acquisition - literally - she had been the main singer for a pop act. She also possessed a complex background, being borne in Iceland, but later recruited to the GRU in Russia and trained in Saint Petersburg and Bulgaria. After many missions, she had bought her way out, but everyone knew that the Kremlin would still regard her as a deep asset in London.

"Hey babe, " said Christina to Clare. They hugged, "You are staying on? There's still more to do at Parliament. - Surely not?"

They both laughed. Jake called them into a glass meeting room. It was a 'Bigsy special', which he'd set up so that no radio waves would be able to get inside.

"Westminster bubble-schmubble. It won't beat this one," said Jake.

"Okay, now we are secure, I can tell you what I know," said Clare.

"Rachel tipped me off that there is still some kind of influence strategy running around Parliament. She thinks it is the reason her brother David was killed a year ago. It seems to be somehow independent from the Medusa set-up, which used simple blackmail to get what they wanted. This seems to be more monetarily operated."

"I'll ask around my contacts," said Christina, "But I doubt even the Kremlin would try the same thing for the third time!"

Jake added, "And Duncan Melship has just taken up a new position as a Minister - for something called Department for Transport Efficiency. I can't help wonder if there is a connection?"

Tessa added, "And Melship knows nothing about cars. Except how to sit in the back of them."

Clare shook her head, "That would be almost too convenient, given my link with Lottie, who is his Research Assistant! More interesting is that Amanda knew about me staying on, and I can only conclude that MI6 somehow hacked Rachel's phone to intercept this information."

"It is a clever hack, too, to be able to find the exact usable information so quickly. It seems to me that someone has been watching Rachel for a while," said Christina.

"We should ask Amanda," said Jake, "I don't think she'll have forgotten how helpful we have been to her in the past."

With that, Jake picked up his phone and dialled Amanda Miller's cell phone.

"Foreign ringtone," he said, "She must travelling,"

"Oh, Hello Amanda! I hope you are well?"

They could all hear the background of Amanda talking, but Jake didn't put it on speaker, so they only heard half the conversation.

"Really? I've never been there - Helsinki."

"Yes, yes, in our office, together."

"We wanted to ask you something..."

"Okay, no, we will."

"So, Clare had been asked to stay on in Parliament. But we think you knew that already. We think there is still some untoward lobbying occurring. Not connected with the previous scams. We wondered how you knew so quickly. We think you found out from Rachel?"

"Indirectly?"

"Could it have been by your phone intercept?"

"And why the interest? Are you following this one too?"

"You are?"

"Proposition? I'll need to explain it to the others."

He listened for a few minutes whilst Amanda explained her idea.

"Everyone. It's a similar setup to last time - working with Amanda - Are we all in?"

Bigsy and Christina nodded and Clare raised both her thumbs, all to signify 'yes'.

"Okay, it's a yes from us. Next time we call we'd

better all be secure."

"Oh, you are secure? Of course, you would be!"

"*Moi-Moi*, Amanda, *Moi-Moi!*"

Jake turned back to the others. "I should really have put that on speaker phone, but I didn't want to put her off."

He looked at Clare. "You were right about Amanda tracing Rachel's phone. And she is interested in this new form of sleaze. Amanda thinks it is something that a few MPs have invented by themselves. Not a state actor in sight, although she thinks it could be a corporate player. However, she wants to nip it in the bud before it blossoms into something unsightly. Amanda says that the whips are useless on this situation. They only want to deal in their own forms of moral suasion, not have ones imposed from outside sources. Self-interest at its finest."

Christina added, "And if your so-called corporate actors discover that this is happening, then they will want to leverage the situation. You have to assume they are in the picture somewhere."

Clare grinned, she looked happy that she had guessed most of it.

Jake spoke, "I've an idea that could help us move this forward. Remember I used to work for Street?"

Clare nodded.

Jake continued, "And that we did items about 'flash-boys' who drove fancy cars? You remember, like Darren Collins? Well, our car expert there was a chap called Tony Brooklands. He knows everything about cars. We used to be great buddies. I could get him to come over to the office and to provide us with a briefing."

"But will he know the kind of thing we are interested in?" asked Clare., "I don't want someone who is a car-bore. You know - someone who can tell us how many horsepower we can get from a Mini-Cooper and likes watching middle aged blokes drive multi-coloured sports cars around racetracks. You know the kind of fella. They are often seen in bars."

"Oh yes, like Toad of Toad Hall? No - I'd say that Tony is about as far from Toad as you can get. Leave it with me."

Lady driver

Duncan Melship was delighted. He had expected to stay resolutely on the backbenches, but this was now his chance! A Secretary of State. He'd be on news segments. He'd probably get some TV spots on 'The Answers' and maybe even some fun appearances on those alternative TV shows. And a Jaguar. Being driven around in a Jaguar. No worries about where to park and always being picked up by his driver.

"Can you check that for me?" he asks Lottie, "If possible, I'd like a female driver for my Jaguar. I'll be one of the top 20 MPs after this so I don't think I should settle for a Pool driver."

Lottie looks at some of the new policy documents in preparation. Somewhat starkly it was presenting the new MP code of conduct for travel.

"It says you'll be using an electric car unless on a very long journey. The PM has also let it be known that it is best for you to have your private vehicle as an electric too. He wants to avoid negative publicity.

In fact, he wants this done quickly so you can issue some immediate positive press releases."

She handed across an A4 sheet. It listed the top 10 all-electric vehicles, with notes next to each one about their country of origin. It looked as if he would have to settle for a Sunderland manufactured e-car instead. It didn't have a very English sounding name and Melship thought it was from the far east.

"Hold on though. Don't Jaguar make an electric car? An SUV?" Asked Melship.

"They make hybrids," explains Lottie, "They are on another list entirely."

"So, what is the difference?" asks Melship.

"They still have petrol or diesel engines inside," explains Lottie, scanning a car brochure from the internet, "They are only partly electric."

"Hmm," says Melship, " I can see there are some downsides with all this climate saving,"

"I think we'd better get you briefed on recent car developments," answers Lottie.

Above the fold

The next day, Duncan Melship makes the newspapers. He was standing next to a plain-looking electric car, surrounded by manufacturer-supplied smiling, pretty women. The announcement described his new post and that he had already changed his Ministerial car to an all-electric model and had plans to do the same with his private vehicle.

"It's a triumph!" says Melship to Lottie, "Look I'm above the fold on several of the papers and the lead story in a couple! And I've already had several helpful people contact me about transport infrastructure briefings."

Lottie looks at the list of offers. It was like a rollcall of the major manufacturers. She has never been this close to blatant lobbying before.

"But I think we have to turn these down," she says to Melship, "They are a little close to briefing jollies."

"Obviously some of them are trying to take a chance,

but I've noticed that several mention that they could provide briefings at the upcoming auto industry Expo. Obviously, I'd need support if I went to that and it is entirely within my purview."

Lottie's mind struggles with this idea. "I suppose if you arrange your own transport and then overtly choose the specific sessions then it might work. Where is it?"

Melship smiles, "Oh, I think it is abroad somewhere - Let me look again, oh yes, it says Gstaad, Switzerland."

Lottie asks, "But that's the Swiss Alps. Most people go there for skiing or to be jet-setters?"

"I know, but the car industry is using it to make a point. There is a main car show in Geneva and then a special satellite Expo two and a half hours away, where they show the latest SUVs and long-range electric cars."

"Does the PM know about this?" asks Lottie.

"Oh, I told him I was going to Geneva on a fact-finding visit. He was entirely supportive. It is accurate as well, my flights are in and out of Geneva, but I'm being met and driven to the Expo from the main show."

Lottie realised that Melship was taking full advantage of his new position.

"Oh yes and they have asked me to present something at the Gstaad Expo. I'll need your help with that."

Colour drains from Lottie's face.

Amanda calls

Back at Parliament, Clare's mobile rang. 'Amanda,' it said.

She picked up. "Hi Amanda," she could hear the soundscape of an airport.

"Sorry, I've just been through security," said Amanda, "But this is my best chance to call you."

"And where are you today?" asked Clare.

"On my way back, via Stockholm, then to LHR. I should be back to T4 by around 8 pm, " answers Amanda, "Look we've been delving into the lobby situation. There's nothing obvious this time. The biggest move I can see is around that new appointment - you know - Duncan Melship to be Secretary of State for - what is it? - Department for Transport Efficiency."

"Yes, we had noticed this as well," answers Clare.

"Well, it sounds as if there's a couple of big players ready to pitch in," continues Amanda, "They have offered Melship various trips to a Swiss Car Expo but he has turned them down. He wants to be seen to have made his own way to Geneva."

"Geneva?" asks Clare.

"Well not exactly. The main briefings are in Geneva but the electric Car Expo is another two and a half hours away in Gstaad. We can get you tickets to both parts of the Exposition, but you'll need to make your own flight and accommodation arrangements. It's not until the New Year, when the Swiss snow is pretty much guaranteed.

"Never a dull moment!" answers Clare.

"And no links back to me," asks Amanda above the sound of plane announcements.

Clare had just hung up the call when Lottie appeared in the doorway of the office.

"Lottie?" exclaims Clare, "Wow - a visit! It must be serious."

Lottie looks at Clare, "I need some help," she says, "I think you can provide it, only I wouldn't usually ask but this is a big deal for Duncan and I don't want to mess up."

"What is it?" asks Clare, "Come on sit down." They were alone in Andrew Brading's office.

"Duncan Melship made that Press Release about using an electric car today. I talked to him some more and it is evident that he knows next to nothing about cars and I'm afraid he will say something ill-advised."

"I need some kind of briefing so that I can keep him on the right track until he goes to a trade show in a few weeks' time."

"Lottie, this is your lucky day! My company is just arranging a briefing from Tony Brooklands the automobile journo. Jake knows him well and we are running it from our office. Why don't you come on over? You can meet the gang and you'll be bound to pick up some useful knowledge."

Lottie answered, "The thing is, we need the Department to be squeaky clean - no lobbying or bribery or anything. You should know this from that last business you were mixed up in."

"Lottie, we'll be squeaky clean. Don't worry! Just come along and take away as much knowledge as you can hold. You know what - bring Tessa as well so you've a good alibi and witness."

Tony Brooklands

Jake had called his ex-colleague and Tony duly arrived at The Triangle offices, and to Clare's relief didn't look like a typical middle-aged motor journalist. Before she sized him up fully, Christina had already whispered in Clare's ear, "He's got the body of a Formula 1 driver, trust me."

Lottie and Tessa had both come along. As well as the electric car briefing, they were both intrigued to see the other place Clare worked, and to meet some of her colleagues.

Lottie smiles across to Tony and then he gave a dazzling smile back across all of them. Tessa whispers, "Clare, you are always full of nice surprises."

Tony could sense the attention and playfully removes his leather jacket.

"Okay now, Jake tells me you need to know something about electric cars? Would someone like to explain?"

"We are helping some people in the government," explains Clare blandly, "but need to be further ahead of the marketplace in terms of our understanding. We are hoping you can provide us with that briefing as well as any personal opinions you might hold about the options."

"Ah, okay; Jake said it would be like a brain dump," he breezily replies, looking towards Jake, "It is lucky that I was talking to the Society of Motor Manufacturers on this exact topic. 'E-cars and their infrastructure' - I brought the slides." He opens a small MacBook and looks for somewhere to plug it into. Bigsy steps forward with a small box and connects everything together.

"These slides are not confidential, nor are they proprietary, but I'd ask you not to pass them on further," Tony begins.

"Say, if you want to find out about the automobile industry you should all go to the Geneva Car Fair. It is supposed to be 'Trade Only' but I'm sure that someone with Jake's resourcefulness can get you all passes."

"We are ahead of you, for once," says Jake, "We are already ticketed!"

"Wow, I haven't even got my ticket yet - but I guess I'll see you all there!" replies Tony.

"Okay Slide One - A Summary" He presses a button and the slide advances.

"Let's remind ourselves: The UK has committed to Net-Zero carbon emissions by 2050."

He continues, "Transport is currently the largest emitting sector of the UK economy, responsible for 27% of total UK greenhouse gas emissions. Within this, cars are responsible for 55% of transport emissions. The UK Government has just appointed a Duncan Melship to lead the initiatives around this area. He heads a new Department called Department for Transport Efficiency- DfTE. You've probably seen it mentioned in the news over the last couple of days."

They all nod, realising that Jake had not told Tony who they worked for.

Tony continues, "Electric vehicles (EVs, sometimes known as Ultra Low Emission Vehicles (ULEVS)) offer one method of reducing emissions, with the Committee for Climate Change (CCC) suggesting that all new vehicles should be electrically propelled by 2035, if not sooner, to achieve the Net Zero target."

"You'd better explain what an EV and a Hybrid is," says Jake.

Tony smiles and puts up the next slide.

"What are EVs? EVs run, either partially or wholly,

on electricity, stored on board the vehicle in batteries or produced from hydrogen. Whilst cars represent 92% of the 432,000 ULEVS licensed (1.1% of all licensed vehicles) at the end of 2020, there are also electric motorcycles, taxis, buses, vans, and heavy goods vehicles.

"The market for EVs is immature, yet growing, with 8.5% of UK registered vehicles ULEVs in 2020. Meanwhile, only 1.8% of used car sales, responsible for approximately 80% of transactions, involved alternatively fuelled vehicles."

And we'd like to know what the government is doing to support all of this?" asks Lottie.

Tony smiles again, "You are a good audience and know all the right questions to ask," He flicks to the next slide.

"Government measures in support of EVs: There have been a variety of strategies employed over the past decade to encourage the uptake of EVs. Since 2011, the Government have supported EV ownership through the plug-in grant scheme. Additionally, the Government plans to ban the sale of new diesel and petrol cars and vans from 2030, whilst only fully zero-emission vehicles will be sold from 2035. This will require significantly increased battery numbers, opening up the potential for the UK to develop battery production facilities."

"And batteries are still a big issue?" asks Clare.

"Yes, UK can't make enough, the technology is like a phone battery and runs down. The last 20% is difficult to charge and they degrade with use, maybe with a life of 5 to 8 years. At present, they also make up to between 40% and 50% of the cost of an EV."

Christina adds, "An example to generate sales: In Russia, the Russian government offers subsidies to manufacturers of electric vehicles and batteries to co-finance the costs associated with the construction of plants and to special investment contracts. Electric cars can drive free of charge on toll roads. As a further incentive, electric cars are to be included in concessionary loan and leasing programmes."

Clare speaks, "That seems strange, with Russia presiding over some of the world's largest oil resources?

Christina replies, "Moscow's push for electric mobility is simply driven by the global market. Like the way Russia plays the energy markets. It is the irony of the way the Russians nowadays like to follow the money."

Tony continues, "Well, getting back to the UK, the Government produced the 'Transport Decarbonisation Plan,' to cover all road vehicles as well as the rail, aviation and freight sectors. I guess that will be an ongoing project for some time."

Lottie looks at her notes.

"What about electricity demand?" she asks.

Tony smiled, "Now you've caused me to go out of sequence! Just a moment." He smiles as he fiddles with the computer, "Here we are - Electricity Demand: Currently, road transport uses approximately 500 Tera Watt hours of energy.

"Although improved efficiencies may reduce this, the shift from petrol and diesel cars could increase electricity demand by 200 Tera Watt hours. That's a lot! The use of smart charging or vehicle to grid technologies could significantly lower peak demands to be approximately only 8% greater than current peak power draw."

"So are EVs the silver bullet then?" asks Lottie, "Will they help save the planet from carbon's environmental impact?"

Tony answers, "No slide for this, but my opinion...EVs improve local air quality and reduce point-of-use emissions; however, they are not net-zero when considering the whole life cycle of a vehicle and its sub- components, as well as the particulate matter emitted on-street."

"Further, batteries for EVs can require rare elements such as lithium and cobalt, which has raised environmental and ethical issues in countries where these elements are mined. There are also concerns over 'peak lithium' and future shortages constraining growth in the EV market."

Tony continues, "It brings me to my next topic: Why do we need Electric Vehicles? "

He was back into his slide sequence.

"As of 2019, transport was the largest-emitting sector of the UK economy at 122 mega tonnes carbon dioxide equivalent (MtCO2e), accounting for 27% of total UK greenhouse gas (GHG) emissions. Of this, cars represented the greatest proportion of emissions within the transport sector in 2019, accounting for 55% of transport emissions."

"So, all of these stories about cows and methane and suchlike?" asks Jake.

Tony continues, "The story and statistics are very garbled on livestock. Not to mention the transport lobby's effect. Past and current governments have supported measures to encourage uptake of EVs as they can contribute to a wide range of transport policy goals. For example, EVs can help to improve air quality, reduce noise pollution and support efforts to reduce carbon emissions."

"So now there is a greater push for electric vehicles, like the 'dash for diesel', back when Gordon Brown was the PM?" asks Jake.

Tony nods, "Exactly. Millions of Britons switched to drive very polluting vehicles, while being told it was less damaging to the environment. Emissions of nitrogen oxides and particulates were linked to respiratory difficulties, heart attacks and lung cancer. It was - is - an unsurfaced scandal."

Then he continues, "But beyond the diesel dash, the importance of EVs was outlined in updated advice on meeting the net zero 2050 target, published in May 2019 by the Committee on Climate Change (CCC) – the statutory advisors on emissions reductions for Government. This said that the market for electric cars and vans should scale up to 100% of new sales by 2035 at the latest (and ideally by 2030) to meet the net zero target."

"Can we believe any of this, given the government's abject performance on diesels?" asks Clare.

"When it is all couched in terms of 'pathways' and other management speak, I'd say it was dubious."

Christina adds, "What is it they say? 'It always works in PowerPoint?'"

Tony continues, "So, to my point, under the older 80% reduction target by 2050, the CCC advised a 'least cost' pathway would need 60% of all new cars and vans sold to be electric by 2030. Management consultancy speak if ever I heard it."

"And don't forget, although electric vehicles offer "clear benefits" for local air quality due to zero exhaust emissions at street level, they still emit particulate matter from road, tyre and brake wear. This means EVs cannot entirely eliminate issues of air pollution in cities."

"Further, they do not address wider issues, such as urban sprawl, inactive lifestyles, or congestion, which may increase due to reduced operational costs of motoring. The CCC has recommended that if the UK is to meet the 2050 net zero target, 100% of new vehicle sales should be electrically propelled by 2035 at the latest (and ideally by 2030)."

"So, has someone got a number in an envelope in a drawer?" asks Jake, smiling.

"You'll have to ask the new man, Duncan Melship, although I've never seen him in any remote connection with the automobile industry up to this point," answers Tony.

"As an example, progress in reducing emissions in the transport sector has been slow. In 2018 the average CO2 emissions of newly registered vehicles was 124.9 grams per kilometre (g/km).

"This is down from 178.8 g/km in 2001 and represents a decrease of around 30%. Between 2001 and 2018 the average CO2 emissions of newly registered vehicles were falling year on year although this then began to rise again from mid-2016. "

"But were some of those numbers faked?" asks Lottie, "Remember the various car scandals about rigging the system to show lower emissions that were actually occurring?"

Tony nods, "Sadly so, and the Americans are running all kinds of class actions about the misrepresentation."

Drily he adds, "And I'm not sure all that many people study the emissions when they are buying their next car. More to do with capacity for ferrying the kids to school or looking good in the car park."

"This is good stuff," says Lottie, who had been taking copious notes, "Can we get your slides too?"

Tony looks at Jake, "I guess so, although I'd need to anonymise them first. But we are on to the next piece. The Road to Zero."

Road to Zero

Tony continues, "Way back in 2009, the Labour Government published its ULEV strategy. It said it would provide £20 million "seed money" to support the development of lead cities and regions in building the necessary charging infrastructure to help increase consumer confidence that would make ultra-low carbon vehicles viable. The Strategy also expected the private sector ultimately to take the lead in infrastructure provision.

"Then the Labour manifesto for the 2010 General Election promised to 'ensure there are 100,000 electric vehicle charging points by the end of the next Parliament'."

Tony grimaces, "It's bunkum, of course. The stats to the end of 2021, show that there were around 48,000 charging points on 28,000 devices at 18,000 locations. Like with everything else, the government can blame the pandemic."

"What happened after that? That all seems to be Labour government policy?" asks Lottie.

"Enter the Coalition," says Tony, " They committed to 'mandate a national recharging network for electric and plug-in hybrid vehicles'. In the June 2011 EV infrastructure strategy, they said the approach was not to mandate 'a ChargePoint on every corner'. Rather, it said most of the recharging is likely to take place at home and at work, so an extensive public recharging infrastructure would be under-utilised and uneconomic.

Tony continues, "Labour said at the time that this represented a renege on the Coalition's commitment to a 'national charging network.' However, others, including manufacturers of electric vehicles, supported the Government's claim that most charging would be done at home or in the workplace and that the need for public recharging points was therefore limited. I happen to think they missed the long-distance driving aspect with this convenient simplification."

Tony smiles, "So then comes the humorously titled Road to Zero strategy."

"Talking Heads anyone?" says Jake, and he quietly sang

"We're on a road to nowhere
  Come on inside
   Takin' that ride to nowhere
   We'll take that ride"

"I know, the consultants they used for this strategy were having a laugh, weren't they? No wonder it is suspiciously low in the mix," replies Tony.

He continues, "The Government published its Road to Zero Strategy in 2018. It shows how the government intends to support the transition to zero emission road transport and reduce emissions from conventional vehicles during the transition. The strategy is 'long term in scope and ambition, considering the drivers of change, opportunities and risks out to 2050 and beyond'. It set out several new measures, including to phase out the sale of petrol and diesel vehicles, and the rollout of a charging infrastructure."

"But isn't that kicking the 2010 objective of 100,000 charging points further down the road?" asks Jake.

Tony answers, "Well spotted, and that's not the end of it. In March 2020 the Government issued a 'Decarbonising Transport: Setting the Challenge' report which details strategies to decarbonise transport, including those for road-based vehicles."

He continues, "It went on to say, '...we do not currently know the optimal path for delivering a decarbonised transport network. We, therefore, intend to work with business, academics, researchers and innovators, environmental NGOs and the wider public over 2020 to design the package of decarbonisation policies...'. Another kick of the can."

"Predictable, " says Clare. Lottie and Tessa both nod.

"Buying time," says Tessa.

Jake comments, "Buying time...Look at the time! We've been going for a couple of hours!"

Tony says, "Okay then, my final thought...Then a November 2020 paper confirmed that the Government would pursue a two-phased approach: Step 1 sees the phase-out date for the sale of new petrol and diesel cars and vans brought forward to 2030; and Step 2 sees all new cars and vans be fully zero emission at the tailpipe from 2035. The announcement said that hybrids could continue to be sold between 2030 and 2035 'if they have the capability to drive a 'significant distance' with zero emissions and this will be defined through consultation.' "

Tony smiles, "This is thirsty work; how about we adjourn to the pub and continue in a more relaxed format?"

Jockey full o' bourbon

Edna million in a drop-dead suit
Dutch pink on a downtown train
Two-dollar pistol but the gun won't shoot
I'm in the corner on the pouring rain

Yellow sheets on a Hong Kong bed
Stazybo horn and a slingerland ride
To the carnival is what she said
A couple hundred dollars makes it dark inside

Hey little bird, fly away home
Your house is on fire, your children alone
Hey little bird, fly away home
Your house is on fire, children alone

Tom Waits

Whiskey Sour

Clare arrives at the office the next morning with a sore head. She knew Jake could drink and normally Clare would be able to keep up, but this time the Whiskey sours had found their way through her defences.

It had been Tony's idea, although she soon realised, he couldn't even take the stuff he was suggesting. They had to pour him into a taxi at about nine-thirty in the evening, but then Jake had suggested 'one more for the road'.

If it was any consolation, she had remembered Lottie and Tessa were worse than her. The concoction of whiskey, lemon juice, sugar, and a dash of egg white with red wine floated on top, was ultimately lethal.

She sits down in a chair in the office and certain that her brain is suspended in alcohol which was taking more time to settle. She looks in the drawer and finds a pack of paracetamol, from which she dutifully takes a couple.

Her phone rings: it is Lottie.

"Hiya Babe," Lottie says, "Thank you so much for yesterday! It was great to get so much information so quickly."

Clare is surprised that Lottie sounds so chirpy after such an evening.

"My pleasure - we were drinking from the firehose, that's for sure."

"Yes, until it turned into boosted Whiskey!" says Lottie, "You know something? Tessa is a wreck this morning. I don't think she'll even go to work. She was huddled up on the sofa with 'Friends' on the telly when I left. I think it's the congeners or something."

"Oh yes, that thing about don't drink dark liquids; I remember that from my Uni days."

"And I remembered to drink about a pint of water when I got back. I tried to persuade Tessa but she was singing '99 Luftballon' in German - and making some of the original Nena moves!"

"Oh dear," said Clare, suddenly realising she was in better shape that she could have been. Although Lottie had certainly won on this occasion.

"Also, a quick 'heads up' from me that when you log on, you'll see the rumpus that Duncan has caused.

He's asking your MP Andrew for some assistance. Anyway - Later Babes!" And Lottie was gone.

Just at that moment, the door to the office opened. Serena appeared, "Oh. What happened? You look somewhat fragile. Almost into 'hair of the dog' territory, I'd say."

"Well spotted. I had rather an evening of it with some boys. They were drinking Sours."

"Oh, I've had the same with Singapore slings. Once experienced, but never forgotten. Look, have you seen the odd request from Duncan Melship? - He's passed it along to The State Secretary for Internal Affairs because he thinks he could save the day with it. It's the Aberdeen Pop-Up Chargers."

Clare has no idea what Serena is talking about.

Aberdeen Pop up chargers

To: Secretary of State for Internal Affairs

Andrew,

Here's an interesting idea, maybe our departments could work together to come up with something like this across the UK?

Duncan

Secretary of State for Department for Transport Efficiency- DfTE

Attachment: (Article)

Aberdeen installs pop-up EV chargers in pilot project ahead of 2030 ban on new petrol and diesel cars

Along Aberdeen's Union Street, two businessmen in suits stride along the street avoiding a slower moving assembly of tourists with wheely bags. The suitcases roll over a row of electric vehicle chargers, and the tourists barely notice their existence.

Unlike bulkier on-street chargers, which draw complaints for clogging up pavements, these "pop up" devices only appear when activated using an app. "A lot of people walk past they don't realise they are there," said Angus Crombie, corporate fleet manager at Aberdeen city council, which is involved in a £5.2m project to test 36 pop-up chargers throughout the city.

Whether the UK will have sufficient charging facilities to meet the government's 2030 ban on new petrol and diesel cars and vans has recently become a subject of deep concern among MPs and policymakers. Aberdeen was chosen for this new initiative because of its close associations with North Sea oil.

The government has already confirmed legislation to ensure that all new homes are built with a charging point but EV experts say the bigger hurdle will be providing sufficient facilities for the estimated 8m-plus households that do not have access to a driveway in which to install their own device.

More than 10 times the current number of public devices, estimated at more than 25,000, would be needed by the end of the decade, warned the Competition and Markets Authority in July.

MPs also said in a damning report in May that they were "not convinced" ministers had "sufficiently thought through" how to expand charging infrastructure "at the pace required."

In 2019, Scotland agreed a 2045 net zero emissions target, five years ahead of the wider UK 2050 deadline.

With projects such as the pop-up EV chargers, Aberdeen has become something of a laboratory to learn how cities can meet the 2030 ban. The council said it had already installed sufficient public facilities to charge almost 10 per cent of the cars and vans passing through the city.

The same percentage for the rest of the UK falls to just 1.9 per cent. But it becomes difficult for local authorities to understand how much costly infrastructure is needed and in which locations, particularly as the technology was changing so rapidly.

EV charging provision is not a statutory duty for local authorities and councils' enthusiasm and skills for the task can vary wildly, according to Robert McHenry, head of e-strategy at Metropolix, a consultancy involved in the pop-up chargers project.

"Because EV chargers are new, they find a different home in every local authority. In some local authorities, it's the fleet section. Some places it's the highways team, in some places it's the sustainability team," said McHenry.

Private companies have engaged in an early battle for market share. Major oil companies have offered to install tens of thousands of on-street chargers in the UK by 2025. One oil major has offered to assist local authorities in England with their share of installation costs to accelerate the rollout. The move was seen by analysts as part of a "land grab" by energy and utilities for prime charging locations, which tend to be in large cities and wealthier urban locations, leaving charging "deserts" in other areas, such as north-west England.

Even though it was "really hard to make money at the moment" from charging networks, said McHenry, companies were "positioning themselves" to control prime locations. "In 10 years', time when the numbers of EVs go up that's worth a lot of money and they are in control of the assets."

A spokesperson for the Department for Transport Efficiency believes charging provision should be included in council's statutory duties, and funding for specialist "charging officers" should be part of future settlements between central government and local authorities. Councils should "bundle" packages of charging locations to ensure that private networks do not pick off prime areas and leave rural and underprivileged communities unserved, according to the group.

The CMA found in its July report that, of 5,700 on-street charge points in place in the UK, only 1,000 were outside London. Drivers' costs and the way in which charging is paid for, often requiring different apps or cards, varies wildly between networks.

Experts fear this could become a barrier to further take-up of electric vehicles. The CMA warned that "local monopolies" of charging networks could also develop "if left unchecked."

But McHenry believes fears about the number of public chargers needed are overblown. Secretary of State for Internal Affairs research suggests half of drivers use their car so little they typically would only need to fully charge their vehicle twice a month. A 'Clear Streets' campaign spokesperson William Dacre said, "People often imagine that what we need is rows of chargers along every street in which cars are parked. The reality is EVs don't need charging that often. We don't need a charge point outside everybody's home."

Clare giggles as she reaches the end of the article. It was helping her lift the fog from her brain.

"Boys' toys?" asks Serena, "Or a practical solution?"

"More things to go wrong," answers Clare, "Even the hire-bikes in London have their share of mechanical, electrical and payment failures. Imagine that when the meters are underground and must be powered to the surface with electric motors. How many pigeons will get inside? And rodents? Oh sorry, I think it is the hangover speaking."

Serena smiles, "No, I happen to think you are right. Putting the charge points under crowded pavements means that they are not in the way when they are not in use. Imagine the same procession of tourists with wheeled luggage traversing the street when the units have surfaced and there are cables connected to cars. A pure case of first-level thinking.

"So, we will need to manage the new-found enthusiasm of Duggie."

Clare realises it was this that Lottie had been warning her about. She was thankful for the extra knowledge imparted yesterday by Tony.

Travel brochures

Lottie was in Duncan Melship's office. He was avidly reading a couple of travel brochures.

"They sent these with some admission tickets for a couple of special events," he says.

"Do you notice that they have kept the business section of the itinerary separated from the leisure section?"

Lottie smiles as she realises why this has been done.

"I guess it makes it easy to submit a business case for attending," she says, "without referencing the Gala Ball, the ski chalet bases for attendees and the sports car drive to the venue. Come to think of it, it doesn't even mention the fireworks display."

"No, none of them!" says Melship, "I see they are doing one display over the lake in Geneva and another one against the mountains, complete with a torchlight procession!"

"And each of the tables for the Gala Ball is hosted by a celebrity. There's dozens: film, music, sport, even television."

Lottie looks through the list. The tables were priced at different levels according to the celebrity hosting it. She wondered whether Melship had even noticed this aspect. Then she spotted a name she recognised. Jallie T. She knew Jallie T. was a friend of Clare's and Christina's.

"Leave it with me," says Lottie, "I'm sure I can - er - explain our various selections. Just don't be too extravagant or you'll get picked up by the paparazzi."

Lottie was already dialling Clare.

"Hiya Clare, I remember your friend Christina was a pop star. Didn't she tour with Jallie once?"

Clare replies, "Yes, we both did, all around the world: Russia, Japan, the USA, I'd say she became a lifelong friend of both of us!"

Lottie sighs, "You are doing it again, Clare, showing me that you have an ever-increasing list of surprises. Can I ask for some more help?"

"Sure, my hangover is now diminishing!

"Well, Duncan Melship has been invited to a trade fair in Switzerland by several car manufacturers. He wants to go, and there's a whole hospitality programme to the side of the main event."

Clare laughs, "So it's a jolly really?"

"Duncan is overwhelmed with offers at present but seems to have his heart set on this particular session in Geneva and Gstaad."

"Gstaad? For a car show? Up all those mountains?"

"Don't even ask. But anyway, there is a Gala Ball at the event in Gstaad, which it seems only the great and the good get to attend. It has been set up with hosted tables and one of the hosts is Jallie T."

"Oh, I get it, you want me to fix it to get Melship on her table?"

"And that means me as well, please?"

"Let me call Jallie and see what is possible."

"Oh - Thank you, thank you, thank you!" says Lottie.

Another Table

Clare was in a taxi on her way back to her apartment. She called Jallie T and notices the foreign ring tone.

Clare speaks, "Hi Jallie - I hope you are well. Touring I guess?"

Jallie explains, "Yay- Clare! Yes, I'm in Brussels, touring with my band, mainly smaller venues, the tee-shirt listing looks more impressive than the actuality of it. Here- I'll read from one of the tee-shirts.

"Flekkefjord, Drammen and Sarpsborg in Norway, then then Switzerland to Berne, Rorschach, Appenzell, then to Germany, Stuttgart, Wuppertal, Hamburg, Frankenberg, Berlin, Rosenberg, Tübigen - wait for it - In Jan's Toolshed, then a bunch in Austria including Graz and Vienna and then back for the last few in Germany but finishing up in Brussels. It's been quite a trip. We'll be back at home for Christmas!"

"Whew, work it, babe."

"I know, but there's something to be said for those big arenas that you and Erebus could command with Christina. I think we'd have the equivalent of the first ten audiences in one of the arenas!"

"Anyway, I've called to ask you a favour?"

"Anything..."

"Well, I don't know if you know that you are doing a celeb appearance at a Car Fair yet? In Switzerland - Geneva/Gstaad?"

"Oh yes, I do actually, one of the car makers has said they will lend me a car for a year in return for attending it."

"Well, my favour is to ask you to request to sit with a few specific people."

"Hold on a minute, let me talk it over with Rishi, he's the band's manager nowadays."

"Rishi?" replies Clare, "Are you two...you know?"

"Yes, as a matter of fact, after that long tour with Christina, we got together. Darius was complaining anyway about his loss of control and we agreed to swap Rishi as the new Manager. He's very switched on - as well as very cute!"

"Okay, Okay, I guess he is within earshot?

"You got it. He's saying to me that they will be bound to want something in return. Wait a minute...He's suggesting that you offer Christina as another celeb on another table...That'd be amazing."

Clare considers it for about half a second. "Oh yes, we'll do it, and I'll be along as her PA or something. It would be brilliant to meet again."

"I'll start practicing Nirvana numbers again! We could do that 'teenage spirit' thing if they will let us!"

"Okay, I'll send over the details in an email, and send my love to Rishi - it will be great to see you all again!"

A visit to Lottie

Now, with the table deal confirmed, Clare decides
to drop around to Lottie's office. It is in Portcullis
House, the more modern part of the Parliament
buildings, and it takes her around ten minutes to
walk across.

She walks into an office bedecked with Xmas lights
and a few cards pinned to one of the notice boards.

Lottie looka surprised and a couple of the other
assistants look up when they see Clare, who was
recognisable as the Research Assistant to Andrew
Brading.

Lottie walks across the small office toward Clare
and then nudges her into the corridor.

Clare speaks, "Okay, I've fixed it for Jallie T to be on
Melship's table and we are negotiating the
attendance of Christina Nott to host another table.
That way I can get some extra people into the event."

"Whoa, you've got Christina as well. I imagine the car event promoters are chuffed!"

"Frankly it was a bartering chip to ensure that we could control Melship's table. Jallie T is getting a car for a year for showing up! - Anyway, the stage is now set!"

Xmas Party

The Department's Christmas Party is in full swing when Clare arrives. It's been done properly. Not just some smuggled-in wine in suitcases and Tesco nibbles. No, this is the real deal and at a hotel. The venue's entrance has been strung with fairy lights and tinsel. She wonders who is 'sponsoring' the event, but soon gets swept into the moment.

Each table has a small white board beside it, and Clare fears the worst - that party games have been included. There are crackers on the table and some are already wearing the cheap hats from inside the crackers.

A local school choir is singing in the entrance and there's mince pies upon entry and the option of mulled cider, or chilled prosecco. Clare decides to avoid anything that will mean she has less hands free.

Then to a table, where crackers are pulled. Jokes read out - not necessarily the ones from within the

Tom Thumb crackers.

The booze is now eggnog and punch but Clare continues with her hands-free rule.

Andrew Brading and Maggie are in a corner by plate-glass windows which look over a stark, brutalist courtyard which screams 'underground car park'. There is a low-level sleet in the grey evening which is fogging the view. Clare slips away from her designated table and joins them. They both look relieved that they will be able to sit with people they know.

She puts on a hat and reads the cracker joke out loud

"What do you get when you cross a snowman with a vampire? ... Frostbite"

Andrew laughs politely and then says:

"What does Santa get when he's stuck in the chimney? ... Claus-trophobia"

Maggie is sipping her eggnog and stares at the hazy view towards the River. She says, half-heartedly:

"Why is it getting harder to buy Advent calendars? ... Because their days are numbered"

Andrew is looking at the other party people in various stages of inebriation. One can sense that he must have a 'hands free' rule too, for such events.

Clare knows that Andrew's wife, Katherine is on a train heading back to their constituency home in Canmore Grenville. Andrew won't leave London until Christmas Eve, heading up on the train with a smattering of gifts from the House of Commons gift shop.

"Are you staying local? Or heading away?" asks Maggie, aware that they seldom have time for such small talk around the office.

"I'll be going back to Hampshire," says Clare, "A family get-together with party games, you know the kind of thing. And you?"

Maggie smiles, "My folk have a pile outside Durham. I'll be hunkering down there, although I expect we'll only have part of the house open."

Clare remembers that Maggie is from landed gentry. Probably Andrew, the Conservative MP, and State Secretary, will have the most modest Christmas of them all who share an office. Serena has already flown off to Normandy to take Christmas in her husband's rural French barn-conversion.

"I've never understood egg-nog. It's like drinking alcoholic custard."

"American," says Andrew. They all burst out laughing.

"No, I think it was the Brits actually," says Maggie, "They took a perfectly good posset and ruined it."

"I still love a good posset," said Andrew. They all laughed again. It was that end-of-term feeling finally creeping in.

"What's happening over there?" said Maggie. She nods sideways. Across the floor Douglas Lessiter is talking to a woman in her late twenties. He has a hand on her upper arm. She has her head down and is shaking her head, her face flushed.

"Does anyone know her?" Maggie asks. Lessiter glances around, like he can feel them looking, then he puts his face closer to the woman's, talking fast.

His grip is making the fabric of her suit jacket wrinkle. She moves her arm. Is she trying to pull away? It is hard to tell through the crowd.

"Only it looks nasty," says Maggie, standing as if to intervene.

Clare says, "I'll help" and they make their way to where Lessiter and the woman are standing. As they pass Maggie mimes recognition of the woman.

The woman moves and even through the crowd Andrew can see the reluctance with which Lessiter lets her go. Then everything has changed: Maggie and the woman are arm in arm and heading further towards the women's' powder room. Clare has peeled off and continues a conversation with

Duggie Lessiter to help ensure some distance, but then she explains that she must get back to Andrew.

Andrew looks around at the apparently happy colleagues raising a glass of Christmas cheer. A few are singing along with the carollers.

Then Maggie is coming back towards them carrying three cups of punch at once in a sort of triangular shape, with elbows out and biting the side of her lip as she concentrates.

"So?" Andrew asks. "How was the damsel in distress?"

"Didn't get much out of her," Maggie says. "I didn't try either, mind you. She seemed pretty shaken up. Something about a Non-Disclosure Agreement"

"She said she'd signed one. But she didn't mention her name. Anyway, she's gone home."

"She didn't tell you what Duggie was pressuring her about?" Andrew asks.

"No. She asked me to walk her out. Still, it gave me an excuse to get to the bar," Maggie shrugs and drinks her punch while Andrew examines his. It is neon red and has bits of what might be orange pith in it. He hopes it won't make the eggnog in everyone's stomach curdle.

Clare notices the phone, then the Parliament WhatsApp group and emails all go quiet.

An hour's drive back to Hampshire and a few days being part of the family. Time to decompress. She knows that Jake, Bigsy and Christina will be doing the same.

She realises that a way to get an awkward reputation is to keep sending emails at this time of year.

It is like a natural end to things, Samhain, Saturnalia and Yule leading to the New Year. A time to reflect before the sun cross wheel starts turning again.

Then a ping. It is from Amanda. "When are you back in London?" it asks. Clare is sure that Amanda must have way of tracing her all the way to Hampshire.

"4th Jan," replies Clare.

"Ok - let's meet. The Wolseley, Breakfast 5th Jan - 9am?"

"Agreed," replied Clare. "Developments," she thought.

Wolseley

Clare made her way through the well-heeled streets of St James, to the grandeur of the Wolseley restaurant.

It wasn't lost on her that Amanda had picked a venue that was once linked to the motor trade. Wolseley Motors Limited had wanted a prestigious car showroom in Mayfair at the site of 160 Piccadilly.

The English architect, William Curtis Green incorporated marble pillars and archways with Venetian and Florentine-inspired details, making for a grand and impressive building befitting of the company's ambitions.

Then, as it said on the menu, by 1926, the cars weren't selling as well as they had hoped and the firm went into bankruptcy. A bank took over the site and their new branch opened in the spring of 1927. The same architect was called upon once again to construct a banking counter and managers' offices either side of the main entrance, which today serve as the bar and tea salon.

From the early 21st Century, it became a restaurant but as testament to the longevity of Green's vision many aspects of his original design, such as the domed ceiling and monochrome geometric marble flooring, are still on view today.

'Great,' thinks Clare, 'to be sitting at one of the best breakfast spots in all of London.'

"Clare!" Amanda walks into the area in a shapely dark grey business-like jacket and skirt and they exchange hugs.

"Happy New Year," says Amanda.

"Happy New Year," responds Clare.

"I thought we should see in the New Year in style, hence the venue," explains Amanda. She leans forward, "And it will be easy to spot unexpected visitors in here."

"Are they yours?" asks Clare, pointing to a corner table where two men were fidgeting with croissants and coffee.

"Yes, and the one over there," she points to a lone woman enjoying a hot chocolate with a Müesli.

"Why so many?" asks Clare.

"I guess it's because I wanted to give them a treat!" confides Amanda, "Really - this could be just the two of us, but they have all done well during last year."

They both smile at this thought. Christina smiles also from the screened-off table behind Amanda.

"Okay, so what have we got then?" asks Clare, "I was intrigued with your sense of urgency."

"What we know and what we don't know," answers Amanda.

"To begin with, there are a couple of companies eager to pursue Melship when he is in Gstaad. They have both made strong bid to be on Jallie T's table. Oh, and by the way it was brilliant that you have managed to infiltrate it."

"Who are the companies?" asks Clare.

"One is that trillion-dollar electric car maker. The other is a relatively unknown startup called Zillian."

"We don't know what either of their agendas would be, but they are certainly different."

"There's also talk of some revaluation of Zillian before it goes public, but no one knows where this has come from."

"But wait, wasn't ZiL the name of an old Russian car manufacturer? They supplied the cars for many Russian leaders?" asks Clare.

"Yes, that thought didn't escape us either, and they did also make trucks with missile launchers and military buses, amongst other things. The cars were all as ugly as sin, by the way. Imagine stretched out versions of those big flat American looking cars and imagine them where curves are banned and all sheet metal has to be black and folded."

"Yuk - it sounds horrible. But you don't think there is any connection?"

"No, the company has been handled by Red Fox from Menlo Park."

"Menlo Park, that's where Facebook/Meta are based, isn't it?" asked Clare.

"Yes, but aside from Sand Hill Road - the investor playground, we cannot see any connection."

"So, what we know is that a couple of companies, one well-known and the other unknown, are going to be at the table with Duncan Melship in Gstaad."

"Correct - but I think we are on to something tangible now. We just need to keep following the thread."

Back to Bermondsey

A few days later, Clare was in a taxi to the old flat share in Bermondsey where she had lived with Lottie and Tessa. They had invited her over for a few glasses of new year celebratory wine.

As well as the opportunity for gossip, she would also be interested to meet the new occupant of her old room.

She climbed out of the taxi into a light sleet and scooted towards the front door. She rang the bell and a skinny long-haired woman in a checked shirt answered it.

"Oh Hi," says Clare, "I'm here to see Tessa and Lottie."

"Oh, come on in," answers the woman, "I'm Cat, and I guess you must be the oft-talked-about Clare? You work in Parliament as well, I gather?"

"Yes, that's right, but from that I'm thinking you

don't?"

"No, I'm a banker. I work for Corax Investments, in the city in their trading department."

"Oh - high finance and all of that?" asks Clare.

She was led into the lounge, which was unchanged from her time there and immediately Tessa and Lottie let off a confetti cannon, which sprinkled the room in glitter.

"There is always time for more glitter!" says Lottie.

"And surprises!" adds Clare. As she turned, she noticed a Christmas tree in the corner, complete with little lights.

"Nicely done!" says Tessa to Cat.

"Well, we'd better all have some bubbly after that!" says Lottie, " And welcome back, Clare."

They sit down with their glasses of Champagne and Clare notices a selection of other wine glasses and realises this could be quite an evening.

"So, Cat, how did you find out about this place?" asks Clare.

'Oh, I've known Tessa for years and she let me know that a spot was available. You might notice that I'm also originally from Germany. My full name is Katharina Maier, which does sound a little more

'Dgerman'. She emphasised a 'D' on the front of German in a pastiche of German pronunciation.

Until then, Clare hadn't noticed. Cat had a perfect Londoner accent.

"But I guess you are in my old room. It's not that large for an investment banker!"

"I agree, but I'm just starting out and this location - Bermondsey - is so convenient for everywhere. I can walk to the tube and be in Canary Wharf in about ten minutes.'

'The travel works for Corax Investments like it did for me travelling to Parliament," answers Clare.

"And the girls keep telling me about your various mysterious surprises. It's one of the reasons they wanted to ambush you," answers Cat.

"So, what's been happening with Duggie Melship over the last couple of weeks?" asks Clare looking at Lottie.

"Unbelievable!" answers Lottie. "Remember Melship was always one for parties and lavish surprises? Well, now he is involved with transport, there is an interesting amount on offer."

"Surely it has to be declared?" asks Clare.

"Yes and no; there are grey areas, like so much in politics. Remember that alleged Xmas Party at

Number 10 during lockdown? It is kind of like that."

Tessa interrupts, "Reality distortion."

Lottie laughs, then adds, "and ahem 'forgetfulness'. For example, Melship isn't directly involved with any of the persistent car companies. They are not providing him with any services, nor even with any, say, vacations etcetera. It isn't as blatant as some of them who 'cannot recollect' where funds or £30,000 holidays came from. And he is not doing anything towards raising funds for the party on the promise of Knighthoods, like some I could mention. By most Westminster definitions he would be squeaky-clean."

"But what about the 'industrial tourism'? " Asks Clare, "Lottie, you have accompanied him to several locations recently. Surely, he can find out about cars without visiting Wolfsburg, Munich and Tilburg."

"Agreed," says Lottie, "But all of these have been Executive Briefing Centre trips. You fly there, stay overnight in a hotel, where a couple of British representatives of the company try to get you drunk whilst telling stories about how great they are.

"Then, next day, you get bussed to their luxurious briefing centre where they offer elaborate breakfasts and then a succession of presenters who have dumbed down everything to fit into 45-minute segments."

Lottie sighed, "A couple of coffee breaks, a lunch

and a spin around a test track in a so-called secret wonder car which has been painted to look like a boulder avalanche in a snow field. Melship seems to enjoy it and often stays on for a couple of days at the end of a visit. I grab the first flight back and feel as if I've been processed like a slice of Kraft cheese."

"There must be so much to do in Wolfsburg and Tilburg?" laughs Clare.

"Actually, there was a well-known sleaze scandal attached to Wolfsburg - 'The Wolfsburg Fortress Mentality' as it was known in the German Press," answers Tessa, " You should google it for the salacious details."

"Well, now Melship is looking forward to the visit to the Motor Trade Show in Switzerland. And a couple of the car companies there are bidding for places on his table. They are targeting him, rather than the celebrity host - Jallie T."

"I suppose it is quite clever really. A form of camouflage to target the influencer under the guise of targeting the celebrity!" says Clare.

"It is surprisingly common actually," says Cat. "I get asked to go to all kinds of events with potential clients. Sometimes it is lavish restaurants, other times it is formal events like theatre and opera. Corax always seems to have a golden key to gain access for our client to anyone."

Tessa brings over a fresh bottle of chilled white

wine.

Lottie laughs, "Tessa - will you never learn!"

"So, Cat, you know about companies and shares and things?" asks Clare.

"Shop!" say Lottie and Tessa simultaneously.

"No let her go on," says Cat, "I'm intrigued."

"Well, we've been following a lead for a company called Zillian. They manufacture cars, mainly."

"Ach, yes, Zillian. A very mysterious company." Answers Cat.

"You know they make electric cars and vans?" asks Cat.

"Erm, I don't really know much about them at all. I was hoping you could help me find out some more."

"Well, it's not my area, but I know someone that trades automotive and he'll probably have the information. Are you planning to invest or something, only you seem to have a very shaky knowledge."?

Clare answers, "No, we were looking at them as part of a company profile, but there seems to be some doubts about their scale of operation." She was determined not to reveal anything about the situation with Melship and she could see Lottie give her a glance, which was like 'you'd better stop now.'

Cat answers, "Leave it with me, I'll get my man to dig into it for you. I expect we have an analyst profile piece or something."

Cat returns with information

Clare's phone rings. She is in Andrew Brading's office in Parliament. It is Cat.

"Hi, it's Cat. I've got the information you asked about, but there is quite a lot of it. Will Hanson is the analyst and he's said he'll provide a briefing for you. I told him you were something in Parliament and he couldn't wait!"

"But it might be difficult to find a briefing room. Leave it with me, and I'll get back by midday tomorrow."

Clare calls Jake.

"I can get a briefing about Zillian, the car company mixed up in the Melship briefing, but the guy concerned - Will Hanson - wants it to be linked with a trip around Parliament. Have you got any ideas?"

Jake pauses and then says, "Amanda wanted to have a catch-up briefing. Why don't I ask her if we can run it from Vauxhall Cross? That way you could meet Hanson at Parliament, but then bring him over to SI6? I could ask Amanda to lay on a car, maybe? - A little theatre thrown in?"

"Brilliant plan. Let me tell Cat about the offer. I'm sure it will work."

Right through you

Wait a minute man
You mispronounced my name
You didn't wait for all the information
Before you turned me away
Wait a minute sir
You kind of hurt my feelings
You see me as a sweet back-loaded puppet
And you've got a meal ticket taste

I see right through you
I know right through you
I feel right through you
I walk right through you

You took me for a joke
You took me for a child
You took a long hard look at my ass
And then played golf for a while
Your shake is like a fish
You pat me on the head
You took me out to wine dine 69 me
But didn't hear a damn word I said

Now that I'm Miss Thing
Now that I'm a zillionaire
You scan the credits for your name
And wonder why it's not there

Alanis Nadine Morissette / Basil Glen Ballard

568

Undetectable Firearms Act

Jake had made sure it was all arranged for the briefing from Will Hanson.

Clare was to meet Lottie, Cat Maier, and Will Hanson at Parliament, but then get them all ferried out in an SI6 SUV and along to Vauxhall Cross.

Clare arranged to meet them at Portcullis House. They could get visitor passes and have a coffee and then she could take the tunnel to the main Parliament buildings. It was a quick way to impress Will.

Lottie smiled when she heard Clare's plan. Amanda Miller had provisioned a couple of Range-Rovers to ferry them along to SI6 and they would be able to come out of the underground car park and out through the main gates of Parliament. Clare knew that there was a regular ferrying of people to and from Parliament and to various buildings around the immediate area.

Lottie asked Jake, "But this must be quite an important meeting if you are involving SI6 and getting us all ferried from Parly to SI6?"

"Oh yes, Amanda is most interested now she thinks we are on to something. I didn't expect to get two cars through!" says Clare.

Sure enough, Cat and Will arrived and Lottie and Clare dished some hospitality on them both. It was all routine for them, but it was impressing Will and Cat. She hadn't told Will that they were heading along the river to SI6's building.

"Time to move, " says Clare, "We're being picked up."

"Where are we going?" asks Will. He looked at Cat, but it was plain that she didn't know either.

"We have to run the briefing at SI6, which is just along the river. We are being taken there in special vehicles."

"Oh, I don't know about this," says Will, looking concerned.

"You'll be going to the building they use in all the James Bond movies," explains Lottie.

"You'll probably need to sign the Official Secrets Act as well," adds Clare.

They were walking to the underground car park

adjacent to the Big Ben clock tower. Standing by a couple of marked bays, Clare rang for the cars.

Two black Range Rovers slipped quietly into the parking spots.

"You'd better climb in and make the most of this journey," says Clare, "People will think you are a diplomat or a spy, travelling like this!"

Clare noticed that there was already someone in the front passenger seat of the first car. She didn't want to admit that it was the first time she had been transported in this manner.

Lottie wasn't as cool and says, "Clare: the friend who just keeps on giving!"

They slip out of the car park, up a short ramp, past some traffic lights and a couple of serious-looking yellow and black-painted barriers and then a couple of policemen open the gates and shoo the pedestrians away so that they can make their exit.

Clare noticed that the cars both had blue flashing lights, but no sirens as they gently made their way along the river's edge towards Vauxhall.

Then over Vauxhall Bridge and in a matter of moments they were in tunnels which led into the security services building.

They were shown out of the cars. Clare realised that both cars had a member of SI6 sitting in the front passenger seat and these two individuals showed the four of them into the building. There was a familiar routine of handing over phones and showing identities.

Clare realised it was some time since she was last in SI6, and that she had been reset to an occasional visitor status.

Then, at last, they were ready to move to a conference room. It was on a low floor and looked out of the back of the building, away from the Thames.

Amanda Miller appeared and greeted Clare.

"You must be Lottie," she asks, " Which would make you two Katherina Maier and William Hanson?"

"It's Cat, actually," says Cat and then adds, "Oh and Will!"

Amanda smiles, "We are going through to another room in a moment. Jake is in there, along with Bigsy and Christina. I thought if you were all involved, then we could cross brief one-another together."

Will looks slightly stunned by all of this. He'd only responded to a minor request from Cat and now, in one day, he had experienced more of the Secret Service than he'd ever watched in spy films.

Cat speaks to Lottie, "Yes, I am beginning to see what you meant about Clare's range of surprises!"

"Okay, before we go further, I need to know that you don't have any weapons?" asks Amanda, "Your colleague Christina was carrying a Glock 17 pistol, which we had to confiscate."

Clare notices Will's eyes go from large to almost pop from his head at this revelation. Cat breathes to Lottie, "Okay, I'll believe everything you say from now on."

Amanda led them along a short corridor. There were a couple of numbered doors on each side as well as the one into the conference facility. Clare noticed they were back on the river side of the building and considered that Amanda must be suitably senior to get these best spots.

Inside, already sitting round a table were Bigsy, Jake, and Christina as well as Grace from GCHQ, who immediately recognised Clare and came around the table to greet her.

"I didn't expect to be working together so soon!" she says smiling, "and this has some curious similarities with those other situations - Medusa and Minerva."

Clare replies, "I thought that at first, but I'm less convinced now. I think the Russians have given up on their attempts to blackmail lobbyists. I think this has the hallmark of an internally generated situation."

Amanda speaks, "Okay everyone, we'll do a quick

around the table introductions. I'll remind everyone that this meeting falls within the Official Secrets Act and that anyone disclosing anything from here can be prosecuted and may face imprisonment.

"When you came through the reception, we asked each of you to sign your MOD 134s which is a full Duty of Confidentiality"

Clare Bigsy, Jake, and Christina were all used to this protocol but Clare could see that Lottie, Cat and Will needed some time to process the information

Then Amanda asked Will about his background.

"I guess I'm just starting out, really. I thought my MBA was really table stakes for this role. Now I'm in it I can see that there are so many graduates and even 18-year-olds attempting to get into the business. It's like an episode of the Apprentice each time a fresh batch arrives.

"They said my role was a senior level position responsible for assisting clients in raising funds in the capital markets, as well as in providing strategic advisory services for mergers, acquisitions and other types of financial transactions.

Will continued, "...And I know I'm in the business, but now there's investment advice channels being run by 20-year-old video-bloggers. It has all become rather scary in a 'JFK's father' kind of way. He said, just before the 1929 stock market crash..."

Jake interrupts, "I know this one, 'If shoeshine boys are giving stock tips, then it's time to get out of the market.'"

"Yes, spot on. You must think like an economist," says Will, "If history is particular; economics is general —it involves searching for patterns which indicate if a cycle is turning. Today's financial system looks nothing like it did before the crashes of 2001 and 2008, yet lately there have been some familiar signs of froth and fear on Wall Street: wild trading days on no real news, sudden price swings and a queasy feeling among many investors that they have overdosed on techno-optimism."

"So, it is really one big casino!" says Clare.

Will continues, "To give you an example. Shares soared in 2021, then, in January 2022 Wall Street had their worst January since 2009, falling by 5.3%. The prices of assets favoured by retail investors, like tech stocks, cryptocurrencies, and shares in electric-car makers, all plunged, like some kind of Stockbroker board game. The once-giddy mood on reddit/wallstreetbets, which is a forum for digital day-traders, slumped.

Will continues, "It is tempting to think that the January sell-off was exactly what was needed, purging the stock market of its speculative excesses. But the global financial system is still loaded with risks. Asset prices are high: the last time shares were so pricey relative to long-run profits was before the slumps of 1929 and 2001, and the extra return for owning risky bonds is near its lowest level for a quarter of a century.

"Many portfolios loaded up on long-duration assets that yield profits only in the distant future. And central banks are raising interest rates to tame inflation. America's Federal Reserve is expected to making regular quarter-point increases.

"Now it would be good to say that this was all under control, but it has become a case of 'no-body knows'. It's all wrapped up in machine algorithms, which automatically micro adjust as part of high-speed trading systems. Analysts invent a new slice of logic, plug it in, and it's like an anti-missile missile chasing its prey. And just as explosive."

"Like the fibre optic shortcut that Michael Lewis described in Flash Boys? The one that cut 5 milliseconds off a high frequency trade?" asks Jake.

"Well, that was a more physical manifestation, along with the microwave towers that followed it, " says Will.

"I see it's like betting on the outcome of a horse race when you know the winner?" says Clare, "Like that Redford movie - The Sting?"

"Correct," said Will, "Although you only have milliseconds in which to accomplish all of this. But of course, the odds are loaded in favour of the Flash Boys. All of the time."

Will continued, "But if we look at the bigger forces, the mix of sky-high valuations and rising interest rates could easily result in large losses, as the rate used to discount future income rises. If big losses do materialise, the important question, for investors, for central bankers and for the world economy, is whether the financial system will safely absorb them or amplify them?"

"Are we all doomed, then?" asks Bigsy.

Will answers, "The answer is not obvious, for that system has been transformed over the past 15 years by the twin forces of regulation and technological innovation. For example, new capital rules have pushed a lot of risk-taking out of banks. At the same time, digitisation has given computers more decision-making power, created new platforms for owning assets and cut the cost of trading almost to zero."

"The result is a high-frequency, market-based system with a new cast of players. Share-trading is no longer dominated by pension funds but by automated exchange-traded funds (ETFs) and swarms of retail investors using slick new apps."

Will continues, "For example, borrowers can tap debt funds as well as banks. Credit flows across borders thanks to asset managers such as BlackRock, which buy foreign bonds, not just global lenders such as Citigroup.

These markets operate at breakneck speed: the

volume of shares traded in America is 3.8 times what it was a decade ago. Many of these changes have been for the better. They have made it cheaper and easier for all types of investors to deal in a broader range of assets.

But, like JFK's father's shoe-shine boy's ideas, the crash of 2008-09 showed how dangerous it was to have banks that took deposits from the public exposed to catastrophic losses, which forced governments to bail them out.

Today banks are less central to the financial system, better capitalised and hold fewer highly risky assets. More risk-taking is done by funds backed by shareholders or long-term savers who, on paper, are better equipped to absorb losses.

And there's the shadow players. The reinvention of finance has not eliminated hubris.

Two dangers stand out.

First, some leverage is hidden in shadow banks and investment funds. I'm talking about the equivalent of nation state funding hidden behind a clever wrapper. Russia and China spring to mind as key actors in this space, but they are using smaller players to legitimise the front ends of their dealings. Charles Abridge-Bois springs to mind.

"I always think his name sounds like a bus route," says Bigsy.

"A Victorian one? With wooden bench seats?" suggests Jake.

Will added, "Laugh all you might, he's still gaining money at a rate that would make some forgers blush. Through an off-shore company where most of it is going to the Caymans or similar places offshore."

"But I've seen him in Parliament, lounging about in the commons," says Bigsy, "He looks louche but not like a spiv."

"Appearances may deceive," infers Will, "And there's plenty with a finger in this pie."

"For example, the total borrowings and deposit-like liabilities of hedge funds, property trusts and money market funds have risen to 43% of GDP, from 32% a decade ago. Firms can rack up huge debts without anyone noticing."

"There's only a few places where this is easier than the UK, and that's where the action is evolving.

"As an example, take Singapore. Singapore is open as an international financial, investment, and transport hub which exposes it to money laundering and terrorist financing risks.

"The country's position as the most stable and prominent financial centre in Southeast Asia, coupled with a regional history of transnational organised crime, large-scale corruption in neighbouring states, and a range of other offenses in those states increase the risk that Singapore will be viewed as an attractive destination for criminals to launder their criminal proceeds.

He adds, "Limited large currency reporting requirements and the size and growth of Singapore's private banking and asset management sectors also pose inherent risks. Among the types of illicit activity noted in the region are fund flows associated with illegal activity in Australia that transit Singapore financial service providers for other parts of Asia."

Jake adds, "Yes, now that London has freed itself from EU legislation, the fat cats are eyeing Singapore as an interesting model."

Will continues, "There's around 40 offshore banks in operation, all foreign-owned. Singapore is a major centre for offshore private banking and asset management.

Assets under management in Singapore total approximately $2 trillion. As of the end of 2014, Singapore has approximately $1.5 trillion in foreign funds under management. Singapore does not permit shell banks or anonymous accounts.

Jake mused, "You don't have to be a sovereign state to be interested in the potential of London, just blend in offshore banking and some Freetrade zones and it all starts to pull together. The likes of Charles Abridge-Bois, will be licking their lips in anticipation of the new prizes on offer."

Will nods, "An example: A Chinese trader created a business in Singapore which had $10 billion under management as of 2020. His previous company had pleaded guilty to insider trading of Chinese bank stocks in 2012 and paid a $44 million fine. The holdings were primarily in the form of total return swaps, a technical financial instrument where the underlying securities (stocks) are held by banks."

Clare speaks, "Hmm, I'm a bit hazy on total return swaps!"

Will adds, "It meant that they did not need to disclose its large holdings, while if it had transacted in regular stocks, it would have had to. The fund was also heavily leveraged and did business with multiple banks which were likely unaware of the large positions held by other banks.

"Like borrowing money against the same collateral multiple times?" asks Clare.

"Exactly," says Will, "Of course, it crashed and several big and well-known banks had to take the financial hit, measured in billions of dollars. Simply put if asset prices fall, other blow-ups follow, accelerating the correction."

Will continues, "The second danger is that, although the new system is more decentralised, it still relies on transactions being channelled through a few nodes that could be overwhelmed by volatility. Exchange-traded funds, with $10 trillion of assets, rely on a few small market-making firms to ensure that the price of funds accurately tracks the underlying assets they own.

Then Will adds, for emphasis, "Trillions of dollars of derivatives contracts are routed through five American clearing houses. These transactions are executed by a new breed of middlemen, such as Citadel for hedge funds and the related Citadel Securities, for 40% of the stock trades in the USA. The Treasury market now depends on automated high-frequency trading firms to function."

"All these firms or institutions hold safety buffers and most can demand further collateral or "margin" to protect themselves from their users' losses."

Cat speaks, "Yet recent experience suggests reasons for concern. The market-based financial system is hyperactive most of the time; in times of stress whole areas of trading activity can dry up. That can fuel panic."

Will speaks again, "Exactly, Cat. Ordinary citizens may not think it matters much if a bunch of day-traders and fund managers get burned. But such a fire could damage the rest of the economy. Fully 53% of American households own shares (up from 37% in 1992), and there are over 100m online brokerage accounts. And of course, it all feeds through into pension plans."

Cat speaks again, "If credit markets gum up, households and firms will struggle to borrow. That is why, at the start of the pandemic, the Fed acted as a "market-maker of last resort," promising up to $3 trillion to support a range of debt markets and to backstop dealers and some mutual funds."

"Maximum score," thought Clare.

Will continues, "In reality, I spend most of my time producing reports like the one I gave to Cat.

"I guess that means your report is quite balanced, then?" asks Amanda.

"I hope so; although this one won't have been re-edited by a Chief Analyst to hit the investment criteria, we need to Value Sell the proposition," answered Will.

Cat smiles, "We both sound like buzz-word compliant corporates, because it's what we do all day!"

Clare and Jake both laugh, and Will continues, "Cat has never asked me for anything before, and I had no idea she related to such people as yourselves. You all seem to be spies or something? I mean one of you was even carrying a weapon."

Christina replies, "Well it was concealed and being made of polymer I didn't think the scanners would see it."

Amanda answers, "We've had plenty of time since the Undetectable Firearms Act of 1983 to perfect better scanning. But Will, you should tell us what you have discovered?"

Will starts to speak, "If you want to gauge the market's feelings towards the future of sustainable mobility, look no further than electric vehicle maker Zillian."

"The company is predicted to have an opening market value greater than Ford or General Motors."

Will looks baffled, "What makes this strange is that it doesn't have any product yet. So far it has produced a total of around a dozen vehicles, half of which were vans.

"Last quarter, it only generated around £2 million in revenue. That's not profits. It's total revenue. Now it isn't the only disruptive new company in the automotive space. There's been that well-known electric car manufacturer which sent one of its cars into space for publicity. And there's at least a couple of other fledgling start-ups.

Christina speaks, "I guess we could say 'powered by twitter' features strong and the Millennial generation of investors."

"And there's something else," adds Will, "The Zillian prospectus looks kinda hokey."

"Technical phrase!" interjects Cat.

Will continues, looking serious, "The thing is, when

I went along to their own corporate website, the bumpf looked suspect. It looked as if it had been lifted from somewhere else by an undergraduate trainee.

"To be honest, I thought it was text from a software company. Nothing about engines, driving experience, comfort etc. All about management, as if it was a systems software purveyor."

"A couple of examples," Will looks at a small notebook.

"Our proprietary management platform helps optimize and automate fleet operations to help improve your total cost of ownership and maximize uptime.

"Cloud-based tools conveniently accessible on multiple devices."

"Our team of experts work with you from initial planning to installation providing a full turnkey site deployment solution"

Bigsy interrupts, "It sounds more like server systems management solution than a car firm,"

"Yes, that's what I was thinking. You could almost edit in the 'car specific' words. Another example, 'Engineered specifically for fleets to help you achieve an exceptional total cost of ownership.'

"Paper Tiger?" Asks Grace,

"Wow, I haven't heard that in a long time," replies Amanda.

Grace adds, "Mao Zedong was keen to use the phrase - 'In appearance it is very powerful but, it is nothing to be afraid of; it is a paper tiger. Outwardly a tiger but made of paper, unable to withstand the wind and the rain.'"

"That was American Imperialism, I think?" says Cat.

"Ah, so you are breaking cover as a historian?" asks Amanda.

"PPE at Uni," says Cat, "Don't ask me how I ended up doing banking!"

"So, what do we think?" says Jake. He looked toward Amanda's analyst Grace.

Grace says, "Yes, I agree with Will's analysis, but we need to think why, ask a few 'and then what?' type questions."

Christina suggests, "Maybe someone is starting a new money laundry? This could be huge in scale. It would need some state backing to be able to start it up. I could see the Kremlin making a play like this."

Grace speaks again, "Yes, if someone is thinking of how to fire up a semi-state type enterprise, then this would be a way to raise funds."

Will looks at them both, "You are thinking about this as if it would be used illegally. There's all kinds of legislation around to prevent those kinds of things."

"Just like the no-plastic guns legislation?" says Amanda.

"Exactly," says Grace, I can show you several sites where the software instructions to print plastic guns are stored. To be honest, plastics are being superseded by CNC-milling operations nowadays. Take a block of metal and machine it to make an untraceable semi-automatic. A ghost gun."

"Jake chimes in, "Rules: For the obedience of fools and guidance of wise?"

"More like 'proceed until apprehended,' "says Clare

"But the sheer scale of a company share floatation?" asks Will.

"Precisely, its what's called 'hiding in plain sight,' " says Amanda.

"Okay, what else do we know?" asks Amanda.

Lottie speaks, "There is some sad news. Isabella Stevens, who worked for Douglas Lessiter, was found in the Thames this morning. She was spotted by one of the commuter boats. It's in the papers now." She opened her phone and displayed a front page from one of the London news feeds.

"My god!" says Clare, looking startled, "it's the woman that was with Lessiter at the Xmas party. I didn't know her, but I got involved in rescuing her from a difficult situation during the party. There was some kind of an argument."

Lottie looks over, slightly shocked, "Yes, I know Hannah from Lessiter's office. I'd seen the two of them around together. I'm sure Hannah is shaken up by this, but I'll see if there is any other news."

Grace looks at her laptop and reads, "Early statements suggest that there was no foul play and it looked like tragic accident. She appeared to have a high Blood Alcohol Content level of 0.35."

"0.35 is enough to induce a coma," says Amanda, "It is an unrealistically high amount to get from an office party, unless the drink was massively spiked."

"There will be big attempts to decouple this from a government office party," says Clare, "Brace yourselves!"

Lottie speaks, "Back to Melship. Since he has been Secretary of State for the Department for Transport Efficiency, he has been inundated with requests from every car manufacturer. They all want to wine and dine him, then spring some influence. They play him like a fool. The ultimate sweet back-loaded puppet."

Clare laughs, then Jake says, "I'm not quite sure what that means."

Grace says, "There's nothing else out of the ordinary about Zillian, that I could spot. It looks just like generic corporation positioning for a floatation."

Will nods, "Exactly. It looks almost too generic. Where's it's unique selling points that all make the market want to buy it?"

"Where are its existing products?" Adds Grace, "The Emperor has no clothes."

"We'll find out soon enough," says Jake, "The Geneva Car Expo approaches."

Kotyonok

Saturday at Heathrow Airport and Clare waited for the plane with Christina and her 'table group'. Douglas Melship had gone through to the business lounge with Lottie.

Christina Nott was with her car show 'second table' treating the whole trip as if it was part of a road tour. Jake and Bigsy accompanied her, with Jake as a surrogate Road Manager and Bigsy as technical support.

They had taken a small corner of the lounge and were keeping themselves to themselves when a stranger appeared and motioned Christina to one side.

"My god!" uttered Christina in amazement, "I didn't expect to see you here!"

A leather-jacketed man strode towards her. He had a military haircut and grabbed Christina in both arms.

"Ha, kotyonok, what mischief are you in this time?"

It was Antanov Chekeryn, who Christina originally

knew from the Academy in Arkangelsk. They had worked together a few times and she knew that Antanov was entirely dependable.

"Kotyonok - kitten! - But you. You bring memories of good times on helicopters! I guess this has something to do with Blackbird?"

Blackbird was Fyodor Kuznetsov, her handler. Although she had always thought that Kuznetsov's code name was just a little too close to 'blacksmith', which was the English translation of Kuznetsov.

"Yes, " smiled Antonov, "After you reported back to Blackbird about this suspected attempt at lobbying, Blackbird was asked to intervene. Because your operational style is somewhat unusual, zvezda moya, he asked me to also take a look."

"Usually, The Kremlin is all over these situations," said Christina, "Not this time," replied Antonov, "In fact Blackbird wondered if it was something from China."

"Okay, so that also rules out Russian organised crime," said Christina, "and the United States. This could be a wholly new operative?"

Antanov replied, "Well, I'm going to Geneva as part of the Radiant Tyre Company. Radiant produce 20% of the radial tyres in Russia, apparently. I'll be checking up on things while I'm there. I wanted to let you know so that we can stay in touch whilst you are there."

"You know what, you are still in my cellphone," said Christina and to prove it rang the number. Sure enough Antanov's phone rang."

He held it up so that she could read the name. 'Kotyonok', it displayed - Kitten.

"Okay, well I guess you know we are also going to Gstaad as part of the VIP Programme?" asked Christina.

"Yes, me too. Although I'm borrowing a helicopter to get there. I'll fly myself from Geneva. And you never know when a helicopter becomes a useful field asset."

Christina smiled. Antanov was still a man of action.

Geneva

As they landed in Geneva, Clare could see snow and various types of de-icing system being deployed on planes getting ready for take-off.

Then, through Arrivals and onward to the bag check.

There were many delegates queuing at the various luggage belts. Clare, Christina, Jake and Bigsy decided to share a taxi to the hotel. Most of them had 'Bus Line A' tickets from the organisers except Christina's preferential 'Bus Line B'.

Sure enough, Bus Line A's queue stretched a long way from outside and back into the terminal building.

Bigsy hailed a large VW taxi, which was some kind of minibus and they loaded their luggage on board and then sat in tidy rows of seats. "It's like a mini-road tour!" said Clare and Christina laughed.

Then Clare noticed from the corner of her eye the signs for Bus Line B. It led to a taxi rank, except instead of taxis, there were high-end saloon cars to whisk the privileged to their hotels. She noticed Melship and Lottie waiting in the line but decided not to wave.

Their taxi driver was polite, but slightly bemused that the group wanted to be driven to the hotel.

"It is only a few minutes' walk from the airport and from the Palexpo.", he explained. But they asked him to drive them anyway, and Bigsy made sure he received a good tip.

"The advantage of this hotel is that it is right by the Expo and the airport yet is only around 15 minutes to get into the centre of Geneva'" explained Bigsy, who had made the detailed logistical arrangements.

The driver added, "It is quite clever of the organisers because many visitors will stay around here, and the main thing to do is visit the show, rather than getting a diffusion of visitors into Geneva. Most people will go into the city maybe once, or twice, but mainly they will be immersed in the car industry and all of its charms."

Sure enough, the hotel had various prestige cars parked outside and inside there were a couple of brightly coloured exotic-looking sports cars raised into the air.

As they checked in, Clare noticed a row of

hospitality desks, arranged by various well - known car companies. It was clear that many guests were to be pampered at this event. No wonder Duncan Melship was so eager to attend.

Then, at check-in, they were each handed a bag of complementary products. Clare expected it to be brake fluid or anti-freeze, but it turned out to be expensive perfume from France and delicious-looking chocolates from Switzerland.

Christina was given a larger bag as well, which contained a sleek red leather backpack by Wenger - a Swiss manufacturer.

They were all given registration instructions. As well as checking into the hotel, they needed to check in for the event.

"You've hit the jackpot," said Jake, smiling as Christina and Clare cooed over the bag.

Then they noticed Melship and Lottie arrive. They were with Douglas Lessiter and his assistant Hannah. Duncan Melship was looking harassed. Lottie smiled to them but her expression indicated they should stay away.

Melship was saying, "How could they lose my bag so quickly? I mean it was a short flight from London and yet my bag with all my briefing papers for the conference has gone missing."

They could hear Lottie speaking, " The organisers

have a 'perte de bagages' room. I'm sure yours will turn up there. In the meantime, I have everything on my laptop. But I think we'll need to be ready for tonight's meeting with Express Fleet Management. I think the reception for it starts in about an hour."

Jake realised what was happening. "They must have filled Melship's itinerary. It's a common trick to swamp the target with receptions, meeting, and meals. Almost like sensory overload. He'll be flagging by time he is scheduled to visit Gstaad."

"Yes, but I think his disappearing baggage might be something else," said Christina. "Someone wants to see or get inside it."

"What? Read what is in it, or bug it?" asked Jake.

"That's my theory," said Christina, "and it is not a very subtle attempt."

"Does that mean you are suspicious of your shiny new luggage?" asked Jake.

"Not really, look around. There's already a handful of others with the bags - even Lottie, look!"

"She must have been on the same kind of privileged ticket as Melship," said Clare.

"Just a moment," said Christina. She walked back to the registration desk and talked for a few minutes to the person controlling it. Then she returned.

"Clare, go back to the desk, see that man on the left-hand end position. Say you are my personal assistant."

Clare did as she was asked and to her surprise, the man presented her with the larger complementary bag. Clare could not believe her luck. "Oh yes, and we have these for assistants too," he looked behind him and produced a small white box containing an iPod Touch. "It's been preloaded with the itinerary and you can use it to select the sessions for Ms Nott."

Clare happily received this electronic goody and returned to the others.

"It's a bit embarrassing, I've now got one of those excellent bags, which has the same perfume and other things in it as my original one, plus a complementary iPod to help us get around the show!"

"Did you see the piles of those bags behind the registration desk?" asked Jake, "They must be immune to the value they are handing out!"

"And it shows how much this industry is awash with marketing budget!" added Bigsy.

Clare's' phone pinged. It was a message from Lottie.

"Busy tonight, will see you for breakfast tomorrow. 8am."

"Lottie is busy with Melship's itinerary; I guess at

least we have someone on the inside," said Clare.

"Like us; we need to be on the inside of a bar right now, " said Jake, "Let's get to our rooms and meet up in, say, half an hour. We can go to that bar over there."

Breakfast

Next morning, they assembled for breakfast.

"The discussion yesterday evening was entirely out of my comfort zone," says Clare, "Those guys in the bar, the salesmen, were so sure of themselves and they all seemed to be running on unlimited expenses."

Jake nods and says, "It was an interesting dilemma, for them. They could see two attractive women sitting with us but were torn when they felt that there was a fleet buyer around or someone important from a government."

Clare smiles, "Christina or a fleet buyer. Honestly!"

Jake smiles also, "Yes, no contest. Christina and Clare, every time."

Clare playfully elbows Jake in the ribs, "But seriously, do you think you can continue to talk about cars for a whole week?"

She adds, "Wheels. Tyres. Doors. Engines. Litres per 100km. Sunroofs. Satnav. Electricity. Environmental impact."

"Something I learnt is that most of the new electric cars look like my old toy car racing set," says Bigsy, "One chassis can take many car bodies."

"Yes, and the chassis is entirely made of little batteries," adds Jake.

Clare speaks, "I guess the whole automotive industry will have to find new things to talk about. Open the bonnet, it's empty! Luggage space. Open the boot, it's also empty! More luggage space. No dials since they made the dashboard look like a smartphone. Then the two or three electric motors on each of the axles. They don't even make a noise. It's not like talking about a 3-litre V6 or a V12. What will men in pubs discuss?"

Jake replies, "That's easy... I drove silently all the way from London to Hull and only had to stop once for a very long coffee break whilst I recharged. I took plenty of luggage with me because of all the storage space."

"Maybe that's why they were giving away free bags to Christina and Clare yesterday?" adds Bigsy, "encouraging greater luggage use?"

Lottie arrives. She looks harassed. "Melship was at a meeting last night with the people from a fleet management company. I thought this was an almost missable meeting, but it turns out they want to do something like the bikes in London and have a lot of hire-cars on street corners. It's a taste of things to come."

"What was Melship's attitude?"

Lottie explains, "Well he had been placed next to a gorgeous blonde who seemed to be explaining what the various 'key points' from the discussion were about. Melship was caught in her headlights, so to speak, and didn't really know what to say."

She continues, "They were asking for his agreement in principle to support a new kind of charger. It was proprietary, so it would only work with their hire cars. It all sounded like a nightmare to me."

Bigsy says, "I see what they are doing. Trying to sew up London's streets with their own private design of vehicle. It's like a land grab."

"Have you been into the main hall yet?" asks Lottie. Everyone shook their heads.

"It is immense and full of cars. I say full, but there is quite a lot of room to walk around the vehicles and even climb in them. There's also a whole range of smart-suited salesmen and a few women out there. I thought the sexist battle about car marketing had been fought, but there still seem to be a lot of lightly clad bodies draped over bonnets."

"We used to call them 'booth babes' and 'grid girls' for the Formula One, when I worked for Street," says Jake, "And I'm pretty sure that exhibitors are still free to choose how they want to present their vehicles."

Jake continues, "I dated a model who used to work for car companies. She told me they had secret signals, such as tucking hair behind their ears, when they wanted help in fending off overly eager patrons.

"And some of the car companies said it makes more sense to use product specialists who knew about the cars."

Bigsy adds, "It's like those silly giveaways - they also do it at tech shows. Some show visitors grab a big bag and then try to fill it up with all the freebies on offer. What use is it if you manage to capture their business card. Are they a serious buyer? I think not."

Clare speaks, "I guess #METOO has had some impact then? On this most exploitative of industries."

Jake, "Yes but it will take a long time to work its way into an industry that top to bottom has glamour calendars - even for car tyres."

Bigsy adds, "And think about the lack of interesting things to talk about with new cars: '...It's battery operated!' "

Clare asks, "So, did we learn anything new?"

"Only that Duncan Melship is a liability," answers Jake.

Rinse and repeat every breakfast

Clare, Christina, Jake, Lottie and Bigsy had agreed to meet at 08:00 each morning to compare notes. It was an hour ahead of when Melship would appear and gave Lottie a chance to get some input from the rest of them.

The next morning, they met.

Clare was just saying, "In that old song it goes something like ' cars don't talk back.' - Well guess what, they do now. I didn't want my car to keep reminding about closing the doors and putting on the handbrake - and so many variations of bing bong noises."

"I'm with you on that," says Bigsy, "Although most of the newest cars have automatic handbrakes now."

Lottie laughs, "I think this was supposed to help Duncan, but I think it might be confusing him."

At that moment, Hannah appears, "Hi guys, I

thought I saw you here yesterday morning. Clever to get in to breakfast before our esteemed bosses."

"How are you?" asks Lottie. She looks concerned, "It must have been quite a shock when Isabella disappeared like that? Our condolences."

Hannah looks toward the group eating their croissants and Swiss cheese.

"I'm not convinced about that whole situation," she whispers, "Look, I don't know all of you sitting here, so maybe I shouldn't say more..."

Lottie replies, "Hannah, you remember Clare, from Andrew Brading's office? And these other people are my trusted friends. Jake, Bigsy and Christina. They all have the highest clearances, one could say, right through to Vauxhall Cross."

"Oh, you are agents?" asks Hannah, "And Lottie is vouching for you, so I'd just remind you about secrecy if I carry on explaining."

Jake, Bigsy and Christina all looked suitably sombre and Jake says, "Yes we heard about your colleague."

"I was there, at the party, when Isabella was last seen," says Clare, "As a matter of fact I was helping her to get a taxi home. Andrew Brading and Maggie Shannon were there too and we saw events unfolding before Isabella asked me to help her leave the event."

"Did Izzy seem at all drunk to you?" asks Hannah.

"Not especially. I mean we'd all had a few drinks by that time."

"But not enough to push into chronic intoxication. The kind that could induce a coma?" asks Hannah.

"No, I didn't recognise Isabella, nor did I know her name," answers Clare, "But she seemed quite capable of lucid conversation and could walk herself to the exit."

"So, what were you doing with her?" asks Hannah, looking intrigued, "I mean, if that isn't too personal a question."

"No, no," says Clare, "As a matter of fact, I was rescuing her from an altercation with Duggie! - Maggie and I were both helping her out. She seemed to be in an intense argument with Duggie. It seemed to be more than his usual wandering hands. We could hear her saying something about an NDA."

Hannah thinks for a moment, "Oh yes, I think I know what that was about. A company that Duggie has a tie-in with. He asked us all to sign Non-Disclosure Agreements before they came to present something they were working on to us."

Clare continues, "Well, Duggie had been holding her, I'd say hard enough to bruise her skin. When Maggie and I approached, she broke away and shortly after that asked me if I would accompany her to the exit."

"I escorted her outside, and conveniently a black cab approached us and she hailed it and headed for home."

"I wonder if the entrance had any form of CCTV?" asks Hannah.

'I imagine so if that evening's comings and goings were in any way normal," says Clare.

Hannah's phone buzzes and she says, " I must run, I'm being summoned to Douglas Lessiter."

Christina speaks, "The cab. It could have been a fake. Used to pick up Isabella without raising suspicions."

Jake speaks, "I think we should handle this via Amanda, rather than getting the local police involved. I'll call her when we finish breakfast."

"Okay - We'll see you later at the 'Battery Presentation,' says Clare. Bigsy laughs.

Range anxiety

Clare, Christina, Bigsy, Lottie and Jake trooped their way to a main Ballroom area, which was a floor higher than the main Expo. Sure enough, inside the vast ballroom were many seats - mainly occupied - with large screen repeaters either side of a brightly lit stage. They sat near to the back, well out of direct earshot of the presenters.

Then, Saul Chadnitz walked onto the stage to 'The Power' by Snap, followed by Angela Rolls. They were both in white tee shirts and blue jeans, like a corporate dress-down code.

"Industrial Theatre," breathed Bigsy, and the others agreed.

Angela Rolls opened the session:

"Evangelist, luminary, writer, presenter, marketeer, teacher. Saul has spent most of his professional life on hot relevant topics.

"Saul is the publisher of around 20 best-selling books and I'm sure most of this audience have read at least one."

"Lately, Saul has been working around the area of autonomous vehicles and today's topic is batteries."

Chadnitz stood and paced across the stage.

He spoke, "Hmm, there's a lot of you here. I wonder how many are really interested in batteries? I know, let's do a show of hands."

"He's using voice boosting software," murmurs Bigsy, "Compression and subtle reverb."

Yet no one put their hand up to his request for a show of hands.

"Not yet. I haven't asked the question yet.

"Here we go. How many you are anxious today right now? Show of hands?"

He looked around.

"What? Nobody? I can't believe that, Ah Sir, you there - thank you for being honest."

"Well, look at the numbers... only maybe 5% of this hall is anxious right now.

Undaunted, he continued, "Now another question. If you'd come here by electric vehicle and knew you needed to get back to, say, Paris, but you had parked without a recharge, then who would be anxious?"

"More of you, maybe half."

"Now let's say you had to get back to, say, London. It's around 1000km." Would any more of you put up your hands. Maybe that's three quarters of the people in the ballroom."

He studies the hall, "And we have a name for it...Range Anxiety."

"Invented by a man," says Lottie to Clare. They both giggle.

"How come no Melship today?" whispers Clare to Lottie.

"Oh, he's off doing something with Lessiter. They are being give a special briefing about a new company. They have been asked to restrict numbers. It's all very hush-hush. Actually, I think Hannah is going along with Lessiter."

Christina says, "We should find out what they have been doing."

Chadnitz continues, "First time EV buyers are often worried about range anxiety - that feeling of being caught short on flat batteries miles from a charging point."

Christina whispers again, "Ideally we should know

who they are meeting, then we can run some background checks."

Chadnitz keeps talking, "Yet also of concern is the actual life of the battery pack. Experience with mobile phones, tablets and laptop computers has taught consumers that, over time, the batteries powering them can lose efficiency, resulting in the need for more frequent charging.

He looks around the packed hall, "So should you be worried?

"This is good marketing," whispers Clare "Educate the punters and at the same time terrify them. They will be wanting these new batteries or whatever it is Saul is about to offer."

Chadnitz continues, "Well the good news is EV cells are more resilient than you'd think, plus there are ways to make sure your car's batteries will survive better than most."

He adds, "And another thing is just how long will those batteries last?"

"Oh no!" says Clare with her arm wrapped onto her forehead, "Now I've got range anxiety but I've also got to worry about battery life!"

Chadnitz continues, "After range anxiety, battery life is one of the most common concerns for people making the jump from internal combustion-engined cars to EVs. All batteries degrade over time and with use, meaning they become less efficient as they age and, ultimately, the range of your car is reduced."

"Will the batteries still go the distance!" asks Lottie.

Clare smirks.

Chadnitz adds, "Furthermore, battery technology doesn't come cheap, and by the time the cells are in need of replacement they will cost far more to buy than the car will likely be worth - which is why we tend to replace mobile phones in their entirety rather than replace the battery pack."

Clare whispers, "I buy the car, which costs more, use the batteries, which don't go as far as advertised, so my longer journeys take even longer and after a few years the whole car is worn out because the batteries are such an expensive part." Lottie giggled.

Chadnitz continues, "Yet it's not all bad news, because there are ways to increase the lifespan of your car's battery, keeping it healthier and more efficient for longer. More importantly, while performance may degrade over time, ultimately the cells should still be providing at least 70 percent of their capacity even after 200,000 miles."

Bigsy plays with his phone, "Say a manufacturer says 260 miles range. Maybe it's a 10% exaggeration, then only top up the battery to 80%, but it degrades by 10% per year. Let's see now:

"Assume the manufacturer quotes 260 miles range.

260*.9*.8*.9 = 168 miles. So, I could get 100 miles less after the first year and 260*.9*.8*.7 = 131 miles after three years. About half the original quote. Allegedly."

The others all pull faces. "Well, it's only a rough calculation," said Bigsy, "But I'm not seeing it from any of the manufacturers."

Chadnitz continues, "As an example, a number of e-taxis operating from a London airport racked up over 300,000 miles each over three years, with all retaining at least 82 percent of their charge."

Then he adds, "Perhaps the biggest single contributor to the decline in efficiency is the cycle of use and charging. Frequent draining of the cells followed by a full charge can, over time, damage the battery's ability to maintain its optimum energy storage - it's why manufacturer's typically recommend charging only to 80 percent and never letting the range drop to zero miles."

Clare whispers, "Oh no! I've got to worry about over-filling the batteries as well - Maybe there will still be things to talk about with new-style electric cars!"

Then Chadnitz picks up something from behind the podium. "This is a new type of battery. This battery features graphene, a sheet of carbon atoms bound together in a honeycomb lattice pattern."

"It looks like a regular battery to me," says Jake.

Chadnitz continues, "Let me introduce Dr. Jerrit Petrozewitz, from PowerLite Associates, based in Israel and The Netherlands. They are co-developing this new form of battery with several car companies.

Petrozewitz steps forward. "Good afternoon, everyone. Yes, it is me standing between you and lunch, but I'll hope you have something interesting to think about over your buffet selection."

"Graphene is recognized as a wonder material due to the myriad of astonishing attributes it holds. It is a potent conductor of electrical and thermal energy, extremely lightweight chemically inert, and flexible with a large surface area.

"I imagine some of you are thinking that this battery looks no different to any other but let me assure you it is. A graphene battery is light, durable, and suitable for high-capacity energy storage, as well as shortened charging times.

"Graphene will extend the battery's life, which is negatively linked to the amount of carbon that is coated on the material or added to electrodes to achieve conductivity, and graphene adds conductivity without requiring the amounts of carbon that are used in conventional batteries.

Petrozewitz adds, "Graphene can improve such battery attributes as energy density and form in various ways. Li-ion batteries can be enhanced by introducing graphene to the battery's anode and capitalising on the material's conductivity and large surface area traits to achieve morphological optimisation and performance."

"We are being evangelised to now," says Jake, "BTWBS - Baffle them with bull-shit!"

Petrozewitz adds, "It has also been discovered that creating hybrid materials can be useful for achieving battery enhancement. A hybrid of Vanadium Oxide (VO2) and graphene, for example, can be used on Li-ion cathodes and grant quick charge and discharge as well as large charge cycle durability.

Lottie whispers, "Yikes, this has turned into a science lecture. I thought VO5 was a styling gel?"

Petrozewitz contines, "In this case, VO2 offers high energy capacity but poor electrical conductivity, which can be solved by using graphene as a sort of a structural "backbone" on which to attach VO2 - creating a hybrid material that has both heightened capacity and excellent conductivity."

Then Petrozewitz reaches down and brought out another battery.

"I'm inwardly groaning," says Clare, "I'm not sure that I can take many more batteries."

Petrozewitz continues, "Another example is LFP (Lithium Iron Phosphate) batteries, that is a kind of rechargeable Li-ion battery. It has a lower energy density than other Li-ion batteries but a higher power density. Enhancing LFP cathodes with graphene allowed the batteries to be lightweight, charge much faster than Li-ion batteries and have a greater capacity than conventional LFP batteries."

"So, he's telling us that battery technology still has a way to go!" summarises Jake, "And there's some new wonder substances to make it all work."

"So, roll on the battery breakthroughs, " says Clare.

"Roll on lunch," says Bigsy.

The Raft

"This is so well organised," says Bigsy, "I'm impressed that with our badges we can just roll into the restaurant and get marvellous food."

"You should see what they lay on for assistants!" says Lottie, "Shorter queues and waitress instead of self service."

"It's like Parliament; you just have to have the right badge!" observes Clare.

They grab a table and Hannah comes over to join them, "Hey, Hannah, you look as if your session was as dire as our one - about batteries!"

Hannah answers, "Not really, but it I'm not sure how pally Duggie and Duncan Melship are getting with a certain company. It's teetering on the edge of sleazy if you ask me!"

"Come on, you'll have to tell us. We can put you right," says Lottie, "I'm sure Duncan will spill the beans as soon as I see him, anyway."

"Well, it was all somewhat strange. It was mixed meeting. We were with Zillian and a CGI computer company - you know - the sort that makes animated space craft for use in the movies. It turns out they have something called the Raft, which is a car that runs on electric motors. Then it has cameras all over it and reference points for animators. They can drive it around and then paint onto it any computer-generated body they like. So, it could be a sports car in one shot and then an SUV in the next."

"Is that legal?" asks Bigsy, "I mean making adverts without the real car even present?"

"Apparently. It used to be more expensive than having the actual cars on location, but when some of the cars are hard to source or even still in prototype, then the Raft makes sense."

"Or so goes the marketing spiel!" says Clare.

Hannah nods, "I agree it is good to be sceptical, but my issue is putting this together with a few other things we've been briefed about. To be honest, I wondered if it is something that Isabella knew about!"

"So, what is your thinking? " Asks Christina.

"I'm wondering if the car company is trying to hype their product," answers Hannah. "Suppose they don't have anything to present? I mean, that would reduce their public perception and share price somewhat!"

"I'm not so sure," answers Bigsy, "When I went onto the show floor earlier, there were three brightly coloured Zillians on display: Yellow, Red and Blue. I agree they had been rolled into position in the hall, but I think they are being made available for test-drives to certain reviewers later in the week."

"Okay, so how can we get closer to Zillian?" asks Christina, "To try to work out if some kind of number is being played on Melship and Lessiter."

"We've got the two tables at the Gstaad event," says Clare," I seem to remember that Zillian bid to be on Melship's table, with Jallie T."

"Well, I'm looking forward to the trip to Gstaad in a supercar, tomorrow afternoon " says Jake. "After all of this hanging around being well- fed and briefed about batteries and eco-friendly non-dusty brake pads here in Geneva, we need some light relief."

The others nodded agreement, "I just hope the drivers are not going to want to talk to us about batteries," says Jake.

"Fireworks over the lake tonight, and Jallie T's band are playing close to the fountain," says Bigsy.

"Yes, she's asked me to join her for one number," says Christina, smiling.

"Not that Nirvana thing you two do?" asks Bigsy, "I suppose you'll want Clare on stage too!"

Lottie and Hannah looked intrigued.

"See, I told you, "Says Lottie to Hannah.

Firework Nirvana

Evening by the lake. Everyone had been bussed to the waterfront and it was busy with many dark-suited men in starched shirts with bow ties and women in long dresses.

Clare, Hannah, Lottie, and Christina decided to style it out with black leather jackets and dark outfits. Christina had added a red with black tartan mini-skirt, gold chains and sunglasses.

Clare was wearing her black outfit, when Cristina says, "You'll need these," and produced a pair of black round sunglasses and a small, black-rimmed hat.

"Very cool," says Lottie, and Christina looked in her bag and produced a purple bandana which she handed to Lottie and then says to Hannah, "Come with me, I've an idea!"

Ten minutes later they return and Hannah was now resplendent with faded green hair and a couple of chains.

"Sub-zero!" says Jake as he appeared with Bigsy. By comparison, they were very conservatively dressed in jeans and tee-shirts but with big coats for the bracing Geneva air.

"Christina loaned me this wig," says Hannah.

"Erm, what will Lessiter say?" asks Bigsy.

"Excellent, " says Christina ignoring the banter, "now we look like this, we should get some AAA Badges."

"AAA?" asks Hannah.

"Access All Areas, silly," says Clare.

"Clare you are still doing it," says Lottie.

Christina is already at the barrier to the stage.

"Yes, I'm Christina Nott and these are my three backing singers!" she explains. At that moment someone turned around and it was Jallie T.

"Jallie!" calls Christina.

"Make way for pop royalty!" says Jallie and the two of them hugged.

"It's been too long! And now you come equipped with three backing singers. Very cool. Hi, I'm Jallie -

I'll introduce you to my band when I can find them."

Lottie, Hannah, and Clare appear with their newly acquired wristbands - white rubber with the red AAA embossed on each of them.

"We've left lanyard territory now, moving to the next level!" says Clare.

They all laugh and Jallie goes over to greet Clare just as Rishi appeared.

"My god, great to see you, Clare!" They hug, and then Rishi notices Christina, "Babe, you are looking hot!" he says and kisses her firmly on the cheek.

"And who are your friends?" he asks, noticing Lottie and Hannah. "I suppose they are in some kind of adventure with you and it's on a need-to-know basis!" He laughs.

They all introduced themselves, then Rishi says, "And you know what? Those mallets became so popular that I order them for every venue now!"

Christina laughed and thought back to when they had first met and Rishi had persuaded Clare to take neon pink and black mallets on tour as part of a promotional pack, when they toured together with a band called Erebus. Rishi spoke into a handset and within a few moments, a small brown box containing four of the mallets had arrived.

Lottie speaks to Hannah, "See, Clare is the friend

who just keeps on giving surprises!"

Then, suddenly, Jallie T is whisked away towards a floating stage set upon Lac Leman.

"C'mon, Christina," she calls," We'll work out your spot when we are on stage."

A few minutes later, the Jallie T Band struck up their first number and the whole of the shoreline was rocking. Rishi had rigged up a monstrous light show, which Clare assumed he had borrowed from somewhere. And the PA System sounded loud enough to drown an alien invasion.

Clare, Lottie, and Hannah were all in the wings with Christina, when the band went into an extended instrumental section.

"Okay, next song!" says Jallie - "we'll do Teenage Spirit. Rishi has found us some pom-poms."

"Thank god I've been doing some gigging," said Christina, as she strode onto the stage, over a drum beat like a section from 'We will Rock You.' Boom-Boom-Clap. Boom-Booop-Clap.

"And now - for one night only - Pour un soir seulement! - Jallie T is joined on stage by Christina Nott ! - Jallie T est rejointe sur scène par Christina Nott !"

Then, a rattly guitar plays a few chords. E-A-G-C and a pounding drum bursts into the music.

Jallie T sings, on a simmer setting

"Load up on guns
 Bring your friends
 It's fun to lose
 And to pretend
 She's o-ver-bored
 Self-assured
 Oh no, I know a dirty word

By the edge of the stage, Rishi prepares a sweeping broom.

Pom-poms edge their way to the stage.

Hello, hello, hello, how low
 Hello, hello, hello, how low
 Hello, hello, hello, how low
 Hello, hello, hello

Then a guitar slashed through the evening and the next verse, with Christina singing, carves across the stage. Jallie gestures to Lottie and Hannah, to wave the pom-poms around and they both cautiously make their way on-stage.

"Go Large!" shouts Rishi and imitates how they should push and wave the pom-poms around.

With the lights out
 It's less dangerous
 Here we are now
 Entertain us

I feel stupid
And contagious
Here we are now
Entertain us

A mulatto
  An albino
  A mosquito
  My libido
  Yeah

Clare could feel droplets of sweat running down her back from her leather jacket. How could Christina and Jallie do it? But it was exciting!

Jallie was singing again.

I'm worse at what I do best
  And for this gift I feel blessed
  Our little group has always been
  And always will until the end

It was surprisingly difficult to keep energetically shaking a pom-pom, but the audience seemed to like it.

Hello, hello, hello, how low
  Hello, hello, hello, how low
  Hello, hello, hello, how low
  Hello, hello, hello

Then, Jallie and Christina together.

With the lights out

It's less dangerous
Here we are now
Entertain us
I feel stupid

And contagious
Here we are now
Entertain us
A mulatto

An albino
A mosquito
My libido
Yeah

Rishi worked it with the floor broom, like in the original Nirvana video. The video that has been watched over 1.3 billion times on Youtube.

Christina again:

And I forget just why I taste
Oh yeah, I guess it makes me smile
I found it hard, it's hard to find
Oh well, whatever, nevermind

Jallie T and Christina together:

Hello, hello, hello, how low
Hello, hello, hello, how low
Hello, hello, hello, how low
Hello, hello, hello

Christina:

With the lights out
  It's less dangerous
  Here we are now
  Entertain us

They were singing alternative verses now, so Jallie took over:

I feel stupid
  And contagious
  Here we are now
  Entertain us

Christina:

A mulatto
  An albino
  A mosquito
  My libido

Then the whole band for the last section:

A denial, a denial
  A denial, a denial
  A denial, a denial
  A denial, a denial
  A denial

Then, with a flourish, the guitar picked out the first line of 'Baby, you can drive my car' and at the end of it, Christina and Jallie sang 'Beep-beep; beep-beep - yeah!'

As the echoes of the last power chord ebb away, it merges with a crashing wave of applause from the audience. They were going wild.

"We've just seen something utterly unique," says Jake to Bigsy, who nods.

"Let's hope Melship and Lessiter are both here somewhere!" says Bigsy.

Jallie T and her band were already rocking their way through the next number.

Breakfast with dark glasses

The next morning, at breakfast, there was no sign of Hannah and Lottie, nor of Christina.

Lottie had texted Clare to say that she and Hannah had both been summoned to their respective MPs, for a briefing before they left for Gstaad.

It wasn't until lunch time that they returned and could explain what was happening.

"First of all, that was a fantastic experience yesterday!" said Hannah, "I mean, to be on stage with Jallie and Christina. To get some part of that applause."

Lottie added, "But I'm amazed how they could just carry on after that single number. It was immense and intense. Oh yes, and I noticed that Tony the Motor seemed impressed too, especially with you Hannah!"

"Did you tell Duncan you were on stage?"

"I wasn't sure about that," answered Lottie, "He might have wondered how I'd come to be in that position."

"To be honest, so was I!" said Hannah, "I've never done anything like that before, never, ever!"

"Stick with us, Hannah!" said Clare, "We may drive a twisty road but it's a lot of fun."

"And now we've got to prepare for the ski interlude! Jake, I know you ski, and Bigsy a bit, since that holiday last year. Christina is a natural, all that time in Iceland and Russia I suppose, and I assume the same for Antanov. But what about you, Lottie? And Hannah?"

Lottie answered, "Growing up, learning to ski was a bit like going to school. Mandatory. My father was able to get over the fact that I hadn't inherited his hand-eye coordination because I let him lead me down La Sarenne – The Alps' longest black run, at 18km (11 miles)—aged 10."

Lottie continued, "A year later, he took me to Gstaad, where he himself had learned to ski. Any photographs I took on our father-daughter trip are long gone, but memories stick in my mind. The chocolates we brought back, our patience waning as the shop assistant diligently wrapped the boxes up in similarly painstaking style to the jewellery salesman in Love Actually. The drive from Vevey, where some of my grandmother's family lived, each bend in the road that hugged the towering mountains revealing another majestic view."

She added, "Finally, Gstaad itself – demure chalets with generations-old, rich decoration along the widely projecting roofs and carved balconies; traditional horse-drawn carriages clip-clopping down the main cobbled street; glamorous women, all kept in check by the impossibly romantic Palace Hotel, from its voyeuristic perch high above."

"And you, Hannah?"

"When I was young, I had a ski-teacher who learned to ski around Chamonix. Like a lot of his colleagues and his father before him, he's a dairy farmer. In summer, he escorts his precious herd – 'his princesses' – into the high, verdant pastures. In winter, as pasture becomes piste, the cows retreat to the warm safety of a hay-stuffed barn, leaving him free to instruct and guide."

"They are both amazing stories," said Bigsy, "So now you'll have to tell us what the big boys wanted?"

Hannah answered, "Lessiter and Melship? They wanted to know the arrangements to get us up to Gstaad - what kind of car - that kind of thing."

Hannah looked in her notepad, "It turns out that the special guests are being ferried up to Gstaad in a variety of supercars and other specialist vehicles. "

"How the other half live," muttered Bigsy.

Hannah continued, "I hope I've got this right...Melship asked for a Bentley Bentayga - which I'd never heard of - but has got a Lamborghini Urus - a silly name designed to appeal to the Russians, I'm told. Lessiter asked for an Aston Martin DBS Superleggera but they had to point out to him that although it has four seats, it is somewhat cosy in the back. He insisted and so he now has two cars to take his party to Gstaad. The Aston and an all-electric Ford Mustang SUV."

"Let's hope that news doesn't get back to the UK then," said Jake, "Embarrassing pictures of MPs in sports cars in Switzerland!"

Hannah continued, "Many of the assistants are travelling on a few all-electric coaches, called eCitaros, which I suppose are more environmentally friendly."

Jake said, "I guess we will hear when the supercars start arriving this afternoon, but first we've got that session about reconfigurable electric drive matrices."

"Oh, I'm supposed to go to that, as well. It's obvious that Lessiter and Melship have brought Lottie and me to be their scribes."

"We'll, at least there is some free time as well," mused Jake, "Rock Goddess or Research Assistant"

"Good point!"

"Maybe more free time when we all get to Gstaad?" said Jake.

"I'm not holding my breath," said Hannah.

Reconfigurable Electric Drive Matrix (REDM)

Jake and Hannah finish breakfast and walk outside and along a snow-cleared route into the main presentation hall. The change to crisp alpine air wakes them both up.

Jake says, "This air when we walk back to the Palexpo; it's like a jolt of coffee."

"I agree," says Hannah, "I'm less sure how some of those lightly dressed female demonstrators are coping."

Jake looks at Hannah, "You know, Tony, he's a good mate of mine, but - how can I put this - he's kind of flexible when it comes to women."

Hannah smiles, "I know, I realised from right back in your office when he was making with the eyes. This is a car show and I'm only taking him for a test run."

Jake smiles back at Hannah, "Good, I'm relieved, I wouldn't want him to be hurting anyone."

"No, I can look after myself. Really."

Jake made to change the subject, "Here we are, Reconfigurable Electric Drive Matrix (REDM) - benefits and applications"

On stage was a car chassis. It had a recognisable front and back, but the part in the middle was a simple flat area.

"Bigsy was right," says Jake, "It does look like a toy Scalextric car without the body on it."

"So, in the future we'll all be buying the same chassis with different styling applied?" says Hannah, "They are determined to make cars boring."

On stage were four 'scientists' in white coats and two other bubbly presenters who looked like they could be on a children's TV show.

"Hi, I'm Greta and I'm Jonas," they said in unison.

Jonas bounced on the stage as if he was about to perform an amazing card trick with balloons and fireworks.

He starts: "The models of the future e-Auto family are currently being developed on the basis of the new reconfigurable electric drive matrix (REDM)."

Jake's and Hannah's shoulders sagged under the realisation that this would be like the batteries, brake fluids, or the tyre presentations that they had previously attended.

Greta picks up and continues with the exposition, "These are vehicles in a variety of classes which have been designed as full electric vehicles and reach ranges of up to 500 km and more. The architecture of the REDM will fundamentally change electric cars and cars in general."

Jake mutters, "Sales pitch,"

Jonas adds, "The REDM Toolkit jettisons all the ballast of the fossil age because it has been designed throughout for electric cars. This leads to fundamental changes in body design, interior design, the package and the powertrain characteristics of electric vehicles."

Now they walk around the car's frame pointing out different and somewhat obvious features.

- The wheels (but thinner tyres than usual for improved economy).
- The engines (electric and on each axle - two for the rear wheels and one for the front because of the complication of steering).
- The wiring (Two big fat cables from the front of the car to the back - for fault tolerance).
- The automatic self-diagnosing display (would alert to errors even before they became serious).
- Autonomous driving (but with plenty of

caveats)

- Safety detectors (even checks whether the driver is dozing off)
- The huge bank of batteries which would give the vehicle a claimed 300 miles.

"I could have written most of this without attending the session," says Jake.

Hannah nods her agreement. "It is pretty basic, and we only have their words for most of these things."

Jonas continues, "We want to establish REDM as an industry standard. We have opened the reconfigurable electric drive matrix to other manufacturers. This makes production cheaper, but also offers further advantages. You will find we are open to e-collaboration.

Greta adds, "The REDM is a decisive plus point"

Then Jonas, "The battery is considered the heart of modern electric cars. We can stretch this floor pan and it becomes a van with a 350-mile range, or a microbus able to seat eight people in comfort. Such a microbus could revolutionise inner city travel."

The first of the white coats was standing. Jake nudges Hannah and looks towards the exit. She nods and they both slink out of the auditorium, along with around fifty other people.

"Coffee?" says Hannah.

They make their way to a small coffee area set up for delegates who were between sessions. There was a 'push the lever' coffee machine which filled small paper cups with strong coffee.

They seated themselves at a quiet table.

"I could have made most of that up from the brochure," says Hannah, "I just hope Lessiter and Melship are becoming more knowledgeable."

"But we've hardly seen them?" observes Jake.

"Haven't you realised?" says Hannah, "They are having a blast, being wined and dined by manufacturers in separate hospitality suites. Several of the hotels around here have been taken over and suppliers and manufacturers have a floor each, in which to schmooze with their clients."

"I should have known," says Jake, "I could have looked out for the signs."

Hannah laughs,"...Martha Ford Suite? Carl Benz Suite? Frank Seiberling Suite? Zündapp Suite? Ford, Mercedes, Goodyear, Porsche. If you get my drift."

Jake laughs, "I may have been out of journalism for just too long," he said.

"Well, here's something else I picked up, " says Hannah. She was just about to begin when Christina and Bigsy appear with Antanov Chekeryn.

"Look who I found in the main hall!" says Christina as Antanov introduces himself to Hannah.

"Er - are you Russian?" asks Hannah, "Only with that name...I could never tell it from your accent!"

"Yes, I'm originally from the far away land, from Perm, which is in the Volga. But when I was quite young, my parents moved to Moscow and then later to Saint Petersburg. I was at the same Akademy as Christina in Arkhangelsk - we run into one another every few years!"

Jake smiled as he thought how difficult it would be to believe that story, yet how true he knew it to be.

"I was just explaining to Christina how I'd found out a few things about one of the car companies that your MPs are going to visit."

Hannah looks surprised, "How could you know about that?" she asks.

"Christina and I trust each other with information. It can be very useful when trying to work out certain complicated situations."

Jake nods, "That's right, I remember when Antanov was in London that time, and provided us with all manner of useful facts and contacts for some work we were doing with another organisation."

"But if you are linked with the secret service?" asks

Hannah, "Surely Antanov isn't as well?"

"No, I'm not," answered Antanov, "But I have my own set of contacts and am very comfortable to work with Christina. When we have flown helicopters together over the Dvina River and the White Sea, then you put trust in one another.

"Kotyonok, you remember when I rescued you from the fishing hut near Kumbysh? and I certainly remember you hauling me back from the Paratov Restaurant in Archangel, to help me avoid a court martial."

Christina laughs, "Yes this is the man who turned up in a helicopter to rescue me when my dingy washed up on an island just before the White Sea. Then at another time, I had to fetch him in a taxi, when he'd fallen in with a crowd of drunken sailors and 'gone fishing' in the city. He was so drunk he could not stand up. I hauled him back to our base, carried him up a fire escape and tucked him into bed."

They both laugh. Hannah looks confused, "Is there anyone who Clare knows that is kind of 'normal'?

Bigsy answers, "If you have to ask then it is probably you - although after your singing and pom-poms on Lac Leman, I think you are safe."

"Well, let me tell you what I found out!" says Antanov, "And I had to pull strings to get some of this. Antanov opened a small laptop and began to read.

"It's a long story all about Zillian's rise from the rubble", he says, "Brace yourselves:

"Weidemotoren was a manufacturer of tractors, agricultural machinery and engines, founded in 1933 by industrialist Tomas Weide in the Landsberg district of Bavaria.

"It was the beginning of considerable development of Weide's factories. Coincidentally, another tractor company was also started in Bavaria around this time. Both companies made tests and carried out competitive work.

"By 1936, the other company - Eicher - built the first diesel tractor with a 20 hp Deutz - diesel engine. The gearbox was attached to the engine and passed the power via a propeller shaft to the rear axle.

"Weide saw the design and a few inherent problems, and built a vastly improved version, with selectable engines and transmissions in 1937.

"In the same year, Weide was represented for the first time at the DLG (Deutsche Landwirtschafts-Gesellschaft) exhibition in Munich. The modular construction of tractors with flexible engine choices was an instant hit and prevailed in the following years. "

"They have a whole show for tractors?" asks Jake.

"Oh, it's immense, says Antanov, "There's even a

spin-off of the show in Russia - It's called 'Potato Days, Russia!' "

Jake looks incredulous.

Antonov continues, "And if you go to one of their DLG Feldtage - sorry, field days - you'll be able to see actual kit operating on real fields. Think of a car show only with tractors!"

He smiles as he notices the look of fear that briefly flickers across the faces of Jake and Hannah.

Hannah interrupts, "Yes, that is consistent with what I found out from a briefing with Douglas Lessiter and Duncan Melship yesterday. It ties in with some things about Zillian, but I'd better let you continue, Antonov," she smiles and then felt the full force of Antonov's charm beaming back.

Jake realises that Hannah and his buddy Tony Brooklands were evenly matched in the flirtation department.

Antonov continues, "Weide decided to diversify and became an automobile manufacturer in 1938 when it purchased Fahrzeugfabrik Nieten, which, at the time, built Morris 8s under licence under the Nieten marque as the well-known Nieten Luxus."

"I've seen pictures of them. I think it was an early example of the use of common running platforms, to build a saloon, a tourer and even a van or small truck," says Bigsy, "It's strange how history is reinventing itself now."

Antanov looks back at his laptop, "The onset of war caused the retooling of the Weide factory for the additional production of armaments and aircraft engines to a generic design also produced in other factories throughout Germany.

"Weide's factories were heavily bombed during the war and its remaining West German facilities were banned from producing motor vehicles or aircraft after the war.

"The company survived by making agricultural tools and bicycles as well as pots and pans. In 1948, following BMW restarting motorcycle production Weide was able to restart its own vehicle production.

"Weide resumed car production in 1952 with the Nieten Weide luxury saloon and a lighter 2-door version. The range of cars was expanded in 1955, through the production of the cheaper Wespe 3-wheeler microcar under licence.

"Slow sales of luxury cars and small profit margins from microcars meant BMW was able to completely outpace Weide until BMW, too, became in serious financial trouble and in 1959 the BMW company was nearly taken over by rival Daimler-Benz.

"The faltering Weide was almost saved by an industrialist, Günther Quandt, but with the influence of his sons, they placed their entire investment with BMW instead."

Antanov continues, "We should note some background. Günther Quandt joined the Nazi party in 1933 and made a fortune arming the German Wehrmacht, manufacturing weapons and batteries.

"Quandt's enterprises were appropriated from Jewish owners under duress with minimal compensation.

"At least three of Quandt's enterprises made extensive use of slave labourers, as many as 30,000 in all. One of his battery factories had its own on-site concentration camp, complete with gallows. Life expectancy for labourers was six months. It is alleged that it was the funds amassed in the Nazi era by his father which allowed Herbert Quandt to buy and rescue BMW."

"Yes," confirms Hannah, "it's like what I heard as well, although they didn't mention the Nazi influence and made the BMW bail-out sound like a rich family purchase."

Antanov continues, "This bleak situation left Weide to fend for itself and without investment, it moved back to its origins, producing tractors. In 1948, the first post-war development was finally presented, the Weide 16.

"This tractor used an air-cooled diesel engine. The same multi-platform technique was used with Weide producing more tractors with increasing horsepower - the imaginatively named Weide 25, 28 and 30 - each able to carry a more sophisticated range of tools."

The Germans seemed to like air-cooled designs," observes Bigsy, "Think of the Volkswagen Beetle or the early Porsches".

"Porsche's last air-cooled car was the 993," sas Jake, "See? I do remember some things from my time at Street. I had to do a filler article on one once, I remember that Keanu Reeves, David Beckham, Harry Styles, Ellen Degeneres, and Antonio Banderas, all had them."

"We are drifting off topic," says Christina, " I know, Jake, you want to prove you haven't lost the street cred,"

Antonov laughs, "Well it's more interesting than me just running through this history lesson. The Weide marque continued through the 50s and 60s, creating tractors and tools such as flail mowers, backhoe loaders, stone buriers, rotovators, hedge trimmers, cultivators, ploughs, log splitters and power harrows."

'Stone buriers?" says Jake.

"We'll be testing you on what each one does, at dinner," jokes Bigsy.

Antonov adds, "But now the clever idea. Their designs retained the modular concept with the advantage that the tractor attachments would work with either the Ferguson 3-point hitch or the Euro adapter using something called the A-hitch."

"I see, so they could hook up to anything, " says Bigsy.

"Story of my life," says Jake.

"Boys, let's be serious," says Christina.

Antanov continues, "Weide A-hitch patents were licensed to many other tool suppliers and the run-rate of licensing deals kept the company alive for the next fifty years.

"In 2016, Weide was sold in a surprise takeover by Zillian Automobile. Analysts declared the takeover as mercenary and that Zillian wanted to buy 'heritage' for its new startup business."

"I see, says Jake, "It's like Lamborghini, able to show its early credentials in tractors and even batteries before moving to automobiles.

"Yes, except these new Zillian credentials would be faked," answers Antanov.

"And they have side-stepped the war implications, too" says Hannah, "And now, I've found out a few things too. It wasn't actually from Zillian, but from one of the well-known car companies trying to run interference on Zillian."

"How so?" asked Jake,

Hannah replied, "Oh, Lottie and I have had a string of invitations to all kinds of 'meet the people' sessions because we are representing Lessiter and Melship. One was with a mega corporation who want to bring ever larger trucks to the UK.

"It was an embarrassing session when someone pointed out that they would not fit under UK's motorway bridges. The bridges are 4.7 metres high, but these new curtain-sided trucks were 5 metres high!"

"However, those present started to chatter about competition and a string of scandals were implied.

Hannah continues, "There was a whole somewhat juicy section about Zillian and Weide. It turns out the combined car maker firm has been mired in controversy, corruption, sleaze, and sex scandals ever since the takeover by Zillian.

"Industry experts say the 'Unterlech Fortress Mentality' - the town where the company has its headquarters - made arrogant bosses feel invincible in the face of competition and regulation.

"To be honest, this didn't ring true with me. It looked more as if the Weide company had been honest manufacturers of tractors and then had a lucky break with that connector licensing deal.

"I felt that the sleaze was being pumped in from the

Zillian direction. As an example, In 2019, it was the centre of a sex scandal which rocked Germany. Zillian's Workers' Council chief, Meik Meindl, received £1.2million in bribes, some of which paid to his Brazilian lover Miriam Conceição de Ávila

"To improve their chances, Zillian organised sex parties for German MPs and union bosses. Former personnel manager Franz Rimensberger admitted his role in the scandal. And this was in the time when Zillian was only making a handful of cars."

"I could see it would be a quick way to climb to the top," says Jake, "That's to the top of a rather sleazy pole, of course."

Hannah continues, "A €5 billion compensation fund was set aside as bosses braced for the raft of collective compensation claims from customers who purchased unfit vehicles - frequently because of emissions claims."

"So what vehicles was Zillian producing at that time?" asks Bigsy, "I thought Zillian was all about electric cars?"

"Yes, it is, " answers Hannah, "The cars in question are all from Weide, but now rebadged as Zillian. The 303, which looks quite like a Mini Cooper, the 404, which is quite like a medium sized BMW, and their bigger car, the 505, which looks like a Range Rover."

Antanov adds, "The cars were only making 'placeholder sales' in Europe and the USA at that time. Enough to keep the marque validated, but not enough to turn a profit. Our investigations suggest that the cars were actually rebadged Chinese copies of European cars."

"Ha," says Bigsy, "A rebadged Chinese car then rebadged as a Zillian."

"That's right," says Antanov, "Zillian are simply buying Chinese cars to resell as Zillian, while they became established in the market."

Jake asks, "What like the JAC A6, which is a rip-off of the Audi A6? - I only learned about it this week!"

"That's right," says Hannah, looking at her notes, "Even the Rolls-Royce Phantom is available as a copycat from China - the Geely GE - although they later had to restyle it and change the name to EmGrand."

Jake asks, "But surely this is another point of suspicion about Zillian, then?"

Hannah continues, "Yes, they wanted keep Zillian looking like a German company, but it didn't help when their chief executive Carl Tisch resigned, saying he wanted to give the German manufacturer 'a fresh start', after the allegations of copycat cloning and emission result faking."

Hannah adds, "But Zillian is no stranger to controversy. The latest to engulf Zillian rakes up painful memories for industry experts as the company's history is blighted by cover-ups, dodgy deals, and collusion. For example, in 2017, through Weide, the company shocked the markets by announcing it was taking a €160 million provision to cover losses it incurred as the victim of a foreign exchange fraud - almost halving its profits.

Hannah adds, "Look, I pulled some papers. That scandal, which led to an international manhunt for the fraudsters, caused Zillian shares to plunge almost a third. After a seven-month search, FBI agents arrested a foreign exchange broker from Frankfurt wanted in connection with the fraud, having tracked him to an apartment in Hollywood."

Antanov nods, "Yes, it is very similar to what I found out. He opened a hard bag and pulled out a small MacBook, which he then opened and turned around for everyone to see.

"I had it translated from German," he says, "It was in all the main papers at the time." He reads from the article:

'Shamed German MP Daniel Honigsman-Bopp attended a sex party organised by Zillian. He was jailed for perjury when he lied and said he hadn't attended.'

"That is hardly enough to discredit the company," says Antonov as he looked towards his next note:

"This situation centres on the collusion between union bosses and corporate bigwigs to keep the workers at the production lines and the profits rolling in."

Hannah interrupts, "Zillian was suffering from high wages, low productivity and increasing competition and wanted to push through harsh staff restructuring plans."

Antanov resumes, "That's what I discovered too, Hannah. Zillian's bosses knew their plans would be rejected if put to the Worker's Council and so set aside a €500,000 slush fund to entertain German politicians and union bosses to force them to agree to the reforms."

"I see, " says Christina, "Buy Weide to recredentialise Zillian, use cheap clone cars to establish a market, weaken the Union position to lay off staff - presumably Weide staff - and use a troubled company profile to weaken the price to make it cheap for a further take-over. These are all Kremlin plays from the old days. The young guys are throwing the old men out - again!"

Antanov continues, "Christina is right...The plan was to weaken the unions' clout by using honeytraps - in other words luring officials into compromising situations."

"This is so like the Minerva and Medusa programmes which ran in the UK, " says Jake.

Antonov adds, "Well this time they used company funds to pay for sex parties for powerful union reps and politicians. It looks like the Russian organised crime method of influence was being used by Zillian to influence German politicians.

"Daniel Herr, Zillian's personnel head, paid millions of euros over several years to the company's works council chief, Meik Meindl.

"Meindl used the money to fund lavish parties and luxury hotel stays in Brazil and Lisbon for shop stewards and disguised the payments as business expenses.

"Some €280,000 of the money was paid to Meindl's Brazilian lover, Miriam Conceição de Ávila, along with jewellery and furs. But the plot unravelled when the parties came to attention of state prosecutors after the actions of a whistle-blower.

"In the subsequent court case, Daniel Herr was fined €500,000, but escaped jail by admitting to his part in the affair.

"The court heard how he paid illegal bonuses to Meindl because Zillian's management 'wanted union acceptance to change of work practice.'

Christina says, "This a much simpler corruption - pure blackmail and payoffs. It comes straight from the age of old KGB training manuals."

Antanov nods, "German MP Daniel Honigsman-Bopp was implicated in the fallout. He sat on the powerful IG Metall Union at Zillian in Augsburg where the workers' committee and staff reforms required his approval.

"Honigsman-Bopp later admitted being present at a Sexworld party in a Hanover club, where champagne and 'other entertainment' were laid on for workers' council directors.

Hannah says, "As far as I can tell, in the same year, Zillian was also caught up in a corruption scandal in India when a senior executive promised to build a factory in the Andhra Pradesh state in return for a €1.4m payment."

Clare smiles. She knows Hannah is an awesome researcher and now Hannah was allowing herself to freewheel, she was finding out all kinds of interesting facts.

Hannah adds, "And further, the company was embroiled in a wider auto industry corruption scandal after executives at some carmakers were accused of taking bribes from suppliers.

"This scandal led to the resignation of the executive chairman of Vitless, a French brake component maker, after Erwin Lang, Zillian chief executive at the time, threatened to sever ties with the company."

Antonov adds, "After this, Red Fox - a subsidiary of Brant Holdings - were raided as part of an investigation into alleged market manipulation by the company's executives during a failed takeover of Zillian."

"Whoa, Whoa, Whoa," says Jake, "Brant. Again, involved in malpractice. I thought we had stopped all of that."

Christina smiles, "Think of that fairground game.... Whack-a- Mole. Brant is like that and will keep reinventing itself to pop up again."

Hannah adds, "Yes. The industry insiders at the briefing suggested that Brant quietly built a stake in Zillian by using a contentious options strategy, which distorted the price of Zillian's ordinary shares over a multi-year period. They used Red Fox to do this, so that they could appear 'hands off' if anything became difficult.

Then she referred to her notes, "Joachim Ganser, president of the association of German industries, BDI, said; 'We strongly criticise any form of manipulation. Any misconduct must be cleared up completely with transparency, openness, and speed.

Hannah looked at her notes again, " 'Made in Germany' stands for excellent products,' Ganser said, adding that German engineering and craftsmanship were 'rightly respected worldwide'. Deutsche Nachrichten, the broadcaster reported that 'Ganser's statement reflects deeper concerns here in Germany that Zillian's breach of industry ethics could do lasting damage to the country's reputation as a producer of top-notch goods.'

Jake summarises, "Okay, so our two MPs are both

chatting away amiably to a remarkably dodgy car manufacturer."

Hannah adds, "I wish that was all. They have also both been happy to visit all kinds of hospitality events whilst here in Geneva and have sent myself and Lottie away to attend seminars about automatic transmissions and the advantages of winter tyres."

Antanov smiles, " I must congratulate you, Hannah, to not be fooled by this although I suspect much of your material also required additional research?"

"Yes, it did, after I knew a few key points and therefore where to start digging. I also borrowed the help of an industry expert who seemed happy to assist my line of enquiry."

Jake smiles, realising that Tony had not been leading Hannah along. It was more the other way around.

Bérénice Charbonnier

Late afternoon, the invited delegates for the Gstaad session had all been transported to Hotel Les Bergues, on the lakeside in Geneva. There was a gentle clinking of champagne glasses while they waited for their cars. They had all gone together and were now working the senior delegates before they made their way to Gstaad.

The outside of the hotel has been dressed to look like a pit-stop, complete with grid girls and even some grid guys. The first of the cars were already being filled with people, and by the sound of them they were powerful petrol driven cars. Polar opposites of the vehicles being promoted by the car manufacturers.

"It's hilarious to watch," says Lottie as a silver saloon with two rows of slit-like headlights came into view. It had a huge V-shaped cheese grater front grill and made a rasping sound with its 3.5 litre twin-turbo V6 engine.

"But listen as they describe the paint colours too," says Hannah, "Dragon Orange Metallic, Sao Paolo Yellow, Thermal Orange Pearl, Cyber Orange, Phoenix Yellow, Ocra Tri-Coat, Lime Essence, Papaya Spark. Imagine ticking the wrong box in the dealership?"

Lottie replies, "I guess they are all televisual colours - like the Mamids wear on those review shows."

Jake queries, "Mamids? - I've heard of Mamils - Middle Aged Men in Lycra - not so much the Mamids?"

Christina answers, "Middle aged men in denim."

Jake smiles, since he'd left Street, he was losing touch with his Urban.

Lottie had been asked to stay with Duncan Melship and Hannah with Douglas Lessiter for the car collection, although they both knew they had been relegated to separate cars for the journey to Gstaad.

Clare was with Christina when she noticed Tony Brooklands among those at the reception and wandered over to say 'Hello'.

"Oh hello, Clare," he replied, "Are you excited to be in one of the most high-value car processions that Geneva has seen?"

Clare smiled back, 'Boys and their toys,' she was thinking.

Tony was talking to another group of people and he briefly introduced them as Bérénice Charbonnier from le Genevois - the Geneva newspaper, Kjeld Nikolajsen, Miller McDonald and Mary Ranzino from Brant and Qiu Zhang and Volvakov Kirill Valeryevich representing Zillian.

"It sounds as if these two companies want to make a big splash with electric cars," says Tony, "It is most exciting."

"My card," says Volvakov Kirill Valeryevich, "And you may call me Kirilka,"

He hands them both an embossed card, with one side printed in Russian and the other in English.

They also notice that Bérénice Charbonnier was adroitly ushering the group, including Tony, away from them both.

Christina whispers, "There's such an obvious Russian-style game-play being used here, although I'd say that Qiu Zhang works for the Chinese MSS and it is a copycat model.

"The MSS?" queries Clare, "That's a new one on me,"

"The Ministry of State Security (MSS), or Guoanbu is the civilian intelligence, security and secret police agency of the People's Republic of China, responsible for counterintelligence, foreign intelligence and political security. MSS has been described as one of the most secretive intelligence organisations in the world. It is headquartered in Beijing."

Christina continues, "I had to check it out once before. The MSS facilities operate from close to the Summer Place in Beijing. The MSS is divided into secretive Bureaus, each assigned to a division with a broad directive. The Enterprises Division is responsible for the operation and management of MSS owned front companies, enterprises, and other institutions."

Clare asks, "You seem to know a lot about this."

Christina nods, "Yes, I'd almost forgotten, but the other time I checked MSS out, it was beginning to copy the way Russia became more gangster-like. Like when the Russian state apparatus created all their offshore companies, sent trusted people to run them, launder money through them and then appoint other people to take over the state banks and heavy industries like oil, minerals, and logistics. The old guard ran everything until the young guns wanted more of the pie and started throwing the old men off balconies. Nowadays, like in so many things, the Chinese are trying to copy the processes."

Christina adds, "I've had a prior run-in with Bérénice too. Don't be taken in by her warm smiles. She has ice running through her veins. I suspect she is in the pay of the Chinese, orchestrated by Qiu Zhang."

"Wow, we got a lot from that 30 second meeting with Tony!" says Clare.

They were nearly at the front of the line to pick up their cars to be transported to Gstaad.

Cars to Gstaad

Duncan Melship's car arrived first. It had a Lamborghini badge on the front but looked like a yellow SUV.

"I doubt if that is what Melship was expecting!" mutters Tony, under his breath.

"It reminds me of one of those Porsche people carriers you see all around London," agrees Bigsy.

"Astute," breathes Tony, "It uses some of the same bits inside."

Melship climbs into the car, along with two smiling women in matching yellow jumpsuits.

"It's the London scene being played out here in Geneva," says Bigsy, "Eye candy for the men in suits,"

"And the research assistants have to follow up on the bus," adds Clare.

The car accelerates away from the hotel, just as a somewhat sleeker car arrives, announced as a lime essence green Aston Martin, followed by a red Ford SUV.

"It must be Duggie's car," says Hannah and watches as he steps forward, along with another two remarkably slim women.

"It's so they can fit in the back," explains Jake, "The opposite of 'supersize'.

Sure enough, Duggie was led by the hand to the low-slung Aston Martin and then had to assist as the two women slid into the small back seats.

"What a business!" muses Bigsy, then looking startled as he realised, he'd said it out loud.

Suddenly, an unmistakable bright red Ferrari appeared to a few gasps from the crowd.

"My ride," says Christina.

"I approve," utters Tony as Christina strode toward the vehicle, "You are looking at a £500k plus car over there," he said, "I think it does 0-60 in under three seconds."

"But can it handle snow?" asked Jake, "Or is it only good along la Croisette and outside Senequier?"

"No ladies for Christina," observes Clare.

"But there's nowhere to fit them," says Bigsy, laughing.

"Shall we make our way to the buses?" asks Clare.

"Good plan," says Lottie.

Snow crunches under their feet as they approached the bus shelters, where a fleet of electric buses was marshalled to take the less privileged assistants to Gstaad.

PART TWO

Toblerone

Ice cream.

That is all.

Bigsy

About Gstaad

"It really is the land of chocolate and cheese, here in this part of Switzerland," observes Bigsy.

"And small ski resorts," adds Jake.

They had disembarked from their coach at Le Grand Bellevue hotel.

Gstaad–once described by Julie Andrews as 'the last paradise in a crazy world'– to find out what lies behind the jet-set façade.

"This isn't for normal people," observes Jake.

"It's amazing," adds Clare.
"Are we really staying here?" asks Bigsy.

A woman appeared, "Welcome to Gstaad. Let's get you sorted out," She handed each of them a small guidebook and yet another lanyard and badge.

Jake scanned the copy on the guidebook cover:

"It's the skiing that many return to Gstaad for, year after year – 200km (124 miles) of immaculately groomed, wide and often empty slopes. Unlike other popular resorts, Gstaad's ski areas are separated by nature reserves and un-pisted mountain faces. Far from being inconvenient, it means spending each day in a new area, exploring new terrain, from the windswept plateau of Glacier 300 – the only glacier ski area in the Bernese Oberland – to the Wasserngrat's Tiger Run, the region's steepest slope with an average gradient of - 45°."

A voice interrupts his reading, "If you could each identify your luggage, we will arrange to have it shipped to your suites and chateaux. Some of you will need to catch further small bus to your individual chateau."

"I guess that will be us, then," says Clare, "I imagine this hotel is for the more well-heeled and influential."

As if on cue, both Lessiter and Melship appear, surrounded by a small posse of cat-suited women. Lessiter seemed to be enjoying the attention, although Clare sensed a look of work-weariness in the eyes of the women.

Lessiter was being shown to a room, and Melship was waiting patiently for his key. Clare noticed that these guests seemed to get a whole carrier bag full of goodies, instead of the guidebook that they had received from the coach disembarkation.

"I feel this is the kind of place that James Bond would like," observes Bigsy.

"Silly, this is exactly the place where Roger Moore, 007, lived in real life," says Lottie, " I think he moved from this side of the mountains to the other side, to

Crans-Montana, which has even more skiing," answers Hannah.

"Impressive," says Bigsy, absent-mindedly, "Oh I'm sorry, I keep saying things I'm thinking, out loud!"

They all laughed. Hannah adds, "I've just been reading the guidebook. It happens to mention Roger Moore in it. But he's not the only celebrity - in fact, there's whole herds of them!"

Jake laughs, "Herds, an interesting collective noun for celebrities! I'm thinking a clique, or maybe a pap?"

An official-looking woman appeared. "You are together?" she asks, "I have a 16-berth chalet which you can occupy."

They all looked at one another, nodded and Jake says, "Yes, do lead the way,"

The woman took them to a Mercedes Coach, and then they made their way a short distance to a huge chalet overlooking the valley.

"I could get used to this life-style," says Bigsy.

They were greeted at the door by Allegra Schrämli, who announced herself as the chalet maid.

"Unbelievable," says Bigsy, out loud. The others smile.

"Willkommen, Bienvenue," said Allegra, "I've fixed for you all to have a fondue this evening made with the finest Gruyere from the Pays-d'Enhaut. After a day like today, it will be something cosy and social for you all before business starts again tomorrow!"

She waved them into the wooden chalet which was stunningly appointed in a modern architectural style, "Oh, wow, I wasn't expecting this," says Jake, "Oops, I've caught Bigsy's speaking out loud thing!"

"It is architect-designed, like many of the larger chalets. I sometimes think the bigger guests miss out when they all want to stay in the major hotels here. This chalet was designed by Chaletwirth Architekten and the inside was furnished by Alexandra Bernardette, that most famous designer."

"But komm," she says, "Choose your rooms; there are few enough of you to ensure that everyone will get a balcony with a view. And there is a ski-room downstairs where you can grab some kit for the slopes."

"Pinch me," says Bigsy to Clare, "Am I dreaming all of this?"

Clare's phone rang. It was Christina.

"Hiya Ms Ferrari, are you nicely settled in your luxury hotel? We've done well with this overspill chalet which is as top of the range as you can imagine. It even includes skis."

"That's what I wanted to call you about," says Christina, "I've met with Antanov again. He's suggested we could all go skiing tomorrow."

"I'll need to check with the others, said Clare, "In case anyone wants to pass on it."

"Okay, well forget all those ski-lifts though. Antanov arrived at the hotel by helicopter. He says we can use it tomorrow to go heli-skiing. Apparently, there are six sites to choose from! What are they, Antanov?"

Clare could hear Antanov call out 'Gstellihorn, Wildhorn, Vordere Walig, Stalden, Gumm, Glacier de Tsanfleuron, but it's not a test!'

Clare realised that Christina and Antanov must be sharing a room, like that time in Germany.

Christina added, "I should also mention that Antanov has brought along a Mil Mi-171A2. It can take quite a few passengers and costs about 20 of my Ferraris!"

"I guess someone is taking this whole car thing quite seriously if Antanov can get hold of such kit?" asks Clare.

"Oh yes, not least because the Kremlin could be dragged through the mud for something it hasn't done. And let's face it with Antanov and me on the case, it has a certain high profile within Russia," answers Christina.

"And you know something? We should take Melship and Lessiter with us, see what we can find out," says Christina.

The right to disconnect

The next morning was Saturday, deemed a non-working day. The car Expo would start again on Monday, giving the delegates the weekend to unwind. This part of Switzerland was close enough to France to mean that some of the French customs of 35-hour working week and the 'right to disconnect' had been informally implemented.

Hannah and Lottie arranged for Melship and Lessiter to join the skiing expedition. Antanov had chosen to fly to the nearby Gsteig bei Gstaad area, which offered some low-risk skiing descents all through the valley toward Gstaad. Antanov estimated it was around 15 kilometres of gentle downhill to ski back and would not require any additional queues at cable stations.

Just as importantly, it ended in Gstaad, so the helicopter could be flown out but would not be needed for a subsequent pickup.

Clare invited Allegra to come along too, and they all

met at the Gstaad heliport, where Antanov's helicopter dwarfed the others present.

"It's difficult to hide something this large," exclaimed Antanov, "but it will give everyone the luxury experience."

Clare noticed that the helicopter's interior was a set of two clusters of four plump leather armchairs and then another two further back. It screamed luxury and she wondered if it belonged to an oligarch. She could not imagine the Kremlin's procurement department buying something so lavish.

Melship and Lessiter took it in their stride, and Clare quickly realised that they were being given the finest treatment by the various companies they were visiting.

They all settled into their newly acquired VIP suite, with Duncan Melship and Douglas Lessiter on the private chairs and then the rest of them filling in the cluster of eight seats, and with Christina Nott taking the co-pilot seat next to Antanov.

Clare noticed that Melship and Lessiter were talking between themselves and that they made little effort to socialise with the rest of the cabin.

Allegra looked in some wonder at the helicopter and appeared to be considering just who these guests were that she was supporting.

The skis and other paraphernalia had all been

loaded and then the 'copter took off and after what seemed like a few minutes was already preparing for a descent at the ski point.

Christina looked at ease in the co-pilot's seat and Clare remembered how Christina had told her about her military training in Arkhangelsk.

After a gentle landing, Antanov walked through the cabin.

"There," he said, "Just 15 kilometres from Gstaad, but a totally different outlook. After you have unloaded, Christina and I will take the plane back to Gstaad and see you in a couple of hours for après ski."

Helipad

They disembarked and Clare noticed the other people around the helipad. In a fashionable ski outfit, Bérénice Charbonnier was standing with Qiu Zhang and Volvakov Valeryevich. Behind them, a small group of additional men, who Clare considered to be their minders.

Bérénice spoke,*"Quelle surprise, Une coïncidence, Et quel plaisir de vous voir. Nous avons pris le premier hélicoptère jusqu'à ce sommet, depuis Gstaad."*

And then realising they were all English, "How great to see you all, we took the early helicopter to the peak, for a gentle ski back to Gstaad! Perhaps we can all go together?"

As if on cue, two more athletic looking women skied into view and joined Bérénice's party.

Clare could immediately spot the difference in ski capability among the group. Allegra, Christina and Antanov all looked fully proficient. Jake looked as if he could handle the skis well and at about the same level as Clare herself. She knew that Lottie took regular skiing holidays, so they should be good on the slopes. She could see that Bigsy was struggling to stay upright, as indeed was Lessiter. She'd judge Melship as a better skier and maybe around her own level.

By comparison Bérénice, Qiu Zhang and Volvakov Valeryevich all looked to be superior skiers, as did their entourage.

"We seem to have some mixed abilities here," said Jake, "I think you may enjoy a faster run toward the village."

"No, no, we wouldn't dream of it. We can probably help your group, too," replied Bérénice.

"Although whoever is last back gets the first round of schnapps!" said Volvakov.

Allegra called out, "I must remind my guests to stay safe. No excess speeds, stay away from the edges and beware equipment, low beams around the cable pylons and other sharp things on the descent."

Clare was impressed that Allegra had spoken up and wondered how mean seasons she had done as an instructor; she certainly moved gracefully on her skis.

Bérénice arranged them all into two rough groups.

"Here, we will make up the forward group and probably go slightly faster than the others. Then can come the middle group but I expect it will detach a few stragglers! No need to decide beyond the basic group yet!"

And with that, Bérénice, Qiu Zhang, Christina, Lottie and one of the minders took off down the slope

Then, the second group formed. Jake, Bigsy, Clare, Allegra, Lessiter and Melship, the two women, a minder and Volvakov.

"Okay, we can start now," said Volvakov, "Here, Douglas, why don't you ask my two pretty зайчонок to ski either side? They can catch you if you start to fall!"

He gestured to the two women, who he had just called 'little rabbits' in Russian. They both snuck up beside Lessiter as the second minder took an Instagram of them all together.

They set off down the mountain, more falteringly than the first group. After two kilometres it was apparent that this group contained several novices including both Melship and Lessiter.

"Don't worry," said Allegra, "There is a cable station about another three kilometres down this slope. Anyone that needs it can hire a sled from that point and ride down the remaining kilometres in style!"

Clare looked toward Melship, who already looked exhausted. By comparison, Bigsy was still looking fresh.

"You know, I'm quietly enjoying this and the pace is not too fast," he confided to Clare.

Soon, they reached the cable station, which had an adjacent Hire Store. From here they picked up several sleds and Melship, Lessiter, Bigsy and one of the women and the minder each put themselves into a sled.

"Lets's go now!" said Volvakov, and they gingerly released the brakes on the sleds and shot forward.

"This is the life!" said Lessiter, while the woman in another sled whooped encouragement.

Clare realised it would now be difficult to keep up and signalled to Jake to slow down.

"This is becoming something of a children's outing," whispered Jake and Clare smiled.

"It sure takes our minds away from the Car Show," said Clare.

In under an hour, they had reached the others, who were seated on a sun terrasse, sipping schnapps.

"Where did you get the karts?" asked Lottie, "Surely not at that cable station? You've hardly skied down at all if that is the case."

"We were just keeping with the transport theme," said Volvakov, waving his arm to attract a waitress, "Schlehengeist all around, please!"

"What's that?" asked Clare.

"Sloe berry spirit - a schnapps," answered Christina, "Perfect after skiing."

Clare sat down at the wooden bench with Melship and Lessiter.

"That was so exhilarating!" said Clare.

"Yes, it's another complicated one for the expenses," said Duncan. Douglas nodded his agreement. Clare looked at the two slightly drunken MPs. The altitude, exercise and schnapps had loosened both their tongues.

She asked, "Don't you ever worry? You know, like when the PM's house was decorated by a party donor? Or that MP who was working in the Caribbean? Full disclosure and all that?"

Lessiter laughed, "Oh yes. Full disclosure, always. But remember there is a difference between transparency and openness.

"It is possible to have the facts visible, but in ways that obfuscate the truth. Commons rules ensure MPs' earnings are publicly declared, but those rules also dictate that in the case of legal work only the firms need be named — not the clients, the people paying the bill. So, this time, to declare anything at all, I only need to show that the trip down the mountain was to support Brant Holdings."

Melship added, "He's right. MPs must declare 'any financial interest or other material benefit which a Member receives which might reasonably be thought by others to influence his or her actions, speeches or votes in Parliament.' And, by and large, they do. Sometimes the context isn't shown, like these lovely sun-drenched ski slopes."

Lessiter continued, "The register was the basis of much of the reporting on MP's second jobs. But the format in which it is published generates a fog that makes it enormously difficult to pick out the answers to many basic questions."

Melship expanded the theme, "For example, no one has been able to work out how much money MPs make from outside earnings since the last general election. And no one has worked out how much MPs made from, say, banking. Or law. The register is constructed as a riddle. Each MP's entry is published as a series of documents. They cover overlapping time periods, so the same interests will be declared time and again, making it rather confusing to unpick."

"But why are you telling me this?" asked Clare, looking confused. "I mean, you know I work in Parliament for Andrew Brading?"

Melship answered, "Yes, we both know. Andrew is one of the MPs who plays a completely straight bat. No scandal, no sleaze, a real goody two-shoes."

"Oh, no disrespect intended," hastily added Lessiter, "And I guess we could say that Parliament invented enigmatic accounting principles!"

Melship continued, "And we're telling you because none of this matters. We get a few presents from our sponsors. They expect to influence us. But the truth is each of us is only one six hundred and fiftieth of Parliament. By ourselves we can't do so much. But lobbying continues, we are just having some fun with it."

Lessiter added, "And the regulators inside Parliament know this too. Except for a few silly duck-houses and moat repairs, most of the system passes unnoticed. Most MPs' statements are a challenge to decipher. The data is unwieldy, unintuitive, and full of traps. To get the figures required for accurate analysis, you would need to manually go through every entry. The latest edition of the register shows MPs made close to 4,000 separate declarations of gifts, hospitality, and other outside interests. Since the last election it has been published and corrected many dozens of times."

Clare asked, "But doesn't this result in pseudo-transparency? Every MP has declared their second jobs. The information is published and accessible. But using that information is too time-consuming. The result? Less accountability and less scrutiny than if it were collected and presented in a modern, structured format."

Melship nodded, "I suppose we could publish it all in a spreadsheet for some of the newspapers, but then we'd lose out on all this sunshine and the rather marvellous schnapps...Cheers!!"

Jake and Lottie had been listening in on the conversation. It didn't leave either of the MPs looking good sat here among the car lobbyists.

Clare looked around. At other tables she could see equivalences of this group. Happy, drunken targets being hit upon with all manner of indiscretion. International lobbying at its finest. One could almost see it as a service industry.

Zopf

Morning. Sunday. The occupants of the chalet were emerging groggily to the breakfast prepared by Allegra.

"Here we are," Allegra announces, "Switzerland is the homeland of muesli, as we know it today. It was invented more than a hundred years ago by the local dietician Maximilian Bircher-Benner. It's so much more than a recovery food, one of the most popular breakfasts in the world!

"I prefer to put dried fruits in regular oat flakes, soaked in some water, milk or fruit juice and left overnight. You can also garnish with whole or chopped raw nuts of your choice.

"And it is Sunday. So, there is a tradition of Swiss braided bread called Zopf, garnished with marmalade and cheeses.

"Add Swiss croissants called gipfeli which are certainly the best company to your morning coffee.

And the king of croissants is His Majesty nusgipfel – A sweet muffin filled with walnut cream, which is generously covered with glaze on top.

"Not forgetting the rösti. A pancake of grated potatoes. it originated from the canton of Bern. The best thing about rösti is that it can be combined with any other type of breakfast such as eggs, bacon and so on. And the secret ingredient? Why nutmeg, of course.

"Enjoy!"

"I won't be able to move after all of that!" murmurs Jake to Bigsy.

"Oh, I will!" says Bigsy, grabbing a plate and moving in on the rösti, to which he added a couple of bacon rashers and a fried egg.

"Officially, today is a 'demonstration day' for the cars," explains Allegra, "You are supposed to go to the main area and select from the available vehicles to then be driven around the area. Why they chose the pedestrianised Gstaad for this I don't really understand!"

Clare smiles, "Maximising client contact time! Although I guess a lot of the people here are influencers rather than actual car buyers!"

"You'd be surprised," says Allegra, "Some of the people who live here or overwinter here are most definitely part of the global jet set. Add in a few of the visitors and there's a crazy full market for these luxury cars!"

"So, what will we do then?" asks Bigsy, "I guess we don't look like their typical car buyers."

"Why not go to the glacier?" asks Allegra, "You could take your MPs with you and they'll have a great time. My friend Jacques is in the company that runs the tours. I'm sure I can get you a Snow Cat and then you can take your group across the snow to the glacier."

"I guess it could 'break the ice' with them, they seem pretty much self-contained when they are around us," observes Clare.

"But how can we persuade them?" asks Jake, "I mean, they seem very plugged in to the official programme."

"Leave that to me," says Allegra.

Studded tyres

Two hours later, there was a commotion outside the chalet. Several cars had arrived. Clare noticed they had studded tyres, signifying they had been kitted out to traverse snow.

"My god!" utters Jake, "Have we stolen the whole car show?"

"No, we've just borrowed and diverted a few cars to come via our chalet. Jacques knows the car marshals and they simply took the next five vehicles and diverted them for us. But we must hurry, they will want them back!"

Jake surveys the cars. A McClaren 570S, a Porsche 911 4S, some kind of Ferrari. It says GTC4 Lusso on the back. That yellow Lamborghini SUV again and a Tesla S, which was apparently plaid, as if that was a good thing.

"It's 1100HP," calls Douglas Lessiter across to them.

Yes, Allegra had pulled off a great heist. Five luxury automobiles and two MPs, along with Christina and Antanov.

"How did you do it?" asks Clare, quietly to Allegra.

"I'm pretty well-known around Gstaad," answers Allegra,"I come from one of The Families, although I keep it quiet with visitors. As is my brother Jacques. All we need to do was ask the hotel concierge to route the two MPs to a special parking lot, where they could choose from five cars to get to the glacier. After that, it was easy. The drivers are all local, the cars are all insured to the best standards and have been booked out for one hour round trips. Speaking of which, we'd better get a move on. It'll take us twenty minutes to get to the foot of the glacier."

Soon enough, everyone was in a car, and as Allegra had predicted, the two MPs were happy to talk to their co-passengers. After all, this was a trip to remember.

And it had the added advantage that Bérénice Charbonnier and her friends were nowhere to be seen.

It's the glacier talking!

Hannah was in the car with Duggie Lessiter and Christina. Lessiter had specifically asked for Christina to join him.

Duncan Melship was with Lottie and Clare. Both MP's seemed entirely at home in their luxury cars, which Clare put down to a combination of over-indulgence in the privileged lifestyle and breakfast champagne.

"This is great!" said Duncan, "I didn't even see this listed in the programme; well done Lottie, for noticing it."

"I wouldn't mention this to too many of the other delegates," said Lottie, "I think we have received some privileged treatment courtesy of our friend Allegra."

"Right, this is happening to me all the time on this trip," replied Melship, "I'm not sure if I'll be able to report any of it when we get back!"

"You'll have my reports on tyre safety, reducing brake pollution and advanced battery technology, anyway," said Lottie.

"Ah yes, you've been doing a great job and the organisers were kind enough to supply a Word document which summarises every session. By the time we've worked that up into a report it should look comprehensive!" Melship smiled.

In the Tesla, which was following behind the Lamborghini used by Melship, Lessiter was talking to Hannah. They were both in the back seats, with Christina in the front passenger seat. Lessiter had insisted and even looked a little frightened by Christina.

"Hannah, thank you for getting those reports for me, you can see how busy I've been over the last few days. Tomorrow is the big meeting with Zillian, and I'd very much like you to attend. It's under the Non-Disclosure Agreement, because I think they want to let us in to some trade secrets."

Hannah nodded her assent, "Where is the meeting?" she asked, "Only it's not one of the ones scheduled?"

"I know; I had to keep it hidden. It was their insistence, a bit like this visit to the glacier doesn't seem to be on any of the schedules."

At that moment the Tesla made a sharp hairpin turn and Lessiter found himself squeezed against

Hannah's frame.

"Oh, I'm so sorry," he said looking awkward. "They say these cars drive themselves, they seem to have a few surprises too," He looked across to the driver, who merely grinned.

'Well, that dashes his hands reputation,' thought Christina. She had heard Clare relay the information from Rachel, which implied Lessiter had an altogether different orientation.

Soon they were at the foot of the glacier and the cars rolled up to the side of a large blue truck with enormous caterpillar tracks.

"That will be your next ride," explained the driver, "It has capacity for twenty people, so you should all be able to get window seats."

They climbed out of the car and watched the others with varying degree of struggle leaving their low-slung vehicles. Clare was quietly astonished that the lowest slung of them all, the McClaren, had even been able to drive through the snow without going aground.

They thanked the drivers and watched as the cars roared off, with the drivers deliberately disengaging the anti-skid devices so that they each threw up white arcs of snow.

"Wow! That was spectacular," uttered Lottie and Hannah nodded her head in agreement. They had all been given bulky red coats to wear for the next stage and as they climbed in, the driver explained, 'It's to be able to easily locate you if you get lost on the ice.'

He gave some other brief care announcements and they were off, bumping across the ice on caterpillar tracks. In the distance they could see another vehicle and the driver explained they would go to where the ice was still safe and where there should not be too many deep fissures.

"We will spend a few minutes walking around the glacier and then return to the Scex Rouge, which has restaurants and a sun terrace. If you want to, you can make an unforgettable walk across a suspension bridge between a couple of the 3000 metre peaks. On a clear day like today, you can see most of the Alps - Diablerets, Mont Blanc, Matterhorn and Jungfrau."

"And how do we get back from here?" asked Jake, "Once we are finished now that the cars have gone?"

"Oh, that's easy," answered Allegra, "I have arranged for a coach to pick us up from Col du Pillon, which is a cable car point. We take a cable car, then change to another one which will take us to the position. It is then a straight run back to Gstaad."

The Cat driver placed a short ladder against the side of the machine. Everyone climbed it and were soon travelling toward the glacier.

"A snow safari!" said Melship.

"Hopefully no wild animals!" answered Hannah.

Everyone laughed. Allegra had been right and the team bonding had begun.

They climbed out onto the ice and could see rivulets of blue water in the warm sunshine.

"Most of the fresh water on the planet is stored in glaciers, " said Allegra.

"But they are melting!" said Clare.

"Yes, the climate emergency is right here to see. This glacier has lost many metres of length in this century," answered Allegra, "Since 1850, the volume of Alpine glaciers has declined by about 60%.

"And in a single recent year, two heatwaves hit Switzerland between the end of June and late July, with around 30 degrees Celcius recorded in Zermatt. In 14 days of high temperatures, Alpine glaciers lost about 800 million tonnes of snow and ice, or the quantity of drinking water consumed by the entire Swiss population (8.5 million people) in the space of a year. But I didn't bring you all here to lecture about global warming! We should look at the view and experience nature."

They were all looking around, standing on the icy surfaces of the glacier, but noticing how much water lay everywhere.

"I suppose in a way all this has something to do with cars," said Melship wistfully.

Monday at the Gstaad expo

A crisp alpine morning and a new venue for the Expo at the hotel. Clare walked to the entrance where she met Christina and they both noticed the row of sparkling colourful sports cars parked outside.

"Someone has a de-icer for these," commented Christina., "Look at the normal cars!" She gestured to a couple of rows further back in the car park, where cars were parked in various states of snow-torment. Some were clear of snow, but others looked as if they had been hurriedly moved and, in some cases, still had snow on their roofs.

"Today it's the big meeting with Zillian," said Clare, "Remember we are only there as assistants."

"Tricky for me," answered Christina, "Remember I already know Bérénice Charbonnier, Miller McDonald Mary Ranzino and Qiu Zhang. I think I'd better make myself scarce."

Clare nodded, just as Lottie and Hannah appeared. They were both sporting new House of Common badges, which Christina noted.

"Cool badges?" she asked.

"The work of Bigsy. He reckoned only a few of us would get into the meeting, so he gave us these little things."

"Listening devices?" asked Christina.

"Yes, but transmitting to our phones, as well," said Lottie.

"You'll be careful in there?" asked Christina, "No heroics."

"Definitely not!" answered Lottie, she unclipped her badge, and showed Clare. It looked solid from the back and didn't show any trace of electronics.

"Bigsy said he got them from 'Amanda'," explained Hannah.

"There seems to be a lot of attention on this session," remarked Christina.

"Time to part company," said Christina as she walked toward the lobby area. She noticed Melship and Lessiter walking in, with someone else whom she didn't recognise. A man in a leather coat, with a small golden lapel badge. She listened to his speech and realised, by his accent, he was Russian.

Melship and Lessiter greeted Lottie and Hannah and the small group walked into the meeting room, except for leather coat man who stayed by the entrance.

"He's got an earpiece too," whispered Clare, who had also noticed the arrival. Christina smiled, "Let's test him."

She walked back through the crowded lobby to the entrance to the meeting room and asked the man, in deliberately broken English, "Excuse me, is this Tesla Meeting Room. I lost."

The man replied, "no, it is not here. You should ask at the information desk," he pointed.

"большое спасибо, bal'shoye spaseebah", answered Christina, and the man instinctively smiled.

"I see what you just did," smiled Clare, "He would have looked confused instead of giving you a polite smile, if he'd not understood."

"Okay, so we know the Russians are guarding the entrance to the meeting."

"There's something off about it though, " said Christina, "It's not how Russia does this kind of thing. We'd always have two people present. A guy on the door and another one to add some muscle if it were needed."

"I think I have your answer," said Clare, nodding to another man around six metres away from the Russian.

"Oh yes, you are right, I can see his earpiece too," said Christina,"You are getting good at this, Clare!"

"I've had lots of practice following you around, Christina!"

"But look," whispered Clare, "Does he look more Chinese to you?" she gestured toward the second man.

"Not necessarily," said Christina. She guided them both back toward the entrance to the building, adding, "Russia is a big place. He could come from the east. Maybe from Siberia. There are people with asian appearance from areas nearer China and the China-Russia border, at either end of Mongolia or the Gobi Desert. And don't forget there's another China-Russia border with North Korea."

They could see Jake and Bigsy now, close to the revolving doors to the building. It looked as if Bigsy was engrossed in a call.

"Hi," said Jake, "Bigsy is listening in, but he suggests that we should go to Christina's suite here in the hotel where we can all hear what is happening."

"It's okay, Christina gave me a key yesterday," explained Bigsy, "it's a pretty good suite too!"

He led the way to the elevators and eventually into Christina's Tower suite.

"It's huge," observed Jake, looking at the separate areas of the bedroom and the lounge area, flooded with light and a beautiful view toward the mountains.

"Yes, I set the speakers up in the lounge area, we can spread out on the sofas and listen to what is happening in the meeting. And don't worry, I'm recording it all," explained Bigsy.

"I'll order some coffee too," said Christina, as Bigsy switched on the system.

The speakers gave a low hum and then a voice came through,

'Before deductions, Zillian will raise approximately $6 billion, making it one of the biggest launches for a US company.'

The voice sounded American, "It's Miller McDonald," said Bigsy, "The Texan drawl gives it away."

'Isn't that a bit high for a car company that's only produced a dozen electric units this year?' asked a woman's voice.

"It's Mary Ranzino," said Clare.

Miller continued, 'You're not alone in thinking that. Indeed, our team says the figure looks incredibly high for any newly listed company, let alone one that only generated $1m of revenue in its most recent quarter.'

Now a Russian voice, 'The immense investor appeal may come from faith in the company's backers - notably that Brant has taken a deep position with Zillian, and soon we will have UK Government approval - so much faster than the EU, but just as marketable. Is that not right, Mr Melship?'

Melship replied, 'Well if these last few days are anything to go by, then I agree. And the share options that you are gifting to me and to Mr Lessiter make such a manoeuvre doubly attractive. If Zillian becomes engineered as a high growth prospect based upon electric vehicles, then we will need to compare it with other electric-vehicle companies and how they have fared after their IPOs.'

Mary Ranzino continued, 'A surge in share price is not unheard of for electric-vehicle IPOs. Tesla, along with Chinese carmakers Li Auto and XPeng, saw their share price increase more than 40 per cent on their first day of trading. Lucid Motors and Nio had more modest gains, but their share prices still closed 10 and 12 per cent higher than their IPO prices respectively.'

The Russian again, "How does this play out long term? If you prove you can deliver, you will be rewarded. But to achieve this you will need to make endorsements. And these endorsements need to come from people untainted with involvement."

"I can see why you have kept this meeting small and select," said Melship.

"And our assistants are very discreet,"

"It was very unfortunate, what happened to Isabella Stevens," said The Russian.

"That is such a clumsy threat," said Christina, "These people are watching too many American movies about making offers they can't refuse."

A new voice on the speakers asked, 'But how will we make this all seem credible? Zillian doesn't have any vehicles."

"I'm guessing that is Volvakov Kirill Valeryevich," said Christina, "he has a hint of a Russian accent."

'Kirilka,' said Mary, 'We may not yet, but the arrangement we have come to with Qiu Zhang means that Zillian can continue to supply plausible petrol cars until the electrics are ready. We will have a few nice but highly popular models which are almost undetectable from their European and American counterparts.'

'That's right,' said Qui Zhang,'We can manufacture any automobile clones required and in any volume. You'll need to provide us with plans, but we can turn the production facilities of several company towns over. They can produce the vehicles and if you want them badged Zillian, it can easily be achieved.'

Miller McDonald asked, 'But the industry and reporters are calling out for Zillian to show vehicles now. Even prototypes. And we need to do that to be able to run a floatation of the company.'

'That should not be a problem, we have two ideas for this,' answered Valeryevich, 'First we can use the Raft CGI platform to demonstrate the car.'

'In other words, you use a virtual car?' asked Melship.

'Secondly, we will acquire, legitimately, several eCar platforms and add new body skins. We'll soon have created the illusion that we are good to go,' said Mary Ranzino.

'Correct. Then a proposal...'

"Faking it?" said Jake, "Faking it to boost the share price."

Miller McDonald's voice continued, 'We will need a seal of approval. That is where you two come in, Mr Lessiter and Mr Melship. You will provide the legitimacy that the venerable Zillian needs to proceed.'

There was a pause. In Christina's room they all looked at Bigsy.

"Nope," he said, "It isn't me. The sound is still working fine."

Then it resumed. It sounded like Melship's voice.

'But how would we do this? Even as MPs we have limited powers...'

Lessiter commented, 'I'm not sure about this...It would be a significant betrayal of trust towards the electorate.'

'You forgot to say, 'financially rewarding',' said Mary Ranzino, 'With your new-found equity in Zillian, suitably placed offshore in a financial institution of your choosing, you can enjoy an oligarch's lifestyle. Once you have resigned from Parliament, of course.'

"FOBFO," said Clare. Christina and Bigsy giggled.

"Nah," said Jake, "You've got me again. I know FOMO - Fear of missing out, but not FOBFO."

"Fear of Being Found Out," chorused Christina and Clare.

"It's far more gangsta," added Bigsy.

Jake did a mock facepalm and groaned, "Children," he said, "I'm working with children."

The conversation from the conference room

continued.

'But how...would this work?' asked Melship.

"Hooked," observed Bigsy.

A two-stage thing

'It is a two-stage thing,' explained Miller McDonald.

'First, we launch Zillian, backed by Brant and touting its long -term credentials through the acquisition of Weide. The entire launch will be handled by Red Fox, as a form of insulation.'

McDonald continued, 'But here's the thing. We'll position the first customer deliveries of the $90,000 Zillian 502 sedan. It will be to a few people from the 'reserved list'. Celebrities and Instagram influencers posed next to one of the shiny new all-electric cars.

It will be just as the IPO goes live and we should get an immediate lift of at least 10% in the share price on the back of it. There will be a feeding frenzy as investors get into the share.

A week later, these same celebrities will announce that they can't believe the mileage they are getting from the vehicles. It is as if the vehicles recharge themselves whilst they are parked. Someone will announce that they have achieved over 450 miles between charges.'

"Impossible," said Bigsy, "Today's battery technology has finite limits."

Mary Ranzino continued, 'The effect of these quotes will be enough to see another rise of the share price. Maybe another 10 per cent.'

'That's when we announce the service vehicles,' explained McDonald. "It may be boring for the average car buyer, but we will announce a range of service vehicles. A van, a minibus, a delivery truck and a full-sized bus.'

Ranzino spoke again, "Maybe only a few points from this announcement, until the UK Government, via Douglas Melship, Secretary of State for Department for Transport Efficiency- DfTE announces it has decided to place a significant order for the UK. All government service vehicles to be provided on a rental agreement from Zillian. The projection of some 20,000 units should be enough to boost the price again."

'And then, a further piece of policy work. I had it prepared, and it will unfold through an announcement by Douglas Lessiter Minister of State for Infrastructure.

They could hear paper rustling and then Mary Ranzino spoke again.

'Here we are:'

'The UK must move away from "20th century thinking centred around private vehicle ownership" and towards shared mobility, Minister of State for Infrastructure, Douglas Lessiter has said.

'Lessiter said that shared mobility must become "the norm" as he outlined support for a future transport system which, he claimed, would introduce "greater flexibility, with personal choice and low carbon shared transport."

'Addressing this week's Collaborative Mobility Conference (CoMoUK), the Infrastructure Minister said it was "staggering" that nearly two-thirds of car trips are taken by lone drivers, and said the UK is at a "tipping point" where shared mobility will soon be a "realistic option for many of us to get around."

'As many industry analysts speculate whether Original Equipment Manufacturers (OEMs) will ever return to the pre-COVID new car registrations highs, a vision of a new transport system where Mobility Hubs become a familiar part of our street architecture, and where all these options will be available to book and pay for at the touch of a smartphone was shared with conference delegates.

'Furthermore, I am announcing the Framework legislation to support these vital changes to the UK's infrastructure, starting with London, in Parliament in the current term. It is a vital element required to meet the Government targets of carbon reduction.'

Mary Ranzino paused, and those in Christina's room realised that it was to give Lessiter and Melship a chance to think.

'That's another boost in share price and politically very enticing for the UK Government who can show they can move faster than the EU or the United States. The shaky Prime Minister will be delighted to have something positive to talk about and it can only do the Zillian share price further good.'

'But how will we get our initial allocations of equity?" asked Melship.

'This is where it becomes a win-win,' said Valeryevich. 'We will take care of your initial stake holding. In fact, we have already done so. My friends from Moscow have already donated £1 million to a private account for each of you, with Bank Rossiya, in Cyprus.'

"Bank Rossiya in Cyprus!" said Christina," I think that has fallen out of favour with Russian Mafia nowadays - it was linked to Putin via Sergei Roldugin and Yuri Kovalchuk - a couple of his close friends who are uncovered in the Panama Papers scandal. I think we might need Amanda Miller's help if we want to dig any further into this."

"What about if they are smart? If the Russians are working with the Chinese but don't want to give too much away?" asked Jake.

Christina agreed, "Sure, that could be grounds for

using some questionable mechanisms in the set-up."

Melship again, 'But how do we gain access?'

Valeryevich, 'You don't, at least not for a while.'

Ranzino, 'You will be able to watch the money as it gets invested into Zillian and grows.'

Valeryevich, 'We are using investments like yours to help seed the growth of Zillian. You will be early purchasers of the Zillian launch and ride the shares all the way up.'

"It's a classic semi-state model," said Christina, "Just the usual Russian game play when they were selling off the State's equities. They sold the banks to their friends and then lent money to one-another to buy other state enterprises at knock-down prices. This is just a variation of the old ways."

"But will the owners get thrown out of tall buildings at the end?" asked Jake.

"Leverage," explained Christina, "Play along and Lessiter and Melship should become very rich very quickly."

"And if they don't?" asked Bigsy.

"Then I'm afraid they would be following Isabella," said Christina.

Gangsta rap

The meeting had ended and there were sounds of scraping chairs from the conference room.

"Stay away," said Christina, "We'll wait for Hannah and Lottie to return. They did well with their microphones. Thank you, also, Bigsy."

"They have some bottle," said Bigsy, "I'm not sure I could have sat through that whole session like that."

Christina's suite's doorbell rang. She walked over to answer it.

Hannah and Lottie walked in.

"My god!" said Hannah, "That was the scariest thing I've ever done! In a room full of global gangsters! When we left, we took a very roundabout route to get here, to ensure we were not followed."

Christina looked at them both and gestured to them to remain silent.

"Bigsy, can you check them for bugs? I'm thinking about countermeasures."

Bigsy retrieved a small orange device from his bag and approached Lottie.

"Ahem, I hope you won't mind?" he asked as he swept Lottie first and then Hannah for electronics, with the small device with what looked like a tape measure made into a 40 centimetre 'U' shaped aerial. He found their phones and his own microphones, but nothing else.

"All clear," he declared.

"Clare, your friends - the adventures - I said it just keeps on giving!" declared Lottie. She eyed the minibar in the room.

"Oh, please, help yourself," said Christina, "You've earned it! I'll call for some drinks to be delivered here."

Jake asked, "So what else did we discover? We could hear the voices but couldn't read the body language?"

"They all looked very serious. Melship seemed more compliant than Lessiter. I'm not even sure that Lessiter would go along with this if it wasn't for how deep he was already into everything," said Hannah.

"I could also see that Valeryevich was playing hard

ball, but he looked as if he was taking a lead from Qiu Zhang. She didn't say much, but I sensed she had the power in the room. What did you think, Lottie?"

"I agree, I had a feeling that the whole show was being put on for Qiu Zhang's sake. I could see several glances from everyone except Melship and Lessiter towards Qiu Zhang. I also couldn't stop noticing her clothes. She was by far the best dressed. I think her dress was Gucci, judging by the discreet brooch in a G shape on the shoulder. And she was so young! I'm guessing early thirties tops."

"Yes, and her arms were sculpted, like she was a fitness instructor," added Hannah.

"As I suspected, she's MSS, for sure," said Christina, "An agent of their Enterprises Division responsible for the operation and management of front companies, enterprises, and other institutions. She is tasked to help China get more control in the west and has the money to support these aims."

Jake looked at his phone. "I've just had a message from Amanda. She wants an update. I'm guessing she must have someone else here. She seems very well informed."

"Shall we do it now, or do we need longer to consider things? " Asked Clare.

"I think we are good," said Jake, "And we can ask whether Grace has found out anything about Qiu Zhang and Volvakov Kirill Valeryevich as well."

Carrots and sticks

"Okay, I'll put the audio through the same set-up," said Bigsy, "Except this time I'll plug in the microphones so everyone here will be heard by Amanda."

Jake dialled Amanda and they waited patiently for her to answer.

"Hi Jake, thanks for getting back so quickly," came Amanda's voice. It sounded as if she was on a speakerphone too.

"Unusual with no video, nowadays," observed Jake.

"To you, maybe. We still use an awful lot of ATCs, Audio Teleconferences," replied Amanda, "Oh and as you can't see her, I should mention that Grace Fielding is here with me! She says hello to everyone."

"Well, here in Gstaad, they - Brant and friends - just finished their meeting with Zillian, the automotive manufacturer, " stated Jake, "Our general supposition was right. Brant/Zillian are trying to influence Douglas Lessiter and Duncan Melship. They want the MPs to help further the cause of Zillian. There are several stages, each of which is designed to boost the base share price of Zillian. This will be at least partly achieved by MP endorsements of Zillian and UK Government policy, and as a reward Melship and Lessiter are both to be given a stake holding in the company."

What sort of stake holding?" asked Amanda.

Jake explained, "Financial, in effect a shareholding. They are being given money, which each of them uses to buy initial shares in the company. Then they see the shares rise significantly in value because of their endorsements. The initial money is being held for each of them, in trust in an offshoot of Bank Rossiya in Cyprus."

"That's Putin's Bank," said Amanda, "I mean he is a major shareholder, said to be worth billions in holdings."

"Well, we thought Russia, but then we also have Qiu Zhang's involvement," added Christina.

"Qui Zhang - she's from MSS, isn't she?" asked Amanda, "So it's a China/Russia alliance at work here?"

"I wondered that as well," said Christina, "I've already set in motion some enquiries. My sense is that it is being bankrolled by the Chinese though. It reminds me of a Russian scheme, but from many years ago. I doubt whether the Kremlin would operate this way now, except if this was some kind of leveraged deal,"

"I wondered too," said Clare, "I mean, £1 million each sounds like a lot for these two MPs, but for a Russian state deal it would be like chicken-feed."

"Exactly," said Christina, "Although I suppose the Chinese are adding plenty to the pot, if they want to quietly assume control of Zillian."

"China already owns several European automotive brands," said Grace, "Volvo was sold to Ford but then bought by China. Geely, I think. Then there was MG, saved by BMW but sold on and then picked up by Nanjing Auto, who in turn sold the brand to a Chinese State company. Pirelli tyres are majority owned by a Chinese chemical company and even Lotus is half Chinese and half Malaysian."

Clare summarised, "So what we get to, is two British MPs helping a scam to boost the share price of Zillian, where part of the funding is from China, but where Russia is still implicated?"

Christina nodded, "Yes, that is what it seems like, but I can't help wondering why Russia would nowadays be interested in such small fry numbers."

"I think the clue might be with Putin's Bank linkages," said Amanda, "That and the Chinese interest in the project."

"Clones!" said Bigsy suddenly, "If the Chinese want to learn how to copy things! This could be a test run by China, under Russia's tuition!"

Grace spoke, "Consider using legitimate companies as a money laundering system. It is already commonplace in Russia, but less so in China. Remember the Panama Papers?"

"Yes, I do," said Jake, "A network of secret offshore deals and loans worth $2bn which laid a trail to Russia's president, Vladimir Putin. The setup made members of Putin's close circle fabulously wealthy."

"That is right," said Grace, "Though the president's name does not appear in any of the records, the data reveals a pattern. His friends earned millions from deals that seemingly could not have been secured without his patronage. Furthermore, the documents suggested Putin's family has benefited from this money including massive unsecured loans to Sandalwood Continental, extending $650m in credit. Sandalwood was a reputed investment vehicle of Putin."

"I see, suddenly it's not a couple of million any longer," said Jake.

"And the laundering has been speculated to run into the billions," said Grace.

Amanda spoke, "This seemed to be the tip of an

iceberg. If Melship and Lessiter play along, then we'll have a worsening situation before we know it. Aside from the money, there must be another form of pressure operating. Carrot and Stick."

"Simple, old-fashioned sleaze," said Christina, "These two boys have been in Geneva and Gstaad for almost a week. They have barely attended any of the Car Expo meetings, instead sending along Lottie and Hannah. They have been out to play, under the guidance of Bérénice Charbonnier, who knows how things go down in Geneva and Gstaad - all the way from Rue Docteur-Alfred-Vincent to Rue du jeu de l'Arc."

Bigsy looked a little surprised that Christina knew so much about Geneva.

"Remember, Bigsy, I've been here before," added Christina, noticing Bigsy's expression.

"So, it really is carrot and stick?" asked Jake, "To Amanda's point, they get money and shares as their carrot, and sleazy smears as the stick."

Pressure Point

"We will need to tempt them to break cover," suggested Jake.

"Or to lean on Melship and Lessiter?" added Bigsy.

"Yes, and I think we have a pressure point," said Christina, "Remember that Lessiter was trying to stop Isabella Stevens before she was found in the river? - I'm sorry, Hannah, to bring this up."

Hannah nodded, "Yes, but I want to find her killers, too; she was a lovely person."

"Well, it may lead to a method to scare Lessiter," said Christina. "We know that Isabella had signed an NDA. The Non-Disclosure Agreement. Now we need to persuade Lessiter that Isabella let something slip. Something that he could also have let slip. It could be a way to rattle him. Particularly if he thinks it was his fault that Isabella was killed."

"But do we know what was in the NDA?" asked

Jake.

"I'm guessing it is very similar to the one that I had to sign," said Hannah, "I'll need to find a copy of it on my laptop, I can send it to you all."

"Amanda, what do you think of the plan? I know it is somewhat tactical," Christina asked.

"You are using the available assets wisely," said Amanda, "And some of them won't automatically be suspected of SI6 links either. I'm sure Qiu Zhang won't have realised that Hannah and Lottie are linked into SI6. It makes this a good plan to exert pressure."

Hannah's disappearance

"Last day today!" said Jake, "Then tomorrow we're back to London. I shall miss the walk from the chalet to the hotel!"

He had just appeared at the hotel's breakfast table, where Lottie and Clare were seated.

"Where is Hannah?" he asked, looking around, "Ah, I know, with her good friend Tony!"

"Not this time," answered Lottie, "As a matter of fact, Tony was here earlier and asking if any of us had seen her. He said he could not reach her on his phone, either."

"Yes, so I tried," said Lottie, "You know, in case there was a reason that Hannah didn't want to pick up for Tony, but no, nothing. It wasn't even going through to voicemail."

"Oh, she must be with Lessiter, then. He probably wants to demand a report from her."

"You might have thought so, but Lessiter also called me to ask of Lottie's whereabouts," answered Lottie.

"After that I decided to let myself into her room - Allegra opened her room for me. It didn't look as if she'd even been back to the chalet," answered Lottie.

"Oh, well that paints a different picture!" said Clare suddenly looking agitated, " I think she may well be missing."

Those around the breakfast table looked at one another, "Are we overreacting?" asked Jake, "I mean she could be -er - with someone?"

"Not Hannah," said Lottie, "Well, if she was, she'd have told me, at least, as a principle of security."

At that moment Christina and Bigsy arrived, "Why the glum faces?" Christina asked, looking around.

"We think Hannah has gone missing," explained Jake.

"I might be able to help with her whereabouts," said Bigsy," I wasn't going to tell any of you, but I added trackers to your jackets, back at the chalet."

"Bigsy?" said Clare, looking aghast, "You've been stalking us all?"

"Well, not exactly, but I realised that we could need to keep tabs one another over here. The ski jackets seemed like the most obvious piece of kit that would be taken everywhere."

"Well, it seems like a good idea now," said Christina, "How quickly can you run a trace, and how accurate is it?"

"I can do it from my laptop and it should be accurate to within a few metres, the tags auto-connect to any nearby phone to relay back their position, using the GPS from the phone. It is a pretty basic system, yet surprisingly effective."

"But why would Hannah want to disappear, or who would want to abduct her?" asked Clare.

"I think there's numerous suspects based upon what we know now, centred around what she knows about Lessiter's plans, and even that NDA she has on her laptop," answered Jake.

"Did anyone receive it yesterday?" asked Clare, "I know I didn't, but I put it down to the late hour."

She looked around the table and could see shaking heads.

"It could be the trigger for her being lifted," said Christina, "To stop us from seeing the Non-Disclosure Agreement. If it is the same as the one that Isabella had signed, then Lessiter seems to care greatly about its content."

"Now, an admission...We all enjoyed that ride in

Antanov's helicopter the other day. No-one asked why he'd brought such a large one along..."

"I did wonder," said Clare, "But it was incredibly useful."

"Well, it was fully loaded with passengers when it first arrived in Gstaad. He brought a squad of eleven soldiers with him, from the 76th Russian Airborne Division and led by a staff sergeant. These soldiers are all professionals and combat hardened. My Russian handler thought that I might need some backup."

"And why was that?" asked Jake.

"Blackbird had received further information. It suggested that the disruption being caused here in Gstaad were designed to lead back to the Kremlin. Blackbird had been told that the Kremlin was as much in the dark about this operation as everyone else."

"What, the Zillian scheme?" asked Bigsy.

"Correct, he said that it looked as if the scheme was designed to make the Kremlin look culpable. He hinted that it could expose some of Putin's own moves as well."

"So, any further idea who is driving this?" asked Clare, "Could it be the Chinese?"

"That's what Fyodor suggested," said Christina, "It

puts Volvakov Kirill Valeryevich under Qiu Zhang's control. He would be working for an agent of the Chinese MSS. And Miller McDonald and Mary Ranzino from Brant appear to be up to their usual tricks, too."

"But there are not so many Chinese/Russian gangsters, though?" queried Clare.

"If we look through post-Soviet gangsters, we find many nationalities," answered Christina, "Russian, Ashkenazi Jews, Estonian, Chechen, Tatar, Georgian, Armenian, Azerbaijani, but I've never seen a Chinese member operating inside the Russian Mafia, nor the Kremlin."

"But could it be the other way around?" asked Clare.

"The Honghuzi?" asked Christina, "They were sometimes called 'The Brothers', but they were silenced by the end of the 1940s. I don't think they have anything to do with 'The Brothers Circle' in Moscow."

"No," said Clare, "I think it is what Blackbird suggested. That the exposure of the Zillian moves could inadvertently lead back to the way that the Russian Central Bank has handled money on behalf of Putin."

Christina continued, "RCB/Sberbank is vast, with sometimes a reported 80,000 branches and numerous spin-offs. They say a close friend of Putin runs the bank nowadays. Add that to Putin's reputed net worth of between $70 and $200 billion and you can see why he won't want anyone looking around his arrangements too closely."

"No wonder they wanted to silence Isabella, and threaten Lessiter," said Bigsy, "Look, I've managed to run that trace. It looks as if Hannah is still here in Gstaad. They must want to use her to threaten Lessiter. They obviously don't think that Hannah knows anything."

"So that means the threat to Lessiter using Hannah only lasts as long as they are both here in Gstaad," said Christina.

Bigsy tuned his laptop and pointed to an area on the map. Clare asked him, "That is in the mountains, it looks close to the cable car stop?"

"Yes, it looks like a machinery depot, where they keep the snow ploughs. But it also has a brilliant outlook." Bigsy switched to a Street View image around the building.

"Look, see, it has a well-fortified position, but there is a fast and wide ski-run that passes almost next to it."

"Yes, I can see it has defence, yet good access as well," said Christina.

"However, we can show this to Antanov and I'm sure he, with an Mi-171, and eleven from 76th Airborne Division can handle Hannah's rescue," said Christina.

"Do we need to tell Amanda?" asked Jake.

"Afterwards, I suggest," said Christina, "Never ask permission from someone with a power of veto, if you are sure it is the right thing to do."

Jake grinned.

Second Order thinking

"But wait," says Clare, "What happens afterwards? If we rescue Hannah? I mean - the consequences?"

"Let's think about it for a moment," says Christina, "We'll be successful, of that, I am sure."

"Right, " says Clare, " So we rescue Hannah and bring her back in the helicopter."

"There will be prisoners too," says Jake, "I don't know how many, but they will be some kind of mercenaries."

"So, we could bring them back on the same helicopter," answers Christina, "It is the simplest thing to do."

"And where do we put them? We now have prisoners," says Jake.

"Misdirection," says Christina, "We must make them think we are from another force."

"Okay, but what kind of force?" asks Jake.

"We can imply the Russian bratva network," says Christina, "That's the organised crime network in Russia. No-one will want to mess with that. And I think we should use a gang like Solntsevskaya to create the impression that we are somehow linked to one of Russia's major transnational criminal organisations -- Vory v Zakone or "ladrones de la ley" - the thieves in law.

"Solntsevskaya has well-documented linkages with Mexican criminal organisations. They ship drugs like cocaine, heroin, and methamphetamines to resorts, hotels or houses protected and owned by their Mexican associates."

"I see," says Clare, "We make it look as if they have moved Hannah to a hideout that somehow crosses a Solntsevskaya line. That they are angry and want to sound a warning shot to move the trespassers out of town."

"Perfect," says Bigsy.

"Just a little complicated, " says Jake.

"So, what do we do with the prisoners?" asks Clare.

"We put them on a plane from Geneva to Juarez," answers Christina, "It's around 20 hours with a Moscow stopover. I can get that authorised through Blackbird. We can turn them loose in Mexico City and let them fend for themselves. If they have any sense they will go to ground, because they will be worried that they are being hunted. And no-one from around here will believe that it isn't a put-up job - In other words that they were paid to let Hannah escape."

"Wow!" says Lottie, "You guys don't mess around! But what about the protection for Hannah?"

"We'll make it known to our charming little gang from Zillian, that Hannah is now under Bratva protection. That can be easily achieved via a few well-placed emails and texts," explained Christina.

"Then, I assume it becomes business as usual?" asks Jake.

"Correct," says Christina, "Although I think Lessiter will be abnormally worried by this turn of events."

"Yes, if one assistant died and another goes missing from his team, it would be sufficient grounds for a full-blown investigation of him," says Jake.

"Yes, although if we do this right, Hannah should be able to return her role without a fear of further reprisals. The time is almost up." answers Christina.

"And, assuming this all works, we are all out of here tomorrow!" says Jake.

Small airstrip, big helicopter

Bigsy drove them in a minibus to a small airstrip on the outskirts of Gstaad. A separate military truck was parked adjacent to what Clare thought of as Antanov's helicopter. Clare watched the helicopter load up with the selected members of Russia's 76th Airborne. She was not going on this flight, although Antanov and Christina were piloting the large helicopter. If everything ran to plan, they would be back within an hour.

Bigsy, Jake and Lottie stood by her side, all of them watching the small mix of tough-looking men and women in black combat gear climb into the helicopter.

Then, the rotors started and the noisy 'copter took to the sky. Soon they could only hear the rotor beats and then what they assumed was the sound of the helicopter descending towards the target building. In the expanse of the valley, it was unlikely that anyone else would even notice the sounds.

Ten minutes later, they could hear the helicopter starting up once more and then, an increasingly loud sound as they could eventually see its three front lights, red, green, and white, as it once more approached the landing strip.

A flurry of snow, and the helicopter landed, further away this time and close to a coach with boarded side windows. They watched, as first the soldiers and then four figures disembarked and they could see what looked like two men and two women herded toward the coach.

A heavy motor started and it was on its way, followed by the original military truck that the soldiers had been delivered in. A smaller group led by Christina crunched over toward them in their cold huddle. Then a single figure broke and ran toward them. Hannah.

"My god!" she called, "Am I glad to see all of you!"

"Okay, let's sit in the bus and you can tell us all what happened," said Jake, gesturing to the nearby parked VW-Transporter. As Christina climbed aboard, he noticed her wink at him.

Suspicion-less

They were all the minibus, with Hannah in the front seat, next to Bigsy, who prepared to drive them back to the chalet.

"So, what happened?" asked Lottie, as Bigsy started the engine.

Hannah began, "It was intense, but also like a dream. A female police officer came to find me during the conference. She had I.D. and said that she needed to take me to Lessiter. That something had happened to Lessiter and he had asked for me. She showed me to a police car, a regular white and orange Hyundai, which had 'Polizei' in big letters on the side - oh, and a blue roof light."

"You weren't suspicious?" asked Lottie.

"Oh, no, I thought that Lessiter had got himself into some bother, maybe something that would require him to be extracted from a jail or something. Anyway, I got into the back of the car and the policewoman sat next to me. There were two heavy set men in the front, although they looked like plain clothes detectives or something."

"Where did this happen?" asked Christina.

Hannah began, "Right outside the Expo, the car was almost at the main entrance...Well, they drove me for what seemed like a long time and I realised we were heading out of town. It was quiet in the car as well; they didn't seem to have radios bleeping or anything like you see in regular cop shows on TV."

"Then they took a turning and the car climbed a way toward the place where they eventually held me. I thought that Lessiter must have been there, maybe with some form of entertainment. I assumed the police were keeping it low-key, maybe to avoid diplomatic embarrassment.

Hannah looked around at the group. Everyone was leaning in, listening to the story, except Bigsy, who was concentrating on driving.

"They showed me into a very modern-looking building, like an architect-designed house, about 5 kilometres from Gstaad, I'd guess. It was on a slope and near to a cable-car."

"That'll be around Videmanette, close to where we landed the helicopter when we came to find you. It's actually about 14 kilometres from Gstaad!" said Christina.

"That's when the policewoman said that they would be grateful for my co-operation, and could I hand over my phone. Now I was suspicious and then another policewoman appeared from one of the rooms of the house."

"Did you notice another police car?" asked Christina.

"No, but I asked what the hell was happening; to be truthful I had no idea. The second police officer asked me to sit down, that they had something important to say."

Bigsy was indicating to turn into the main streets of Gstaad, "Maybe you should move to a less visible seat," said Christina, "Here swap with me."

Hannah and Christina swapped seats and Hannah continued, "Then they explained to me that I was being held, pending deportation. That Lessiter had been involved in a club scandal and that the decision was to simply deport his entire party, to move the problem away. To be truthful, it all seemed kind of believable. Then the first woman told me I was technically being held by Bern Canton, but that they would treat me respectfully so long as I didn't try anything."

Jake asked, "So you were held, in custody, in a safe house?"

"That's what I thought. I could not believe that this was happening. I said I needed to make a phone call, but they said it was not allowed, neither was I to have any form of solicitor privilege. I asked why they were not holding me in the police facility and was told for diplomatic reasons I had been taken to a *sicheres Gebäude* - a safe building - outside of Gstaad to reduce the chance of adverse publicity, particularly involving Lessiter and the Car Expo. It did all seem kind of plausible, what with Lessiter being an MP and these being police officers."

"But you didn't ask for any other form of I.D?" asked Christina.

"No and given that they were in uniforms and I was transported by police car, I was believing them. I asked how long I would be detained, and they said it would be until my planned return to the UK-literally the next day."

"Didn't they offer to tell anyone of your whereabouts?" asked Bigsy.

"They said they would leave a message at the Expo that for diplomatic reasons I had been taken to police headquarters, but that they would ensure I was on the 'plane back to the U.K. I would not be allowed to contact anyone until I was back on the 'plane."

Bigsy was indicating to turn into the road to their chalet. They would be back in another minute. He could see in the distance that Allegra was moving some shopping from her car.

Hannah continued, "The two women spoke good English, but quite heavily accented. They were very kind to me. They said that as police officers there were certain parts of their jobs that they didn't like and this was one of them."

Bigsy switched off the engine, but everyone remained in the minibus.

"That evening, to disarm me even further, the two policewomen rustled up a delicious Tartiflette, with acres of Reblochon cheese."

"Tartiflette?" asked Bigsy.

"It's a combination of thinly sliced potatoes, smoky bits of bacon, caramelised onions and oozy, nutty, creamy Reblochon cheese," answered Lottie, "You missed our evening at Le Flore, in Geneva, Bigsy, when we had that huge round Tartiflette to share!"

"Don't keep reminding me about that evening when you all went out and left me charging gadget batteries!" answered Bigsy - he waved to Allegra from the front of the minibus, then held up a splayed hand as if to signal five minutes. Allegra did a 'thumbs up' in response.

"But you see my point?" asked Hannah, "I might have been held captive, but because they were not being all menacing with duct tape and ropes, and they were feeding me well, I thought it was a pleasurable way to spend about 30 hours in detention. I didn't even know I needed to be rescued by helicopter by a squad of Special Forces until it happened!"

Clare looked around the group. She could see that they were mainly smiling. But she knew it could have gone very differently.

"What has happened to the four of them?" asked Bigsy.

Christina answered, "Antanov has them detained now. They are all from a unit of GRU Spetznaz - that's the Russian Special force used to infiltrate other countries. I assumed they were being shipped back to Russia; if they stay in Switzerland there is a chance that they will cause problems."

"I assume travel is through your friend Blackbird?" asked Hannah, to Christina.

"Yes, although we are as confused as everyone about who is working for whom in all of this."

"And how much does Lessiter know?" asked Hannah, "Does he even know I'd been abducted?"

"Lessiter will know, " said Christina, "The whole point of them taking you is to show Lessiter that they can get at anyone, and any time."

Jake spoke, "So that will be the 'stick' part of the process. He gets a lot of money to assist but knows that if he doesn't then bad things can happen."

Clare added, "Now we must be careful about what we do over the next day. As we fly back tomorrow, we could keep Hannah hidden until the flight, to create the illusion that the plan has worked. Then I could ask Antanov and one of his Special Unit to accompany Hannah to the gangway to the plane. It could look quite theatrical, but should do the trick," said Christina.

"Could we have Hannah delivered to the steps onto the plane, " asked Jake.

"Yes, I'm sure we can arrange that, although we'll need a military vehicle to make it look right," answered Christina, "I expect Antanov will know where to get one."

"And Hannah's back-story?" asked Clare, "It can be almost how she described it, Lessiter won't want to contradict anything, because it can only dig him a deeper hole."

Christina continued, "The difference in the story can be that Hannah stayed in the 'safe house' until the flight. She was well-looked after but had been told Lessiter was at first detained but then released from police custody after a misunderstanding."

She continued, "Antanov found out that Lessiter had been disorderly in 'La Cage' - a gender-fluid club in Gstaad, where he was wearing a purple minidress, with a grey neck swag, black tights, and black silver-tipped platform shoes. He claimed to have been drugged and forced to wear the clothes."

Jake and Bigsy burst out laughing, "Why not make the whole thing improbable?" said Bigsy.

"No, it's a thing," said Clare. Christina and Lottie nodded.

"Yes, it's a part of the scene in London too," added Lottie. Hannah nodded her agreement, "A little too often with Duggie, to be frank, I'm amazed that he gets away with it, he's even hidden it from that reporter Rachel Crosby. She was close to finding out a month or two ago."

Jake and Clare remembered their conversation with Rachel, back at the Caffè Concerto, in London. The oblique reference to the 'Fleet's In!' painting, which Clare had subsequently googled and confirmed her suspicions.

"Okay, so what will we say in front of Allegra?" asked Jake.

Christina replied, "As little as possible. Today, we went sightseeing with Bigsy, in the Minibus, but it broke down. It was ironic, being in Gstaad for a Car Expo. The local TCS (Touring Club of Switzerland) were dispatched to rescue us but we gave them the wrong location and so we lost a couple of hours whilst they located us. It was a minor electrical fault and the man from the TCS fixed it."

"Well, that sounds mundane compared with what actually happened!" said Bigsy. They all climbed out of the minibus Transporter.

"Wow, you all look as if you have been through the wars!" exclaimed Allegra, "You know what, tonight is your last night, I'm making you something simple and typically Swiss. With lots of garlic and cheese! - It's Tartiflette."

They all looked at Bigsy.

Window dressing

Clare sat in a window seat on the return flight. She could see Lessiter and Melship further forward in the Business Class seats at the front of the plane. They appeared to have a row each, with a protection officer sitting discreetly on the other side of the plane in seats JKL.

Clare was surprised that the return flights were on a commercial carrier instead of in a private jet, but then she realised the MPs had been flown out, courtesy of a car industry supplier, but they had been forced to return under their own arrangements.

Clare remarked about this to Lottie.

Lottie answered, "It's window dressing - it looks far less privileged if they come back on their own pocket. Ever since that scandal about the Minister who flew from London to Australia on a private 220 seater A320 jet. It cost the Minister their chance of a run at the top job."

"Yes, I suppose there's those photographers who hang around at Heathrow too, looking out for celebrities and public figures."

Lottie nodded, "Any minute now it should get interesting, when Hannah gets on the plane!"

They could see a black SUV had driven to the left-hand side of the plane. Then she could see several military personnel and a woman - Hannah - climb out. Hannah was shown to a set of steps which wound their way onto the jetway and then they saw her appear at the front of the plane. She was rapidly shown to her seat, which Lottie and Clare noticed was in the same select area as the seats of Lessiter and Melship.

"Look. Lessiter looks surprised," whispered Clare, to Lottie.

"I can just make out what they are saying," said Lottie.

"It seems Lessiter had been told that Hannah had to return early, back to London. He does look surprised to see her here."

"He could have phoned her to check she was okay," answered Clare.

"That's why they have assistants like us - to do those kinds of calls," said Lottie, "Not that I'm bitter."

The rack above the seats made a 'bong' sound and the pre-flight announcements meant they were ready for take-off.

"Goodbye Geneva," said Clare.

"Goodbye Gstaad," echoed Lottie.

Intense

They were back in Heathrow, and Clare could see Lessiter agitatedly taking to Hannah. It reminded her of the scene back at the Christmas party with Isabella Stevens, except this time Lessiter was not grabbing Hannah.

"Whoa! There's something intense going down between Lessiter and Hannah," said Jake. "And look, Melship is talking to Lottie."

Bigsy commented, "It is as if, now they are back in the UK, the two MPs have suddenly remembered that they have assistants. I expect hey are both setting up all the errands they want performed, so that both MPs can go home for a well-deserved rest."

Christina walked over, "It all seems to be resetting. By now Lessiter will have told Hannah that he thought she had to return early. That is why he did not miss her. And Melship will be unloading a range of errands for Lottie."

"Where is Antanov?" asked Jake.

"Oh, he had to escort the four captives back to Moscow," answered Christina.

"And what about Kjeld Nikolajsen, Miller McDonald and Mary Ranzino from Brant and Qiu Zhang and Valeryevich?" asked Jake

"We checked and Nikolajsen and McDonald have flown back to Norway, and Mary Ranzino and Qiu Zhang boarded a flight to Paris, whereas Valeryevich was heading for Moscow," answered Christina, "It was helpful having those Special Forces that Antanov brought."

"Paris seems like a random choice?" said Bigsy.

"Not really, it's a major hub to link with just about any major capital," replied Christina, "Ranzino still lives in New York, for example."

"What about us?" said Clare, "Is there anyone following us at the moment?" she looked at Christina.

"No, I don't think so," said Christina, "Anyway, they already know where each of us lives - or at least where we work,"

"How reassuring," muttered Clare.

Brading's Office

Monday, and everyone was back at work. Clare was in Parliament and back in Andrew Brading's office with Serena and Maggie.

"How did it go?" asked Serena, looking interested, "Did you find out anything fascinating about Duggie and Duncan?"

Maggie looked around, also interested in what Clare was going to say.

"Oh yes, they certainly both know how to freeload. It goes no further but poor Hannah and Lottie were dumped with all the work, whilst Duggie and Duncan were able to visit high-end entertainment in both Geneva and Gstaad."

"You don't surprise me," said Maggie, "There's still a great sense of entitlement with some of the MPs. We all know which Etonian occupant of Number 10 set the tone, and even with some casualties in the fall-out, there are still MPs who will continue to operate from a haughty sense of privilege."

Serena nodded, "Yes, Clare, you've seen your share of such MPs, from when you were here the last time as well. Don't get me wrong, there are some fine upstanding MPs, but there are also both likeable rogues and out-and-out scoundrels."

"Some of them simply fall into the wrong company," said Maggie.

"And others were born this way?" asked Clare.

"But let's face it, I'm not sure how much your time in Switzerland will have helped Andrew," observed Serena, "Have you anything for the Secretary of State for Internal Affairs?"

"We'll, as a matter of fact, I have, " answered Clare, " It looks as if a variation on the Minerva and Medusa scam is being run by an as-yet unknown power."

"Not more bribery and corruption of MPs?" asked Serena.

"I'm afraid so, and both Douglas Lessiter and Duncan Melship seem to be involved."

"Can this go public?" asked Serena, "Is there enough proof?"

"I'm afraid not. Both behaved badly whilst abroad, treating the trip like a 'jolly' but I think we've a developing situation because of some of the people they spoke to."

"Do Lottie Davis and Hannah know about it?" asked Serena.

"Yes, Hannah accompanied Douglas Lessiter and Lottie was with Duncan Melship. Figuratively speaking..."

"No great surprise if Melship was doing the round of the parties. I imagine he threw himself at every opportunity!" said Serena.

"And I imagine Douglas was - er - more selective about the company he kept?" asked Maggie.

"Well observed, Maggie, although Lessiter was also drinking the Kool-Aid. We, on the other hand were learning all about tyre pressures and the five stages of self-drive car evolution. And I can bore for Britain on battery life expectancy - Oh for a full electric car, the bottom line is about 100,000 miles, by the way."

"But as importantly, did you keep an eye on our two MPs?" asked Serena, "Amanda Miller impressed upon me the importance of that aspect of the visit. You are something of a dark horse, Ms Crafts!" Serena smiled at Clare.

Clare was relieved that Serena was prepared to be complicit in the plans briefed by Amanda.

"We're into Official Secrets Act territory now," explained Clare.

"The daring duo are mixed up in a car floatation share price scam," explained Clare, "It could make them both very rich, but I think whoever is running them has something over each of them too."

"Do we know who it is?" asked Serena, "I mean is it - er- individuals or a state action?"

"We don't know, the mix of people includes Americans, Chinese and Russians and there are also different companies in the background."

"I assume you'll be making a report to Amanda Miller?" asked Serena.

Clare nodded, "Yes, actually we were planning to do that today, later"

At that moment Andrew Brading appeared, "Oh, welcome back Clare! Look I am so sorry to be a bearer of some terrible news. Douglas Lessiter was involved in a road traffic accident. Very close to his London apartment. They say he died instantly."

"Oh my god," said Serena, "What happened?"

"A couple of witnesses said he was walking, weaving across the road, looking drunk and then he stepped out in front of a van. It ran straight over him and just kept on going - a hit and run. Apparently, the witnesses were quite shocked but one of them managed to write down the middle part of the van's registration. They didn't get it all and so far, the police can't get a good match on anything. It is supposed to be a white van. I can't imagine the driver will get far, with all the cameras in central London."

"Clare - you look pretty shaken," said Maggie.

"It is the last thing I would have expected!" answered Clare, "I mean, Lessiter seemed to be on the side of the whoever is plotting most of this."

Andrew Brading raised an eyebrow, "What's this? Was Lessiter mixed up in something? And was it with Melship?"

"I was explaining to Serena, it is similar to the previous corruption, with MPs being put on the hook and then offered enticements to do things to line the pockets of others."

"But there isn't sufficient proof," said Serena, "It is mainly supposition. You know what enquiries into MP behaviour can be like. And it has got worse since that shambolic charlatan duped everyone in Parliament."

Brading answered, "Yes, it has made it devilishly difficult for everyone honest since that last pack of lies and corruption was uncovered. It was as if it was all a part of the plan to make investigations of Parliament more convoluted."

"Okay, but what about Hannah? She was working with Lessiter and had a spare room at his apartment?" asked Clare.

"Oh? I didn't know that," said Serena. Andrew Brading also shook his head, but she noticed that Maggie remained quiet.

Clare added, "Yes, Lessiter provided Hannah with some digs in London. It suited him too and provided cover for his unusual predilections. It was all kept out of the press, although some of them knew or guessed," said Clare.

She noticed Maggie nodded at this.

"Are you and Hannah good friends?" asked Clare.

"Yes, we have known each other for several years. I've even been to visit her at Lessiter's place," added Maggie, "But it seemed to be - you know- private and personal. But right now, I wouldn't want anything to happen to Hannah."

"As a matter of fact, something happened in Gstaad," said Clare, "We are still speaking confidentially? Yes?"

"Agreed," said Serena.

"Hannah was abducted as part of a threat to Lessiter. We had to mount a full-blown rescue party to get Hannah back. However, the kidnappers were very refined and Hannah didn't even think she had been abducted. The kidnappers posed as policemen and she thought she was being detained in a safe house."

"So how on earth did you get her back?" asked Andrew.

"Well, remember my friends? A few of them assisted liberate Hannah from capture. There's a longer version of the story, but now is not the time," answered Clare. She thought it better not to mention the helicopter and the Russian Special Forces.

"You lead a very interesting life," observed Brading.

"Well, right now I think we should move Hannah to somewhere safe and secure," said Clare, "and that doesn't sound as if it should be Lessiter's spare room."

Maggie picked up her phone, "I'm calling Hannah. I'll ask her to come to this office. I'll say it's urgent. She should be on the Estate, somewhere."

"I'll authorise you to use one of the secure meeting rooms in Portcullis House. I'm assuming you'll want to bring in Amanda Miller?" said Andrew, "But you'll forgive me if I don't join you, I have another pressing matter at hand, and I'd really appreciate it if Maggie - at least - could join me."

Clare made a few phone calls, she would bring Jake, Bigsy, Lottie and Hannah to the session, as well as Christina.

Portcullis House

Clare started the walk across to Portcullis House. It passed along a few twisted corridors, with strategically placed buckets to collect rainwater. The Palace of Westminster building was still in need of some repairs. By comparison, Portcullis House was modern, with a swooping glass canopy over the atrium-like central space. Its site was once occupied by houses from the 1400s built for the dean and twelve canons of St Stephen's College at the Palace of Westminster. Much later it became the St. Stephen's Club. Underground, the District and Circle lines bisected the site and formed a deep well between the buildings, at the bottom of which was situated the deep tunnels of the Westminster underground station.

After the passing of the London Underground Act, it was deemed necessary to clear the whole corner site to build the new Jubilee Line station. This conveniently opened the possibility of a substantial new, freestanding building and the creation of a secure parliamentary campus extending as far as

Parliament Street and Richmond Terrace.

Sure enough, everyone was waiting for Clare in the visitor's lobby of Portcullis House. Hannah and Lottie have walked across from inside the Parliamentary complex."

"Jake and I came by taxi," explained Jake, "This sounded quite urgent. Although Christina wasn't with us, I expect she'll arrive by helicopter in a moment!"

They laughed, just as Christina made her way in, smiling "No helicopter, just a London cab!"

On this occasion, Clare was leading the group to Andrew's go-to meeting room in the complex. It was one of the more prestigious and secure rooms and illustrated that Andrew had clout as a Minister. They passed a scurrying weaselly 'Pomp' on the way to this session, but this Minister looked blankly ahead as if he was some absent-minded university Professor. It was a long-cultivated look, which he wrongly thought played well to television viewers.

"Bleurgh," whispered Bigsy, "I hate that man."

The others nodded in silent agreement.

"Ever since his back-stabbing play to depose the Prime Minister, he's been the enemy at one's back. As Andrew puts it: 'Remember, the opposition is in front of you; your enemy is behind you in your own party.'

"Oh dear," said Clare, "Another case of only the paranoid survive!"

Clare swiped her access card and they all trooped into the conference room.

"Nice," breathed Bigsy, "Although not quite as fancy as some of those along at SI6."

He pulled a small orange scanner from his bag and proceeded to sweep the room as if looking for surveillance equipment.

"They've done a good job here, not a bug in sight, " he muttered.

"Has someone already contacted Amanda?" asked Clare, suddenly realising that this ad-hoc session might be in vain.

"I'm ahead of you," said Jake, "We've got it set for 11am. In twenty minutes, with Amanda and Grace."

Hannah stared at Clare, "You had something important to tell me?" she asked, "What was it?"

"Oh Hannah, I guess you still haven't heard. I got the news from Andrew Brading. There's no easy way to tell you this. Duggie died this morning in a road accident."

They all looked at Hannah, whose face broke and she moved her hands to brush away slight tears.

"I knew something like this was on the cards, " she said, "Duggie was playing with fire. It's what Isabella was trying to warn him about."

Clare softly took Hannah's hand, "How could you be expecting this?" she asked.

Hannah straightened herself in the chair and put on her best serious Nicole Kidman expression.

"Look you must all know that I've been living in a room in his London apartment. It's purely platonic and came about when we both realised it was taking me too long to get to work. About 90 minutes each way, from deepest Hampshire. Duggie offered me his spare room, and by then, he had shared with me that he was gay - something I'd already worked out. Although he had not 'come out' in the conventional sense and was worried about his electorate's take if he were to suddenly announce it."

"The press were on to him as well," said Lottie, "That Rachel Crosby seemed to know."

"Yes, and actually she came around once to ask Duggie some questions. He asked me if I'd mind being around to provide a bit of camouflage. Of course, I didn't mind - and we'd become quite professionally close over the time that I worked for him."

Hannah continued, "I could see that Rachel was no fool and had scoped Duggie in the first few minutes.

I was trying to cut short her interview with him."

"But how did you know about whatever else Lessiter was doing?" asked Jake.

"He wasn't always that subtle. Izzy had spotted that he was being trapped into a paid lobbying situation and that was when he got all serious about the Non-Disclosure Agreements. To be frank, I think it was Brant that insisted upon them. I have one too."

"So, what happened?" asked Bigsy.

"Izzy wanted to warn Duggie that he was getting in too deep. That Brant was not an organisation to be messed with. If he wasn't careful, he could lose everything. She told me she was going to say it all to Duggie and I guess that as what was happening at that Xmas party,"

"I see, so she warns Lessiter not to be a fool?" asked Jake.

"Yes, but I think she must have threatened to be a whistle-blower too. That would have riled Duggie and been the reason he brought up the NDA."

"But it doesn't explain why she was in the Thames," said Lottie.

"My guess," said Christina, "Lessiter told someone that Isabella was a potential whistle-blower, and they clumsily dealt with her."

"Terrible, but who would it be?" asked Jake.

"It has to be someone involved with the Zillian scheme," said Christina, "And probably from Brant. They have access to all kinds of military contractors."

At that moment, there was a chiming sound in the room, and Clare pushed a button to reveal that Amanda and Grace had now joined the call.

"Hi Amanda, Hi Grace, " said Clare.

"Hello everyone," said Amanda, "And how are things?"

Clare began to summarise everything for Amanda, with additional inputs chipped in from everyone else.

Grace then flicked up a single chart. "So, this seems to be the story?"

LESSITER
- Hannah and Isabella work for Lessiter, both sign NDA
- Isabella discovers Lessiter is potentially compromised
- Isabella confronts Lessiter and threatens to whistle-blow.
- Isabella found in the Thames.

LESSITER AND MELSHIP

- Lessiter and Melship both have influence in transport lobby
- Both taken to Switzerland for Expo briefing
- Both wined, dined and 'befriended'.

BRANT ZILLIAN

- Melship and Lessiter propositioned for Brant/Zillian launch
- They are asked to assist in lobbying
- Both stand to make much money if they do as told.
- Hannah gets abducted, as leverage on Lessiter
- Hannah gets rescued, Lessiter told she is back in the UK.
- All return with apparently Lessiter and Melship prepared to do as told.
- Suspects include Bérénice Charbonnier, Kjeld Nikolajsen, Miller McDonald and Mary Ranzino from Brant and Qiu Zhang and Volvakov Valeryevich

IN UK

- Lessiter dies in Road Traffic Accident.
- Zillian scheme is poised to be executed
- Not clear, beyond Zillian and Brant,

who is running it.

"That is a good summary!" said Clare, enthusiastically.

"I can imagine Bérénice Charbonnier being mixed up in this, but not a ringleader, " said Christina.

"Kjeld is Norwegian and works for Brant, Miller and Mary are both Americans. Qui Zhang is Chinese and Valeryevich is Russian, so take your pick!" announced Bigsy.

"And The Kremlin is denying involvement," added Christina, "Although it doesn't rule it out, nor a bratva gang from Russia in charge."

"So, what are the next steps?" asked Clare.

There was a pause as everyone considered for a moment. It was Christina who spoke.

"I've been checking back, " she said, "Russia doesn't seem to know much about this. They know of the acts of Zillian, but don't seem to have anyone driving this."

"But can you be sure?" asked Amanda.

"Sure, in that my handler has asked me to look into it further. My handler supplied me with a helicopter, pilot and ten Special Force troops to go to Switzerland. I doubt very much whether I'd have got so much attention if the Kremlin new all about it."

"I can't speak directly to your handler, can I?" asked Amanda.

"No, it would be an embarrassing breach of protocol. I don't even think they know I have these occasional conversations with you," answered Christina.

"I have an evolving theory," said Grace, "Start by following the money. Who gains from all of this?"

"Melship and so would have Lessiter," said Clare.

"Yes, but who puts up most of the stake-holding?" asked Grace, "The Chinese. This could be a copycat situation. China is trying to do what the Russians did so successfully in the late 1990s. They can see that investing in the right enterprises could yield them millions."

"They could make money two ways, actually," observed Christina, "First through a share price rise and secondly by sourcing the actual Zillian vehicles in China."

"It could also create a massive money laundering vehicle for Russia," said Grace, "Think about it. It's a win-win for both China and Russia."

"It's like the old schemes we uncovered," said Jake, "Right back when they were operating the so-called green-lanes scams. It is, if you think about it, - ahem

- how The Triangle was formed."

"Yes, but I am sure that you only grabbed some passing 'small change'," said Grace, "In the Russian Federation, the estimates of capital flight frequently serve as a basis for money - laundering estimates because a significant part of the capital flight is presumed to be laundered illicit proceeds. The magnitude of capital flight itself causes suspicions about money-laundering."

"Capital Flight," smiled Bigsy, "I like it! A euphemism for stolen money!"

Grace continued, "In the 1990s, the magnitude of capital flight from the Russian Federation was significant. This was acknowledged by many sources, although there is no consensus about its nature and size.

"A joint project on capital flight undertaken by the Institute of Economics based in Moscow concluded that the average of different agencies' estimates equals a total of $133 billion for the period 1992-1997. Capital flight in the Russian Federation was running at an annual $17 billion. Then, in 1999 the Central Bank of the Russian Federation estimated the size of capital flight to be $54.2 billion for the period 1994-1998, which suggests an annual flow of about $11 billion."

"But hold it," said Clare, "Isn't that the same bank that is now wrapped up in this whole business?"

"It is," said Grace," and many say Putin himself has much equity with the bank. Ad indeed with many of the schemes, which required his sponsorship. They had built a money filtering factory, which was even up-front about the amount of money leaking from the system!"

"Hiding in plain sight!" said Christina.

Grace continued, "It is reasonable to assume that the capital leaving the Russian Federation illegally might be returning to the country disguised as legitimate foreign investment. The relationship between capital flight and foreign direct investment (FDI) appears to be clear-cut."

Christina spoke, "Yes don't you all see? This mechanism for creating huge wealth has been tested by the Russian Federation. Now they are branching out, using foreign companies and foreign investment to disguise what they are doing."

Christina continued, "Few in the Russian Federation worry about money laundering, but many are concerned about the enormous illicit proceeds from the theft and embezzlement of public and private assets. This concern echoes an international perception of the Russian Federation as a source of illicit proceeds, rather than as a safekeeping haven."

Jake spoke, "It's as if they are using the mechanics of the state and the bulk of personal savings to hide the gangster-like quantities of money being laundered"

Grace added, "In an effort to circumvent the legalisation of illegal profits, the Russian authorities have been tightening controls, which have included measures halting financial liberalisation and installing foreign exchange controls. Ironically, China is only just waking up to this."

Jake spoke, " I suppose the immense secrecy surrounding much of what goes on in China also acts a brake on new legislation?"

"Yes, you are kind-of right. You can't administer what you don't know about," said Grace.

"I remember something called S-Special accounts, in Russia," said Christina, "I used to get paid through them."

Grace nodded, "Exchange control mechanisms, including suspension of operations through non-residents, so-called "S-special" accounts, were introduced and prompted innovations circumventing these restrictions. The schemes involved foreign holders of roubles and Russian companies interested in doing business with them. Under the scheme, the shares of the Russian companies sold for roubles to foreign companies were purchased back by the same Russian companies for hard currencies.

"I see, " said Jake, "A Magic Roundabout of money. Put something impure in, wait a while and out pops the equivalent legitimate money."

"Correct," said Grace, "To purchase the shares, the Russian companies use their foreign currency holdings abroad. Zillian would be a good example. The Russian authorities described these operations as of a limited scale and not of a criminal nature. Nevertheless, they raise questions about why and how Russian companies have been able to accumulate and keep abroad assets of such size."

"They started this a long time ago," said Christina, "The sell-off of Russian banks and then state companies using the banks to pay for the shares in the companies, then seeing everything rise in value, so the original bank loans could easily be repaid. A popular Russian pun equates privatisation to the grabbing of State assets. Privatisation is referred to as prihvatization. 'Hvatat' in Russian means to grab, which could be also understood as a robbery."

"Wow, and I assume everyone got rich?" asked Jake.

"Yes, rich or murdered," answered Christina, "Many were killed as the next wave of nouveau-capitalists appeared to take control."

"Hmm, I wonder if that is what we are seeing now with Lessiter meeting his end?" asked Jake.

China, my China

In the haze of the morning, China sits on eternity
And the opium farmers sell dreams to obscure fraternities
On the horizon the curtains are closing
Down in the orchard the aunties and uncles play their games
(like it seems they always have done)

In the blue distance the vertical offices bear their names
(like it seems they always have done)
Clocks ticking slowly, dividing the day up
These poor girls are such fun they know what God gave them
fingers for (to make percussion over solos)

China my china, I've wandered around and you're still here
(which I guess you should be proud of)
Your walls have enclosed you, have kept you at home for
thousands of years (but there's something I should tell you)
All the young boys are dressing like sailors

I remember a man who jumped out from a window over the bay
(there was hardly a raised eyebrow)
The coroner told me 'this kind of thing happens every day'
You see, from a pagoda, the world is so tidy.

Brian Eno

China

"We should talk about China," says Amanda, "Grace, what have you found?"

Grace begins, "As China's growing global role and increasingly hardline policies at home and abroad gain attention, the United States and other Western governments are also taking notice of China's expanding influence in developing countries."

"They should do, with the number of products now made in China," says Bigsy.

Grace continues, "The implications of China's growing investments linked to the Belt and Road Initiative (BRI) which is its global infrastructure and connectivity program, are increasingly debated. So, too, are the nature of Chinese Communist Party (CCP) efforts to popularize its authoritarian model and undermine developing democracies around the world, whether intentionally or indirectly."

Jake adds, "Belt and Road? The Belt is the 'Silk Road

Economic Belt' referring to the proposed overland routes for road and rail transportation through landlocked Central Asia along the famed historical trade routes of the Western Regions. I remember 'Road' is short for the '21st Century Maritime Silk Road', referring to the Indo-Pacific Sea routes through Southeast Asia to South Asia, the Middle East and Africa. Examples of Belt and Road Initiative infrastructure investments include ports, skyscrapers, railroads, roads, bridges, airports, dams, coal-fired power stations, and railroad tunnels."

"Great answer!" smiles Clare, "Worthy of Mastermind!"

Grace continues, "The Chinese administration, through its Indo-Pacific strategy, intends to bolster the rule of law and human rights in regional countries facing growing influence from China. Such attention is welcome, and it has spurred numerous analyses on the drivers of China's growing influence efforts especially ones with external focus."

Christina adds, "Yes, China seeks influence due to many geo-strategic considerations, such as the protection of sea lanes critical for the transport of energy and the establishment of military facilities to protect China's growing global interests. However, much of the foundation for China's growing influence in developing countries is found inside China, where the CCP faces a mounting set of challenges to its rule that dominate its attention. It is very focused on the centralisation of power."

Grace continues her briefing, "The centralisation of power has been more an accelerant rather than the main driver of China's more assertive influence efforts. It is the Party's obsession with preserving its rule that more fundamentally drives China's growing influence in developing countries. Mounting threats to CCP control have occupied Chinese leaders as they have come to terms with the unravelling of the core factors that characterised China's reform era—relative political stability, ideological openness, and rapid economic growth."

Christina chips in, "It is different from the Russian situation. Chinese leaders have sharpened their focus on those aspects of developing country relationships likely to bolster the Party's fortunes. Two significant areas in which the CCP has stepped up influence efforts to benefit Party control are the economy and information management."

Jake frowns, "I see it differently. There isn't the same form of central governance with China, so now it wants to assert itself."

Christina nods and adds, "Yes - First, Beijing wants to mitigate mounting economic challenges and slowing growth in China through overseas investment and the creation of markets abroad for Chinese goods and materials. It's an ideal way in for China to assert itself. The Party's legitimacy depends on the health of China's economy. Access to resources needed to feed China's growing economy has long driven its engagement with the developing world, but China's economy is now struggling. Chinese leaders are looking to further boost overseas investment and trade, which have been growing for years but have been partially rebranded under the Belt and Road Initiative."

Clare looks around the room, "So what we get is China trying to copy Russia. To manipulate privatisation to such a degree that they can create a huge profit. But then to have a company which can be used for other purposes. As a laundromat for money."

Amanda speaks, "Yes, Clare, and Russia is happy to see it happen, in the knowledge that they too can leverage the situation for their own ends."

Grace adds, "And Melship and Lessiter as two hapless MPs - Only one now - used as a catalyst to generate the growth in Zillian."

"But will someone else replace Lessiter?" asks Bigsy, "Surely it can't be Andrew Brading?"

"No chance," says Clare, defensively," But I think you are on the right track. It must be someone who operates in the same circles as Melship and Lessiter."

"How about Michael Tovey?" asks Amanda, "Remember when he tried to oust Andrew Brading? He was also involved in the Elixanor situation which almost wound up with him being taken down by that hitman Yaroslev."

"He has gone to ground since then, mainly behaving as a low-key back-bencher," says Grace.

"I expect your warnings to him did some good then?" asks Bigsy.

"Or the two men that ran at him with loaded pistols. They had the larger influence," answers Amanda.

"Who are Tovey's assistants?" asks Amanda.

"I can help with that," answers Lottie, "One of them is Matt Stevens. Charming, loudmouthed, but slightly dim, actually."

Clare and Hannah both smile. They remember when Lottie had a short fling with Matt. He thought highly of himself, but inevitably crashed out under the influence of drink.

"Oh - I think I remember him too," says Jake, "He was at that Chinese in Soho. Totally out of it if I remember correctly. Oh - wasn't he your boyfriend for a while, Lottie?"

"Not something I'm too proud of," says Lottie, smiling.

"Oh yes, he was quite a loudmouth, or at least after he'd had one or two," answers Jake, "Oh, no offence Lottie"

Hannah smiles and Clare sees that Hannah knew

Matt's reputation too.

"Okay, it doesn't look as if Matt would be much help as we try to investigate Tovey."

Grace speaks, "As a matter of fact, Tovey has prior form too. He set up a trust fund in the Cayman's. The idiot gave it his own name and it all got revealed when the Panama Papers broke and exposed offshore fund hiding was big business. Of course, there were bigger fish to fry and he managed to wriggle clear of everything."

She presses another button and a list appears, illustrating some of the Panama Papers people involved.

Politicians
- Retired Member of the House of Lords
- former Member of the House of Commons
- MP and former Chief Scientific Adviser to the Ministry of Defence
- former Member of the House of Commons
- Member of the House of Lords

Relatives and associates of government officials
- Duchess and former wife of Royal.
- father of Prime Minister
- son of Baroness
- son of former Prime Minister

Businesspeople

- British political donor to the Tories and UKIP
- British retail and media moguls
- British hotelier
- British banking business executive and CEO
- former chairman of major oil company
- British-Russian oil and uranium business manager
- A Reverend and former operating officer
- British-Syrian businessman
- British entrepreneur and environmentalist
- British industrialist
- British businessman

Grace adds, "You can see from this incomplete list that there are many other higher profile people who would get 'the treatment' before Michael Tovey came to light. The list only shows part of the British involvement, altogether there are hundreds of individuals and organisations involved in dubious off-shore equity management and funds concealment."

"But what did you find out about Qiu Zhang, Grace?" asks Jake.

"Not a lot to begin with, " answers Grace, "But then I discovered that Qui Zhang was an alias. She is really known as Zhao Hu, and comes from Hong Kong, where she is linked to the (義安) Yee On triad.

"The Yee On triad is distinct from mainland Chinese criminal organisations. In ancient China, this triad was one of three major secret societies. It established branches in Macau, Hong Kong, Taiwan, and Chinese communities overseas.

"Known as 'mainland Chinese criminal organisations', they are of two major types: dark forces (loosely-organised groups) and black societies (more-mature criminal organisations).

"Two features which distinguish a black society from a dark force are the ability to achieve illegal control over local markets and receiving police protection. The Yee On triad refers to traditional criminal organisations operating in Hong Kong, Macau, Taiwan and south-east Asian countries and regions.

"We were lucky to find out anything, but four years ago, Italian police arrested 33 people connected to a Chinese triad operating in Europe as part of its Operation China Truck. The structure of the Triad placed Zhao Hu as the 'Vanguard' or Operations Master - a rank of 438, which is very close to the top. The triad were active in Tuscany, Veneto, Rome, and Milan in Italy, and in France, Spain, and Germany. The indictment accused the triad of extortion, usury, illegal gambling, prostitution, and drug trafficking. It was said to have infiltrated the transport sector, using intimidation and violence against Chinese companies wishing to transport goods by road into Europe. Police seized several vehicles, businesses, properties, and bank accounts.

Grace continues, "For this detention, it was noted

that there was a close relationship between the Triads and the Camorra, and the port of Naples is the most important landing point of the trades managed by the Chinese in cooperation with the Camorra.

Then, Grace chuckles, at what she is about to reveal, "Here's the stupidity of the system at work: Zhao Hu avoided detention, partly as a woman and because there were also two other similar ranks (both 438) which were the so-called Deputy Mountain Master and the Incense Master. A woman ranked 438 alongside two other exactly similar raked individuals. In China, you can just sense how this will play out.

"She left Hong Kong for New York the day before the arrests and there was nothing which could be done to detain her. Some say she may have shopped the triad, but there is nothing to prove it."

Grace continues, "Among the illegal activities in which the Camorra and Yee On work together are the human trafficking and illegal immigration aimed at the sexual and labour exploitation of Chinese immigrants into Italy, synthetic drug trafficking and the laundering of illicit money through the purchase of real estate.

"Then in 2017, like something from The Sopranos, investigators discovered an illicit industrial waste transportation scheme jointly run by the Camorra and Triads. The waste was transported from Italy to China, leaving from Prato in Italy and arriving in

Hong Kong - a scheme which prior to its discovery had been netting millions of dollars' worth of revenue for both organisations."

"Where there's muck there's brass," says Bigsy and Lottie laughs.

"But aren't we forgetting something?" asks Amanda, "Where that original lead that there was something off-kilter came from?"

"Oh yes, our favourite Parliamentary reporter. I've only given her very little since we returned from Gstaad. I was worried just how much could turn up in the Press," says Jake.

"Time for some disclosure, then," says Amanda, "but she must know that she cannot publish anything. Would you like me to come along?"

"That would be excellent!" says Jake, "And she will be intrigued because I think she suspects you of wiretapping her phone."

"I could not possibly comment," says Amanda.

Deflect, Distract, and Brazen it out

Jake, Clare, and Christina agreed to meet Rachel Crosby at the Cinnamon Club, a modern Indian restaurant just a short walk from Parliament.

"I was worried by the ominous words '£1 million facelift' and 'new look'," says Rachel.

"Yes, the Old Westminster Library, certainly had a refresh," says Jake.

Rachel adds, "I remember when it first launched, the Cinnamon Club became an instant London landmark. It was like an established, convivial, exclusive, old-school members' club that also happened to serve exceptionally good, high-end, modern Indian food. And women were as welcome as men. Pitch-perfect."

"I used to visit with people who thought it had been here much longer - as a restaurant, I mean," says Jake.

"I like the way the books line the main dining room as well as that gallery - most colourful," observes

Christina, "And a light touch comes from the butter-soft teal leather seating!"

"We sound like Sunday supplement restaurant critics," says Clare, "But we are here to update Rachel,"

"You know what," says Jake, "This food is so good, I think we should order one starter and one main each and then share!"

There was a pause as they considered and Jake made a list, ready for the waiter.

"If only Bigsy, with his appetite was here!" says Clare, "We wouldn't have to worry about the quantity," They all laugh.

Rachel suggests they all try the Twisted Tea, combining Tanqueray No10 gin, saffron-steeped Galliano and both chamomile liquor and tea.

"This is going to be one of those evenings," says Jake, as the small wagon arrived with the drinks.

They start to recount their story of the trip to Geneva, and then onward to Gstaad. Rachel was most interested, but when they mentioned the names of the people they had met in Gstaad, she stopped them.

"My brother David knew Miller McDonald and Qiu Zhang," she says. "He met them both in London a couple of times. It was something to do with UK

Government business. He explained it to me once, but it seemed to me to be secret-squirrel type surveillance."

"I can't properly understand why he would be talking to those two about UK Government business?" says Clare.

"To be truthful, neither can I," answers Rachel, "I think he was trying to set up a combined deal with Brant Industries. Using his computer technology and their existing 'ins' to the UK Government. If it had worked, they would have had a compelling proposition, although I'm not sure most MPs would like the idea of being monitored."

"What happened?" asks Jake.

They all paused the conversation as a couple of waiters appeared. The waiters set up a small table next to their own and then carefully place an array of starters upon it. The lead waiter then produces four small plates which he ceremoniously distributes around the table. Then, in turn, each of the starters was brought forward.

"Here we are," he explains, "Spiced aubergine steak, pumpkin chutney, masala peanut and moutabal; Tandoori octopus with chutney potatoes and tomato lemon dressing; Char-grilled Zeeland kingfish with carom seed, samphire and pickled radish and Lamb mille-feuille – Hyderabadi black spiced lamb escalope, Awadhi lamb galouti!"

"Amazing!" says Clare, "I can't think why I've never been here before!"

Rachel continues with her story, "Well the whole deal with Brant collapsed when David died. The only record of it was on his laptop, and although I still have it, it has proved impossible to get into with his passwords and other security measures. Remember, he was in the business!"

"I know this is delicate," says Jake, "So please excuse me for asking, but do you suspect foul play for your brother's death?"

The normally professional Rachel looks a little tearful, "Yes, I do, actually. David was too positive in his outlook to have driven all the way to Liverpool and then killed himself in a dockyard pool."

Christina nods, "I assume the police were involved in full investigation?"

Rachel nods, "Yes, they were, and said they would leave no stone unturned, although I was not convinced. The un-investigated laptop is a case in point. The same with his forensically clean car, found parked near to the scene. That short log file I was sent by email from him. None of it makes sense. I think I said the police left it as an open verdict."

Jake answers, "We could get our technical whizz on to this. To look at the log file and to see if it is possible to break into David's computer."

Clare realises that Jake was suggesting Bigsy could take a look.

"You are most welcome, but please remember that this was all looked at by the police at the time," replies Rachel.

"Where is the computer now?" asks Christina.

"It's in my apartment," says Rachel, "In the bottom of my wardrobe, actually."

"Okay, we'll send someone around tomorrow to pick it up."

"The same rules still apply to all of this," says Clare "Just to be clear, we can't have any of this in the press - at least not at the moment,"

"We are long past that moment," says Rachel, "Rest assured that we are good. I'm treating this as a personal situation rather than part of my investigative journalism."

"Okay, so that's what we need to pick your brains about next, Rachel. I'm hoping you'll be outspoken because this is simply between the four of us. We'd like to know what your opinion is of Michael Tovey, MP?"

Rachel grimaces, "Tovey? A snake, I'd say. A privileged Etonian with no moral compass."

"Oh, we've hit a nerve?" asks Clare.

"I'm afraid that Tovey's behaviour and attitudes are typical of some parts of the British establishment. If the ruling party has a shared culture, it's entitlement and shamelessness, a conviction that wrongdoing should meet consequences only if you are poor and powerless."

"He sounds like a few others I could mention!" interjects Jake.

"When Tovey joined the old leadership during the pandemic, he made it very clear that he believed that the rules had to accommodate his needs, rather than vice versa,"

"I remember - he was one of the people caught partying during the lockdowns," says Clare.

Rachel adds, "He was the same with the multitude of expenses scandals: he was one of the MPs who railed against 'benefit cheats' while milking hard-pressed taxpayers. His immediate circle of friends believed they were not sufficiently remunerated and that offshore tax havens were the way to go. All the time he was cultivating party donors – the City hotshots and top lawyers with whom he clinked champagne glasses. "

"The penalties were so light for most of them," said Clare.

Rachel continues, "Why shouldn't they just help

themselves to extras they deserved? A handful of MPs went to prison, but for most, being personally winded by some adverse newspaper headlines did not prove a roadblock to their future political careers. In a few cases they even made political capital because it raised their profile."

Jake considered, "The revolving door between the fourth estate and politics has enjoyed a bit-part in this scandal. Remember the press officer/woman journalist who ended up being thrown under the ex-PM's bus (metaphorically) to keep some others in power. Still, I suppose she owned up, which is more than can be said for most of the inner circle."

Rachel nodded, "Yes - Tovey discovered that spreading myths and outright lies about benefit claimants, refugees and Muslims was largely consequence-free. Tovey is one of the MPs who emphasises the establishment's unofficial motto: 'rules for thee and not for me.' He is adept at firing chaff like some lumbering warplane to deflect any arguments, whether against him or in defence of his party leaders. One of the Pomps – pompous – oh - I'll let you guess what the 'S' stands for."

"I like the imagery of the warplane with sparks flying out from it to confuse incoming missiles," chuckled Jake.

Rachel continues, "Tovey boasted that nobody 'stuck up for the bankers as much as I did' after the last financial crash. Indeed, Tovey has been a longstanding and unapologetic champion of the wealthiest, who he once described as a 'put-upon minority' who made a 'heroic contribution'. They barely needed his defence."

"I assume he was richly rewarded for running to their defence?" asks Jake.

Their table had been cleared and now the main course arrived. Jake noticed that the waiters had assembled two small serving tables for this.

"I think we may have over-ordered!" he said, smiling.

The waiter patiently explains the new dishes: "Now the main courses: Achari gobhi - Tandoori cauliflower with pickling spices, yoghurt sauce, pilau rice; Kokum crusted halibut on the bone, shallot and tamarind sauce, lemon rice; Grilled New Caledonian Obsiblue king prawns, Alleppey curry sauce, rice vermicelli; Vesavara spiced free range chicken breast, chicken leg stew, stir-fried greens. And, of course, the accompaniments: Tandoori breads; Potato paratha, garlic & coriander naan, tandoori whole wheat roti; Homemade chutneys; Pilau and lemon rice."

Clare comments again, "It all looks amazing!"

Rachel continues her story, "Then, to Jake's point, after the financial crisis, over 300 financiers were convicted of crimes after the financial system nearly collapsed in the US. Here in the UK, the number of bankers who went to prison was just five. Five!

Again: terrible behaviour, minimal consequences. Aided and abetted by the softly spoken words from Tovey."

She adds, "There are good reasons why members of the establishment like Tovey may believe their power and connections are a bullet-proof vest. "

"But I thought Tovey had been hunted any gunmen and rescued by Amanda Millers' people?" asks Jake.

Rachel nods, "Yes, if the rumours are true, but I think the source of those incoming gangsters was more connected with his other shady dealings."

Then she pauses before saying, "I know I can't publish this but consider that in the UK, you are over 20 times more likely to be prosecuted for benefit fraud than tax fraud. Benefit fraud may inflict far less economic and social harm, but our society hysterically demands that it's the sins of the poor that must be punished. Oh yes, Tovey is an arch exponent of 'deflect, distract and brazen it out.' "

Committee Room

Clare was back in Parliament with Lottie and Hannah. They were sitting in a deserted meeting room on a quiet Friday afternoon. Conventionally Fridays were quiet in Parliament. Like a public school, sitting was scheduled only from 9.30am to 3pm and no debates were scheduled for Fridays, so many MPs did not even bother to stay around the buildings.

It meant that there were usually free rooms around the Estate and Lottie had co-opted one, via the W4MP website. They were in a Committee Room and the electronic diary indicated that it would next be used for a Formal Meeting of the Health and Social Care Committee on the following Monday afternoon.

Lottie, Hannah, Clare, Bigsy, Christina and Jake were all present and they had the session listed by Lottie as the 'Transport Technical Committee debrief of Working Papers.'

"I wanted to make it sound boring, so we don't

attract any attention," explained Lottie.

"Doesn't sound boring to me!" chipped in Bigsy.

"Bigsy, you are sometimes special," commented Clare.

The room's capacity was much larger than the assembled group and a set of ancient wooden tables and chairs had been pulled into a 'U' shape which took up much of the room. The carpeting was like something from a 1970's pub, and the wallpaper above the panelling on the walls was a swirly salmon colour. A TV annunciator on one wall was soundlessly playing back the empty chamber from the House of Commons.

"I drove over to Rachel's and brought back her brother's PC," explained Bigsy, "I took a quick look, but have given it to someone else with some specialist knowledge to 'spring the catches' on it. Then we'll be able to look for anything interesting. I also got the file that had been sent to Rachel. It looks like a tiny file from a PC almost like a serial number or something, so I don't think I'll have any trouble decoding it, especially when we have the PC 'opened,'

"But can you trust your friend?" asked Lottie, "I mean, he won't start publicising what we are doing or anything like that?"

"No, Luke is a good guy - a friend with whom I have been involved in numerous scrapes over the year. I trust him implicitly - as does he, towards me."

"When do you think it will be ready?" asked Clare, "I mean that we can access it?"

"Knowing Luke, it will be ready this evening. I'll have to collect it from him."

"What else do we know?" asked Clare, "Or at least suspect?"

"It looks to me as if Michael Tovey might be taking the place of Douglas Lessiter in the Zillian scheme," said Lottie, "I was in the office yesterday and who should walk in? None other than Tovey. Embarrassingly he had Matt Stevens with him. But Tovey and Melship were making jokes and it was clear that they are old drinking buddies. It seems they go back a long way."

"Right the way back to Oxford, by the look of it," said Jake who was looking at his laptop, "They were both members of the same drinking club, where they had to meet in a pub, carrying a diamond and a toy squirrel and order a pint of Champagne."

"Boy's toys," said Clare, and Christina agreed.

"It all makes sense of the big parties that Melship had, too. Cultivating his chumocracy," said Lottie, "I used to go to them in the early days, but then I felt I'd heard every chat-up line ever invented and decided to stop going. I know, I still ended up with Matt, but that's another story."

"Hmm. I seem to remember a few others too," said Hannah, smiling, "Both before and after Matt..."

"Okay, point taken!" said Lottie, "But how's this relevant?"

"Only in much as if you can remember any of them, for their backgrounds?" asked Christina.

"Oh yes, they were mainly well-heeled, well turned out, polite," answered Lottie, "But they all had serious defects,"

"Ooh, interesting..." Said Clare, "Like what?"

Lottie opened up, "Well, Davy was a serial buffoon, like a clown act. All the time. He thought it endearing. Matt was a loudmouth who couldn't hold his drink and was totally indiscreet. Brian (yes that was really his name) was charming but ran out of interesting things to say after about three sentences. Denzil was funny but had a chip on his shoulder. Not the obvious one, but one about how his family had treated him badly. I could go on, but you get the picture, without me even going upstairs."

"Going upstairs; That's a great euphemism," said Jake.

"Oh, we used it all the time around at the flat," said Clare.

"And elsewhere," added Hannah.

Clare summarised, "Okay, so Tovey has replaced Lessiter in the scam, which requires the combined - er - talents of Melship and Tovey. At the end of it, they both stand to make decent off-shore money."

"Yes, that's the sum of it," said Jake, "We could take it back to Amanda, but I think she's already reached that conclusion."

Recording

Bigsy was in the Triangle offices. His friend Luke had returned David Crosby's computer. Sure enough, Luke had defeated the laptop's security and been able to access the hard drive. Bigsy had made a copy of the hard drive and was pouring through the emails.

"Nothing unusual," he said out loud, when a ping arrived on his text.

It was from Luke and said, "Not sure whether you noticed the second partition?"

Bigsy hadn't. He had made a simple copy of the disk to work upon, but somehow didn't spot that the disk had been divided into two sections. A readily accessible one and another, smaller hidden section.

"Luke - Thank you!" he sent and proceeded to copy the second section to another hard drive, so that he was sure to preserve the original.

"Encryption Key Required:" said his copy routine. He typed in a string of characters and noticed that a dash was being inserted by the system after every fourth keystroke. He needed a 20 character-long key to allow the disk to be read and copied back in an un-encoded state.

He remembered the key that had been sent to Rachel in the mystery email. It was the right length. He typed it in.

'AHfg-1265-WeUI-7602-QmaL'

"Encryption Key Accepted:" said the copy routine. He watched as a giant copy operation began. In around half an hour he would have the contents of the secret folder stored on David Crosby's computer.

PART THREE

Ed Adams

lived in bars

We've lived in bars
And danced on the tables
Hotels, trains and ships that sail
We swim with sharks
And fly with aeroplanes in the air

We know your house so very well
And we will wake you once we've walked up all your stairs

There's nothing like living in a bottle
And nothing like ending it all for the world
We're so glad you have come back
Every living lion will lay in your lap

We know your house so very well
And we will bust down your door if you're not there

We've lived in bars
And danced on tables
Hotels, trains and ships that sail
We swim with sharks
And fly with aeroplanes out of here

Charlyn (Chan) Marie Marshall

Partition revealed

Bigsy waited and could see the file structure emerging on the new disk. Much of it was references to other companies, but then he noticed Zillian appear. He should be able to start from there.

Once completed, he dug into the Zillian folder. There were several documents, mercifully without any additional passwords.

He selected the one that said 'IPO of Zillian' which included a Process folder.

There was a form S-1 registration statement; the list of SEC technical requirements; A Registration Statement filing, then the S-1 Filing and the complete execution timeline mapped out. The whole Zillian flotation was poised and ready to roll.

Bigsy noticed the Tactics folder. It included several small recordings in it as well as a couple of documents.

He clicked the first recording.

"Hi, this is David Crosby, I'm in trouble related to the Zillian launch and am putting my statement on record. It is also saved away to a DropBox folder in the Cloud, so even if the original data here on my PC is compromised, it should still be available from the DropBox backup."

Bigsy knew that using DropBox for a backup was a rudimentary solution, but could understand why Crosby, in an emergency, had done it.

Crosby's voice continued, "I've discovered some big irregularities with the Zillian launch. The documents in this folder prove the accusations I am making on this recording."

"Firstly, Zillian doesn't have any vehicles of its own. The ones it is selling are from a Chinese factory making clones of other vehicles.

"Secondly, the electric cars are a sham. Zillian is buying chassis from another well-known German car manufacturer and adding their own bodies to them. They only need a few to prove the point for their share valuation.

"Thirdly, the contracts being entered into by Zillian, for example, with the UK Government are being made under a mixture of threats and bribery. Threats because they had compromised information about some key MPs and bribery because they are also providing the same MPs with cash to invest in the new company.

"I don't know who orchestrated this, but I suspect the Chinese are putting up most of the capital for the equity launch. With good management, the shares should rise considerably.

"Then, I believe there will be some kind of 'good news' press release which will add even more to the share prices. My suspicion is that this will be because the UK Government wants build good relationships and an order book with Zillian."

The recording stopped. Bigsy considered for a moment. It seemed as if David had been prepared to whistle blow this whole situation. Instead, he had paid with his life.

Bigsy realised this was dangerous knowledge. He would move the laptop to his off-site store where he kept the disaster recovery used by The Triangle. It was in a vault in north-east London.

Bigsy emailed the recording to himself, carefully changing its filetype to that of a spreadsheet first, to make it harder to track. Now was time to convene a meeting with everyone.

What we've found

Bigsy arranged to meet everyone in the Triangle's own offices on Thamesside, in their office building in Hays Galleria. Everyone knew the location and he considered it to be even more secure from wiretaps than the Parliamentary Estate.

He invited Amanda Miller and Grace Fielding to join remotely, as well as Hannah, Lottie plus the usual gang of Christina, Clare, and Jake. Amanda would patch Grace in from GCHQ. Because of the sensitive nature of the meeting, he decided not to invite Rachel Crosby.

Bigsy described the situation to everyone, including a playback of the recording from Rachel's brother David. Jake named the two MPs now suspected of involvement in the scheme to float Zillian and to make a huge profit for themselves.

"I can't deny that this is well-researched," said Amanda, "But the burden of proof still runs against us. Ever since that smoking gun when a one-time

Prime Minister attempted to lie his way out of a situation. Remember even when 300 photographs appeared, he was still saying he'd broken no rules, and that he didn't know anything about it. It was like an upgrade of 'plausible deniability', through "I cannot recollect" and onwards to bare-faced denials."

"What are you saying, then?" asked Christina, "It sounds as if we need to catch them in the act of their scam?"

"I'm afraid so, and there are several moving parts. However, if we catch them and can prove that we have evidence, then I think events would take their own course. Neither the Chinese nor the Russians like failure, nor being found out!"

"Well, we have good access," said Christina, "I mean Lottie has a direct line to Melship and we also have a link to one of Tovey's assistants."

"We do, although that is less helpful, because he is an unreliable blabbermouth," said Jake, speaking up on Lottie's behalf.

"That's right, but I think his weakness could become our strength," said Lottie, "Matt Stevens always likes to hear good gossip and likes to think he hears it first. What could be better than an old 'ex' of his asking him for some advice, ideally over copious amounts of alcohol."

"Will he still meet you?" asked Hannah, "You know

how you left it?"

"Oh yes, I think so, time will have played its part and I think he'd have a certain dry pleasure in seeing me asking his opinion of something. It will need to be work-related though..."

"What about something to do with the car industry? You must be so well briefed by now?" suggested Jake.

"I know, something about electric cars and their chargers being prepared for widespread distribution in London?" suggested Bigsy, "But that London is to be made even more car-free?"

"That could work." said Grace, "Especially if part of the share price launch is predicated on doing a big deal with London."

"It would ruin the IPO share launch of Zillian, which would not make the big money after all."

"So why are you asking Matt about this?" asked Christina, "There has to be a very plausible reason?"

"You can say you want to know whether to stop Melship from making a fool of himself, not with the share deal, of which you can be ignorant, but because you think Melship is about to advise the PM to make some kind of stirring speech in Parliament, which would all be wrong a few days later and lead to a massive U-turn."

"I like it," said Jake.

"Oh yes, that could very well create a meltdown and see the way open for Opposition attack," said Grace, "Back-bench Tories are looking for an opportunity to move the PM, to get someone more likeable before the next election."

Amanda spoke, "Conservative governments in the past have regularly suffered humiliating meltdowns. In 1990 Margaret Thatcher's premiership ended in tears after months of plotting against her. Then her successor, John Major, resigned as leader and sought re-election in a failed attempt to silence his critics."

"Oh yes, we forget that it has always been so," acknowledged Jake.

Amanda continued, "More recently, the crises have come faster and faster: David Cameron's resignation after losing his Brexit referendum in 2016; Theresa May's disastrous attempt to increase her parliamentary majority in 2017; the failed effort to remove her through a no-confidence vote in 2018; her repeated Brexit defeats before her resignation in 2019."

"Yes, they seem to speed up in more recent times, " added Clare

Amanda added, "Curiously, none of these episodes led to the Conservatives losing office. On each occasion, for days, weeks or months, the party's future appeared to hang in the balance. We've all seen the journalists reporting excitedly from Downing Street, or outside meetings of the Tories' much-mythologised 1922 Committee. Opposition parties seized on Conservative divisions and disarray. Labour politicians began to believe they might soon take office."

Now Clare spoke, "Every time, the sense of crisis gradually ebbed away. The Conservatives changed their leader, or some of their policies, or just played for time, exploiting the opportunities in Britain's parliamentary calendar for evasion and delay. With its frequent recesses, the House of Commons is not as tough a place for wounded prime ministers as is traditionally claimed."

Amanda looked serious, "I have to remain impartial in this because of my role, but it's easy to note that Tory governments survive their disastrous phases partly because voters lose interest. Not just because most people only follow politics closely for, at best, a few days at a time. But also, because these very social media compatible crises can be emotionally and politically satisfying in themselves - like some tawdry soap-opera."

Lottie smiled, "This could be a great story for Matt. The potential overthrow of the Conservatives because of his own Minister's avoidable mistake. I like it!"

Breaking up with a drunkard

Lottie was about to meet Matt Stevens. She had not seen him since their break-up, which she had engineered to be on a commuter train, early evening, before he had a chance to get drunk.

It hadn't gone especially well, although it had created a fascinating spectacle for those sitting in the adjacent seats. Lottie had also enlisted Tessa's support and she had sat across the gangway from Matt and Lottie when the event occurred.

Of course, in the style of the best breakups it was all done in a very public place, to avoid the worst of Matt's protestations. Lottie decided that Matt must have had a liquid lunch, in any case, because he didn't have too much logic in his replies, and the whole scene was over between Vauxhall and Putney, where Lottie and Tessa left the train.

Lottie had called Matt plaintively this time:

"Matt? Its Lottie...I hope we are still able to talk.

Look I've found out something. It's about your boss, Michael Tovey. I think you need to know and maybe give me advice about what I should do with what I've found out."

"Lottie?! I didn't expect to hear from you again! This is quite a surprise! How are you doing? Erm, you know I'm with Charlotte Mendez now? That's Charlotte from Banca Cariba. She doesn't work on the Estate. But sure, if you think I can help, then fire away!"

"I'm doing fine, by the way. This topic is rather sensitive, I'll need to meet you for half an hour somewhere close to Parly. Do you know Cafe Churchill on Parliament Street?"

"What the place near to Downing Street? Near the traffic lights?"

"That's the one. Can we meet there for breakfast, say tomorrow? At 8.30?"

"Sure, I'll be along. Mine's a latte and a croissant!"

Lottie had picked a low-key place to meet, one that most resembled a work venue.

Cafe Churchill

The next morning, Lottie was early to arrive at the Cafe. There were a few tables with chequered tablecloth along the pavement and a couple of other consultant/refugees from Parliament sitting hunched over another table, engrossed in a pre-bid discussion.

Then she saw Matt arrive. He was walking briskly and looked fresher than Lottie could ever remember. Maybe this Charlotte was having a good effect upon him.

But then, as he approached the table, she sensed the aroma of peppermint, aftershave, and stale beer. At least he had made some attempt to disguise it, but she realised that this was the same old Matt, still spending his evenings in bars.

"Hello, my darling," he said, and Lottie remembered that Matt was originally from Cornwall and that 'Darling' was part of his workaday vocabulary, just like 'My beauty'.

"I was inside and ordered your latte and a croissant," answered Lottie, "I haven't got long to explain this to you,"

"Okay, it sounds like some juicy gossip, especially if it has to be delivered in person," said Matt.

The coffees and croissants arrived and they both paused to take a bite and to realise that the lattes were too hot to drink.

"Okay, here's the situation," said Lottie. "You know I am working for Duncan Melship? Well, I recently went on a trip with him and Duggie Lessiter to Switzerland."

"Oh wow, you are moving up in the world!" said Matt.

"Well, Melship is now involved with the car industry, and I think Michael Tovey has now taken over from Lessiter, since Lessiter's tragic accident."

"Yes, it was tragic. First Isabella and then Duggie."

"Yes, well my friend Hannah also worked for Douglas Lessiter, and we heard some of the inside story. We heard that electric cars and their chargers are being prepared for widespread distribution in London? - It's some big propaganda push announced by the PM, driven by Michael Tovey's agenda and briefings."

"Yes, it's almost good to go. It will make quite a lavish splash," said Matt,"I know it is technically insider trading, but there's a few companies who will see share prices rise on the back of this story. In fact, I have heard Tovey talk about a particular company - Zillian - which he thinks could go through the roof."

"Well, I'm not so worried about share prices, " lied Lottie, "But I am interested in stopping the PM from making an absolute fool of himself in Parliament."

"How so?"

"Well, there are strong rumours that London is to be made even more car-free," explained Lottie "It would seem crazy to roll out a massive infrastructure to one part of the country that didn't need it. The red wall towns in the north could have a field day - 'Wasting money on London when the rest of the country is crying out for new infrastructure.' "

Lottie could now sip from the latte. She paused to look at Matt's expression. Was he taking it all in?

She continued, "I can see that there is something very 'profile enhancing' for someone to stop the whole process before it goes too far. It would save the PM from getting more egg on his face at a time when his support is somewhat beleaguered."

"I can see that. How reliable are your sources?"

"It's not so much about the sources, as about the ability to put the big picture together. Look in yesterday's Metro, you'll see the story about how London plans to reduce the number of cars still further. Look, I brought the article."

Lottie fished in her bag and brought out a press cutting from yesterday's paper.

"Wowowow. Okay, Lottie, so what do you want?" asked Matt.

"Matt, I don't want anything. I'm just concerned that your Minister doesn't make a huge mistake that could bring the whole government crashing down. I guess you, rather than me will be the hero of the piece, but I'll bank that for another time," Lottie smiled, sipped the last from her latte and then stood.

"I need to go now, Matt," she said as Matt hastily stood and then made a motion as if to shake her hand.

"So formal, Matt, but I shall now leave this in your capable hands," she turned and rapidly walked back along Parliament Street in the direction of the Houses of Parliament. Matt was still clutching the press cutting as he stood and then scurried away towards The Treasury buildings in Whitehall.

"That went well," said one of the two consultants sitting at the adjacent table. Bigsy nodded back at Jake, "Yes and I think we should have a good video of the entire encounter."

Clare's article

Rachel Crosby's phone rang.

"Hi Rachel, it's Clare. We've found something out about your brother now and we want to share it with you."

"What? Have you found something on his laptop?"

"Oh yes, it's in his own words too, a recording that show he was into the situation quite deep."

"Oh, okay, I knew it, does it shed any light on his death?"

"It adds to the evidence that he was murdered," said Clare, "And Rachel, I've written an article which it would be good to get into the papers under your by-line. It is a prediction of some stormy water ahead for the current Prime Minister."

"Won't that be yesterday's news?" asked Rachel, "I mean he is only just clinging on as it is!"

"This might just be enough to tip it over the edge when some other news breaks," answered Clare, "It should be in your in-box."

Rachel read Clare's article:

"By exposing the errors and shortcomings of our usual ruling class, and by forcing them into U-turns, changes of leadership and displays of sometimes embarrassing contrition, Conservative crises can feel like a rebalancing between politicians and citizens — and make more fundamental change seem unnecessary.

"The 1992 and 2019 elections both came after particularly protracted periods of Tory upheaval. Yet they saw the biggest total Conservative votes of the past half-century.

"Many people seemed to feel that the Tories had listened and adapted sufficiently to their discontents. The government had been punished enough, so ironically a new one was not needed.

"In pre-democratic times, the status quo was protected by brief, pressure-releasing ruptures in the established order. In medieval France, for example, the annual Feast of Fools would be when low-ranking clergy temporarily swapped places with their superiors and mockery of church practices was permitted.

"There is something similarly ritualised in today's Tory crises: from the theatrical sending of letters to the 1922 Committee by MPs seeking a leadership contest, to the inauthentic-feeling attacks on the government by the right-wing press, which flare up and then suddenly cease.

"These protagonists may well be playing their roles on the understanding that uncomfortable periods for the Tories are the necessary price, paid every few years, for the party's long-term dominance. And during these crises British politics becomes, more than ever, mostly about the Conservatives.

"They know how to do theatricality and how to cling to Power.

"For non-Tories, trying to work out who would be the least awful new Tory leader is a familiar routine — in effect, a partial acceptance of continuing Conservative rule.

"Many voters and journalists probably know more about the rules of Tory leadership contests than they do about Labour's policies. And that's not just because they don't have enough compelling ones. There is an English preoccupation with Tory politics that is a kind of self-fulfilling prophecy.

"In one-party states, it's common to ridicule or feel contempt for your government without being able to envisage its removal.

"Our politics isn't that stuck, yet, despite the Tories' ongoing efforts to tilt the electoral system in their favour, such as making it harder to vote for social groups who tend not to support them or gerrymandering political boundaries.

"But the deepening cynicism about politicians means that a chaotic government no longer shocks and alienates voters as much as it did

in previous eras with struggling prime
ministers were ejected from Downing Street for
smaller errors than those of the current
gangster-like incumbent.

"Nowadays it's widely expected that our leaders
will be out of their depth, as well as entirely
out for themselves.

"Yet it's too early to be sure that the Tories'
current troubles will recede in the usual way.
There is another, rarer kind of Conservative
crisis. It is less exciting to follow, but
longer lasting and more lethal. It involves
enough voters firmly deciding that the Tories
have been in power for too long, and then
fitting every government scandal and mistake
into that template.

"The last time this happened was in the 1990s,
when Labour's return to office was preceded by
almost five years of Tory calamities and failed
relaunches. Tony Blair was Labour leader for
the most decisive part of the period, and his
ability to promise a better future helped make
the Conservative government look obsolete.

"Current Labour doesn't have the same
salesman's gifts. Nor does it get much of a
hearing from wavering Tory voters and the
right-wing press.

"We live in a more tribal age.

"It's also a more impatient one, jittered by
social media when the political mood quickly
changes. The Tories could be in the early
stages of a terminal crisis. But if you're
hoping that they really are doomed this time,
it's going to be an anxious wait."

"Wow, Clare" said Rachel, "That's not bad, I can tell you have written PR for corporates! - I might need to ease the tone a little for a leader article, but it is quite do-able."

"And the consequences?" asked Clare.

"Quite acceptable, we have for a long time tried to course-correct the government, so this won't seem out of place."

Floundering

Things were chaotic in Michael Tovey's office at Parliament. Here was a man tipped for the very top, but now floundering around about what to say and whether to warn the Prime Minister of what he had just heard from Matt Stevens.

"Matt, you are absolutely sure about this?" he asked again, "I mean, so far I have remained loyal to the Prime Minister during the scandals. I even called him an 'exceptional leader' who is 'good at thinking things others aren't thinking' - but let's face it, he is no Churchill.

"Churchill always had new ideas. The PM may eschew conventional thought, but his increasing desperation is driven by his own self-interest, and forgetfully he will change positions between interviews to suit the cameras."

He added: "I'm just saying that the politicians who succeed are the ones with a willingness to make decisions and to then persuade people. I think it might be time for us to up the ante."

"What are you suggesting?" asked Matt, somewhat confused.

"I'm just considering letting the PM announce the cars and chargers plan for London. It could be my chance for a crack at the main job."

Matt asked, "But won't the London initiative blow up in his face? Apart from the lower car targets for London, there's the whole Levelling Up of the north. It would look doubly stupid to announce a major investment plan for London when the north is crying out for infrastructure. And it could easily annoy the London Mayor too!"

"Yes, but that is the beauty of our Prime Minister. His crowded brain is overflowing with scandals, and the web of lies that he spins. He is also without any bright tacticians in his office now, just 'yes men and women' prepared to take the money whilst secretly loathing the way he is running things."

"Matt, can you run that advancement of the London Infrastructure up into a speech, which the PM could give in the House. Notice how I am trusting you with something big here."

Matt nodded, pleased at the privileged position that he had attained, but worried that this was not the plan he had envisaged after the coffee with Lottie.

Safe to cross streets

An hour after Matt's exchange with Michael Tovey, an incoming phone call to Tovey's office was answered by Matt.

"Hello, this is Miller McDonald, from Brant. I need to speak urgently to Michael Tovey. He will know the topic."

Matt relayed the information and ten minutes later Tovey was on his way to a meeting with McDonald. Matt noticed that Tovey didn't use a pool car, but instead ordered a regular London Taxi.

Tovey arrived at the nearby St Ermin's hotel in St James a few minutes later and was shown to a room, set up for a conference. There were several people in the room. He recognised Miller McDonald, and thought he recognised another woman, but had no idea about the others, all in suits but looking just a little like they were back from a battle-zone. Before he had a chance to run introductions, another door opened and in walked Duncan Melship, also unaccompanied.

"Oh, hello Duncan, I hadn't expected you to be here."

"Gentlemen, gentlemen, and ladies, of course," said Miller McDonald. He looked across to Melship and Tovey, "It is a great honour to have two of UK's Members of Parliament present, and even more so that they followed instructions to come alone.

"Let me introduce the rest of us here today, "Miller McDonald and Mary Ranzino from Brant and Qiu Zhang and Kirillka Valeryevich representing Zillian."

"Let me come straight to the point," said Miller.

He continued, "We have been preparing this New York Stock Exchange launch of Zillian for some time now, and it is ready for next week. We have also been preparing a few press releases to assist its price go up upon launch. Both of our dear colleagues, the two MPs, have an important part to play for that reason.

"Firstly, Douglas Melship, Secretary of State for Department for Transport Efficiency- DfTE must meet his obligation to place a significant order for the UK, with Zillian. Some 10,000 government service vehicles will be provided on a rental agreement from Zillian.

"Then, Michael Tovey, will provide the Prime Minister with the House of Commons announcement to provide framework legislation to support vital changes to the UK's infrastructure, starting with London.

"But that could ruin the Prime Minister," said Tovey, "London is trying to drastically reduce the number of cars."

McDonald continued, "It doesn't matter. The Prime Minister is well-known as a serial liar. If he says one thing today and does something completely different tomorrow no-one - and I mean no-one - will be surprised."

"But he could lose his job over this. Too much accumulated reputational damage?" said Melship.

McDonald again, "But think of the upside. You both get rich on next week's share price lift and then you also get a crack at the top jobs in Parliament following a leadership contest."

Melship asked, "But what about the company? Zillian. It can't actually manufacture the vehicles, can it?"

McDonald answered, "No, but how long will it take before that is discovered? Plenty of time to divest and cash in big time. And China gets a ready-made laundry mechanism for cleaning cashflow. Converting cloned inexpensive vehicles into cleaned money."

"Not to mention the vast requirement for

component parts," added the Mary Ranzino, "They can be cleared through the same laundering process."

"You learn well," said Valeryevich, "It is an approach we have used in Mother Russia since after the fall of the USSR."

"This has become bigger than I expected," said Melship.

"Well, you can soon enjoy your good fortune. And you need to know you are safe crossing those busy London streets," said Valeryevich.

The threat was not wasted on Tovey nor Melship.

Badge engineering

Christina was in The Triangle offices with Jake, Clare and Bigsy.

"There's still something about all of this situation that doesn't quite ring true," she said.

"How so?" asked Bigsy, "I mean, we've found the two shaky MPs about to pull a stunt to raise Zillian's share price and walk away with a tidy profit."

"I know," said Christina, "That's the obvious situation. I think there must be something more."

"Okay," said Clare, "Let's think about it...A car company launched on the American stock market, but only making its cars in China. Owned mainly by Chinese."

"But with indirect links to Russia," added Christina, "But not to the Kremlin, instead to a bratva gang."

"And making its cars look as if they are British,

European and American," added Jake, "Like, say Ford or BMW,"

"It means they will have a lot of cars in transit," said Bigsy, "You know, ships filled with them,"

"So, they will bring these cars halfway round the world to sell into local European markets?" asked Clare.

Jake said, "Before they invest in local factories, like Nissan still do, from Sunderland and Honda did, from Swindon - until mid 2021. I expect they will wait until there's some form of deal available."

Clare added, "Yes, but Honda closed the factory and turned it over to a logistics developer. The developer makes tin-shed depots and then leases them out to mega-online retailers. Companies like Amazon."

Jake said, "Yes, and Honda will make its new cars in Japan, to ship to Europe. It was fall-out from Brexit. The EU cut a new deal with Japan."

Clare agreed, looking at her laptop, "It is interesting to notice that Zillian wants to copy some of this process. They already make cars in Guangzhou, China, for example. Honda Accord, Honda City, Honda Crider, Honda Crosstour, Honda Fit, Honda Odyssey and Honda Vezel,"

Bigsy said, "I've never heard of some of those makes. Are you sure they are not motorcycles?"

Clare answered, "No, I'm certain they are all types of cars. Look - here's some pictures from the Honda website."

"So have we got any closer to working this out?" asked Christina, "There has to be an angle on it."

Jake ventured, "Something to do with the importation of cars? Re-branding them to look British? Remember when General Motors used to call their cars Vauxhall in the UK and Opel in Europe? It implied they were made in Germany."

Bigsy added, "And come to think of it, they were Holden in Australia and Buick, Saturn, and Cadillac in the USA. Badge engineering, they call it."

Clare added, "And since 2021 they are owned by that well-known brand Stellantis!"

"Stellantis?" queried Bigsy, "Never heard of them!"

Clare added, still looking at her laptop, "Stellantis is the sixth-largest automaker worldwide, they design, develop, manufacture and sell automobiles bearing the brands of Abarth, Alfa Romeo, Chrysler, Citroën, Dodge, DS, Fiat, Jeep, Lancia, Maserati, Opel, Peugeot, Ram and Vauxhall, and Mopar auto parts!"

"Okay, so now we are on to something," said Christina, "Zillian joins the ranks of shadowy companies owning big brands and shipping their products quietly around the world."

"I can think of some other organisations that would like to be able to stealthily move product around," said Clare.

"Exactly," said Christina.

"And I think I need someone else to help us now," said Clare, "It's another flatmate, or at least it would have been if I still lived in Bermondsey!"

Advice

Clare called in on her old flat. Tessa was beside herself with excitement and had clearly been told of recent adventures by Lottie. Clare wondered how much Katharina Maier - Cat- would know about what was happening.

"Hey everyone, I think I'm going to need some help!" said Clare, opening a cool bag containing three bottles of chilled wine.

"That wine should help us all think," said Lottie.

"I want to know about an IPO, " explained Clare, "The one for the car company, Zillian."

Cat smiled; Clare realised that she must know most of what had happened.

"Oh no, I swear I haven't told anyone else," said Cat, "But it is a great story."

"I had a look at Zillian's offering as well. It reads as

if the figures have been highly manipulated, like they are really trying to make this seem good. Almost too good."

Clare asked, "So, will traders buy it?"

"I'd say it is a slender share. It is one of those which looks too good to be true, which could put a lot of people off. I can see you might get some high-volume trades at the start of the day, but they will all have disinvested by the end of the day."

"But what about if the company received some good news?" asked Clare.

Cat answered, "Ew, that could be illegal. It could smack of insider trading. The company would have the SEC down on them."

Cat continued, "It's being launched next week, isn't it? On the New York Stock Exchange? I guess they are hoping it will be a rocket ship like some of the other car companies."

"Can you take the day off? I mean when it launches, to be in our office and to give us some guidance?" asked Clare.

"What? A chance to be in on one of Lottie's friend's schemes? How could I turn it down?"

"Great! That's settled then, we'll order you a car to come around our office on Monday, well ahead of the US launch. Now, about this wine!"

Process, not Event

It was Monday, the day of the Zillian IPO. Cat, along with Lottie and Tessa had just arrived at the Triangle Offices.

Clare, Jake, Bigsy and Christina were already in a meeting room.

Jake spoke, "Welcome, Cat, I think you know some of us, but we'll all introduce ourselves. Then for our education and sanity it would be good if you could explain the process to us."

Formalities over, Cat began, "Having an IPO is not so much an event as it is a process. It takes months of planning to prepare a company to go public. A board of directors must be assembled, accounts audited for accuracy, consultants and advisers hired. In fact, a whole cast of characters must take the stage to help an IPO happen."

Cat continued, "The most important character is probably the underwriter, an investment banker who works for an investment company. Our company - the one for which I work - will sometimes be involved in getting underwriters allocated."

"But you use other people to provide the actual money and investment?" checked Bigsy.

"Yes, that's right. Underwriters have the distribution channels and business community contacts that can get a company's shares out to the right investors.

"They will also help set the initial offering price for the stocks, work to create enthusiasm for the stock, and assist in creating the prospectus. The prospectus is an important document that describes the company in detail to potential investors. Once the prospectus has been drafted, it is reviewed by the SEC."

"That's a big deal, to ensure that the IPO is legitimate?" asked Jake.

Cat answered, " Kind of. SEC approval only means that the prospectus follows the regulations for such documents -- it says nothing about the quality or future profitability of the company. When I looked at Zillian, it had the aura of something just 'too good to be true'!"

"As we also thought!" said Jake.

Cat continued, "Following SEC approval, company executives go onto a road show, otherwise known as the dog-and-pony show. This is a tour of major cities and cities where important brokerage houses have their headquarters."

"I think we had our share of those events in Switzerland!" said Lottie.

Cat continued, "At these invitation-only slide shows, potential investors are given "goodie bags" containing trinkets elaborating the company's product, and whatever else might help investors think favourably about the company."

"So that's where all the toy cars came from!" said Tessa, laughing.

"We were having a competition to see who could get the most, but then we realised they were quite heavy in our luggage," explained Lottie.

Cat continued with the briefing, "The road-show crew also includes a tame Wall Street analyst who will give positive opinions about the company's future profitability. However, no one involved with the company is allowed to talk publicly about anything that isn't in the prospectus in the period leading up to the IPO."

"I think Google got caught out with something like that," muttered Jake, "Something about a Playboy article..." His words trailed away, "I can't believe I just said that out loud,"

Cat smiled, "You are right about that article, by the way. Then, the day before the stocks are issued, the underwriter and the company must determine a starting price for the stocks. It is what they have done with Zillian."

"But it isn't the same as the target price?" asked Jake.

Cat nodded, "Quite right, a target price will have been set early in the process, but IPOs are rarely stable. Obviously, the higher the price, the more money the company gets; but if the price is set too high, there won't be enough demand for the stocks, and the price will drop on the aftermarket."

Then she added, "The ideal stock price will keep demand just higher than supply, resulting in a stable, gradual increase in the stock's price on the aftermarket. This will lead to praise from market analysts, which will in turn lead to increased value down the road."

"Peachy," said Jake, "But can anyone buy shares in an IPO?"

Cat answered, "Not really. Who gets to buy the shares during an IPO is a complicated matter. In most cases, your typical, individual investor doesn't get access to these offerings. Instead, the underwriter gets to allocate the shares to associates, clients, and major investors of his choosing. In effect it is a closed shop."

"So, what type of people get the shares?" asked Clare.

Cat answered, "Most of the shares - up to 80 percent -will go to institutional investors, typically it is major brokerage firms and investment banks, and a few high-profile individual investors. And, by the way, in this case it looks as if Brant are one of them.

Cat explained, "After the initial offering, the stocks hit the open stock market, where they begin trading at a price set by market forces. IPO stocks tend to trade at a very high volume on that first day -- that is, they change hands many times. Some IPOs can jump in price by a huge amount -- some more than 600 percent. However, many IPOs do poorly, dropping in price the day of the offering. Others fluctuate, rising and then dipping again -- it all depends on the confidence the market has in the company, how strong the company is vs. the hype surrounding it, and what outside forces are affecting the market at the time."

Shea added, "I'd be very surprised if Zillian went up because of the window dressing around their numbers which will put many people off."

"So, this doesn't look very promising for our two MPs?" asked Clare.

"Not on Day 1," answered Cat, "But after about a month, the underwriter issues a report on the IPO, which is always positive. This tends to give the stock a slight boost. After 180 days have passed, people who held shares in the company prior to its going public are allowed to sell their shares."

"But why would I want to sell shares, if they haven't done very well?" asked Jake.

"Well, if I was given the initial money to buy the shares, that could be one reason," answered Cat, "Although I might be better off hanging in there if I knew that an uplift was likely,"

"Precisely, " said Christina, "Firstly, If the MPs and other inner core of shareholders know that some good news is coming. Secondly, if the investment has been hidden in a tax haven."

"What? So, no-one knows about the investments?" asked Bigsy.

"Exactly!" said Cat.

"Then it is truly a magic money tree!" said Jake.

Bigsy had rigged up a stock ticker for the share in the office. It blinked on the launch price. "ZILL $17.00"

"Is that a good launch price?" asked Clare.

"It is almost impossible for me to say," answered Cat, "There are a few other car companies to compare with, but they are each their own self-contained valuation. It'd be like trying to compare two bank share prices. For example, Lloyds Bank shares at 52p and HSBC Bank valued at £5.59, some ten times larger. By itself the figure means very little."

"I can see that with Tesla," said Clare, "It ran at $50 for years - but then spiked up to nearly $1000."

"Exactly," said Cat, "And that must be what the Zillian inner-core shareholders are hoping too. Presumably on the back of good news announced by those two MPs!"

They all looked at the ticker, trading had started, but the ZILL price was now $16.52.

"It doesn't look like a mover and shaker, " announced Jake, "And after all of this effort!"

They watched and the price moved to ZILL $17.22.

"Hmm, that's a 1% increase!" said Bigsy.

The price fell back to $17.14.

"It looks as if the initial take-up of the offered shares was what set the original price. The later trading isn't making much of an impression," said Cat.

"We'll need to see what tomorrow and the next 4 weeks bring," said Cat, "Of course those MPs can cash out after a month and still get their tax-free $1 million each."

Unbelievable

You burden me with your questions
You'd have me tell no lies
You're always asking what it's all about
But don't listen to my replies
You say to me I don't talk enough
But when I do, I'm a fool
These times I've spent, I've realised
I'm going to shoot through and leave you

The things you say
Your purple prose just gives you away
The things you say
You're unbelievable

You burden me with your problems
By telling me more than mine
I'm always so concerned
With the way you say you always have to stop
To think of us being one
Is more than I ever know
But this time, I realize
I'm going to shoot through and leave you
The things you say
Your purple prose just gives you away

You burden me with your questions
You'd have me tell no lies
You're always asking what it's all about
But don't listen to my replies
You say to me I don't talk enough
But when I do, I'm a fool

Dench / Atkin / Brownson / Decloedt / Foley

You're Undetectable

The next morning, Bigsy was reading a news feed:

FINANCE WORLD NEWS

In February, Red Fox Capital — a special-purpose acquisition company (SPAC) — announced a deal to take automobile manufacturers Zillian public, valuing the company at $8 billion. The company is going public "to accelerate into the next phase of our growth," Zillian CEO Miller McDonald said.

A SPAC, also known as a blank-cheque company, is an alternative to a traditional initial public offering. These blank-cheque companies have no assets beyond cash. They trade on stock exchanges and then merge with private companies, taking those companies public.

Zillian began trading under the ticker symbol ZILL on the Nasdaq.

Zillian started delivering its Zillian 502 — a high-performance, ultra-efficient luxury EV sedan four months ago, according to the company. The company expects to roll out its Zillion 602 performance luxury SUV within the next year. The Zillion 302 started in production a month ago.

In a slide deck filed with the U.S. Securities and Exchange Commission Zillian Motors touted more than 10,000 reservations for the Zillian 302, representing $700 million in anticipated sales. It claimed the 302 beats the Tesla Model S and Amazon-backed EV startup Rivian's R1T in battery efficiency, which it calls the ultimate measure of EV technology. It also claims the Zillian 302 beats luxury EVs from Jaguar, Porsche, and Audi on that metric.

Zillian touts EV technology it developed in-house. It describes the Zillian 302 as the 'quickest, longest-range, fastest-charging electric car in the world,' delivering 500 miles of range.

The Environmental Protection Agency hasn't certified that range yet. The 302 also boasts high-end features such as a 'glass cockpit.' The Zillian 302 features an autonomous driving system using 32 sensors, including long-distance Lidar, a safety technology that Tesla long avoided.

The first fully loaded 302 will cost around $160,000, including federal subsidies. Cheaper versions will be released, with a $70,000 version expected within a year.

ZILL Stock Technical Analysis

According to the IBD Stock Checkup, ZILL shows a weak 30 out of a perfect 99 IBD Composite Rating. The Composite Rating helps investors easily measure a stock's fundamental and technical metrics. Weak IBD Composite Ratings are normal for new issues.

The SEC could be alerted to the unusually intense buying and selling of Zillian shares following the IPO. Conventionally, the short-term profit taking is frowned upon for a new company launch.

Zillian Motors Stock News

Before the IPO, Zillian Motors shareholders voted to approve the merger of the blank check company.

The company said it had finished its preproduction phase after a series of delays. "The testing and validation of Zillian 302 is progressing well," CEO Miller McDonald said on the call. "It's on track for the start of production for customer deliveries."

"This all looks pretty direct for investors," said Bigsy, "one car produced in limited numbers and another couple on the way. The share price was hijacked by shot term traders in for a quick buck and now the share price is floundering round its original launch level."

"I agree," said Jake, "Except that people who invested dirty money can still pull out clean money, and in the case of those MPs there isn't even taxation to worry about."

"Yes," said Clare, "It's tantamount to a massive dirty bribe to both Melship and Tovey, in return for which they will boost the value of the Zillian shares."

"Mega-sleaze, " said Bigsy.

"And almost undetectable," added Jake.

Infrastructure Improvement Committee Session

Matt Stevens and Lottie Trevethick had been asked to support Michael Tovey and Duncan Melship at an upcoming Infrastructure Improvement Committee Session.

"Hmm, this is awkward," said Matt, as his arm grazed Lottie's shoulder on the way into the session."

"Only as difficult as you want to make it," returned Lottie.

Humphrey Morris (Conservative, Brampton and Blissett) brought the committee to order. There were eleven MPs present, and Lottie only recognised a couple beyond Melship and Tovey. She realised that as an Assistant, she was invisible to most of the MPs, except the patently lecherous one who was eyeing her rather too intently.

Matt whispered, "I think you have a follower," into

Lottie's ear, which helped her decide she would sit elsewhere in the room.

The Committee rumbled into a discussion of Levelling Up, a topic only known to Sonic the Hedgehog gamers until it became political capital. The phrase "levelling up" had steadily proliferated across Whitehall, and the committee was expecting a landmark "levelling up white paper."

Ahead of that publication, MPs published a report concluding that the concept 'has yet to be defined', adding to widespread narrative that 'levelling up' is an empty political slogan.

"Oh dear," thought Lottie, "this committee will need light speed shoes, crystal rings and a bounce bracelet to get out of this conundrum."

Then, one of the MPs Robert Bighampton (Conservative, East Pagentree), presented a levelling up example based upon the Humber Bridge, which connects Hull with the East Midlands. It commenced construction in 1966 and opened to traffic in 1981.

It cost £385 million to build at 2021 prices. It was financed by Government loans, which accrued interest. Those loans have yet to be fully repaid despite a toll being levied on bridge users. In 2012, former Chancellor of the Exchequer George Osborne reduced toll charges on the bridge from £3 to £1.50 each way for cars and removed motorcycle tolls. The lower tolls were introduced following the

Government's writing down almost 50% of the outstanding £330 million.

"This is before levelling up was a thing," thought Lottie, "Surely they can't be trying to claim it?"

The presenter droned on, "According to the Infrastructure and Projects Authority's (IPA's) Annual Report on Major Projects 2020–21, major projects on the Government Major Projects Portfolio are 'typically those where approval is required from The Treasury, either because the budget exceeds a department's delegated authority level and/or because the project is novel, complex, contentious, or requires primary legislation'.

"Although the bridge reduced journey times for the local population and connected families and businesses, it did not produce tangible economic returns."

"Yes, and today, Hull has one of the highest unemployment rates in the country," thought Lottie.

The presenter added, "The Department awaits the Government's forthcoming Levelling Up White Paper' which must clarify how major transport infrastructure projects can contribute to levelling up."

'We are all stuck in the glue of an enormous machine, ' thought Lottie, 'Where every report and its conclusions is dependent upon something else. Only a few projects escape to conclusion, and if they are like Humber Bridge, then the results are not altogether conclusive. It becomes a great place to hide anything.'

The presenter continued, "The Department plans to develop proposals for the 'robust assessment and presentation of distributional and place- based impacts to support decision makers in better understanding impacts on priorities such as levelling up'.

'Jargon-central,' thought Lottie, tapping notes on her iPad.

"It is also reviewing its "rebalancing toolkit" and wider strategic case guidance to correspond with the latest updates to the Green Book. If those reviews are to be meaningful, the Department will need to define the "levelling up" policy agenda in a transport context to set a benchmark against which to test business cases.

Lottie thought again, 'A rebalancing toolkit! It sounds as if something is being developed, but it could just as easily be a playpen activity designed to obfuscate.'

Then the Presenter added, "To allow Parliament and the public to judge the effectiveness of the Government's infrastructure plans, the Government must publish detailed metrics that define and measure the 'levelling up' concept.

"We are concerned that the Department did not

explain how the construction of major transport infrastructure projects can support the 'levelling up' policy agenda. We would be reassured if the Department were to set out a worked example illustrating how investment in major transport infrastructure projects drives growth and productivity."

'Oh yes,' thought Lottie, 'After we've just seen an example of a project which built a bridge, didn't recover its costs and still the area of the UK is one of the poorest. It makes a great case for levelling up.'

The committee moved on, under the guidance of Humphrey Morris, who thanked Robert Bighampton and moved on to discuss costs and timescales. Sarah Blackburn (Labour, Kingston Turnberry) stood to present the HS2 costings.

"It's a simple case study," she began: "The first estimates for the cost of HS2 were published in the February 2011 HS2 economic case. Phase One costs were estimated to be £19.6 billion, with the full network estimated at £37.5 billion. Phase One from London to Birmingham is now estimated to cost between £31 billion and £40 billion, an increase of between 14% and 47% from the £27.1 billion funding allocated in 2013."

'A mighty increase,' thought Lottie, 'but it is difficult to pick through strings of recited numbers like this. A couple of charts would be better.'

Sarah Blackburn continued, "A target cost for Phase

One has been set at £36 billion, or £40 billion in 2019 prices. Originally due to open in 2026, the full opening of the Phase One into Euston station is now expected between 2031 and 2036, although services from Old Oak Common are due to commence between 2029 and 2033."

'They've published two completion dates; it'll be the last one with more added slippage,' thought Lottie, 'Instead of 2026, its seven years later at double the cost.'

Sarah Blackburn continued, "The estimated cost of Phase 2a has also increased from £3.5 billion in 2013 at 2015 prices, to between £4.5 billion and £6.5 billion, an increase of between 29% and 87%."

'It will be over 100% cost increase and take years longer. Burn rate is a consultancy's friend,' thought Lottie.

Sarah Blackburn added, "Phase 2a is now due to open between 2030 and 2031, three to four years later than expected. The cost of Phase 2b is now estimated to be between £29 billion and £41 billion, an increase of between 15% and 63% on the £25 billion previously allocated in 2013, and three to seven years behind schedule. The current estimate is for services to open between 2036 and 2040, compared with the original target date of 2033."

'Hilarious, if it wasn't so gross,' thought Lottie, 'Now they will be blaming the original estimates for being wrong. Estimates which they were put under political pressure to provide within certain parameters.'

Sarah Blackburn added, "Those statistics suggest that initial costs and timescales were not properly assessed. The various Ministers with responsibility for HS2 who signed off those estimates have not been held to account for their miscalculations at taxpayers' expense."

'Nor will they,' thought Lottie.

Humphrey Morris stood, thanked Sarah Blackburn, and called Duncan Melship.

'Light blue touchpaper, ' thought Lottie, 'now for fireworks.'

Fireworks

Duncan Melship began.

Lottie realised he was speaking from a well-worn talk track that he used when presenting to schools and general citizen briefings.

"The government sets the objectives and funding for Highways England through a periodic Road Investment Strategy (RIS), which covers a five-year Road Period.

"The first RIS was published in 2014 and applied to the first Road Period, 2015 to 2020. RIS2 was published in March 2020 and applied to the second Road Period, 2020 to 2025. We are now gathering evidence to inform RIS3, which will apply to the Road Period starting in 2025.

"During this first Road Period we:
- Started work on 67 major road schemes, opening 36, with 21 of these schemes opening ahead of schedule.

- Stayed within our funding agreement.
- Delivered £1.4 billion of efficiencies.
- Provided £2.50 of public benefit for every £1 we spent on our major schemes.
- Made the SRN safer and reduced casualties in line with our ambitious targets to cut the number of people killed or seriously injured on our network by 40%.
- Invested over £650 million in projects which have reduced noise, alleviated flooding, protected biodiversity, reduced air pollution, and provided alternative routes for walkers and cyclists. This includes 113 safety schemes, 160 cycling schemes, 124 biodiversity schemes and 1174 noise mitigation schemes: and
- Improved how we work with our supply chain, creating new commercial models, driving efficiency savings, investment, and innovations. In April 2020, we entered the second Road Period and we started to deliver RIS2. We are investing £27.4 billion into England's Strategic Road Network over the next five years."

Lottie thought, 'Melship is making his department seem on-the-ball after the prior two presentations.'

She waited for the Big Ask from Melship. First, he described the Strategic Road Network and its important social role, bringing people together and connecting communities and regions.

Then, "As a key infrastructure delivery partner of the government, our plans for this second Road Period (2020-2025) and beyond will see us play an important role in realising the priority outcomes set out in the NIS. Our operation, maintenance, and improvement of the SRN over the next five years and beyond will support:

- Rebuilding the economy.
- Setting a new carbon-light agenda for roads in the Capital.
- Procurement of exclusively carbon-light government vehicles, from preferred and reliable suppliers.
- Supporting the government's 'levelling-up' agenda by connecting all parts of the country, the Union, and provision of better access to international gateways in support of trade.
- Decarbonisation and adapting to climate change.
- Delivering better infrastructure more efficiently; and
- Protecting and enhancing the environment.

"In its second Road Investment Strategy (RIS2) published in March 2020, the government set out its vision for a safer, more reliable, and greener SRN that uses new technology, supports the country's economy, and is an integrated part of the national transport network. Our Departmental aims are in support of this vision."

Melship looked across to Humphrey Morris, who stood thanked Duncan Melship and moved toward the next Agenda item. "But before we do that, I think we all deserve a break!"

'There,' thought Lottie, 'He has said it. Buried in a Committee speech. Two bullets built into the next Strategic Road Network Plan, which give Zillian their keys to the British economy, and give Melship and Tovey around £1 million each.'

China

China all the way to New York
I can feel the distance getting close
You're right next to me
But I need an airplane
I can feel the distance as you breathe
Sometimes I think you want me to touch you
How can I when you build a great wall around you
In your eyes I saw a future together
You just look away in the distance
China decorates our table
Funny how the cracks don't seem to show
Pour the wine dear
You say we'll take a holiday
But we never can agree on where to go
Sometimes I think you want me to touch you
How can I when you build a great wall around you
In your eyes I saw a future together
You just look away in the distance
China all the way to New York
Maybe you got lost in Mexico
You're right next to me
I think that you can hear me
Funny how the distance learns to grow
Sometimes I think you want me to touch you
How can I when you build a great wall around you
I can feel the distance
I can feel the distance
I can feel the distance getting close

Tori Ellen Amos

700 per cent

The session continued in the Committee Room for another three hours. It was almost 5 pm when they broke and Lottie was back online.

She and Matt were both immediately greeted with a torrent of messages. She wondered what could be so important, but as soon as she opened the first message she realised.

Zillian had run a press announcement the same afternoon as Melship's speech. Whilst he and Tovey were locked away in committee, Zillian had announced their deal with the UK Government. The UK was to procure up to 10,000 vehicles from Zillian and additionally was declaring that most of Greater London would become a petrol and diesel-free zone.

Both Melship and Tovey had finely crafted press statements extolling the virtues of these decisions and the Prime Minister appeared to be in on the process too, virtue signalling that the UK would be the first major nations to deliver an ecologically positive set of reforms.

Lottie checked one of the monitors inside the Commons. A TV show from London Today was running and showed a hubbub around Parliament's gates and another one outside Downing Street. This was the story of the day. The opposition were finding it difficult to be critical because it is something that they had theoretically promoting for the last few years.

At this rate, Melship and Tovey could come through this looking like political heroes, and the Prime Minister would be tugging at their coattails to get profile-enhancing draught.

Lottie wondered about the ZILL share price. It had been around $17.50 the last time she had looked. She gasped when she clicked it on her phone. $122.53. A rise of some 700%. Zillian shares had rocketed on the combined news. And it would also mean that Melship and Tovey had earned a cool and undetectable £6million extra during that Committee session. Something like £1 million per hour, and no tax to worry about.

Lottie called Clare.

"Have you seen it?" she asked, "Oh yes," said Clare, "We are all looking at it now. Zillian has turned from a cheeky ape into an 800-lb gorilla."

Clare continued, "Bigsy asked us: 'Where does an 800-pound gorilla sit?' and you know the answer:

'Anywhere it wants to.' "

"I was called by Amanda Miller as well," said Clare, "She wants to put a stop to this. I've never heard her sound angry, but she did this time."

"Shall we pay her a visit?" asked Lottie, "I was in Melship and Tovey's committee meeting."

"Good idea," said Clare.

Generous donors

Amanda Miller usually worked from the Thames location of the SIS-(MI6) building based at 85 Albert Embankment, Vauxhall Cross.

For this meeting, she opted to cross the river to the MI5 building at Thames House, situated on Millbank and only a short walk from the Houses of Parliament.

"I wonder why we are meeting here?" asked Clare.

Bigsy shrugged his shoulders.

Jake answered, "Well, she has plenty of sites to choose from, I suppose."

Clare, Bigsy, Jake and Christina also knew about the other Secret Service buildings spread around London. One in the Square Mile of the City, a network control centre on the 17th floor of Euston Tower and a spy training school in South London. A few buildings had been closed too, notably

Kennington Lane, with its bubble doors like the ones in the TV-show Spooks and the old GCHQ building in Palmer Street.

Bigsy explained, "It's always good to look for a BT Openreach Monitoring Station, if you want to know where the secret services are operating. There's one by Parliament, another by the Stock Exchange, one in the City close to the Bank of England and then there's that whole warren around Holborn in the West End."

"I thought the big tunnels under Holborn and Kingsway were used for something else?" queried Clare.

"Monitoring of individuals," answered Bigsy, "Both landline and cellular,"

"Are we really living in a police state?" asked Jake.

"Well monitored, but you've seen how the Met has been perceived," answered Bigsy, "but I doubt we will ever find out what really happened."

Christina smiled, "It not just the UK that monitors in London. The US, the Kremlin and the Chinese have listening posts too.

"I sometimes wonder with all those phones and ancillary communications manufactured in China," said Bigsy, "How difficult would it be to add a few backdoors?"

Amanda appeared, with Grace.

"Oh ladies, this is indeed an honour to have you both here, in person, I have such memories of this place!" said Jake.

Amanda smiled, "Jake, Ah yes, when we had to lock you up in this building a few years ago!"

"But you let him out, when we returned from Arizona!" smiled Clare.

"Okay," said Amanda, "I used this building for a good reason. It is far easier to bring Members of Parliament here, than it is to take them across the River. It could be a simple security matter here; over the water it implies dealing with foreign agents."

"So, who have you got locked up this time?" asked Jake.

"It has to be Melship or Tovey," said Christina, "I'd go for just one of them, probably Tovey to exert the most pain," said Christina.

"Christina, you are right. Although we have Duncan Melship held in the Annex, with Lottie Trevethick."

"What is the angle?" asked Jake.

"We need to put a stop to the Zillian plan. Melship is going to help us," answered Amanda.

Grace flicked on a presentation.

"Here we are: Melship with Miller McDonald, Mary Ranzino, Qiu Zhang and Volvakov Kirill Valeryevich. And in the background is the Zillian logo."

Jake spoked, "Yes, but that's circumstantial? Can't prove anything from the group of them standing by a car stand at an exhibition."

"I agree," said Grace, "but we are building a picture."

She moved to the next slide. It showed a transaction. Banca Cariba, in the name of Duncan Melship. A deposit of £1 million.

"Where on earth did you get that?" asked Jake.

"We were very lucky," answered Grace, "Let's say a recent friend of Matt Stevens helped us."

"Charlotte Mendez?" said Christina, "I thought there was something unusual about her sudden relationship with Matt."

"Correct," said Grace, "Our associate Charlotte had to persuade Matt that it was simplest for Tovey to bank with Banca Cariba. He did and then persuaded Melship to do the same."

"It was so simple for them to open their Banca Cariba accounts with no tax returns in an offshore tax haven."

"So, you have got a similar sword hanging over Tovey?" asked Christina.

"Yes, but we don't want to reveal that part yet, especially because it will illustrate Matt Stevens' gullibility. This way it looks like an unfortunate circumstance."

"Em, this is delicate, but it looks as if the Prime Minister may also be involved in some of this," said Clare, "He and his immediately surrounding Cabinet of Ministers seem to have turned a blind eye to way that the original deal for Zillian was passed by the Commons, without any difficult questions."

"The PM is a friend of Miller McDonald. He has provided the Tory Party with some immense donations in the past," answered Grace. "According to press sources just 10 wealthy people account for a quarter of all donations made by individuals to the Conservative Party."

"But how much?" asked Jake.

Grace continued, "The 10 super-rich donors – nine of whom are men – have given a combined sum of just over £10m to the Tories equalling more than 25 per cent of the £38.6m received from all individuals in the past two years."

Jake added, "I know it is a lot of money, but somehow, in the scheme of this Zillian scam, it doesn't seem so much to pay to be in control of the direction of the United Kingdom."

Grace added, "Yes. Fears have been expressed about the power held by the very wealthiest Tory donors after it emerged that a group known as the Advisory Board had been developed to connect the party's biggest financial backers with ministers."

Grace continued, "One of the 10 most generous donors is Miller McDonald, CEO of Brant Industries, who has given almost £1,000,000 to the Tory party in the last two years. MacDonald's ties with the Tories came under scrutiny earlier this year when it emerged his company was a co-investor in a failed bid to buy a Premier league football team."

"That could be an interesting additional source of money laundering," mused Clare.

Grace added, "Other wealthy Tory donors on the top 10 list include an online trading tycoon who has given the party just over £870,000 in the past two years. He was handed a peerage last year – sparking accusations of cronyism from Labour. It is rumoured that Miller McDonald is also in line for a peerage."

"But I thought Miller McDonald was American?" asked Bigsy, "I mean he sounds American when he speaks?"

Grace answered, "No. Miller McDonald is actually British - Scottish to be precise. He hails from Braemar, which is quite close to the Royal residence at Balmoral. It means he is free to donate to the party and can bag a peerage when the party shows sufficient gratitude."

"I guess that is after several years of consistent donations?" said Jake, "I remember Street - that's my old magazine - did an article once about Quintessentially, a luxury concierge service, which offered (among other things) to connect Tory donors to senior figures - like the Prime Minister and the Chancellor. I suspect the so-called Advisory Board was copied from that idea."

"Well, we should bring Duncan Melship into play now," said Amanda, "Although I'm going to run that session from another interview room. You'll all be outside, but still able to see what happens. And Grace, you'd better come with me."

Grace flicked a few buttons and a different scene appeared from the projector. It was of a small interview room, like the ones used in TV police interviews, but with slightly more opulent furniture.

"They won't be able to hear you," said Grace, "although you'll be able to hear everything."

Free-for-all?

Bigsy, Clare, Jake and Christina watched, as Douglas Melship and Lottie appeared in the new interview room. Then Amanda and Grace walked in, along with a third, suited and rather serious looking man."

"It's Jim Cavendish," said Clare, "Amanda is bringing in the big guns for this meeting."

Cavendish was Amanda's boss and they had known one another for many years.

"Another reason to pick this side of the River," said Jake, "Jim can do a drop in for the interview."

Jim opened the session.

"Douglas! It must be three years since we last met, how time flies!"

"Hello James, yes it has been a while, and look at you now, a centre Chief here at MI5!"

"That's right, I get involved when there seems to be a major situation developing."

"Not one with me, I hope?" said Melship.

"Well, yes, actually. You seem have stumbled into something quite big. It could even be considered as a plot to overthrow the government."

"It must be some kind of mix-up," answered Melship, "I've done nothing out of the ordinary, my life continues on its usual routine way."

"Not quite, said Jim, "We can see you are mixed up with this company called Zillian. You even recommended them in the House to be a UK supplier of vehicles."

"Well, it was after the usual due-diligence, James,"

"Was it Duncan? I mean, you seem to like the company so much you had shares in it?"

"No, I don't think so," said Melship.

"Curious then, that we found your offshore account where you'd purchased almost £1 million of Zillian shares,"

"No, it must be some mistake, to be handling such a large quantity and just before that announcement from the UK Government that it would be investing in Zillian? You spoke to the House and even had the

Prime Minister later signing the deal's praises."

"I don't recollect any stake holding in the company and I'm sure I will have followed all government guidelines on any investments."

"Well, that is a relief, someone else must have planted that money offshore and used your name to attempt to hide it, otherwise it would be ruinous to you, both financially and reputationally."

"Something else has come to light too, about Zillian."

Those watching could all see that Melship wasn't the best at hiding his concerns.

"He is wriggling, " said Christina, "Can't take the pressure of being found out. Classic lack of interrogation experience."

Jake and Bigsy laughed, Christian was viewing this with her professional eye.

"Grace, I think you'd better show Duncan here what else we have discovered,"

Grace pulled up a couple of line drawings of cars.

"It's the Zillian 302, and next to it is the Lotya M300, which is built as an electric taxicab in Hangzhou, China. The two cars are identical, right down to the Wanzijiang Group manufactured battery cells. Same length, width, height, wheelbase, weight and stated performance."

Melship was looking at the car as if it was the first time he had seen one.

Grace continued, "Look I found a couple of photos too, they are almost indistinguishable from one another."

Then she flipped to another picture. It showed a road accident.

"This is one of the Lotya M300s on fire. The battery pack overheated. Fortunately, the driver and passenger were able to get out and walk to safety."

Amanda spoke now, "Due to the incident, the Hangzhou city authorities decided to halt all electric taxis on safety concerns. Fifteen of them were Lotya M300 EVs out of a fleet of 30 electric taxis."

Melship looked surprised to hear this, but he had also looked surprised to see one of the Zillian 302s in the earlier picture.

Grace started again, "The city's official investigation team found the cause of the fire was the car's defective battery pack due to lack of quality control during manufacturing. According to the investigation report, the battery pack problems include leaking of battery cells; damage of the insulation between battery cells and the walls of the aluminium container in which the cells were stacked; short circuits occurred within certain containers and those involving supporting and connecting parts."

She added, "One of the stronger short circuits ignited the car's back seats. The lead investigators said that '...in sealing and packing the battery cells, in loading and unloading the battery stacks, insufficient attention had been paid to several safety factors; monitoring procedures had been inefficient or neglected in the process of manufacturing, battery charging/switching, and vehicle driving, failing to detect anomalies.'

Amanda spoke, "The report added that the battery cells on the car were made by Wanzijiang Group."

Jim continued, "Okay Duncan, we can see that one occurrence would be an unlucky event; even Tesla had some early problems with their first Roadster in 2006. There were some thermal issues when accelerating fast and pushing the car to its limits. Clearly, a risk of fire or overheating is not something which Tesla was looking for when developing an electric car which would prove the technology to the world.

Grace picked up the description: "Consequently, Tesla developed the Battery Management System (BMS), a system which is still used as a similar design in the Model S, 3 and X today."

She added, "Whatever type of BMS Tesla uses, it needs to be powerful to cool all of the 7000 battery cells. Tesla patented a battery cooling system for the Model S which allowed each of the cells to make contact with a coolant pipe."

Then Jim Cavendish again, "Now the difference with EV car fires is the use of high voltage lithium-ion batteries which can short, break down and spontaneously combust, and also that lithium-ion fires both are difficult to extinguish and produce thick toxic smoke."

Grace continued, "The running temperature of an EV is perfect for short, peak performance like rapid accelerations and top speed runs. Subsequently, the battery pack must be both heated and cooled to create the perfect temperature range. This is done with the BMS (battery management system)."

Jake spoke from the monitor room, "Melship looks as if he needs a Battery Management System." Tell-tale beads of sweat had broken out across Melship's forehead.

Grace continued, "Furthermore, when the V3 superchargers were released, a new Model 3 setting was engaged which would allow batteries to be 'preconditioned' before receiving maximum charging speeds. This preconditioning will include heating or cooling to get the battery to about 30 degrees Celsius or a little more for superfast charging. It is a clever design and must add considerably to the manufacturing costs of the vehicle. Any equivalent design is notably absent from the Zillian 302 EV and the Lotya M300 EV."

"And Melship," said Bigsy.

Grace continued, "We decided to dig further. We found that the designs of the next two Zillian cars were based upon clone cars manufactured in China. Both the Zillian 502 and the 602 are copies of Chinese car models. None of the ones copied had any form of BMS. There were no statistics for the Zillian's safety record, but we substituted their original close cars to get a safety breakdown.

Grace continued, "It was truly shocking. For the 302, there were 137 fires: for the 502 another 22 fires and for the limited production 602 another 8 fires. These statistics were eared across a large area of China and it may because of this that the trend had not been identified."

Jim again, "Our conclusion? The cars are not safe and the fires generated - of a chemical nature - are huge pollutants."

Douglas Melship looked towards Lottie as if asking her to say something. It was clear that his time in Gstaad hadn't given him a grasp of the technology.

Lottie asked, "But won't that make our government look awkward. We've just agreed, in principle, to procure 10,000 of these Zillian cars and vans?"

"Yes, but we have already sought legal advice and are to cancel the contact. It's called Rescission.

Jim continued, "And if we have to cite anything, then it will be the ultimate safety of the vehicles being provided. That the ones offered did not have suitable built-in safety features and that the manufacturer did not have sufficient oversight of the production process."

Melship spoke again, "But what will this do to the share prices of Zillian?"

Jim answered, "I should think it will destroy it, but they are selling a worthless product and are a company that cannot be trusted."

"And the effect upon the Prime Minister?"

Jim answered, "Well, it is no secret that he is already on shaky ground. He can tough this out and re-invent the storyline, but fundamentally, he must have gone into this with his eyes opened, perhaps with an eye upon the next big donation from Miller McDonald. I think you should ask about yourself too, I'd imagine your reputation in government will be in tatters after this, and I suspect that your 'investment' with Banca Cariba will have dwindled away."

"When will this all happen, the cancellation of the contract, I mean?"

"Today. It has already occurred. You are very lucky that we have cancelled for cause. It means you are not directly implicated. You will have kept your side of the bargain with Zillian and Red Fox so they should not feel the need for revenge."

"And what about Tovey?" asked Melship.

Jim answered, "He knows even less about what has happened. Zillian will go to him first, but it will be obvious that he knows nothing. Unless you tell him, of course, although that would be mighty stupid. I shall leave you now, Mr Melship."

Jim rose to leave the room.

"Wow," said Bigsy, "He doesn't mess around."

Bigsy looked at the ZILL ticker on his iPhone, "The ZILL share has dropped 26% since start of trading. It is still going down."

Clare's phone rang. It was Cat.

"What have you done?" she asked, "Only Zillian's share price is crashing. The guys around here say it is a dead man walking. It has just been suspended from trading. That's like it has just hit an iceberg and is about to do a long-drawn-out Titanic. It will ripple through to the political forums too, they are saying."

Bigsy asked, "But it is still working here?"

Cat replied, "Trust me. It is dead, your feed must have a 15-minute delay."

Amanda and Grace re-entered the room, "You've heard?" asked Amanda, "The Shares have been suspended?"

Grace flicked the presentation screen to display a news channel.

Christina looked at the screen, still showing the interview room. "It's all been too simple," she said, "I think there is still some other play out there."

Clare summarised,

- "Car firm inflates its share price through tricks."
- "Chinese and Russians invest in leveraged deal - smaller money invested but bigger returns"
- "They blackmail, coerce and bribe two MPs to talk up the share price"
- "Share goes up, and China/Russia make money on covert markets."
- "Car firm discovered as a sham."
- "MPs challenged and deny knowledge"
- "Car firm crashes because of discoveries."
- "Car firm suspended - is worth nothing."

"There is your key window," said Christina, "When the share price rose, all the hidden money could be moved and cashed. That's the money laundering part, but it was so short lived. It has to be a diversion for something else."

The television was running implications of the failure of Zillian and the embarrassment to the UK Government, where the Prime Minister himself had backed the investment. Then it cut to a UK map. It showed several UK locations, designated as Freeports.

The narrator continued to explain their use.

"That's it," said Christina, "They've used the potential import of Zillian cars to secure two of the UK Freeports. Thames and Freeport East. If all of those cars were to have been imported on container ships, they would have needed somewhere to land."

She added, "You watch, even if Zillian gets cancelled, those Freeports will survive."

Grace nodded agreement, "Yes, a white paper for the Centre for Policy Studies outlined ideas for post-Brexit free ports like those in the United States. The paper titled The Free Ports Opportunity suggested that creation of such ports could create 86,000 jobs and help fuel the Northern Powerhouse by bringing increased trade to deprived areas.

"That's the other play," said Christina, "Most of what we've seen was a decoy manoeuvre, but it has secured the Free Ports and has let through the legislation to create them as casinos for the rich and powerful. Deregulation of the tax base, aimed at facilitating tax havens, smuggling and removal of worker's rights."

Clare spoke, "No wonder the Prime Minister didn't look too upset."

"Nor the Pomps and the hyphenated," added Jake, "It will become a free-for-all!"

Wrap up

Jake, Bigsy, Clare and Christina were all in a wine bar within some railway vaults. Jake had invited Rachel but urged her to remain off duty. Lottie, Hannah, and Tessa had been invited and were intrigued to see sawdust scattered on the floor.

"How should we feel about this? Did we learn anything?" asked Clare.

"I wish we'd spotted it earlier, " said Christina, "You know; the real game was to create the Freeports which can be exploited like giant casinos by the Russians and Chinese."

"And certain UK politicians," added Bigsy.

"David, my brother, was on to them and paid with his life, " added Rachel, "I'm so glad you have found

875

out what they were doing and have brought some of them down."

"The Russians and Chinese managed to launder money through Zillian before it went belly-up," added Jake, "But slow-moving Melship and Tovey saw their shares go up and then crash again."

"These Russians were being run by bratva gangs, " added Christina, "they are utterly ruthless, and now the Chinese are starting to copy them. Isabella and then Douglas both killed. It even got the Kremlin agitated, although I suspect it was partly in case any of Putin's secrets were about to be revealed."

"But he's covered his tracks," said Bigsy, "Unlike the Brits involved in all of this."

"The Brits won't ever learn about how to cover their tracks fully," said Christina, "It was too easy to find those two MP accounts in Banca Cariba."

Jake said, "They are both finished as MPs now, though, with corruption charges attached to both of them, although the PM has managed to bluff his way through with plenty of denials."

"The charges will last all of maybe a year," said Bigsy, "Then they will be back in the swamp."

"Something about 'tea break's over, back on your heads!' " said Jake, "Oops! I just said out loud what I was thinking, again."

He paused, then said, "I learned to never buy a cloned electric vehicle, and to check for fire retardants!"

Lottie added, "And being around Clare never creates a dull moment."

"Although it can be dangerous," added Hannah.

"Cheers, everybody," said Clare. They chinked their 150th Cuvée Claret wine glasses together.

Ed Adams

Corrupt

Now choose your next Ed. A. Dams novel!

Now choose your next Ed Adams novel!

Triangle Trilogy		Link:	Read?
1	Triangle	https://amzn.to/3c6zRMu	
2	Square	https://amzn.to/3sEiKYx	
3	Circle	https://amzn.to/3qLavYZ	
4	Ox Stunner	https://amzn.to/3sHxlgh	
		(all feature Jake, Bigsy, Clare, Chuck Manners)	
Archangel Collection			
1	Archangel	https://amzn.to/2Y9nB5K	
2	Raven	https://amzn.to/2MiGVe6	
3	Raven's Card	https://amzn.to/2Y8HLgs	
4	Magazine Clip	https://amzn.to/3pbBJYn	
5	Play On, Christina Nott	https://amzn.to/2MbkuHl	
6	Corrupt	https://amzn.to/2M0HnOw	
		(all feature Jake, Bigsy, Clare, Chuck Manners)	
Now the Science Collection			
1	Coin	https://amzn.to/3o82wmS	
2	Pulse	https://amzn.to/3qQlBvL	
3	Edge	https://amzn.to/2KDmYOW	
4	Now the Science	https://amzn.to/3iG5Nc2	
Edge of forever Trilogy			
1	Edge	https://amzn.to/2KDmYOW	
2	Edge Blue	https://amzn.to/2Kyq9au	
3	Edge Red	https://amzn.to/2KzJwjz	
4	Edge of Forever	https://amzn.to/3c57Ghj	

www.ingramcontent.com/pod-product-compliance
Lightning Source LLC
Chambersburg PA
CBHW010246030426
42336CB00022B/3315